Martin Luther never sat down to write ~~...~~ that modern systematic theologians w. ~~... recognize~~, and sure enough, modern scholars have overlooked or misconstrued Luther's understanding of the Trinity as a result. But he hid it in plain sight, in the unexpected genres of medieval-style academic disputations, hymns that echoed the Psalms, and wide-ranging expository sermons keyed to the liturgical calendar. Helmer's book, ahead of its time when originally published and still on the leading edge of scholarship in this paperback edition, offers a very close reading of a handful of texts that surprise, illuminate, and suggest ways forward for theology today.

Fred Sanders, Professor of Theology,
Biola University

Christine Helmer's *The Trinity and Martin Luther* prompted a new interest in the classical roots of the Reformation. This new and updated edition of Helmer's seminal work discusses the most recent scholarship, offering a cutting-edge view of what we know today.

Risto Saarinen, Professor of Ecumenics,
University of Helsinki

Dr. Christine Helmer places Luther in the venerable company of the speculative theologians of the Trinity. She interprets both the novelty and the continuity of Luther's reason-able faith-language within the spectrum of centuries of attempts to penetrate the mysteries of the Divine Three in One. Diagnosing philosophically the questionable directions of past Luther scholarship and the hermeneutical decisions that have underscored the 'newness' of the reformer's Christ-centricism, Helmer presents a convincing argument for the Trinitarian foundation of Luther's theology as expressed in various genres. An intelligent, compelling, and inspiring contribution that belongs in the front row of scholarly examination of the core, and ecumenical promise, of Luther's theology.

Kirsi Stjerna, Professor of Lutheran History and Theology,
Pacific Lutheran Theological Seminary

All too long, Luther research has been shaped by the paradigms of the Luther Renaissance. Christine Helmer's *The Trinity and Martin Luther* is a challenge for these traditional views. According to her, Luther is more medieval, more philosophical, even more catholic than usually supposed. Combining intricate text analysis in different genres of Luther's work with a broader approach to their systematic impact, this book is a thrilling read.

Volker Leppin, Professor of Church History,
Universität Tübingen

The Trinity *and* Martin Luther

The Trinity *and* Martin Luther

Revised Edition

CHRISTINE HELMER

STUDIES IN HISTORICAL AND SYSTEMATIC THEOLOGY

LEXHAM PRESS

The Trinity and Martin Luther, Revised Edition
Studies in Historical and Systematic Theology

Copyright 2017 Christine Helmer

Lexham Press, 1313 Commercial St., Bellingham, WA 98225
LexhamPress.com

First edition published by Verlag Philipp von Zabern, Mainz am Rhein (1999).

Print ISBN 9781683590507
Digital ISBN 9781683590514

Lexham Editorial Team: Todd Hains, Abigail Stocker, Danielle Thevenaz, Joel Wilcox
Cover Design: Bryan Hintz
Typesetting: Joel Wilcox, Abigail Stocker

For Brevard S. Childs

"You have set my feet in a broad place" (Psalm 31:8).

Contents

Preface to the New Edition

My interest in the subject of Martin Luther's theology of the Trinity was initially inspired by the "Trinitarian turn" in Protestant theological writing of the 1970s and 1980s. Christian theology at the time was still largely taking its cues from German theologians, who had taken up Karl Barth's placement of the Trinity into the prolegomena of theological systems. While traditional systems of theology had situated the doctrine of God as significant for these introductory sections, Barth had changed the order. He understood the doctrine of the Trinity—the content of divine revelation—as the necessary ground for systematic theologies. The Trinity was very much on the minds of Protestant theologians after World War II.

Barth's vision was a powerful one. It identified both the content of Christian theology and its method. Christian theology would be introduced by the speculative doctrine of the Trinity revealed to be differentiated already in eternity; methodologically, the Trinity functioned as the principle of coherence for systematic theology's work of organizing doctrine. The Trinity fulfilled two crucial criteria for systematicity. The first was *coherence*. As Barth had learned from Georg Wilhelm Friedrich Hegel (1770–1831), the immanent Trinity was the condition for economic revelation. The second was *comprehensiveness*, specifically at the level of the economic Trinity. A doctrine that functioned as the principle of both coherence and comprehensiveness could serve as content for the theological system as it had developed since Gottfried Wilhelm Leibniz (1646–1716). But the role of the Trinity in the prolegomena of systems of theology would not come until Barth. Friedrich Schleiermacher's (1768–1834) understanding of the doctrine of the Trinity as such was too far ahead of its time, and it earned for him the opprobrium of Trinitarian theologians; situated in the conclusion of his system, it was mistaken for an appendix.

When I began my studies of Luther at Yale University in the early 1990s, the doctrine of the Trinity constituted a vibrant field of research—everywhere, that is, except in Luther scholarship, which maintained that Luther was above all else a theologian of the cross. Basing their research on the portrait of Luther worked out in the early twentieth-century Luther Renaissance, Luther scholars focused primarily on the young Luther. They identified the young monk's experience of grace and salvation as leading him to the doctrine of justification by faith that was the theological breakthrough precipitating the Protestant Reformation. Christ's cross was the place where God revealed divine mercy. It was this revelation that, when preached to sinners, confronted them with both the inefficacy of any human works and the sufficiency of divine forgiveness. Likewise, it was this perception of a seismic shift from the Catholic to the Protestant paradigm that resulted in my interest in the topic of Luther and the Trinity being greeted with little more than quasi-polite skepticism. Luther was a theologian who preached Christ, not the Trinity. His theology had to do with the word of divine promise that announced as it created the reality of divine forgiveness.

To maintain that Luther might be regarded as a Trinitarian theologian, as I hoped to do, would require a lot of theological spadework. First, I had to find the texts to make my case. Luther scholarship focused on his early writings, those before 1520, principally his early exegetical works on Romans and his polemics against Rome. But these were the very works that led to the consensus on Luther as theologian of the cross in the first place. These early writings, moreover, most often arose in contentious exchanges between Luther and his interlocutors, and so because the Trinity was never a point of contention, there were no texts of Luther's specifically concerned with this doctrine.

I was fortunate that by the time I began researching Luther, German Luther scholar Oswald Bayer, under the new methodological rubric of genre studies, had made the specific and varied genres of Luther's writings uniquely productive for theological reflection. I still recall my impression upon hearing Bayer lecture on the genre of catechism, a text Lutherans learn as youngsters in confirmation class. The assumption had been that catechism was a genre for children, not academic theologians. But Bayer argued that it was precisely such practical theological texts—meant to be sung, preached, taught, and memorized—that had distinct and revealing theological perspectives. I found myself thinking how interesting it would be if the Trinity might be detected in these genres!

This seemed unlikely, however. Consensus among Luther scholars and Lutheran theologians said that the Trinity was a speculative doctrine. Barth's Trinitarian turn, on the one hand, had situated the immanent Trinity, or the Trinity in eternity, at the start of his theological system, before the doctrines of creation and redemption. For Luther scholars, on the other hand, the Reformer's oft-cited polemic against "speculation" into the divine majesty was taken as fundamentally prohibitive of such speculative theologizing. Furthermore, Lutheran theologians in the twentieth century had doubled down on Luther's insistence that knowledge of God is available "under the opposite" (*sub contrario*). It was to be found at those places where God reveals the divine mercy under its opposite, specifically at the cross of Christ. Any speculation on aspects of the divine being in eternity was to disobey God's injunction against being concerned with matters with which humans ought not to be concerned.

But what emerged as my study moved forward through a process of educated guesswork and textual discovery was the opposite of what had been so long maintained as Luther's Reformation theology. In the sermons, hymns, catechisms, and exegetical works I was reading, I found not only expositions of the Trinity but evidence that Luther viewed the Trinity in eternity as essential to Christian piety as well as necessary for knowledge of God. What I did not find was any anxiety about theological speculation!

Discovering the disputations of the later 1540s opened up a new area of research for me. These later disputations provided evidence against the antispeculative direction supposedly authorized by Luther's focus on Christ on the cross, calling into question many of the assumptions about Luther's theology as it was presented at the time. Luther hated philosophy, it was said. He was a theologian, not a philosopher! He insisted on faith, not reason, as the instrument for appropriating the gospel. As a theologian of the word, he had articulated a new language of faith. This was the Reformation breakthrough!

But this was not the stance I saw in the later disputations. Instead, I found a theologian who insisted on using philosophical tools to make theological truth claims; a theologian who was interested in communicating to his students and hearers the need for understanding Trinitarian relations and processions and who used reason to articulate these claims; and a theologian whose new language deployed medieval semantics, in which language in any one field of communication or understanding signified in relation to a particular subject matter while allowing for signification in other fields. In other words, I found in the later disputations a Luther who was most interested in the speculative Trinity and who not only did not prohibit such speculation but actively encouraged it as belonging to Christian life and understanding.

I needed help to get to this point, because as a Protestant theologian taught to regard Luther in modern Protestant terms, I was unprepared for what I was seeing in the disputations. Another Luther scholar interested in Luther on the question of philosophy, Theodor Dieter, recommended to me Graham White's book *Luther as Nominalist*. In this important study, White had done groundbreaking work on Luther's disputations. He had researched many of the medieval theologians whom Luther explicitly and implicitly cited in conjunction with his developing articulation of Christological and Trinitarian doctrines, namely Duns Scotus (c. 1266-1308) and William of Ockham (1285-1347), Robert Holcot (c. 1290-1349), and Pierre d'Ailly (c. 1351-1420). White had shown, furthermore, that Luther had appropriated and reworked late medieval questions of logic in order to articulate Trinitarian syllogisms. White's book, together with the work of medieval philosopher Marilyn McCord Adams, whose expertise on Ockham coincided with Luther's own, were instrumental in shaping my interpretation of Luther in the disputations.

By the time I finished my research, I had a Luther who was more medieval than modern, more Catholic than Protestant, and more philosophical than theological than I had anticipated. In *The Trinity and Martin Luther*, I highlight these reorientations by means of the disparate genres Luther used as media of his thought. The genre of disputation is the foundation for the second chapter, for example. Here I show that in developing his Trinitarian thought, Luther engaged medieval debates between Peter Lombard (c. 1096-1160) and Joachim of Fiore (c. 1135-1202), which prompted the Fourth Lateran Council (called in 1213, convened in 1215). Regarding the debates of his own day, Luther was especially concerned with rejecting an imposition of Aristotle's natural philosophy as a template for thinking about Trinitarian relations in eternity. But this was not a case of theology contra philosophy. Rather, it was Luther using a distinct philosophical *and* theological reasoning to work out the logic, semantics, and metaphysics of the "inner Trinity" (rather than the "immanent" Trinity, which is a post-Kantian designation). Chapter two makes the point that Luther uses philosophy in doing theology—as any other late medieval theologian would have done. Nor did he shy away from speculation: his discussion of the language for adequately representing the relations of the inner Trinity was philosophically sophisticated while at the same time doing justice to the particular theological content of the Trinity.

Since the original publication of *The Trinity and Martin Luther* in 1999, an international community of Luther scholars has advanced the understanding of Luther in continuity with medieval theology. The ecumenical accompaniment to this scholarship was the signing of the Joint Declaration on the Doctrine of Justification between Lutheran and Roman Catholic Churches, also in 1999, which introduced a new, if at times fitfully advanced, era in Roman Catholic and Lutheran relations. Scholars in Finland—in particular, medieval philosopher Simo Knuuttila, ecumenical theologian Risto Saarinen, and historical theologian, Pekka Kärkkäinen—have been at the forefront of international scholarship on Luther's doctrines of the will, of Christ, and of the Trinity, in relation to late medieval and nominalist philosophy. German church historian Volker Leppin and Danish systematic theologian Else Marie Wiberg Pedersen, both scholars of medieval German mysticism, have drawn attention to Luther's appropriation of this distinctive medieval tradition. A new generation of Luther scholars in North America, among them Candace Kohli, David Luy, and Aaron Moldenhauer, are likewise approaching Luther's later disputations from the perspective of medieval thinkers, focusing especially on Luther's predecessor, Gabriel Biel (d. 1495).

Scholarship on Luther and the doctrine of the Trinity thus upended established paradigms and cherished dualities (for example, medieval versus modern, Catholic versus Protestant, philosophy versus theology), and there is still work to be done in this vein. The stakes remain surprisingly high—though perhaps it's not so surprising, given how deeply implicated the historical narrative of Luther and the Reformation breakthrough has been in modernity broadly and modern nationalism in particular. As I have argued in my later work, especially in *Theology and the End of Doctrine*, the earlier paradigm has veered towards insisting on word without a speaker, theology without philosophy, and faith without reason, all of which are dangerous to notions of a common public sphere where religious and nonreligious people may come together to discuss and decide on shared problems. Most pressingly in our times, these issues include income inequality, global climate change, sexism, and racism. The Luther of familiar opposites is indefensible on historical and philosophical grounds. Yet he endures in a lineage of thought, stretching from the early twentieth century to the present, that is antimetaphysical and insists on the law-gospel polarity as the systematic principle of Luther's theology. When the Luther of familiar opposites is seen as the product of twentieth-century historical and intellectual developments rather than as a historically accurate portrait, perhaps this constructed Luther will fade away. Then again, who knows which version of Luther, these or ones not yet anticipated, will emerge as primary in what may be the waning days of our planet? In the short term, we can only hope that reason, mercy, and faith in a living God who is the referent of doctrine will prevail.

Christine Helmer
Cambridge, Massachusetts, 2017

Select Bibliography of Recent Literature on the Trinity in the Middle Ages and Early Modernity

THE TRINITY IN MEDIEVAL PHILOSOPHY

The Trinity as Christian dogma is recognized as the content of revelation, although its normative traditional formulation is found in the Nicene Creed and not in scriptural articulation. The fate of the doctrine of the Trinity depends on its capacity to generate theological meaning in new religious contexts. The theological task thus queries how to communicate the Trinity as experientially meaningful for Christians, whether as object of prayer, confession, or hymns. It also requires that theologians make generative use of intellectual tools to understand, explain, clarify, and establish the meaning and referent of Trinitarian phrases, such as for example the Trinitarian term popular in the Middle Ages, that three things are one thing (*tres res sunt una res*).

Philosophy was the dominant intellectual tool deployed in the production of Trinitarian theology in the late Middle Ages. Studies of Luther on doctrine generally and on the Trinity specifically require engagement with research in medieval philosophy. Over the past decade, studies in the medieval philosophical theology of the Trinity have emerged as indispensable for work on Luther's doctrines of the Trinity and Christology. These studies have a common conceptual basis: Augustine's (354–430) understanding of Son and Spirit as the two movements of intellect and will. Anselm of Canterbury (c. 1033–1109) later situates the intellectual productions of intellect and will in the divine monologue. Thomas Aquinas (1225–1274) focuses on the processions. Duns Scotus (c. 1266–1308) is significant for conceiving divinity as perfect power production: the product is as perfect as the producer, hence the Son is perfect product of the Father, and both together produce the Spirit. Scholars agree on the significance of the relations of origin, which are metaphysically heavy. The following studies complement Marilyn McCord Adams's indispensable two-volume work on William of Ockham (1285-1347).

Emery, Gilles. *Trinity in Aquinas.* 2nd ed. Translated by Matthew Levering, Heather Buttery, Robert Williams, and Teresa Bede. Ypsilanti, MI: Sapientia Press of Ave Maria College, 2006.

Friedman, Russell L. *Medieval Trinitarian Thought from Aquinas to Ockham.* Cambridge: Cambridge University Press, 2010.

———. *Intellectual Traditions at the Medieval University: The Use of Philosophical Psychology in Trinitarian Theology Among the Franciscans and Dominicans, 1250-1350.* Studien und Texte zur Geistesgeschichte des Mittelalters 108/1-2. 2 Volumes. Leiden: Brill, 2013.

Paasch, J. T. *Divine Production in Late Medieval Trinitarian Theology: Henry of Ghent, Duns Scotus, and William Ockham.* New York: Oxford University Press, 2012.

Thom, Paul. *The Logic of the Trinity: Augustine to Ockham.* Medieval Philosophy: Texts and Studies. New York: Fordham University Press, 2012.

Williams, Scott M. "Henry of Ghent on Real Relations and the Trinity: The Case for Numerical Sameness Without Identity." *Recherches de Théologie et Philosophie Mediévales* 77, no. 1 (2010): 35-81.

———. "Augustine, Thomas Aquinas, Henry of Ghent, and John Duns Scotus: On the Theology of the Father's Intellectual Generation of the Word." *Recherches de Théologie et Philosophie Mediévales* 79, no. 1 (2012): 109-48.

LUTHER AND THE TRINITY

There is a growing body of research in Luther studies on the relation of his theology to medieval philosophical theology. This research originates predominantly in North America and Finland, where Luther scholars are contributing to an emergent consensus concerning Luther's indebtedness to late medieval thought. At the University of Helsinki, scholars mentored by Simo Knuutilla and Risto Saarinen have maintained an active agenda in the philosophy and theology of the late middle ages and early modernity. The studies noted here offer an introduction to this new work. Pekka Kärkkäinen's dissertation and Heinrich Assel's work focus for the most part on the early Luther. Other works by Risto Saarinen, Mickey Mattox, Dennis Bielfeldt and my own research take the Luther's later Trinitarian disputations as object of study. The 2017 commemoration of Luther's *Ninety-Five Theses* has inspired other publications on Luther on the Trinity, most recently articles by Lois Malcolm and Christoph Schwöbel.

Assel, Heinrich. "Der Name Gottes bei Martin Luther: Trinität und Tetragramm—ausgehend von Luthers Auslegung des Fünften Psalms." *Evangelische Theologie* 64 (2004): 363-78.

Bielfeldt, Dennis. "Luther's Late Trinitarian Disputations: Semantic Realism and the Trinity." In *The Substance of the Faith: Luther's Doctrinal Theology for Today*, by Dennis Bielfeldt, Mickey L. Mattox, and Paul R. Hinlicky, 59-130. Minneapolis: Fortress Press, 2008.

Helmer, Christine. "Luther's Theology of Glory." *Neue Zeitschrift für Systematische Theologie und Religionsphilosophie* 42, no. 3 (2000): 237-45.

———. "Luther's Trinitarian Hermeneutic and the Old Testament." *Modern Theology* 18, no. 1 (2002): 49-73.

———. "Gott von Ewigkeit zu Ewigkeit: Luthers Trinitätsverständnis." *Neue Zeitschrift für Systematische Theologie und Religionsphilosophie* 44, no. 1 (2002): 1-19.

    This article is also available in English: "The Trinity: God from Eternity to Eternity." *Harvard Theological Review* 96, no. 2 (2003): 127-46.

———. "Trinitarische Ekstase—Göttliche Liebe: Reflektionen zu Luthers Lied, 'Nun freut euch, lieben Christen gmein.'" *Theologische Quartalschrift* 183, no. 1 (2003): 16-38.

———. "Trinitätslehre." In *Das Luther-Lexikon*, edited by Volker Leppin and Gury Schneider-Ludorff, 702-5. Regensburg: Verlag Bückle & Böhm, 2014.

Kärkkäinen, Pekka. *Luthers trinitarische Theologie des Heiligen Geistes*. Veröffentlichungen des Instituts fur Europäische Geschichte; Abteilung Abendlandische Religionsgeschichte 208. Mainz: Zabern, 2005.

———. "Trinity." In *Engaging Luther: A (New) Theological Assessment*, edited by Olli-Pekka Vainio, 80–94. Eugene, OR: Cascade Publication, 2010.

Kärkkäinen, Pekka, ed. *Trinitarian Theology in the Medieval West*. Schriften der Luther-Agricola-Gesellschaft 61. Helsinki: Luther-Agricola-Society, 2008.

Knuutilla, Simo, and Risto Saarinen. "Luther's Trinitarian Theology and its Medieval Background." *Studia Theologica* 53 (1999): 3–12.

Malcolm, Lois. "Martin Luther and the Holy Spirit." In *Oxford Research Encyclopedia of Religion*. Online Publication Date March 2017: http://religion.oxfordre.com/view/10.1093/acrefore/9780199340378.001.0001/acrefore-9780199340378-e-328?print=pdf

Mattox, Mickey L. "From Faith to the Text and Back Again: Martin Luther on the Trinity in the Old Testament." *Pro Ecclesia* 15 (2006): 281–303.

———. "Luther's Interpretation of Scripture: Biblical Understanding in Trinitarian Shape." In *The Substance of the Faith: Luther's Doctrinal Theology for Today*, by Dennis Bielfeldt, Mickey L. Mattox, and Paul R. Hinlicky, 11–58. Minneapolis: Fortress Press, 2008.

Saarinen, Risto. "The Merciful Trinity in Luther's Exposition of John 1,18." In *Trinitarian Theology in the Medieval West*, edited by Pekka Kärkkäinen, 280–98. Schriften der Luther-Agricola-Gesellschaft 61. Helsinki: Luther-Agricola-Society, 2008.

Schwöbel, Christoph. "Martin Luther and the Trinity." In *Oxford Research Encyclopedia of Religion*. Online Publication Date March 2017: http://religion.oxfordre.com/view/10.1093/acrefore/9780199340378.001.0001/acrefore-9780199340378-e-326

LUTHER AND THE MIDDLE AGES

Luther's inheritances from the Middle Ages include medieval philosophical theology, particularly the thought of William of Ockham, Gabriel Biel
(c. 1418–1495), Robert Holcot (c. 1290–1349), and Pierre d'Ailly (c. 1351–1420),
and also the ways in which they took up earlier medieval debates on doctrine. The following studies are exemplary in explaining how earlier philosophical discussions were crucial to Luther's theology.

Dieter, Theodor. "Luther as Late Medieval Theologian: His Positive and
    Negatie Use of Nominalism and Realism." In *The Oxford handbook
    of Martin Luther's Theology*, edited by Robert Kolb, Irene Dingel,
    and L'ubomír Batka, 31–48. New York: Oxford University Press,
    2014.
———. "Scholasticisms in Martin Luther's Thought." In *Oxford
    Research Encyclopedia of Religion*. Online Publication Date
    March 2017: http://religion.oxfordre.com/view/10.1093/
    acrefore/9780199340378.001.0001/acrefore-9780199340378-e-265.
Frank, Günter and Volker Leppin, eds. *Die Reformation und ihr Mittelalter*.
    Melanchthon-Schriften der Stadt Bretten 14. Stuttgart-Bad
    Cannstatt: Frommann-Holzboog, 2016.
Helmer, Christine, ed. *Luther and the Middle Ages*. Forthcoming.
    The articles are contributed by speakers of the con-
    ference, "Beyond Oberman: Luther and the Middle Ages"
    (November 2-4, 2016 at Northwestern University); avail-
    able online at http://sites.northwestern.edu/luther2016.
Kärkkäinen, Pekka. "Nominalism and the Via Moderna in Luther's
    Theological Work." In *Oxford Research Encyclopedia of Religion*.
    Online Publication Date March 2017: http://religion.oxfordre.
    com/view/10.1093/acrefore/9780199340378.001.0001/acrefore-
    9780199340378-e-266.
———. "Philosophy Among and in the Wake of the Reformers: Luther,
    Melanchthon, Zwingli, and Calvin." In *Routledge Companion to
    Sixteenth-Century Philosophy*, edited by Henrik Lagerlund and
    Benjamin Hill, 189–202. London: Routledge, 2017.

Kohli, Candace. "Help for the Good: Martin Luther's Understanding of Human Agency and the Law in the Antinomian Disputations (1537-40)." PhD diss., Northwestern University, 2017.

Luy, David J. *Dominus Mortis: Martin Luther on the Incorruptibility of God in Christ*. Minneapolis: Fortress Press, 2014.

— — —. "Martin Luther's Disputations." In *Oxford Research Encyclopedia of Religion*. Online Publication Date March 2017: http://religion. oxfordre.com/view/10.1093/acrefore/9780199340378.001.0001/ acrefore-9780199340378-e-285

Moldenhauer, Aaron. "The Metaphysics of Martin Luther's Christology." Unpublished dissertation, Northwestern University.

HANDBOOKS ON THE TRINITY

Two recent handbooks on the Trinity include specific treatments of the Trinity in the Protestant Reformation.

Chun, Young-Ho. "The Trinity in the Protestant Reformation: Continuity within Discontinuity." In *The Cambridge Companion to the Trinity*, edited by Peter C. Phan, 128–48. Cambridge: Cambridge University Press, 2011.

Swain, Scott R. "The Trinity in the Reformers." In *The Oxford Handbook of the Trinity*, edited by Gilles Emery and Matthew Levering, 227–39. New York: Oxford University Press, 2011.

Foreword to the Original Edition

One measure of Luther's greatness is his versatility as a conversation partner. Certainly, human being is historical. Like all of us, Luther was a "product of his time." His words and deeds, his ways of thinking were deeply shaped by the cultural contexts in which he "lived and moved and had his being." Nevertheless, the Spirit of God is always calling us to break out of the molds of merely human roles and institutions. Because Luther responded, his person, his thought, and work have a capacity to transcend that culture and to furnish fresh insights, not only to his contemporary followers and enemies, but also to successive generations down to the present day.

Christine Helmer's book takes these facts for granted, and exploits them to startling effect. Helmer's own work was formed and informed by the Yale School of theology of the eighties and nineties, whose major premiss was that the work of a Christian theologian must be steeped, first in Holy Scripture, and then in the theological tradition. In its curriculum, Bible courses laid the foundation, a four-semester history of doctrine sequence (from patristics down through the end of the nineteenth century) raised the walls. During that time, the wider university at Yale was the scene of lively debates about literary criticism, about the construction versus the deconstruction of texts, as well as the rhetorical power and function of different literary genres. Sensitivity was heightened to how words do more than make assertions, to how the same words may be deployed by different genres with strikingly contrasting effects. Helmer's own work was strongly influenced by Brevard S. Childs and his program of canonical criticism, which recognizes how the pericopes of the Bible itself have been told and re-told, read and re-read in many different literary and cultural contexts. These ideas were made vivid in the present by the ecumenical environment of Yale Divinity School, whose students come from a variety of confessional backgrounds—not only Protestant, but also Roman Catholic and Jewish. The nineties at Yale also re-engaged—both from a continental and an Anglo-American analytic point of view—the relations between philosophy and biblical interpretation on the one hand and theological formulation on the other.

Thus, Helmer turned to Luther and his writings, as to a figure in whom one can always find more than has already been systematically codified and appropriated. Removing the interpretative spectacles of the God for us (*Deus pro nobis*) against the hidden God (*Deus absconditus*) dichotomy, Helmer proposed to investigate Luther's own rich treatments of the inner Trinity itself. The methodological move—of abstracting from the later polemical setting of later Lutheran theology to examine Luther in his own historical context—freed her to recognize the stamp of Luther's own debts to medieval scholastic philosophical theology. Thus, Helmer examines how—despite the sometime vehemence of his antipathy for Aristotle—Luther actually deploys the scholastic genre of the disputation to explore this most intimate of doctrines, and takes his philosophical stand with Ockham against Scotus so far as its correct explication is concerned! Her analysis of Luther's theological practice is a contribution towards a more complex picture of how philosophy relates to biblical interpretation and theological formulation in Luther's own work. Again, by letting the hymn text sound its own dominant chord of the Spirit's initiative, Helmer reminds us how Luther's writings are too rich and various to be captured by any single—however theologically important—theme. Likewise, Helmer's treatment of the sermon illustrates yet another way how speaking of the inner Trinity advances Luther's concrete pastoral aims.

If pre-Vatican II discussions featured Luther as the hero of a distinctive reformation faction, Helmer's book confronts us with a Luther with whom all parties to those disputes can find points of continuity. Her choice of topic and sampling of texts illustrates how Luther paid his respects to the inconquerable difficulty of the subject matter of theology, by approaching it with methodological versatility and experimentation. Helmer also shows how Luther repeated the compliment, insofar as he found himself unable in practice to communicate what he had learned about God within the confines of a single literary genre or the limits of a single rhetorical strategy. Helmer thus presents us with a Luther of attractive complexity, a figure from whom scholars and theologians of widely diverse commitments and interests can expect to learn.

Marilyn McCord Adams
Horace Tracy Pitkin Professor of Historical Theology,
Yale Divinity School, New Haven, Connecticut, 1999

Preface to the Original Edition

The story of my search for "holy speculation" began with a question posed by Eva Bayer on a train from Stuttgart to Tübingen. The idea spontaneously came to mind, for the first time: Luther's doctrine of the Trinity. Since this momentary outburst, time has witnessed a gradual change in my own understanding of both the Trinity and Luther's articulation of this mystery. Luther continues to fascinate generations of theologians with his witness to the cross. But it is his Trinitarian theology of glory that compels speculation on God in eternity: to know who God is with the utmost certainty of a necessary truth, and to know the inmost thoughts, the triune essence, and the divine delight in all of creation. Dynamic speculation takes narrative form, structured by the fullness of time in which the beloved Son is sent, and in which the Spirit perpetually works to transform a creation whose end is to glorify the living God. If this work inspires its hearers, in some small way, to speculate more precisely, it will have achieved its aim.

To my teachers, on both sides of the Atlantic, I extend my deepest gratitude. Each has contributed an irreplaceable perspective in the constellation that has shaped my thinking and writing; each has taught me, in unique ways, the integrity of "unconventional orthodoxy," the passion for truth, and the freedom to transcend. I would like to thank Brevard S. Childs for his advising that was more than sterling silver. It was pure gold. To him I dedicate this book as a gesture of my deepest appreciation, admiration, and esteem. Prof. Childs's own work has shaped my view of Luther's Trinitarian interpretation of passages in the Old Testament (chapter three), as well as my adaptation of a "canonical-approach" to study the exegetical unfolding of Luther's sermon (chapter four). I am grateful to Oswald Bayer, who recommended this study's method, launched the category of the *promissio* in his own Luther research, and provided sound advice that suddenly cleared paths through what often seemed to be an untraversable jungle of

Luther's works and works on Luther. I thank Cyril O'Regan, not only for his conceptual powers to heal a chapter threatening to fall apart, and for pointing out the mistakes I would never have been able to detect, but also for his kind dedication to teach me, from the very beginning. The first words Marilyn McCord Adams ever said to me became a metaphor for the extent to which her guidance has radically changed the study's form and content. "Take off your sunglasses," she said to me! In the encounters that followed, she helped me to take off those glasses that had obscured my view of Luther's rootedness in the medieval tradition, and invited me to explore a new and complex world of medieval theology and philosophy. I am especially grateful for all her work in patiently discussing with me each layer forming chapter two, for recommending its many revisions, and for communicating to me a model of scholarship and character infused with clarity and humor. I also thank her for writing the foreword that introduces the book to an international audience.

There are many people whose contributions are, in many ways, inscribed into the study's text. I would like to thank them for their enduring encouragement, and for those wild moments that make a difference. My parents, Greta Helmer and Paul Helmer, instilled a religious curiosity before I had ever heard of Luther, and loyally accompanied more than this work's span. Kay Brown, Edward Conyers, Carol Delisle and my great-aunt, Lydia Girrbach, spoke profound words on a quest that was often confused. Professors, whose academic advocacy helped to overcome the obstacles, were: Rowan Greer, Martin Hengel, George Lindbeck, Jürgen Moltmann, and Thomas Schattauer. My friends who carried me when I was unable to walk, and who held my hand when we could walk together: David Brown, Alice Chapman, Stefanie Cochrum, Alice Fertig, Gabi Kramer, George N. Malek, Waltraud Naumann, Anke Rüdinger, Bettina Opitz-Chen, Chu-Hsien Chen, and William T. Lee.

Christine Helmer
Bad Urach, Misericordias Domini, 1999

Acknowledgments

It was a delight to work with Todd Hains, editor of Lexham Press, in the preparation of this edition of *The Trinity and Martin Luther*. I thank Todd for the opportunity he offered me to make the book available as a paperback to a broader readership. My thanks also go to Candace Kohli and Aaron Moldenhauer, both exceptional Luther scholars, for assistance with translation. Over many years, Marilyn McCord Adams kept me informed about new publications on the Trinity in the Middle Ages that I included in the select bibliography. I am glad that her foreword to the original publication of this book with Zabern Verlag accompanies this edition. *The Trinity and Martin Luther* spans the twenty-five years of my friendship with Marilyn. What began as a tutorial on Ockham in her office in Seabury Hall at Yale Divinity School turned into a research program on Luther's continuity with the late medieval thinkers. I am grateful to Marilyn for her intellectual mentoring and inspiring brilliance. She well embodied her own proverb that "good pals are hard to find." I am grateful to her above all for her constant love for my family—Robert, Anthony, Clarence—and for me. Marilyn passed away as this edition went to press. She is very much missed.

Abbreviations

AWA   *Archiv zur Weimarer Ausgabe der Werke Martin Luthers: Texte und Untersuchungen.* Cologne: Böhlau, 1981–.

BSLK   *Die Bekenntnisschriften der evangelisch-lutherischen Kirche.* 11th ed. Göttingen: Vandenhoeck & Ruprecht, 1992.

CCL   *Corpus Christianorum: Series Latina.* Turnhout: Brepols, 1953–.

CHLMP   *The Cambridge History of Later Medieval Philosophy: From the Rediscovery of Aristotle to the Disintegration of Scholasticism 1100–1600.* Edited by Norman Kretzmann, Anthony Kenny, and Jan Pinborg. Cambridge: Cambridge University Press, 1982.

CHRP   *The Cambridge History of Renaissance Philosophy.* Cambridge: Cambridge University Press, 1988.

CSEL   *Corpus Scriptorum Ecclesiasticorum Latinorum.* Vienna: Verlag der Österreichischen Akademie der Wissenschaften; Berlin: De Gruyter, 1866–.

DS   *Enchiridion symbolorum definitionum et declarationum de rebus fidei et morum.* Edited by Heinrich Denzinger. Translated by Peter Hünermann with Helmut Hoping. 37th ed. Freiburg: Herder, 1991.

EG(H/N) *Evangelisches Gesangbuch: Ausgabe für die Evangelische Kirche in Hessen und Nassau.* Frankfurt am Main: Spener Verlagsbuchhandlung, 1994.

EKG   *Evangelisches Kirchengesangbuch: Ausgabe für die Evangelische Landeskirche in Württemberg.* 40th ed. Stuttgart: Gesangbuch Verlag, 1990.

GNT   *Novum Testamentum Graece.* Edited by Eberhard Nestle, Kurt Aland, et al. 27th ed. Stuttgart: Deutsche Bibelgesellschaft, 1993.

LBW — *Lutheran Book of Worship*. Inter-Lutheran Commission on Worship. Minneapolis: Augsburg Fortress, 1991.

LW — Luther's Works [American Edition]. 82 vols. projected. St. Louis: Concordia; Philadelphia: Fortress, 1955–1986; 2009–.

MO — *Philippi Melanchthonis Opera*. 28 vols. Corpus Reformatorum 1–28. Edited by C. G. Bretschneider. Halle: C. A. Schwetshcke and Sons, 1834–1860.

NPNF — *Nicene and Post-Nicene Fathers of the Christian Church: Second Series*. Edited by Philip Schaff and Henry Wace. Buffalo, NY: Christian Literature Company, 1896.

OPh — *Opera Philosophica: Guillelmi de Ockham*. 7 vols. St. Bonaventure, NY: St. Bonaventure University, 1974–1988.

OTh — *Opera Theologica: Guillelmi de Ockham*. 10 vols. St. Bonaventure, NY: St. Bonaventure, NY: St. Bonaventure University, 1967–1986.

PL — *Patrologia Latina*. 226 vols. Paris: Migne, 1878–1974.

RAC — *Reallexikon für Antike und Christentum*. 18 vols. Bonn: University of Bonn, 1950–1998.

RGG — *Die Religion in Geschichte und Gegenwart*. 7 vols. 3rd ed. Tübingen: Mohr, 1957–1965.

TRE — *Theologische Realenzyklopädie*. 29 vols. Berlin: De Gruyter, 1977–1998.

Vaticana — *John Duns Scotus: Opera Omnia*. 19 vols. Studio et cura commissionis scotisticae ad fidem codicum edita. Vatican City: Typis Polyglottis Vaticanis, 1950–1993.

Vulgata — *Biblia Sacra Vulgata: Iuxta Vulgatam Versionem*. 3rd ed. Stuttgart: Deutsche Bibelgesellschaft, 1983.

WA — *D. Martin Luthers Werke, Kritische Gesamtausgabe: [Schriften]*. 73 vols. Weimar: Hermann Böhlaus Nachfolger, 1883–2009.

WABr — *D. Martin Luthers Werke, Kritische Gesamtausgabe: Briefwechsel*. 18 vols. Weimar: Hermann Böhlaus Nachfolger, 1930–1985.

WADB — *D. Martin Luthers Werke, Kritische Gesamtausgabe: Deutsche Bibel*. 12 vols. Weimar: Hermann Böhlaus Nachfolger, 1906–1961.

WATr — *D. Martin Luthers Werke, Kritische Gesamtausgabe: Tischreden*. 6 vols. Weimar: Hermann Böhlaus Nachfolger, 1912–1921.

1

Introduction

AIM OF THE STUDY

The Trinity comes to view as both mystery and doctrine. As a mystery, the Trinity surpasses comprehension in its groundlessness, yet it provides the surest foundation for those who live from it ecstatically. As a doctrine, the Trinity invites the use of reason's tools only to limit the mind's expansion to what can be confessed in ancient words of faith. Where the limits are encountered, contemplation merges with awe, and the mystery is adored once again. That Martin Luther (1483–1546) can be associated with the Triune mystery and doctrine is, perhaps, a curiosity for those accustomed to a Reformer who preaches Christ on the cross rather than reflecting on the eternal Trinity and who asserts on the basis of Scripture rather than conversing with his theological predecessors. Yet Luther is not silent on this subject of "holy speculation"; he articulates a doctrine of this glorious mystery.

The aim of this investigation is to study Luther's understanding of the Trinity as he articulated it from 1523 to 1546 in the language particular to three theological genres: the disputation, the hymn, and the sermon. In order to approach and tease out Luther's Trinitarian understanding, a method will be applied that is an adaptation of what could be called the "hermeneutical model" of Luther research to fit a systematic-theological theme. This study intends to show how the genre that presents the subject matter shapes the language Luther uses to convey, explain, and interpret the Trinitarian dogma. In each genre-language constellation, I examine how Luther arranges the two factors, *promissio* and narrative, in order to infuse the articulation of the subject matter with a specific Trinitarian content.[1] This study suggests that the interplay between *promissio* and narrative determines the theological structuring of the subject matter that, in turn, is accessible by investigating the relationship between genre and language. Presented in the genres of the disputation, the hymn, and the sermon, Luther's Trinitarian understanding is seen to be a consequent explication of the *promissio* of the Triune God and is conceived as a narrative of the Trinitarian movement towards creation.

In this study, I prefer to use the term "understanding of the Trinity" rather than "doctrine of the Trinity." Luther himself does not use the terms "doctrine" or "doctrine of the Trinity" (*Trinitätslehre*) in the modern sense of a systematic-theological locus, which implies a logical or material relation to other doctrines. For Luther, the Trinity is the object of the confession of faith, the name of, rather than the doctrine about, the Christian God. Luther refers to the Trinity in a variety of ways. He uses the technical term Trinity (*Dreifaltigkeit* or *trinitas*) and discusses the "article of the Trinity" as "the important article of the divine majesty."[2] As the article of the confession of faith, the Trinity forms the center of the Christian faith. When it is contested, its truth must be explicitly articulated, and when doubt terrifies the conscience, its certainty must be confessed. Diverse

---

1. Oswald Bayer's historical-genetic study of Luther's writings between 1518 and 1520 shows how the development of Luther's Reformation breakthrough is oriented to the concept of the *promissio*. According to Bayer, the *promissio* is constitutive of Christ's address in Matt 16:19 as the divine word of forgiveness that is localized in the sacraments of penance, baptism, and the Lord's Supper. Its competence is grounded in Christ's testament that is set into effect by his death and resurrection. Oswald Bayer, *Promissio*, 347, also 323 where Bayer suggests that the "theology of the *promissio*" in Luther's sermon on John 16:23ff. (dated possibly to May 13, 1520) is articulated explicitly as the doctrine of the Trinity.

2. WA 26:500.27 (Vom Abendmahl Christi: Bekenntnis, 1528). In the Schmalcald Articles (1537), Luther also refers to the Trinity and the Christological dogma by speaking "von den hohen Artickeln der Gottlichen Maiestet." WA 50:197.2-3. Luther uses the term, "Dreifaltigkeit," synonymously with the Latin, "trinitas," but prefers the term, "ein Gedritts." "Dreyfaltigkeit ist ein recht bos deudsch. Inn der Gottheit ist summa concordia. Quidam vocant dreyheit, laut spottisch. Augustinus conqueritur etiam se non habere idoneum vocabulum. Non solum est pater, sed etiam etc. Non possum dicere: sunt 3 homines, angeli, dei, kein pra(e)dicat. Das gedritts. Sind person, non 3 dii, herrn, schepffer, sed ein Gott etc. ein einig gottlich wesen. Nenne es ein gedritts. Ich kan im keinen namen geben." WA 46:436.7-12 (Sermon on Trinity Sunday, June 16, 1538). For an example of Luther's use of the term, "Dreifaltigkeit," see: WA 41:270.3, 6 (Sermon on Trinity Sunday, May 23, 1535). In the following excerpts, Luther uses the term, "trinitas." "Trinitas, unitas sunt vocabula mathematica, et tamen non possumus aliter loqui." WA 36:184.17-18 (Sermon on Trinity Sunday, May 26, 1532). Also: WA 17,1:278.6, 7 (Sermon on Trinity Sunday, June 11, 1525). Luther does not refer to the Trinity as "Dreieinigkeit." Emanuel Hirsch, *Hilfsbuch zum Studium der Dogmatik*, 17.

genre-language constellations present different understandings of the Trinitarian article of faith. Each constellation sheds particular light on the subject matter in different ways that depend on Luther's biographical context, the historical context of his utterances, and the communication structure of the genre that generates a particular language of articulation. The term "understanding" underlines how each genre-language constellation offers a unique shaping of specific Trinitarian-theological factors that remain constant in each constellation. It seeks to avoid the connotation that Luther proposes one normative doctrinal summary that can be formulated in discourses other than the confession of faith and the proposition that three *res* are one and the same as one *res*.[3]

The perspective of the present study is oriented by what I perceive to be Luther's own understanding of the theological task. For Luther, the Trinitarian article articulates the object of the Christian faith in a way that circumscribes a particular area on which the work of theology takes place. As the rule of faith (*regula fidei*), the Trinitarian article demarcates the border of the area, distinguishing the "inside" from the "outside." At the center of the "inside" is the Trinitarian article that in the Middle Ages was considered to be composed of the revealed articles of faith.[4] Luther reflects a distinctly medieval position when he considers the articles of faith to be the summary of what is contained in Scripture.[5] Scripture is not regarded solely as a historical document, whose isolated and contingent references to a binity or a trinity are only later articulated by the church as the necessary Trinitarian dogma or creed. For Luther, the article of faith summarizes the content of Scripture in assertions that are formulated, and to which assent is given, under the Spirit's guidance.[6] Mutually related to

---

3. In Latin *res* means thing.

4. Eeva Martikainen, *Doctrina*, 25–26, 69n28.

5. "Das ist nit an ßonderliche ordenung gottis geschehen, das fur den gemaynen Christen menschen, der die geschrifft nit leßen mag, vorordenet ist zu leren und wissen die tzehen gepott, den glauben und vatter unßer, in wilchen drey stucken fur war alles, was in der schrifft stett und ymer geprediget werden mag," WA 7:204.5–10 (Eine kurze Form der zehn Gebote, eine kurze Form des Glaubens, eine kurze Form des Vaterunsers, 1520); "Totum Euangelium est in symbolo," WA 11:48.23–24 (Sermon on the First Article of the Symbolum, March 4, 1523); "In his brevibus verbis omnia habes, quae in tota scriptura habentur." Ibid., 54.34–35 (Sermon on the Third Article of the Symbolum, March 6, 1523).

6. "Spiritus sanctus non est Scepticus, nec dubia aut opiniones in cordibus nostris scripsit, sed assertiones ipsa vita et omni experientia certiores et firmiores." WA 18:605.32–34 (De

each other by virtue of their identical subject matter, Scripture and dogma circumscribe the area in which reason is engaged in the theological task.

Reason is used to understand the object of faith in an area formed by the center and circumscribed by the boundary. When attacks from the boundary threaten to erode the center, or when the certainty of the center is shaken, the theological task begins. In Luther's case, the tension between center and boundary becomes painfully apparent in the work of his later, more vitriolic years. Litanies of early church heretics and harsh statements directed with one fell swoop against philosophers and other religions appear against the backdrop of Luther's own desire for a council to rehabilitate his excommunication from the church and ban from the empire. Luther considers urgent what he perceives to be the attacks of ancient heresies clothed in sixteenth-century dress: the elevation of reason above the revealed word (2 Thess 2:4)[7]—by Jews;[8] by Muslims;[9] and by philosophers.[10] Luther argues against these positions with rhetorical vigor, excluding any philosophical or religious attempts to undermine the

servo arbitrio, 1525).

7. Ibid., 685.8–9. This subject matter will be treated more fully in ch. 4, "The Hidden God."

8. The four works known in scholarly circles as anti-Jewish treatises are, "Daß Jesus Christus ein geborner Jude sei (1523)" (WA 11:314.1–336, 37), "Von den Juden und ihren Lügen (1543)" (WA 53:417.1–552.38), "Vom Schem Hamphoras und vom Geschlecht Christi (1543)" (WA 53:579.1–648.15), and *Von den letzten Worten Davids* (1543) (WA 54:28.1–100.27). These texts are exegetical treatments of Jesus' genealogy, and they represent Luther's understanding of Christ in relation to the Father's promise of the eternal kingdom. The first treatise deals with the dogma of the virgin birth, and the fourth, an exegesis of 2 Sam 23:1–7, is the only exegetical work that Luther devotes entirely to the Trinity. It cannot be disputed that Luther's dangerous rhetoric and anti-Jewish position cannot be uncritically received in contemporary theology. In view of his polemic, a critical approach to Luther's Trinitarian understanding requires exploring the complex matrix of biblical and theological issues, as well as Luther's historical location in the late medieval world. A differentiated article treating Luther's anti-Jewish statements to be part and parcel of "Luther's central convictions and concerns," his apocalyptic worldview, his understanding of political involvement in matters of blasphemy, and his specific target of rabbinic exegesis is the following: Mark U. Edwards, Jr., "Toward an Understanding of Luther's Attacks on the Jews," 15–16.

9. Luther's rhetoric against the "Turkish threat" as a military enemy and his statements against the religion of Islam must be judged in a critical light. In early 1543, a Latin-German translation of the Koran was published in Basel to which both Melanchthon and Luther wrote prefaces. For Luther's preface in which he recommends reading the Koran, although with a polemical purpose in mind, see: "Vorrede zu Theodor Biblianders Koranausgabe (1543)" in WA 53:570.27–28.

10. A differentiated interpretation of Luther's encounters with the philosophers will be discussed in ch. 2, "Luther and Aristotle" and "The Inner Trinity," and ch. 4, "The Homiletical Disputation."

certainty of faith in the divine mercy.[11] If the crassness of Luther's rhetoric can be excused as medieval custom, its denigrative and destructive intention must be received more critically. In a modern context sensitive to absences of interreligious and ecumenical conversation, central claims debated on the boundary are not to be confused with extratheological matters. Great care must be taken to interpret any judgments made about groups or positions that are incompatible with the basic soteriological core of biblical faith. If caution is exercised, Luther's responses to attacks from the boundary can be studied in ways that do not discredit reason, as the surface polemic suggests, but in ways that appreciate the use of reason to articulate the truth.

The theological task is concerned with the articulation of truth. For Luther, the Christian doctrine is the "most certain conviction of the truth."[12] Its formulation in the confession of faith makes a truth claim that falsifies any other statements uttered in the situation of extreme trial (*Anfechtung*) or madness.[13] That God does not lie does not condemn the theologian to silent worship of mystery but compels reason to articulate the truth in ways that are multivaried and genre specific.[14] The academic form of the disputation brings this truth to light in a way that unpacks the proposition

---

11. Particularly Luther's debate with a medieval Aristotelian concerning the term, "infinity," sheds light on the way Luther defines the eternity of the Triune God by eliminating specific natural philosophical and metaphysical determinations from the theological region. See: ch. 2, "Luther and Aristotle."

12. "Absit a Christianis, ut eorum doctrina sit incerta, cum apud eos debeat esse certissima persuasio veritatis et infallibilis lux." WA 40,2:385.13, 386.1-2 (Enarratio Psalmi LI, 1532/1528, to v. 8).

13. Luther claims his "theological testament," recorded in the third section of "Vom Abendmahl Christi: Bekenntnis (1528)," to be a confession of his faith in the Triune God. The Apostles' Creed is used in this text, as well as in the famous Catechisms of 1529, as the basis for his interpretation. Luther acknowledges the radical objectivity of the subject matter articulated by the confession of faith. For Luther, the truth of the confession stands; the confession remains valid in spite of both Luther's own imminently perceived death and other words he might utter in the extreme situation of trial (*Anfechtung*). "So wil ich mit dieser schrifft fur Gott und aller welt meinen glauben von stu(e)ck zu stu(e)ck bekennen, darauff ich gedencke zu bleiben bis ynn den tod. ... Denn (da Gott fur sey) ob ich aus anfechtung und todes no(e)ten etwas anders wu(e)rde sagen, so sol es doch nichts sein, und wil hie mit offentlich bekennet haben, das es unrecht und vom teuffel eingegeben sey," WA 26:499.19-21, 509:24-27.

14. Luther grounds his confession in the truth of the divine word by often citing two New Testament passages. Both Romans 3:4 and Titus 1:2 claim that God does not lie. For example: "Esto autem Deus verax, omnis homo mendax. ... Et Tit. 1: Quam promisit Deus non mendax," WA 18:619.10-11, 13; "Christianorum enim haec una et summa consolatio est in omnibus adversitatibus, nosse, quod Deus non mentitur," Ibid., 619.19-20.

that three persons are one and the same as the divine essence. The saving congruence of this truth is rendered in the nonacademic and nondisputational form of hymnody. Finally, preaching articulates this truth in language that is at once language of belief and of glorification. Each genre-language constellation represents a facet of the theological task that employs reason to understand the truth of the Triune God.

REVIEW OF LITERATURE

The subject matter of Luther's Trinitarian understanding has inspired few scholars in the history of Luther research. This gap in the field of Luther scholarship is surprising, given the current interest, at least since Barth, in orienting theology toward Trinitarian doctrine as a matrix for systematic-theological reflection.[15] The potential of Trinitarian thinking has been recovered by recent theologians in order to structure the theological enterprise as a whole, to apprehend the mystery of the divine essence of love, and to propose social models of freedom and political justice.[16] In spite of the current favor bestowed on the doctrine of the Trinity, the case of Luther's contribution to the history of this doctrine has been neglected. The subject matter of this study, Luther's understanding of the Trinity, has not figured significantly in many nineteenth- and twentieth-century reconstructions of his theology. Nor has investigating the late Luther and his theology been the object of great scholarly interest.[17] Some Luther scholars

15. Karl Barth, *Die kirchliche Dogmatik*, vol. I/1, *Die Lehre vom Wort Gottes* [Hereafter referred to as KD.]; Barth, KD, vol. I/2.

16. Barth's *Church Dogmatics* is a representative example of the effort to ground all theological reflection in the doctrine of the Trinity. Both Jüngel and Pannenberg offer interpretations of the Trinitarian dogma by relating the biblical accounts of Jesus to the proposition in 1 John 4:8 that "God is love." Jüngel discusses God's identification with Jesus on the cross as the narrative extension of the proposition in 1 John. Pannenberg poses the question of the unity of the divine nature on the basis of the self-differentiation, revealed in Scripture, between the Father, Jesus, and the Spirit. He shows how the concrete attribute of divine love can be understood, on the one hand, to motivate the economy of divine activity and, on the other, to explain the eschatological unity between the immanent and economic Trinity. See: Eberhard Jüngel, *Gott als Geheimnis der Welt*, 409–543; Wolfhart Pannenberg, *Systematische Theologie*, vol. 1, 283–364. Although in different ways, Moltmann and Boff both propose the Trinity as a model for freedom and social justice, respectively. See: Jürgen Moltmann, *Trinität und Reich Gottes*; Leonardo Boff, *Trinity and Society*.

17. Bornkamm and Junghans regret the lack of scholarly interest in the late Luther and recommend the fruitfulness of this object of study. "Ebenso fehlt es auch an Einzeluntersuchungen sowohl biographischer wie theologischer Art [des alten Luthers (1532–1546)]." Heinrich Bornkamm, "Probleme der Lutherbiographie," 19. See also: Helmar

have noticed the gap in their field.[18] Could it be that Luther himself had little to say concerning the Trinity? Or is it the case that Luther scholars have been prevented from seeing Luther's commitment to teaching, singing, and preaching about the Trinity?

The initial task of this study is to examine what has prevented scholars from accessing Luther's understanding of the Trinity. By reviewing the history of why Luther scholars have traditionally overlooked this study's theme, I critically investigate the way in which Luther has been, and is being, interpreted. For the purpose of this introduction, I intend to clarify, in a series of observations, the presuppositions underlying Luther scholarship since Ritschl that have led to the neglect of the topic of the Trinity in Luther's thought.[19] The question regarding how scholars have determined the "new" in Luther's thought, and its relation to the "old," will guide the preliminary look at the characteristic lens through which Luther is viewed and obscured. Scholarly positions have been caught between presenting

---

Junghans, "Interpreting the Old Luther (1526–1546)," 271–81. Haile's biography of the older Luther after 1535 presents, with sensitivity, Luther's rhetorical and literary strengths, and interweaves historical events with Luther's personality as well as humor. See: H. G. Haile, *Luther: An Experiment in Biography*.

18. "Luthers Trinitätslehre ist in der Lutherforschung allzu wenig beachtet worden, da die Tendenz vorherrscht, alle Aussagen Luthers zu 'christologischen' oder 'existentiellen' zu machen." David Löfgren, *Die Theologie der Schöpfung bei Luther*, 35n54. "Im ganzen sind die Auffassungen Luthers über die Trinität nur wenig oder ungenügend untersucht worden." Marc Lienhard, *Martin Luthers christologisches Zeugnis*, 237. "Les ouvrages consacrés à étudier sa doctrine sur Dieu ne nous présentent pas une théologie trinitaire tant soit peu élaborée;..." Yves M.-J. Congar, "Regards et réflexions sur la christologie de Luther," 476. "Dabei muß insbesondere auch bedacht werden, daß Luther wesentliche Lehrstücke wie das trinitarische und das christologische Dogma vergleichsweise selten erörtert, ihnen aber zweifellos für die gesamte Theologie schlechterdings fundamentale Bedeutung zuschreibt." Bernhard Lohse, *Martin Luther*, 151. "Die Behandlung der Trinitätslehre ist in den meisten Darstellungen von Luthers Theologie besonders schwach. Sieht man von einigen Darstellungen ab, die auf eine Würdigung von Luthers Trinitätslehre entweder völlig oder doch fast ganz meinen verzichten zu können, so scheint es eigentlich nirgends gelungen zu sein, das Gewicht, welches Luther selbst diesem Lehrstück beigemessen hat, angemessen zu würdigen." Lohse, "Zur Struktur von Luthers Theologie," (1985), 48; reprint, *Evangelium in der Geschichte* (1988), 244. [In subsequent notes to this text, the 1988 article will be cited.] In his last book on Luther, Lohse devotes a section to Luther and the Trinity. Lohse underlines the importance of the early church for Luther's own understanding of the Trinitarian and Christological dogmas, remarks on the relative paucity of texts in which Luther treated the subject matter of the Trinity, and chooses to subsume the Trinity under other categories, such as the divinity of God and the distinction between the *deus revelatus* and the *deus absconditus*. Lohse, *Luthers Theologie*, 223–35.

19. Detailed work on the conceptual presuppositions of Luther research has been undertaken by: Martikainen, *Doctrina*; Risto Saarinen, *Gottes Wirken auf uns*; and Graham White, *Luther as Nominalist*.

Luther as the champion of the new—whether theologically, as the proponent of evangelical freedom, or philosophically, in the neo-Kantian shape of a new metaphysical and epistemological paradigm. The old—Luther as the proponent of the Christological and Trinitarian dogmas—is viewed in less favorable terms. I suggest that the determination of the intersection between "new" and "old" is related to a neo-Kantian philosophical conception. Formed by neo-Kantian presuppositions, Luther scholarship is characterized by privileging Luther's "new" evangelical principle, eroding the significance of the "old" Trinitarian dogma in his theology.

OBSERVATIONS ON THE RECENT HISTORY
OF LUTHER SCHOLARSHIP

The historical and theological interest in the so-called Reformation breakthrough is motivated by the question concerning the determination of the "new" in its relation to the "old." Historians are not theologically neutral when they approach the seemingly genetic question of what is defined to be a key Reformation concept. Differing theological perspectives contribute to the various dates scholars assign to Luther's breakthrough.[20] By looking at what he calls Luther's transcendentalism, Reinhold Seeberg dates the breakthrough early, to the summer of 1509.[21] Bizer, and more recently Bayer, show that Luther arrived at the Reformation shape of the concepts of the righteousness of God (*iustitia dei*) and the *promissio* relatively late, respectively by 1520/21.[22] The historical dating dovetails with the theological determination of the "new" to be what is specifically Protestant. Elert captures a wide scholarly consensus when he labels Luther's breakthrough to be a distinctive Protestant approach, carrying the weight of the history of Lutheranism that follows.[23] From the fresh perspective of the "new," the

---

20. The historical task of dating the assumed breakthrough is not theologically neutral. The determination of where Luther's Reformation theology begins is a function of the interpreter's method of periodization and own theological interest. For a lively discussion of two historical-theological approaches to Luther, see Oberman, who prefers to situate Luther in continuity with his historical predecessors and Grane, who is interested in isolating the theological factors contributing to the breakthrough. Heiko A. Oberman, "Reformation: Epoche oder Episode," 56–109; Leif Grane, "Lutherforschung und Geistesgeschichte," 302–315.

21. Reinhold Seeberg, *Lehrbuch der Dogmengeschichte*, vol. 4/1, 73.

22. Ernst Bizer, *Fides ex auditu*, 174–77; Bayer, *Promissio*, 225.

23. Werner Elert, *Morphologie des Luthertums*, vol. 1, 8.

"old" is consequently painted in drab, pejorative colors. The "old" is determined to be the "unchanging and monolithic" block[24] of "metaphysical theology," the specifically medieval shape of theology from which Luther, in the eyes of his interpreters, is distanced.[25] When the "old" is distinguished from the "new" in this way, Luther's rootedness in the medieval period seems to be discredited; proclaimed is the freedom of the early modern Christian. The effort to locate the historical-theological intersection between "new" and "old" in the Reformation breakthrough ends up distancing Luther from what precedes him.

In the trajectory of nineteenth- and twentieth-century Luther scholarship, Luther's Reformation insight has been discussed in terms of his "new" understanding of justification. From Ritschl's focus on the concept of reconciliation to Bayer's study of the *promissio*, scholars have shown Luther as championing the "new," justification by faith in Christ, against what Oberman has called the Pelagianism of Biel's late medieval or nominalist soteriology.[26] Even scholars who criticized Ritschl, such as Theodosius Harnack, did not deviate from the common focus on Luther's doctrine of reconciliation and redemption.[27] In his breakthrough article, Karl Holl used the historical approach to study Luther's religious development in terms of a religion of conscience (*Gewissensreligion*).[28] Holl defined justification

---

24. White, *Luther as Nominalist*, 55.

25. Martikainen, *Doctrina*, 5–28. Of course, the label "metaphysical theology" or in German, "Substanzmetaphysik," is used by scholars in a pejorative, rather than in a precise sense. The type of metaphysics represented by different theologians during the Middle Ages varies considerably; different types cannot be subsumed easily under the one label of "substance metaphysics." Medieval theology is not limited to the study of metaphysics; it also includes logic and semantics, as ch. 2 will show.

26. Heiko A. Oberman, *Spätscholastik und Reformation*, vol. 1, 168.

27. Theodosius Harnack's two volume work on Luther aimed to criticize Ritschl's approach by providing a distinction not made by Ritschl: the distinction between the God outside of Christ and the God revealed in Christ. Both theologians, however, oriented their studies of Luther to the systematic locus of reconciliation and redemption. Theodosius Harnack, *Luthers Theologie mit besonderer Beziehung auf seine Versöhnungs- und Erlösungslehre*, vol. 1, 18.

28. Karl Holl, *Gesammelte Aufsätze zur Kirchengeschichte*, vol. 1, 35. It is the contribution of Karl Holl who observed the keystone of Luther's theology to be the first commandment. "Mit dieser Entdeckung der eindeutigen Größe des göttlichen Gebots richtet sich zum erstenmal der künftige Reformator vor uns auf." Ibid., 19. The first commandment reveals God in the law that drives the conscience to despair. Holl describes the turn from this point of the sinner's desperation to its justification in terms of the unity of two wills. Faith unites the human will with the Father's will, and the first commandment is fulfilled. Ibid., 35–36. 73–79.

as the fulfillment of the first commandment, which is brought about when faith unites the human will with the Father's will. While arguing against an "orthodox" view of faith as assent (*assensus*), Adolf von Harnack advocated a position whose turning point, at least, he detected in Luther's understanding of justifying faith. For von Harnack, faith was less knowledge (*notitia*) than trust (*fiducia*), the certainty of the forgiveness of sins as well as the personal and constant giving of the self to God.[29] The Reformation turn towards a doctrine of faith (*Glaubenslehre*), prompted by Luther's discovery of faith as trust in God's justifying activity, represented a break with the "whole of traditional doctrine," the "teaching of the councils," or the "infallible teachings" that von Harnack associated with the spirit of Greek speculation.[30] Since Holl's study of religious conscience and von Harnack's polemic against the Greek conception of Christian dogma's birth, Luther scholars have tended to link Luther's determination of justification to the subjective element, the experience of faith. Althaus, for example, opposed Luther's "salvific faith," as the trust in the divine benefits, with "dogmatic faith," as a cognitive assent to objective dogma.[31] What justifies is the former; the latter, being theoretical and without existential relevance, does not. By setting up the distance between "new" and "old" through the opposition between salvific faith and dogmatic faith, a dilemma emerged that was to affect seriously the evaluation of the place the Trinitarian dogma occupies in Luther's theology.

Arising within the conceptual framework that distanced justification by faith from the nonjustifying objectivity of dogma was the problem of assigning a location to the Trinitarian dogma in Luther's thought. For some scholars, such as Ritschl, the metaphysical vocabulary of *res* and substance

---

29. Adolf von Harnack, *Lehrbuch der Dogmengeschichte*, vol. 3, 825.

30. Ibid., 896–97.

31. Bizer describes Althaus' twofold understanding of faith as the opposition between the "Heilsglauben" and "Dogmenglauben." "... - aber ob und wie sie [the doctrine of the Trinity] zu seinem reformatorischen Glauben gehört oder ob sie diesen bloß stört, bleibt mir als Leser so unklar wie das Verhältnis des Heilsglaubens zum Dogmenglauben." Bizer's review of Althaus in Ernst Bizer, "Neue Darstellungen der Theologie Luthers," 320. Althaus explicitly uses the term, "Heilsglauben." Instead of using the term, "Dogmenglauben," Althaus writes about this faith as one that assents to historical facts. "Dadurch unterscheidet er [der Heilsglaube] sich von einem nur theoretischen, historischen und metaphysischen Glauben, der die historischen Fakta der Geschichte und seine Gottheit für wahr hält, ohne sie auf die eigene Existenz zu beziehen." Paul Althaus, *Die Theologie Martin Luthers*, 170.

(*substantia*) could have no place in a discussion of the "subjective religious experience" that reduced faith to the "instrument of and capacity for all Christian life and work."[32] For von Harnack, Luther did not go far enough in ridding his vocabulary and conceptuality of the "worst fantasies of nominalist Sophists."[33] The Reformation could finally arrive at closure only when the nominalist vestiges of dogmatic discourse were banned.[34] Elert sums up the line of thinking that regards the Trinity as an uninvited "erratic block,"[35] standing at considerable distance from the Protestant approach.

Other scholars did not perceive a problem in Luther's carpentering the "new" faith onto the "old" dogma. Wernle, for example, suggests that Luther united the early church's "dry, stiff" dogma to the warm-blooded New Testament witness, without being conscious of their difference.[36] Luther was seen to breathe new life into a dogma that had been turned to cold stone by the Scholastics.[37] Although scholars, such as Wernle and Prenter, gesture sympathetically to Luther's view of the Trinity, they betray, at a deeper level, a suspicion explicitly articulated by Ritschl and von Harnack. For proponents from both sides, dogma, both in its early church and medieval forms, is represented as cold and lifeless. Either a breath of fresh Reformation air or a thorough pruning is required to assign a place to or

---

32. Ritschl writes, "meint er [Luther] mit der Rechtfertigung durch den Glauben an Christus eine subjective religiöse Erfahrung des in der Kirche stehenden Gläubigen ... zugleich [der Glaube] auch das drastische Organ alles christlichen Leben und Thuns ist." Albrecht Ritschl, *Die christliche Lehre von der Rechtfertigung und Versöhnung*, vol. 1, 141, 157.

33. "Indem er dabei seine Grundgedanken doch nicht preisgeben wollte, gerieth er auf Speculationen, die den abenteuerlichsten und schlimmsten Phantasien der nominalistischen Sophisten nichts nachgaben." A. von Harnack, *Lehrbuch der Dogmengeschichte*, 3:875. A taste of von Harnack's rhetorical force is offered by the following quote. "Das Dogma erscheint erstarrt - elastisch nur in der Hand politischer Priester - und in Sophisterei verwildert. ... Da erschien Luther," Ibid., 902.

34. Albrecht Ritschl, *Theologie und Metaphysik*, 19.

35. Elert, *Morphologie*, 191.

36. "Seltsam sind hier von Luther das altkirchliche Dogma vom Geist und das lebenswarme Zeugnis des Neuen Testamentes vom Geist addiert worden, trockenste, steifste Theologie mit begeistertem Zeugnis des religiösen Erlebens, ohne dass Luther die Verschiedenheit dieser Elemente empfunden zu haben scheint." Paul Wernle, *Der evangelische Glaube nach den Hauptschriften der Reformatoren*, vol. 1, 274.

37. Prenter claims that the Trinitarian dogma was rendered lifeless by the Scholastics. According to Prenter, the Scholastics connected a Pelagian understanding of salvation with immanent Trinitarian speculation. In continuity with the early church, Luther breathed new life into the Trinitarian doctrine by relating the notion of a lively faith in the Trinity with the theology of the cross. Regin Prenter, *Spiritus Creator*, 180-83.

purge the Trinitarian dogma from Luther's theology in a way acceptable to those reconstructing it.

Some scholars have linked the appearance of the Trinitarian dogma in Luther's theology to his reception of the early church's Trinitarian formulations and terminology. Instead of dismissing the Trinitarian dogma outright as a distinctly medieval subject of speculation, scholars have argued for harmony between Luther's understanding of the early church's lively faith in the Trinity and the "new" element of his theology. Remarkable variation characterizes the interpretations of Luther's reception of the early church dogma. On the one hand, Koopmans has suggested that Luther tends towards a Greek Trinitarian model because he defines the Trinitarian persons as relations of origin from the Father, the ἀρχή.[38] On the other hand, Luther has also been placed in the trajectory of the Latin Trinitarian model. Peters has suggested that Luther's understanding of the immanent Trinitarian relations as "from/out of both" (ab/ex utroque) is part and parcel of the Latin tradition of Trinitarian theology.[39] Having commented on the De Trinitate in 1509, Luther continued to hold onto Augustine's view that God's unity is preserved in outer-Trinitarian works. The classic phrase, the external works of the Trinity are indivisible (opera trinitatis ad extra sunt indivisa)—never found word-for-word in the Bishop of Hippo's works—is mentioned in the only treatise Luther devoted entirely to the Trinity.[40] A minimal investigation into Luther's Trinitarian understanding has been undertaken by a few scholars. Assured in the research is, at least, Luther's reception of the early church dogma. Whether cast according to an Eastern or a Western model, the Reformer's continuity with Catholic tradition is supposedly safeguarded.

The more daring, and perhaps more mistaken, line of interpretation saw an appropriation of early church heresies in Luther's Trinitarian theology. Holl initiated a debate when he suggested that Luther's understanding of the relationship between Christ and the Father was subordinationist.

---

38. "Es ist nur eine Tendenz in dieser Richtung festzustellen." Jan Koopmans, Das altkirchliche Dogma in der Reformation, 64.

39. Albrecht Peters, "Die Trinitätslehre in der reformatorischen Christenheit," 567. Lienhard shows that Luther receives his understanding of the inner-Trinitarian relations from Augustine. Lienhard, Martin Luthers christologisches Zeugnis, 241–42.

40. Mentioned in, for example, WA 54:57.35–36 (Von den letzten Worten Davids, 1543).

According to Holl's interpretation, the subordinationist element comes to the fore in Luther's exegesis of 1 Corinthians 15:24. Christ, as the Father's instrument (*Werkzeug*), accomplishes salvation in history. Christ's subordinate status will be disclosed at the eschaton, when he will return the kingdom to his Father.[41] Holl further identified a modalist tendency in Luther's translation of the Old Testament, which attributed to Christ the divine titles of "Jehovah" and "Lord of Hosts" (*Herr Zebaoth*). Erich Seeberg joined Holl in noting a modalism that corrected the subordinationist heresy.[42] If the Son is regarded to be ultimately subordinate to the Father at the eschaton, the divinity of the Son must be safeguarded in time in order to correctly claim that salvation has been accomplished. Modalism, according to Holl and Erich Seeberg, secures the divine status of the Son's historical dispensation.

In addition to being accused of subordinationism and modalism, Luther has also been charged with another Trinitarian heresy, "tritheism." Peters has noticed a "naive tritheism" in Luther's Trinitarian theology, both in the economic Trinitarian emphasis of Luther's explanation of the Creed and in the discussion of the inner Trinity as a conversation of love between three distinct speakers.[43] The relegation of Luther's description of the Trinity to a distinct heresy is, in Peters's case, too swift. In terms of classic Trinitarian theology, tritheism, as an accusation, is properly located at the level of the inner Trinity. Modalism, on the other hand, is a charge that can be ascribed

---

41. Holl, *Gesammelte Aufsätze*, 72.

42. "Es ist kein Zweifel, daß die subordinatianischen Züge in der Christologie Luthers, ... durch einen altertümlichen und frommen Modalismus korrigiert werden, der mir wirklich für die Anschauung Luthers von Christus konstitutiv zu sein scheint." Erich Seeberg, *Luthers Theologie in ihren Grundzügen*, 88, see esp. 86–88; See also: Ibid., *Luthers Theologie*, vol. 2, 52–53.

43. Peters attributes the "naive tritheism" of Luther's explanation of the Creed to the catechism's simplicity and ease for memorization. "Um der katechetischen Einprägsamkeit willen nimmt Luther das Mißverständnis eines 'naiven Tritheismus' (Karl Thieme) in Kauf." Peters, "Die Trinitätslehre," 564. Peters also claims that with "Luther könnte man eher von einer Neigung zum Tritheismus sprechen. Ihm sind Vater, Sohn und Geist gleichsam die drei Träger des innergöttlichen Liebesgespräches, in welches uns die Offenbarung einbezieht ... Handlungsträger sind hier die Personen; so gewinnt der Ternar einen personal-tritheistischen Anklang." Ibid., 568. Peters makes a similar claim concerning the tritheistic "coloring" of Luther's portrayal of the immanent Trinity. According to Peters, Luther understands the immanent Trinity to be constituted by three independent "Personzentren," or centers of personhood. Idem, "Verborgener Gott—Dreieiniger Gott," 87. What Peters neglects to consider in his study is Luther's reception of the Western theological definition of the term "person." For this reception, see: ch. 2, "The Inner Trinity." The inner-Trinitarian conversation of love in the hymn, "Now Rejoice, Dear Christians," also studied by Peters, will be investigated in ch. 3.

only to the outer Trinity. If it can be shown that the inner-divine life is not adequately differentiated as three persons, and that the outer manifestation of the divine is parsed according to three dispensations or modes, then modalism, not tritheism, might be detected at the level of the outer Trinity. Peters is correct insofar as he locates the charge of tritheism at the level of the immanent Trinity. However, Peters is mistaken in his position because he too quickly dismisses Luther's understanding of the inner-Trinitarian conversation of love. Peters neglects to locate Luther's conception in continuity with a particular exegetical and theological tradition of Trinitarian reflection that cannot be regarded as heretical.

The demonstrations of Luther's continuity with the early church present Luther's Trinitarian theology in ways that are varied, if not conflicting. Claimed to be in continuity with the early church dogma, Luther's understanding of the Trinity has been seen as reflecting the heresies of the early church as well. A difficulty is exposed when various investigations of Luther's thought end up charging Luther with heretical tendencies of modalism, subordinationism, or tritheism. In the following discussion, I locate this difficulty as a function of the conceptual framework in which Luther's Trinitarian theology has, until now, been treated.

A common horizon can be detected behind the diverse accusations of heresy. Whether modalist, subordinationist, or tritheist, these charges seem to issue from a conceptual frame of reference incapable of adequately defining the inner-Trinitarian unity and its distinctions. In Holl's case, Christ works in time as the instrument by which the human will is united with the Father's will. Holl's concentration on Christ's work at the level of the economic Trinity detracts from making the necessary Trinitarian distinctions in the immanent Trinity. Problems in his portrayal of the outer Trinity result. As Prenter has pointed out, Holl does not sufficiently distinguish between Son and Spirit.[44] The charge of modalism, on Holl's terms, is a result of both diverting the theological attention from the immanent

---

44. A defense of Luther's Trinitarian orthodoxy against Holl's charges is undertaken by Prenter, who, on Trinitarian grounds, shows that Holl does not sufficiently distinguish between Christ and the Spirit as persons. According to Prenter, Holl posits a "sign of sameness" [*Gleichheitszeichen*] between the Christian's new life and the Holy Spirit, as well as between the Holy Spirit, understood in this way, and Christ. Although, according to Prenter, Holl unjustly accuses Luther of modalism, Prenter suggests that Holl's conclusion is warranted on the latter's own terms. Prenter, *Spiritus Creator*, 183–87, 356–57n25. For a discussion of the Holl-Prenter debate, see: Kjell Ove Nilsson, *Simul*, 177n29.

to the economic Trinity and collapsing the divine economy into the work of Christ. Subordinationism, according to Erich Seeberg and Holl, is supposed to rehabilitate modalism. This accusation, however, complements the modalist view. If the unity of the divine essence cannot be adequately maintained at the level of the inner Trinity, then the persons cannot be determined to each be one and the same as the divine essence. An inadequate description of the inner-Trinitarian unity is also characteristic of the tritheist charge. Peters's problematic position seems to arise from the application of an agency model that misunderstands or omits the traditional determination of the inner-Trinitarian unity.[45] The definition of personhood—or, in this case, subject of speech—must include both the personal characteristic, or the relation, and the divine essence, or the *res*.

Where the diverse charges of heresy can be seen to converge is on a common privileging of the economic Trinity as the site of Trinitarian differentiation. Fascination with the incarnation as the site of this differentiation could, as Lienhard has suggested, explain the charge of modalism.[46] More precisely, the lack of attention paid to the inner Trinity has to do with its elimination from the range of the scholar's view.[47] The marginalization of the inner Trinity seems to result from the current preoccupation with the economic Trinity as the site of the "new" in Luther's theology. By determining the "new" to be justification by faith, scholars have tended to privilege the divine economy as the location where the "new" is accomplished and imputed to the sinner. Why does this convergence between soteriology and the divine economy contribute to the overlooking of the inner Trinity? Related to the Trinitarian-theological claims advanced by interpreters of Luther is the philosophical-theological lens through which the Reformer is viewed, a lens whose focal power is not to be underestimated.

The conceptual link between the "new" in Luther's theology and its assignment to the divine economy is, to a large extent, a function

---

45. In ch. 3, I will show how Luther understands the inner Trinity to be constituted by three subjects of speech in a way that does not merit the charge of tritheism. When Luther conceives subjects as speakers, he is appealing to an early church type of exegesis, prosopographic exegesis, that has its biblical source in the royal psalms.

46. Lienhard, *Martin Luthers christologisches Zeugnis*, 112, 121.

47. Lohse's remark captures the opinion of many scholars. "Über die innertrinitarischen Beziehungen der drei göttlichen Personen hat Luther sich kaum irgendwo geäußert." Lohse, *Luthers Theologie*, 227.

of neo-Kantian philosophical presuppositions. Iwand has noticed the neo-Kantian shape of the "for me" (pro me) discourse that characterizes interpretations of Luther,[48] and Saarinen has explicated this observation in detail.[49] Distinct from any "for itself" (für sich) statements regarding the nature of the divine essence is the novelty of conceiving the Trinity in terms of its effects or the "for us" (für uns) address.[50] The turn in language towards the "for us" (pro nobis) reflects a theological shift toward privileging the epistemological accent of what Saarinen has classified as neo-Protestant, Luther-renaissance, and Barthian dialectical theology.[51] In individual theologians from all three groups, Saarinen has shown that the two concepts of effect and the transcendental have formed a theological epistemology that accounts for the ways in which the divine works can be known to be "for me" (pro me).[52] Beginning with Ritschl and Herrmann, an uncritical rejection of what was assumed to be substantial metaphysics was coupled with an appropriation of Lotze's concept of a web of phenomenal effects that mediated an unknown cause.[53] Later scholars followed Ritschl in using the Kantian distinction between nature and spirit in order to work out a transcendental theological metaphysics oriented toward conceiving the divine economy. The divine transcendent will could not be identified with the empirical world known by the senses, nor could it be determined by abstracting the metaphysical cause from the order of

---

48. Iwand argues that much Luther scholarship is colored by this assumption. According to Iwand, the *pro me* has emerged as the determining figure in the Kantian reception of Luther. The *pro me* is understood to be a principle of knowledge that is applied in order to articulate a "Werturteil" concerning God's relation *pro me*, rather than to make a "Seinsurteil" about God. Hans Joachim Iwand, "Wider den Mißbrauch des 'pro me' als methodisches Prinzip in der Theologie," 123.

49. Saarinen explains that the aim of his study is to analyze the conceptual framework of Luther research undertaken until now. He writes, "Eine rein forschungsgeschichtliche Studie ist nicht in der Lage, über die Richtigkeit der Lutherinterpretationen zu urteilen. Wenn die Analyse der Forschungsgeschichte die Denkformen der bisherigen Untersuchungen sichtbar macht, schafft sie nur eine notwendige Voraussetzung für solche kritische Prüfung." Saarinen, *Gottes Wirken auf uns*, 4.

50. A. von Harnack, *Lehrbuch der Dogmengeschichte*, 3:860.

51. Saarinen, *Gottes Wirken auf uns*, 6.

52. Ibid., 229.

53. Ibid., 80–85.

nature.[54] Knowledge of the transcendent will was available through its effects revealed to faith.[55] Faith was regarded as the quasi-epistemological instrument by which the divine benefits were "known" to be the effects of the divine cause. Once a transcendental metaphysics was linked to faith as the subjective reception of the divine effects "for me" (*pro me*), reflection on the Trinity was limited to the Trinitarian differentiation at the level of its works—most importantly, the work of Christ on the cross.

Within the neo-Kantian paradigm, the connection emerged between faith and Christ on the cross. Both the metaphysics of effects that character-ized earlier Luther studies and the existentially construed relational ontol-ogy that forms much recent scholarship establish a correlation between the work of Christ on the cross and its effect in faith.[56] Two moments can be seen to constitute what Luther scholars have termed the "theology of the cross" (*theologia crucis*).[57] The first moment points to the divine hid-denness on the cross; hidden underneath the blood sacrifice is the divine mercy. The effects of this event determine the second moment of the cor-relation. The concept of justification includes its subjective reception in faith, a concept discussed by scholars in various ways. Elert, for exam-ple, attributes transcendental status to the "I" who is justified by faith.[58]

---

54. Ritschl argues against a metaphysical determination of the objects of knowledge. He claims that a metaphysics of "things" erases the distinction in the object between nature and spirit. Ritschl, *Theologie und Metaphysik*, 31. It remains to be argued whether metaphysics can be immediately identified with epistemology that, on Ritschl's terms, leads to discussing objects as substantial essences.

55. Several examples of the metaphysics of effects connected with Luther's transcen-dentalism are: R. Seeberg, *Lehrbuch der Dogmengeschichte*, 47–48, 152–57; E. Seeberg, *Luthers Theologie in ihren Grundzügen*, 48–52. 216. On the metaphysics of the law of opposites, see: Idem, *Luthers Theologie. Motive und Ideen*, vol. 1, 124–33.

56. For lack of a more precise label, I use the term, "relational ontology," to refer to those interpretations of Luther that make claims for different kinds of theological identities, or relations. A more detailed explanation of a "relational ontology" as the conceptual frame-work in which Luther's sermons are interpreted, is offered in ch. 4, "Luther and the Sermon."

57. It is to von Loewenich that Luther research owes the thesis that the theology of the cross forms the overarching rubric of Luther's thought and theology. Von Loewenich states the thesis of his well-known book. "Wir verfechten dem gegenüber [Otto Ritschl] die These: *die theologia crucis ist ein Prinzip der gesamten Theologie Luthers, sie darf nicht auf eine besondere Periode seiner Theologie eingeschränkt werden.*" Walther von Loewenich, *Luthers Theologia Crucis*, 14–15. [Italics in the original text.] On a discussion of Luther's subjective and soteriological reception of the dogmas of the early church, see: Ibid., *Luther und der Neuprotestantismus*, 407–415.

58. Elert, *Morphologie*, 60, 62–63, 72–73.

Ebeling conceives justification as the existential reception in faith of the word from the cross.[59] Christ on the cross, rendered present to the believer through the word, becomes the existential content of faith in the divine mercy. Whether conceived according to a metaphysics of effects or a relational ontology, Luther's theology of the cross is seen as grounded in the Christ-faith *Grundrelation*,[60] or word-faith relation.[61] The cross becomes the economic Trinitarian site at which the soteriological crux of Luther's theology is concentrated; preoccupied with a Christologically reduced understanding of justification and the "for me" (*pro me*) reception in faith, Luther's view of the Trinity—the inner-Trinitarian essence as well as its creation-theological and pneumatological breadth—is obscured.

The fixed lens of the Christ-faith correlation is not the only source of detraction from a Trinitarian view. Difficulty conceiving of the relationship between scriptural statements and church dogma is evident in Luther scholarship, as it is in contemporary theological discussion. For Luther scholars working within the neo-Kantian paradigm, the reduction of Luther's understanding of God to Christology is a function of privileging the cross as the epistemically accessible location of divine self-disclosure. In view of this theological insight, the New Testament Gospels become the source for perceiving the revelation of the divine mercy to faith under its opposite, the cross.[62] Tied together with this biblical-theological program is a conviction that Luther's biblical hermeneutic cannot account for a witness to the Trinity in the Old Testament that is either more complex than

---

59. Gerhard Ebeling, *Lutherstudien*, vol. 1, 24–25; Martikainen, *Doctrina*, 15.

60. Ebeling writes, "Neu ist… vor allem die Erfassung der Korrespondenz von Christus und Glaube als der darin wirksamen Grundrelation." Gerhard Ebeling, "Luther II: Theologie," 500.

61. Idem, *Luther: Einführung in sein Denken*, 73.

62. I am not disputing that Luther grounds knowledge of the Triune God in the Second Person of the Trinity. ["Qui scrutando non volet errare, nec a maiestatis gloria opprimi, is fide tangat et apprehendat Filium Dei in carne manifestatum." WA 39,2:255.20–21 (Die Promotionsdisputation von Erasmus Alberus on Aug. 24, 1543, thesis 37).] What I am suggesting is that the constellation formed by the *theologia crucis*-faith relation ends where I would like to start: a Trinitarian movement beginning with the Spirit, who guides the church to know Christ and Christ who, in turn, incorporates believers into his person on whom the Father's good pleasure rests.

a series of proof texts of the Trinitarian dogma,[63] or more unique than the voices heard in the New Testament and in the dogma.[64]

The hermeneutic poverty in conceiving the Old Testament in relation to the Trinity is not indigenous to Luther scholarship. In contemporary theological discussion, the New Testament records of Jesus' life and death are regarded as the site where Trinitarian self-differentiation and identification are accessible.[65] Although theologians attempt to consider the Old Testament witness to the Trinity in relation to that of the New,[66] a peculiarly modern difficulty haunts the exegetical work of systematic theologians. The discussion is hard-pressed by the insistent question of how to conceive the move from the various biblical statements in both Testaments to the necessity of the Trinitarian dogma.[67] Related to the privileging of

63. In the only monograph to date on Luther's doctrine of the Trinity, Jansen treats the question of the Trinity and the Old Testament under the heading, "Weitere Schriftbeweise aus dem Alten Testament." Reiner Jansen, *Studien zu Luthers Trinitätslehre*, 171. Jansen studies various passages as "proofs" of the Trinity in the Old Testament, such as the Christological-prophetic texts (2 Sam 23:1–7), and the grammatical "proof" of the plural name for God (for example, Gen 1:26; Exod 33:19). Ibid., 171–77.

64. In his renowned book on Luther and the Old Testament, Bornkamm concludes that the Old Testament does not contribute significantly to Luther's doctrine of the Trinity. "Es bietet ihm nur eine Reihe willkommener Belegstellen, gestaltet die dem Neuen Testament und der kirchlichen Überlieferung entnommene Lehre aber bei ihm nicht." Heinrich Bornkamm, *Luther und das Alte Testament*, 102–103.

65. Jüngel discusses Jesus' death in terms of both God's identification with Jesus, or God's relation to Jesus, and the distinction between "God and God." Jüngel, *Gott als Geheimnis der Welt*, 480–82. 510–11. Jüngel states that the "faktische Begründung des trinitarischen Dogmas" is grounded "im Kreuzestod Jesu..." Idem, "Das Verhältnis von 'ökonomischer' und 'immanenter' Trinität," 268. Pannenberg begins to ground his understanding of the Trinity in the New Testament record of the Jesus-abba distinction, and then moves to discuss their unity in terms of Christ's eternal sonship, Pannenberg, *Systematische Theologie*, 287–89. Pannenberg does betray a privileging of the New Testament revelation of the Trinity. "Eine Begründung der Trinitätslehre aus dem *Inhalt* der Offenbarung Gottes in Jesus Christus muß ausgehen vom Verhältnis Jesu zum Vater, wie es im Zusammenhang der Botschaft von der Gottesherrschaft seinen Ausdruck gefunden hat. Die Aussagen des Neuen Testaments über die Gottheit Jesu setzen nämlich seine Gottessohnschaft voraus und sind damit letztlich begründet im Sohnesverhältnis Jesu zum Vater." Ibid., 331. [Italics in the original text.]

66. Jüngel suggests that the "fact of the biblical narrative of promise" is to be understood, not as witness or document, but as the phenomenon belonging together with the concept of God. Jüngel, *Gott als Geheimnis der Welt*, 480. Pannenberg claims that the God of Jesus is the same God witnessed to in the Old Testament. The distinction between the two testaments rests on the specification of the name and person, "Father," in the New Testament. Pannenberg, *Systematische Theologie*, 283–87.

67. The problem of relating New Testament statements concerning the relation between Father, Spirit, and Jesus to the Creed's formulation of the Trinitarian dogma is distinctly modern. See: Jüngel, "Das Verhältnis von 'ökonomischer' und 'immanenter' Trinität," 268;

the New Testament as the source for epistemic access to the distinction between Jesus and his Father could be the avoidance—perhaps even the rejection—of the Old Testament as the warrant for the Trinity. When studying the exegetical elements feeding into Luther's understanding of the Trinity, it becomes apparent that Luther's use of Old Testament passages, particularly the royal and penitential Psalms, figures significantly in his view of the inner Trinity. Luther's Trinitarian hermeneutic—operating in both Testaments—rests on his understanding of the relation between Scripture and dogma, built on late medieval soil.[68] Laying this foundation makes it possible to study the potential Luther assigns to both Testaments to disclose distinct yet harmonious representations of the Trinity.

Privileging the economic Trinity is related to the question of its dispensation. Epistemic access to the cross is decisively soteriological; what is known on the cross is God as God acts and not God as God is.[69] In conceiving God as God acts, an ontological status must be assigned to the dispensation so as not to compromise the soteriological efficacy of the divine economy. When it comes to resolving conceptual difficulties regarding the Trinity, none other than Hegel, or various versions of him, can be brought into the discussion. The so-called Hegelian figure of a "salvation history" (*Heilsgeschichte*) has been used to interpret Luther's Trinitarian thought. According to this figure, the dispensation of three distinct divine acts is elevated into a metalevel narrative.[70] At this level, the theological category of salvation history (*Heilsgeschichte*) borrows from what is assumed to be a Hegelian account of the Christian narrative that extends through the three points plotting the three divine acts.[71] Each divine act is allocated

---

Idem, *Gott als Geheimnis der Welt*, 480–81. For Luther, the Trinitarian article, as it is articulated in the Apostles' Creed, consists of the summary of what is contained in Scripture; the article is not viewed at the level of necessary dogmatic formulation for which Scripture contains only the possibility of its articulation as dogma.

68. This theme will be addressed in ch. 2, "The Inner Trinity as the Subject Matter of the Disputation."

69. This is Lienhard's formulation in Lienhard, *Martin Luthers christologisches Zeugnis*, 239.

70. For an appreciation and a criticism of the *Heilsgeschichte* category in contemporary biblical theology, see: Brevard S. Childs, *Biblical Theology of the Old and New Testaments*, 16–18.

71. For a uniquely detailed, sensitively nuanced, and powerfully argued study of Hegel's Trinitarian narrativity, see: Cyril O'Regan, *The Heterodox Hegel*, esp. 319–23. O'Regan argues that the attribution of the *Heilsgeschichte* model to Hegel is actually a misinterpretation of the Swabian philosopher. In sublating the religious *Vorstellung* into the philosophical *Begriff*,

a place in the history of salvation; the economic order of the appropriations follows the order of the Trinitarian persons confessed in the Apostles'
Creed.[72] In view of Luther's catechetical texts, both Löfgren and Peters
interpret Luther's Trinitarian understanding according to such a "salvation-historical" structure.[73] The three acts are appropriated to the three
persons—Creator, Redeemer, and Sanctifier—and a narrative order plots
the progression in the divine economy. When Luther's understanding of
the Trinity is reduced in this way to an economy and conceived as a progressive unfolding of salvific acts, then it becomes clear why the charge of
modalism is easily bandied about.[74] This charge of modalism, however, is

---

Hegel makes use of "various denarratizing operations" in order "to remove any hint in discourse that the divine movement can be viewed as a sequence of discrete actions strung
together on a temporal line," and to effect the "erasure of suggestions of contingency," and
to erase "the tendency in representation to construe divine activity in terms of discrete acts
of will." Ibid., 340.

72. The idea that the periodization of history into three "tempora" of Father, Son, and
Spirit is associated with Joachim of Fiore, whom Hegel received in his Trinitarian thought.
On Hegel's transformative reception of Fiore, see: Ibid., 265-70. Luther also alludes to Fiore
on the subject of the Trinity, although not in the context of discussing the economy. For
Luther's reception of Fiore's criticism of Lombard regarding the inner Trinity, see: ch. 2, "The
Semantics of the Inner-Trinitarian Proposition."

73. Löfgren sees the economic activity of the Trinity in creation as the salvation-historical
"Betrachtungsweise" of God as continuous creator. Löfgren, *Die Theologie der Schöpfung bei
Luther*, 35n54. Peters also speaks about the "heilsökonomische Bewegung des [trinitarischen]
Symbols" [Peters, "Die Trinitätslehre," 563], and the "heilsgeschichtliche Dynamik" of Luther's
Trinitarian conceptuality. Peters, "Verborgener Gott—Dreieiniger Gott," 83. The conceptual
limitation to a salvation history might be, in Peters's case, a function of the texts chosen in the
analysis. Peters concentrates on Luther's confessional writings with their decided emphasis
on the economy of God's activity.

74. The usual warrant for a modalist reading of Luther's Large Catechism is the following
excerpt taken from his explanation to the third article of the Creed, "Das ist nu der Artickel,
der da ymerdar ym werck gehen und bleiben mus. Denn die schepffung haben wir nu hynweg,
so ist die Erlo(e)sung auch ausgerichtet, aber der Heilige geist treibt sein werck on unterlas
bis auff den iu(e)ngsten tag," WA 30,2:191.17-20 (Der Große Katechismus, 1529). Jenson suggests that the charge of modalism results from confusing the names Luther gives to the three
persons of the Trinity with their proper names. "In einem anderen Kontext würde ich die
offensichtlich modalistische Form, die Luther für diese Anordnung gibt, beklagen. 'Schöpfer,
Versöhner und Heiligmacher' ist natürlich kein Äquivalent für 'Vater, Sohn und Geist', wie
Lutheraner weithin denken, es aus Luthers Katechismen gelernt zu haben." Robert W. Jenson,
"Die trinitarische Grundlegung," 15n12. A discussion in ch. 4, "Luther and the Sermon" will
challenge the metaphysics of effects that scholars have used to conceptualize the identity
between person and work in such a way as to interpret Luther's explanation of the Creed in
the Large Catechism in a modalist fashion. This discussion also takes into account the genre of
the catechism in which Luther derives the names of the three persons from the verbs of their
appropriations. In his explanation to the second article of the Creed, Luther uses the name
"Erlöser" rather than "Versöhner" (*contra* Asendorf's translation of Jenson!) and subsumes

premature; in order to represent what Luther would stress as the eternal relations on the inner side of God, genres other than catechetical writings, such as the disputation, must be considered.

If Luther's Trinitarian understanding has appeared in studies of the catechetical genre, it has all but disappeared in many systematic theological reconstructions of his theology. Some theologians have ordered the doctrine of the Trinity after the doctrine of God, usually after the themes typically associated with the Reformation, such as sin and law.[75] Others have entirely neglected to include the Trinity, as Bizer has remarked.[76] These reconstructions possibly order Luther's theology according to the structure of Protestant Lutheran orthodox dogmatic manuals. In the prolegomena to these manuals, the Trinity follows a section on natural theology (theologia naturalis), in a section on sacred Scripture (de scriptura sacra) that includes a summary of the articles of faith and symbols of the

---

this name in the confession of faith under the biblical name, "Herr." "Antwort auffs ku(e)rtzte: Ich gleube, das Jhesus Christus, warhafftiger Gottes son, sey mein HErr worden. Was ist nu das 'Ein Herr werden'? Das ists, das er mich erlo(e)set hat von sunde, vom Teuffel, vom tode und allem unglu(e)ck." WA 30,1:186.10-13.

75. Some examples of ordering the Trinity under the concept of God are: R. Seeberg orders a discussion of the Trinity together with Christology and the work of Christ (§79) only after the concept of God (§77) and the doctrine of sin (§78). R. Seeberg, Lehrbuch der Dogmengeschichte, 230-36. The theme is picked up again in a discussion of Luther's reception of the early church dogmas (§86). Ibid., 426-32. In part 1 of his Morphologie, Elert discusses the evangelical Ansatz under the related themes of sin, law, wrath, and natural theology, and only in part 2 discusses the doctrine of the Trinity under the doctrine of God in a section entitled, "Dogma und Kirche." Elert, 190-95. E. Seeberg's systematic reconstruction of Luther's theology begins with the doctrine of God, first hidden, then concretely revealed in Christ; a discussion of the Trinity is lacking. E. Seeberg, Luthers Theologie in ihren Grundzügen, 74-81. Althaus structures his reconstruction of Luther's theology in two parts, knowledge of God and God's work. A short excursus on the Trinity is squashed between these two sections. Althaus, Die Theologie Martin Luthers, 175-77. The structure of Pinomaa's reconstruction of Luther's theology follows a similar pattern, moving from the doctrine of God and the particular revelation in the word received by faith, to Christology and pneumatology; in Pinomaa's reconstruction, a treatment of the Trinity is lacking. Lennart Pinomaa, Sieg des Glaubens, 31-34.

76. Focusing on the twofold word of law and gospel, Ebeling's introduction to Luther omits a treatment of the Trinity altogether. In his introduction to Luther's thought, Ebeling only mentions one statement on Luther and the Trinity. The citation, from the Dictata (1513-1515), refers to the Trinity in the context of the spirit/letter distinction [WA 4:365.5-14 (Dictata super Psalterium, Psalm 118/119, to v. 135)]. Ebeling, Luther: Einführung in sein Denken, 108; Bizer criticizes Ebeling with humorful irony. "Aber die einzige theologische assertio, die dort ausgesprochen wird, ist Gottes Verborgenheit... So wird auch von 'Luthers Reden von Gott' gehandelt und dabei die Trinitätslehre nur unter den vorausgesetzten einstigen Selbstverständlichkeiten erwähnt (S. 281) — als ob der christliche Gott jemals ein anderer sein dürfte als der dreieinige und als ob Luther nicht mehr und mehr gerade darauf Wert gelegt habe!" Bizer, "Neue Darstellungen," 345.

church.[77] In the main portion of the works, the Trinity is only ordered after discussions of the natural and supernatural knowledge of God, the divine essence and its attributes.[78] By reconstructing Luther's theology to fit the structure of seventeenth and eighteenth-century dogmatic theology, a view is blocked as to the possibility of locating Luther in the tradition of thought in which he is historically located. Recent scholars, searching for the "Catholic Luther" have come up with original insights on the medieval shape of Luther's thought.[79] For the purposes of looking at the Trinity, a difference can be detected between medieval and early-modern treatments of the Trinity in their respective systems and the side of God that these treatments emphasize. Medieval theologians, commenting on Peter Lombard's *Sentences*, assigned great importance to discussing the inner Trinity in detail at the beginning of their works.[80] Only in books three and four do the topics of Christology and the sacraments, generally associated with the economic Trinity, come to the fore. If a balance can be found in interpreting Luther's thought between the late-medieval and later orthodox systems, then perhaps a more differentiated and richer view of his contributions can be appreciated.

Such failure to regard the significance of the immanent Trinity in Luther's theology may be related to disregard for Luther's Catholic or medieval roots. It also may reflect a particular line of interpretation that uses Luther's own words to emphasize the "new." On heated occasions, Luther

---

77. Heinrich Schmid, *Die Dogmatik der evangelisch-lutherischen Kirche*, 73–79.

78. Ibid., 96–114.

79. In Roman Catholic scholarship on Luther, efforts have recently been oriented towards discovering the "Catholic Luther," or the Luther in continuity with elements of the Catholic tradition. Following the lead of Joseph Lortz and in the company of Otto Hermann Pesch whose monumental work brings Luther into conversation with Aquinas, Peter Manns suggests that the Catholic Luther can be found in two areas. Manns traces the common bond between Luther and Clairvaux by situating Luther in the monastic tradition, and he also recovers aspects of early scholastic theology in Luther's thinking. Peter Manns, "Zum Gespräch zwischen Martin Luther und der katholischen Theologie," 441–532. See also: Otto Hermann Pesch, *Theologie der Rechtfertigung bei Martin Luther und Thomas von Aquin*; and Denis R. Janz, *Luther on Thomas Aquinas*.

80. Book One of Peter Lombard's *Sentences* is devoted to the inner Trinity, a precedent followed by theologians, such as Ockham. Lombard begins Book I with "De Mysterio Trinitatis" and entitles d. 2, c. 1 (4), "De mysterio trinitatis et unitatis." See: Petrus Lombardus, *Sententiae in IV libris distinctae, Tom. I, Pars I, Liber I et II*, 55, 61. The themes of Book III are Christology and pneumatology, and Book IV treats the sacraments. See: Ibid., *Tom. II, Liber III et IV*.

himself warns against "ascending higher" (*hoher steigen*),[81] "over and above this revelation [in Christ]" (*hinuber uber diese offenbarung*).[82] A position that elevates such statements to a governing interpretive key, however, would do Luther a disservice. Prescription to the limits of reason may be more a modern than a premodern worry. Luther's antispeculative bent against specific determination of the hidden God cannot be confused with thematizing the immanent Trinity as a theological task of reason in obedience to faith.[83] In fact, Luther preached regularly on the immanent Trinity, and his disputations document lively exchanges concerning this locus in great detail.[84] It remains to be seen how Luther speculates on the inner Trinity in ways that he considers to be not only theologically legitimate but pastorally necessary.

Reflection within the limits of reason takes place, more specifically, through the application of a Trinitarian category that is decisively modern. A category that appears consistently throughout discussions of the Trinity is the distinction between the immanent and the economic Trinity. It is a distinction that appears long after Luther's death, in the eighteenth century.[85] The distinction presupposes the neo-Kantian distinction between epistemological and essential order. In explaining his understanding of this distinction, Jüngel affirms both a real identity and a distinction of reason between the immanent and the economic Trinity.[86] Jüngel's explanation of

---

81. WA 45:95.32. This passage is cited from the second of two sermons Luther preached on Rom 11:33–36. This sermon preached on Trinity Sunday (May 27, 1537), together with its second part that Luther preached on the First Sunday after Trinity (June 3, 1537), are the representative texts for ch. 4. The texts are found in Ibid., 89:16–93.33; 94:1–98.8.

82. Ibid., 95.30.

83. "Ebensowenig wendet er seine Aufmerksamkeit den trinitarischen Fragen zu. Die Spekulation über die Dreifaltigkeit verbietet er von vornherein." Pinomaa, *Sieg des Glaubens*, 115. White, in an otherwise excellent study of the nominalist sources of Luther's doctrine of the Trinity, mistakenly correlates the distinction between the temporal and the non-temporal with the hidden and revealed God. White, *Luther as Nominalist*, 383. Ch. 2 shows how Luther considers the eternity of God to be a subject matter revealed in time, as eternal.

84. Many of Luther's most passionate sermons on the Trinity are preached on the feast of Epiphany for which the gospel text was the baptism of Jesus (Matt 3:13–17). See: ch. 4, "Luther and the Sermon."

85. Pannenberg has located the eighteenth-century origin of the distinction between the *trinitas oeconomica* and the *trinitas essentialis* in Johannes Urlsperger's treatises entitled, *Vier Versuche einer genaueren Bestimmung des Geheimnisses Gottes des Vaters und Christi* (1769–1774), and *Kurzgefaßtes System meines Vortrages von Gottes Dreieinigkeit* (1777). Pannenberg, *Systematische Theologie*, 317n22.

86. "Die Einheit von 'immanenter' und 'ökonomischer' Trinität zu behaupten ist theologisch nur dann legitim, wenn diese Einheit nicht in dem Sinne *tautologisch* verkannt

the real identity and the distinction of reason betrays a more modern use of the terms than what Scotus would have meant by the "formal and real distinctions."[87] But Jüngel's use more accurately reflects the way Luther is viewed by contemporary theologians. Although an anachronism when applied to Luther, the distinction between the immanent and the economic Trinity seems to be a significant category in which Luther's conception of the Trinity is represented.

Two construals of the immanent-economic Trinity in Luther's theology are historically distinct, yet both betray a common conceptual backdrop. I suspect a similarity exists between a transcendent view of the immanent Trinity, held by Holl, and a transcendental view, held by Jansen. The transcendent view conceives of the immanent Trinity within the framework of a metaphysics of effects. Holl locates the Father in a transcendent realm: the Father sends Christ and the Spirit as two instruments (*Werkzeuge*) who, in time, unite the human will to the Father's will in order for the human to fulfill the first commandment.[88] The Father's will is seen to be the cause of the unity between the human and the divine will, a unity effected at the level of the economic Trinity by the Spirit and Son. It is the Father who transcends the economy of effects that reveal the divine essence of love. Treatments by Kattenbusch[89] and Theodosius Harnack are also examples of this position.[90] Although the immanent Trinity is allocated a transcendent status, the discourse of cause and effect seems to privilege the order

---

wird, daß die *Freiheit* und ungeschuldete *Gnade* der Selbstmitteilung Gottes und also deren *Ereignishaftigkeit* undenkbar wird. Es sollte deshalb, gerade um die *reale* Identität von 'immanenter' und 'ökonomischer' Trinität als *Geheimnis* aussagen zu können, die *distinctio rationis* von 'ökonomischer' und 'immanenter' Trinität theologisch beibehalten werden." Jüngel, "Das Verhältnis von 'ökonomischer' und 'immanenter' Trinität," 275 (thesis 9). [Italics in the original text.]

87. On Luther's controversy with Scotus on the terminology of the formal and real distinctions, see ch. 2, "The Scotus-Ockham Trajectory."

88. In Holl's interpretation of Luther's theology, the persons of Christ and the Spirit are understood to be the effects of the transcendent Father's will that are left behind when the unity of the human will with the Father's will is perceived as a religious feeling. Holl, *Gesammelte Aufsätze*, 71–81.

89. "Jesus Christus und der Geist, das sind die Erkenntnißgründe der Liebe Gottes," Ferdinand Kattenbusch, *Luthers Stellung zu den oecumenischen Symbolen*, 28.

90. "God ist ihm die Liebe nur als die trinitarische." Theodosius Harnack, *Luthers Theologie mit besonderer Beziehung auf seine Versöhnungs- und Erlösungslehre*, vol. 2, 9. The central category in Harnack's work is the distinction drawn between the God outside of Christ and the God in Christ. Harnack claims that the distinction is one based on human sin and does not insert a wedge between a God without Christ and a Trinitarian God, See also: Ibid., vol. 1, 51–61.

of knowing. The cause is inferred from the knowledge of the effect, even though the latter is seen to ultimately transcend the effect.

The transcendental view also privileges the economic Trinity as the starting point for reflection. In the only monograph to date on Luther's doctrine of the Trinity, Reiner Jansen appropriates wholeheartedly the distinction between the immanent and economic Trinity. Jansen concludes that Luther's doctrine of the Trinity is cast in the mold of Barth.[91] Luther, according to Jansen, begins with the economic Trinity at the level of actuality and then conceptually moves back into the immanent Trinity in order to claim the latter's necessity.[92] The immanent Trinity is the condition for the possibility of its economy; the economy is the "noetic" revelation of God as three persons in salvation history, and on the basis of this revelation, the triune essence of God is known to be a necessity of the divine nature. When Luther is observed through this lens, it does not appear surprising that Jansen regards the immanent Trinity to be of minimal soteriological value.[93] Both the metaphysics of effects and the transcendental model converge by locating soteriological relevance at the level of the economic Trinity; they agree, at the immanent Trinity's expense.

When the economic Trinity is privileged and the immanent Trinity is overlooked, the question needs to be asked regarding the fittingness of the distinction both to Luther's thought and to the many texts in which Luther discusses the Trinity in eternity. The initial discomfort seems to be the lack of a conceptual fit between a distinctly modern, neo-Kantian category and Luther's own thought and language. Arising from the criticism would be the question of how one can best represent Luther's Trinitarian understanding. This question motivates the present study.

Luther scholarship since Ritschl has, at best, discussed Luther's Trinitarian understanding in a neo-Kantian framework and, at worst, has entirely ignored it. I began by reviewing what was determined to be the

---

91. See especially: Jansen, *Studien zu Luthers Trinitätslehre*, 194–205.

92. Ibid., 203–204.

93. By posing the following question, Jansen uncovers his presupposition relating the economic Trinity to existential faith that excludes a similar soteriological value for the immanent Trinity. "Hat ein Glaube an Sätze über die immanente Trinität noch irgendetwas mit dem Existenzvollzug zu tun?... Etwas grundsätzlicher gefragt: Hat Luther genügend bedacht, daß die Lehre von der immanenten Trinität wohl eine theologische Lehre ist, nicht aber ohne weiteres eine Glaubenswahrheit?" Ibid., 202–3n282.

"new" in Luther's work, and its relation to the "old." Regarded as Luther's break with the past, the new was isolated in Luther's articulation of the "for me" (*pro me*) relation of Christ present in work or word to effect justifying faith in the believer. A Protestant leap over the medieval scholastic and nominalist schools attempted to ground Luther's commitment to orthodox dogma in the early church, an endeavor that, on second glance, exposed the situatedness of the interpretation in the neo-Kantian paradigm. By taking a closer look at the privileging of the "for me" (*pro me*) novelty, the common philosophical presupposition coloring the theological correlation between faith and the theology of the cross was shown. The theological-epistemological account of the Christ-faith correlation led to a Trinitarian understanding that privileged the salvation-historical economy of the Trinity. Trinitarian differentiation at the economic level, seen as an implication of the Reformation discovery, betrayed an aversion to the immanent Trinity as a significant moment in Luther's Trinitarian understanding. The immanent Trinity was regarded to be epistemically inaccessible, soteriologically insignificant, and forbidden to speculation by reason. The question emerged regarding the distinction between the immanent and the economic Trinity, which scholars have applied to Luther's Trinitarian theology. In the next section, I will show how the approach of this study will be used to gain access to the subject matter in a way that challenges the conclusions drawn by scholars and in a way that conceives of the Trinity at the two locations of the inner and outer Trinity.

TESTING THREE APPROACHES: THE HISTORICAL-
GENETIC, THE SYSTEMATIC-THEOLOGICAL, AND
THE HERMENEUTICAL APPROACHES

In order to begin the study of Luther's understanding of the Trinity, a particular method must be chosen that is suited to gain access to the subject matter. The approach I am committed to using—that of showing the relationship between genre, language, and Luther's theological articulation—offers an alternative growing from more traditional models of Luther research. Lohse has summarized two classic methodological strategies used in Luther scholarship: the systematic-theological and historical-genetic models.[94] The systematic-theological approach was established by Harnack's two-volume study on Luther's understanding of reconciliation and redemption in relation to the doctrine of God.[95] Harnack's precedent was followed by the majority of Luther scholars who oriented their investigations of Luther on systematic-theological themes and showed the internal relations of the center to related aspects. The historical-genetic model, favored by those in search of a date for Luther's Reformation breakthrough, traced lines of doctrinal development[96] that intersected with significant historical controversies.[97] Each of these two approaches, which are not as cleanly distinguished as the typology suggests, have associated problems specific to the way in which a conceptual perspective guides the view of the vast and dynamic terrain of Luther's texts.[98] Systematicians desire theological-aesthetic unity and tend to problematize one theme. They reconstruct a picture of Luther's theology in which occasional writings and oscillating conceptuality do not quickly lend themselves to crisp systematic structuring. By constructing a space in which Luther is engaged immediately in conversation with the researcher's interest, this approach tends to mirror the contemporary author's own intention at the expense of historical accuracy, as Lohse and Bizer remark.[99] On the other hand, the historical-genetic approach aims to reconstruct the relation between Luther's texts and their historical context in order to describe and explain

---

94. Lohse, "Zur Struktur," 239.

95. See 9n27, 25n90.

96. An example of the historical-genetic model is Lienhard's dissertation, *Martin Luthers christologisches Zeugnis*, which traces the development of Luther's Christology from the earliest lectures on the Psalms to the interpretation of Isa 53 in 1544. See 7n18.

97. Lohse, "Zur Struktur," 239–40.

98. Each model adapts the elements of the other model to fit the primary frame of reference. The historical-genetic approach appropriates theological categories that it traces through various controversies and conversely, the systematic-theological approach should situate the theological analysis of texts in their historical context.

99. "Tatsächlich kann nicht der mindeste Zweifel bestehen, daß die systematisch angelegten Darstellungen von Luthers Theologie eigentlich alle in hohem Maße von der jeweiligen theologischen Ausgangsposition des betreffenden Verfassers geprägt sind." Lohse, "Zur Struktur," 240; "Die Ursache für die Verschiedenheit der Lutherbilder aber scheint mir darin zu liegen, daß sich jeder unserer Autoren mehr oder weniger mit Luther identifiziert, mindestens aber sich dessen bewußt ist, daß er den eigenen Standpunkt nicht ohne Luther gewonnen hat... Es sind nicht nur Lutherbücher, sondern zugleich Bekenntnisbücher moderner Theologen, die zur Not auch ohne Luther bestehen könnten." Bizer, "Neue Darstellungen," 348–49.

the emergence and development of a particular theme. Although this model tends to focus on the controversies in which Luther was embroiled as constitutive of his theological formation, it tends to neglect what is articulated in less polemical and more pastoral situations.

Recent Luther scholarship has proposed that a hermeneutical approach is best suited to engage the theological subject matter together with the literary force of Luther's texts. This approach acknowledges that the occasionality, liveliness, and sheer quantity of Luther's work resist both ultimate structuring by a systematic-theological framework and definitive developmental tracing along a historical-genetic trajectory. Proceeding by way of immanent analysis, the hermeneutical approach investigates Luther's texts on the basis of a contemporary theological sensitivity to Luther's own insights into the nature of theological language. According to the central position of this approach, Luther locates the historical communication of salvation in the divine word of forgiveness. Bayer discusses the scientific-theological implications of privileging the temporal performance of the saving word. Theology, as a "science of language," aims to investigate the competence of the literal word, which is itself integrally related to a distinct literary form.[100] On the linguistic level, the hermeneutical approach offers ways of appreciating Luther's literary achievements. The investigation of Luther's texts borrows from research in literary-linguistic disciplines and from rhetorical[101] and reception-aesthetic studies.[102] If Luther's passionate certainty that the word communicates the benefits of Christ is placed at the center of his theology, then any study must, at some level, include an analysis of the speech in which Christ is rendered present in the word.

---

100. "Theologie als Sprachwissenschaft analysiert die Performanz dieses Satzes ["Ich bin der Herr, dein Gott!"] und expliziert die in ihm aktuelle Kompetenz." Oswald Bayer, *Autorität und Kritik*, 145.

101. Steinlein's early article on Luther's picture-language has been followed by the excellent work of Birgit Stolt on the rhetorical differences between Luther's Latin and German texts, as well as on Luther's use of classical rhetorical tools: *ethos* and *pathos*, *movere* and *delectare*. Hermann Steinlein, "Luthers Anlage zur Bildhaftigkeit," 9–45; Birgit Stolt, "Neue Aspekte der sprachwissenschaftlichen Luther-Forschung," 6–16; Idem, *Studien zu Luthers Freiheitstraktat mit besonderer Rücksicht auf das Verhältnis der lateinischen und der deutschen Fassung zu einander und die Stilmittel der Rhetorik*; Idem, *Wortkampf*.

102. Albrecht Beutel, "Offene Predigt," 518–37.

Various studies have demonstrated the complementarity between a theological claim regarding the divine word and a literary focus. Ebeling's dissertation—which, in an effort to distinguish the hermeneutical from the systematic approach, probed Luther's exegesis of the Gospels for their theological content—set the stage.[103] In his later development, Ebeling popularized Fuchs's term "speech event" (*Sprachereignis*), a concept dovetailing nicely with Ebeling's own existential construal of Luther's understanding of the word.[104] Bayer criticized the transcendental status of the speech event in Ebeling's interpretation and argued that Luther understood the word to be embodied in the distinct, liturgical form of the *promissio* of forgiveness.[105] Following Bayer's persuasive thesis, work has begun under the theme of new words (*nova vocabula*). The study of new language (*nova lingua*) inquires into the specific nature of Luther's theological discourse,[106] of which Jüngel's metaphorical theology,[107] Beutel's work on Luther's understanding of language,[108] Streiff's analysis of the mediality of Luther's language of faith,[109] and White's study of Luther's theology in a nominalist

---

103. In his dissertation on Luther's exegesis of the gospels, Ebeling distinguishes his hermeneutical method from the systematic-theological approach. "Es soll sich nicht darum handeln, aus Luthers Evangelienauslegung, wie man das methodisch meist bei Untersuchungen über Predigten oder exegetische Vorlesungen tut, die wichtigen theologischen Gedanken in systematischer Zusammenordnung vorzutragen. ... Es soll nicht den theologischen Gedanken als solchen nachgegangen werden, sondern der Weise, wie sie aus dem Text gewonnen werden." Gerhard Ebeling, *Evangelische Evangelienauslegung*, 359.

104. Ernst Fuchs, "Das Sprachereignis in der Verkündigung Jesu," 281–305. Ebeling comments on his indebtedness to Fuchs' work in *Wort und Glaube*, vol. 1, 319n1.

105. Bayer claims that Ebeling's understanding of Luther's hermeneutics is "dem transzendentalen Denken Kants und Schleiermachers verpflichtet ... mithin von der Methode des Rückgangs hinter alle ontisch-konkreten Sätze." Oswald Bayer, *Freiheit als Antwort. Zur theologischen Ethik*, 99.

106. Jörg Baur, "Luther und die Philosophie," 13–28; Dennis Bielfeldt, "Luther, Metaphor, and Theological Language," 121–35; Bengt Hägglund, "Martin Luther über die Sprache," 1–12; Peter Meinhold, *Luthers Sprachphilosophie*; Risto Saarinen, "Metapher und biblische Redefiguren," 18–39; Reijo Työrinoja, "Nova vocabula et nova lingua: Luther's Conception of Doctrinal Formulas," 221–36.

107. Eberhard Jüngel, "Metaphorische Wahrheit," 103–157.

108. Albrecht Beutel, *In dem Anfang war das Wort: Studien zu Luthers Sprachverständnis.*

109. Stefan Streiff, "*Novis Linguis Loqui*", *Martin Luthers Disputation über Joh 1,14.* The major weakness of Streiff's work consists of slotting Luther into the contemporary literary-linguistic category of medial language. Streiff pits Luther's medial language or language of faith against what Streiff characterizes as the "instrumental" language of Luther's nominalist teachers. Streiff does not distinguish between Luther's rhetorical polemic against the

paradigm are examples.[110] The hermeneutical approach has proved its ability to adapt to a variety of entry points to Luther. It has been used in combination with the historical-genetic model to trace the hermeneutical development of Luther's breakthrough (i.e., the work of Ebeling and Bayer). The hermeneutical model can also include systematic interest. Indeed, it can deepen investigation by drawing out dogmatic themes hidden below the surface of Luther's texts, while being responsive to the rhetorical knit of Luther's literary patterns.

An approach to Luther's understanding of the Trinity evolves by testing the fit between preliminary methodological suggestions and the nature of Luther's texts. Since the Trinitarian theme is explicitly problematized only in the final disputations of Luther's life, a historical trajectory reconstructing its development in Luther's thought would uncover little more than the surface fact that the Trinitarian article functions as a horizon beyond more pressing issues. Not a topic in controversy with Rome, Luther's Trinitarian articulation is embedded in the deep structures of his writings. It is neither so explicit that an entire doctrinal treatise is devoted to its thematization nor so implicit that it cannot be accessed. A version of the systematic approach is favored in light of the way in which Luther himself articulates the subject matter in a plenitude of texts. By initially viewing Luther's texts through the lens of a systematic locus, the reader's perspective is sharpened by recognizing the enormous variation in expression that emerges from the nature of the subject matter itself. Luther's understanding of the living God, ranging from the comforting emphasis on the unity of the divine mercy shown in Christ to the divine hiddenness threatening to stretch the unity to the breaking point, cannot be subsumed under a static concept. The variation in articulation resists a unifying drive towards metalevel systematic reflection and invites an approach to the subject matter that is localized in diverse texts and in sundry ways. Investigating Luther's texts on the premise of his own understanding of theological language is the strength of the hermeneutical approach. When the systematic lens is focused on the range of the subject matter that is articulated in texts according to text-immanent criteria, a vantage point is created, and the study can begin.

---

intrusion of philosophy into the theological region, and Luther's actual reception and use of philosophical concepts and language.

110. See: White, *Luther as Nominalist.*

INTRODUCING THE STUDY'S APPROACH

THE RELATIONSHIP BETWEEN GENRE, LANGUAGE, AND THE TRINITY

The ordering of the dynamic diversity of Luther's texts written after 1523 turns on the issue of genre. Luther's texts, characterized by variable terminology and shifting conceptuality, resist comparison both on the elementary level of word studies and on the more abstract level of contrasting concepts independent of historical context or communication web. An approach is sought by dividing the terrain of theological discourse into distinct spaces. From the academic lectern to the church pulpit, from the private cell to the public marketplace, spaces of life are occupied by particular forms of the oral word.[111] In Luther's thought, theological discourse, marked by its public and oral nature, is assigned a concrete location in which its language is generated and lived out. Each genre is considered to shape a specific Trinitarian articulation circulating around a set of biblical, semantic, grammatical, narrative, and theological elements; in each constellation, the elements distinctly emerge in ways that differ from other genres.[112] The subject matter's contours are peculiar to the genre-language relationship: the academic disputation thematizes the logic of the eternal Trinitarian relations; the hymn praises the wondrous Trinitarian turn toward the despair and captivity of the human being's existence; and the sermon proclaims the Triune God's way with the church. In conceiving the subject matter from different vantage points not duplicated in other genres, breaks and tensions cannot be simply harmonized and flattened

---

111. Oswald Bayer receives this insight from Franz Overbeck as a crucial methodological premise of his own genre approach to systematic theology. Oswald Bayer, "Worship and Theology," 159; Franz Overbeck, "Ueber die Christlichkeit unserer heutigen Theologie (1873)," 179. In the fascinating article entitled, "The Problem of Speech Genres," M. M. Bakhtin investigates what he defines to be speech genres. For Bakhtin, a speech genre belongs integrally to a distinct sphere of human activity. It differs from a form of language by virtue of its existence in reality as an utterance that, as semantically complete, is bounded on both sides by "others" as speakers or as anticipated responders. See: M. M. Bakhtin, "The Problem of Speech Genres," 60–102.

112. By investigating a variety of genre-language constellations, I seek to adequately reflect a balance between Luther's representation of the outer Trinity and that of the inner Trinity.

into one layer of interpretation.[113] Each genre-language constellation bears a distinct witness to the God who is Lord of all areas of life,[114] interrupting and transforming fragments of human reality to reflect God's glory.

The particular texts in this study are representative of three genres in which many of Luther's later writings can be classified: the disputation, the hymn, and the sermon. For each genre, a representative text will be selected according to the criteria of text length,[115] amount of Trinitarian material, inclusion of both the eternal and temporally disclosed Trinity, an acknowledged minimum of scholarly familiarity with the text, and finally, if the text is a record of Luther's speech, the version regarded to be most faithful to the original speech situation.[116] Comparison between the selected text and other texts of the same genre is offered with the intent of showing thematic continuities specific to the genre. In addition, texts written in other genres but located in historical proximity to the representative

---

113. The distinction between first order and second order theological discourse, for example, the distinction between the praise of God and the propositions about God, is less rigorously maintained.

114. Analogous to a genre-language approach to Luther's texts, Childs suggests that the biblical-theological task is to study the distinct voices of both testaments as witnesses to the scope of Scripture itself, Jesus Christ. "The dialogical move of biblical theological reflection which is being suggested is from the partial grasp of fragmentary reality found in both testaments to the full reality which the Christian church confesses to have found in Jesus Christ, in the combined witness of the two testaments. ... [B]oth testaments bear testimony to the one Lord, in different ways, at different times, to different peoples, and yet both are understood and rightly heard in the light of the living Lord himself, the perfect reflection of the glory of God (Heb 1.3)." Childs, *Biblical Theology of the Old and New Testaments*, 85.

115. Many of Luther's Table Talks, too short to be used in this study, illustrate the Trinity. "Praeterea etiam in creaturis trinitas reperitur: In sole substantia, splendor et calor; in fluminibus substantia, fluxus, potentia. Sic in artibus quoque, ut in astronomia motus, lumen et influentia, in musica re mi fa, tres tantum notae, in geometria tres dimensiones: linea, superficies, corpus, in grammatica tres orationum partes, in dictione apud Ebraeos tres literae substantiales, in arithmetica tres numeri, in rhetorica dispositio, elocutio et actio seu gestus; ceterum inventio et memoria non sunt artis, sed naturae; in dialectica definitio, divisio, argumentatio. Sic res quaelibet habet pondus, numerum et figuram. Ita in omnibus creaturis licet invenire et cernere istam divinam esse impressam." WATR 1:395.8-18 (no. 815, first half of 1530's). "1. Pater in divinis est grammatica, dat enim voces estque ipse fons. 2. Filius est dialectica, dat dispositionem rerum estque verbum, λογος, et disponit omnia, so sol es sein. 3. Spiritus Sanctus est rhetorica, bleset vnd treibet vivificando etc." WATR 1:563.26-29 (no. 1143, first half of 1530's). On the *vestigia trinitatis* in Luther, see: Barth, "Das vestigium trinitatis," in KD, I/1:355-56.

116. In the case of Luther's sermons, the bilingual Rörer version is judged to most accurately reflect Luther's preaching. Ebeling, *Evangelische Evangelienauslegung*, 20. In the case of the *disputatio*, sufficient text material is gleaned from the theses that Luther himself wrote and the student records of the disputation.

text are brought into the discussion. This method is used to explore inter-
textuality between the representative text, other texts of the same genre,
and texts of different genres in order to unearth the elements Luther prefers in articulating his understanding of the Trinity. The elements—such
as biblical-theological constellations, the broader arena of philosophical
concerns, the historical context, and the confession of faith in the Triune
God—are continuous across the distinct genres, yet their continuity is
differently shaped by the location of the elements within the respective
genre's contours.

In this study, a systematic-theological orientation that resists ultimate
systematizing is combined with a hermeneutical approach that looks at
texts written on the levels of first- and second-order theological discourse.
This approach can be seen to challenge classic objectives of systematic
thinking while suggesting new directions for further reflection. As Bayer
suggests, systematic theology is "like a morphology ... a kind of grammar
for the language of the interpreted Bible, for the living and life-creating
voice of the gospel."[117] The genre-language approach neither intends to
establish the Trinity as the key to Luther's thought[118] nor subsumes the
constellations under a single doctrine of the Trinity, either as a propositional summary abstracted from primary discourse or as a salvation history (Heilsgeschichte) that identifies the Trinitarian self-disclosure with
three distinct stages of history. In this particular approach to what I have
named Luther's understanding—rather than doctrine—of the Trinity, the
intention is to show the various shapes his understanding takes within
genre-language constellations. This view of the theological genre, in distinction to Ricoeur's literary genre, operates on the premise of Luther's

---

117. Bayer, Autorität und Kritik, 187. Bayer's proposal for a systematic theology as a doctrine
of literary genres takes, as its focus of interest, specific genres in Scripture (such as praise
and lament) and the communication that occurs between God and humans [Wortwechsel]
(such as the promissio and prayer). Reciprocal communication takes place in different forms
of speech that Bayer identifies with forms of life [Lebensformen]. Bayer suggests that the genre
approach to theology is distinct from other forms of systematic theology, such as Hegel's
concept. Bayer, Autorität und Kritik, 187–89.

118. "Damit ist die Trinität das organisierende Prinzip der Theologie Luthers und der
Generalschlüssel zu allen ihren Aussagen." Ulrich Asendorf, "Die Trinitätslehre als integrales
Problem der Theologie Martin Luthers," 129.

understanding between the identity of the human word and divine speech.[119] More than a literary genre that is either identity-forming[120] or experience-expressing,[121] theological genres shape the range of discourses into which God enters and acts. Language is present in spaces established by Scripture and determined by the liturgical forms of worship.[122] What White names Luther's "epistemology of access"[123] is, in theological terms, Luther's insistence on the nature of theological language as a creation and gift of both the Holy Spirit and Christ.[124] As a theological enterprise, the systematic reflection on forms is an exercise in discovering the power of theological language to disclose facets of understanding about God in the acts of articulating that understanding under the guidance of the Holy Spirit.

---

119. By using the designation, "theological genre," I am suggesting a critical theological reception of Ricoeur's work on the literary genres of Scripture. Ricoeur situates the literary genres of prophecy, narrative, wisdom, and hymn at a site closest to the original human experience of a historically significant event. These genres, or "modes of discourse," generate discourse at a level attributing the event to God behind the text. By distinguishing between the historical and literary levels, Ricoeur aims to criticize a monolithic concept of revelation and "to guard ourselves against a certain narrowness of any theology of the Word which only attends to word events. In the encounter with what we could call the idealism of the word event, we must reaffirm the realism of the event of history." Paul Ricoeur, "Toward a Hermeneutic of the Idea of Revelation," 80.

120. For a criticism of an approach to canon in functionalist terms, see: Childs, *Biblical Theology of the Old and New Testaments*, 668–72.

121. For an example of this position, see: Paul Ricoeur, "Philosophy and Religious Language," 75.

122. "to pursue theology as a linguistic discipline—or to be more precise, a doctrine of linguistic forms. ... It is directed to the forms of specific worship." Bayer, "Worship and Theology," 158.

123. White, *Luther as Nominalist*, 328.

124. When discussing the way Christians speak, Luther often refers to the Holy Spirit as the teacher of this special "angelic" grammar and speech "Denn weil sie [Christians] ander leut sind, die nicht mehr jrdisch leben noch reden, sondern himlisch als Gottes kinder und der Engel gesellen, so mussen sie auch andere sprache fu(e)ren, Darumb haben sie auch einen andern meister, den Heiligen geist, der sie durch Gottes wort leret diese sprache verstehen und reden, die man jm himel redet," WA 36:644.15–19 (Sermon on the Fourth of Advent, Dec. 22, 1532). In the context of discussing theological speech, Luther can also refer to Christ, who gives the theologian a mouth and wisdom: "vobis os et sapientiam ... eo ipso [Christ] commendat nobis sacram theologiam, ut sciamus esse donum divinum," WA 39,1:260.17, 21–22, 23–24 (Oratio Lutheri composita in promotione Petri Palladii, 1537).

PROMISSIO AND NARRATIVE

An approach to Luther's texts that organizes them into theological genres, each producing a unique discourse, requires the help of text-immanent criteria that measure the change and difference of Luther's understanding of the Trinity across the genres. By rejecting an overarching systematic template applied to investigate each theological genre, controls for interpreting the particular shapes of Luther's Trinitarian articulation must be gleaned from the content of Luther's texts themselves.[125] I have chosen two criteria as integral to Luther's understanding of theological language and the subject matter it constitutes.[126] The application of these criteria steers my view of the continuity and discontinuity in Luther's Trinitarian understanding across the theological genres. As text-immanent guides, *promissio* and narrative shed light on how Luther conceives of the subject matter in genre-specific ways.

The *promissio* has emerged in Bayer's work on Luther's Reformation breakthrough as the theological key to Luther's understanding of the divine word. In Luther's word-oriented theology, the category of the *promissio* integrates Luther's construal of the word-*res* relation with a Christological construal of the concept of testament.[127] Bayer locates Luther's breakthrough

---

125. One could suspect that the disputational form elevates theological language to a conceptual level that then possibly serves as a stable point of reference from which the other genres can be viewed. In spite of the more abstract level of discourse constructed by the disputation, this genre specifies the subject matter in view of the concept of eternity that is not duplicated in other genres.

126. The emphasis on the theological content of the *promissio* and the narrative is to be distinguished from a functional use of these criteria.

127. In the foreword to the second edition of his book, *Promissio*, Bayer insists that the concept of the *promissio* has become the "matrix" of his entire systematic-theological work. "'Promissio' ist zur Matrix meiner gesamten systematisch-theologischen Arbeit geworden; diese orientiert sich an der die reformatorische Theologie Luthers bestimmenden promissio Dei, an Gottes Heilszuspruch." Bayer, *Promissio*, 1. In his book, Bayer observes the shift from the early Luther to the early Reformation position to turn on the *promissio*. The study traces the shift in this concept from an early sermon on the Prologue to John (1514) to "De captivitate Babylonica (1520)." According to Bayer, Luther's Reformation discovery initially took place during the process of reflecting on the sacrament of penance. In the final form of his discovery, Luther understood the word of absolution to be a declarative assertion of forgiveness. The identity between the divine word of forgiveness and the human word is conceived as the identity between *signum* and *res* so that the oral utterance of the *promissio* constitutes the activity of which it speaks. The word issues into reality what it articulates. Its competence is attributed to the nature of the testament Christ speaks on the occasion of the Last Supper. See: Ibid., 247. Bayer also shows that the concept of the *promissio* is constitutive for the first order discourses of baptism, meditation, and prayer. The term, *promissio*, Bayer

in the Augustinian paradigm of a sign theory. Whereas the tradition generally draws the distinction between sign (*signum*) and *res*, Luther's breakthrough sees the *promissio* as the collapse of that distinction. Identity consists of the literary sign, the absolution based on Matthew 16:19, and the *res*, the sinner's forgiveness.[128] The identity, the *promissio* of forgiveness and the certainty of its actuality, is localized in a liturgical address from the first-person subject of speech to the second-person hearer: "*pro te, pro vobis*." The competence of this liturgical performance, to use Bayer's terminology, is grounded in Christ's testament, sealed by his blood, and put into effect by his resurrection.[129] Initially treating the word of absolution in the sacrament of penance, Bayer's study extends Luther's insight into the *promissio* to other genres, such as baptism, meditation, and prayer. Bayer's work exposes the sacramental quality of Luther's understanding of primary-order religious language, an insight comparable to Grönvik's observations on Luther's view of the Trinity in baptism. According to Grönvik, the presence of God during baptism is rendered by the invocation of the Triune name; the liturgical rite localizes the identity between sign and signification.[130] In light of Bayer's thesis, it is recommended for any further work on Luther to investigate the nature of the *res* that is constituted by the *verbum*. If the *verbum* is the location at which the *res*—in the case of this study, the Trinity—is accessible, then the possibility is opened to explore the determination of the Trinitarian essence together with an understanding of that nature as word, speech, and speakers.

The *promissio* is grounded in the mystery of the cross, the silent word of death that is transformed, through the resurrection, into an address

---

claims, is not to be translated as "promise" that connotes a salvation-historical category of revelation. Rather, the Latin is used to convey the central concept of proclamation: the death and resurrection of Christ. Luther's understanding of the divine word as the concrete and certain declaration of the forgiveness of sins has implications for the doctrine of God and the concept of history. "Damit ist ein ganz bestimmtes Gottes- und Geschichtsverständnis und eine ganz bestimmte Sicht des Alten Testaments gegeben: Die Einheit Gottes gewinnt sich nicht erst in der Totalität einer jeweils noch unabgeschlossenen Geschichte, sondern schenkt sich ganz in der Eindeutigkeit seiner Zusage und wird in deren speziellem Glauben bekannt." Ibid., 347.

128. For a historical-genetic summary of the development of the concept of the *promissio*, see: Ibid., 339–51.

129. Bayer sees the performance of the word, "ein Wort, das etwas veranstaltet," to be in identity with its competence, "was es tut." Idem, *Autorität und Kritik*, 145.

130. Lorenz Grönvik, *Die Taufe in der Theologie Martin Luthers*, 180–81.

redeeming the world. At the heart of Luther's word-preoccupied theology beats his conviction that the speech of God is bound together with the divine act of forgiving and creating anew. Forming the *promissio* is the *verbum* constituting the *res* and, conversely, the *res* creating the effect of the word. Each time the *promissio* is spoken, the identity between *res* and word secures the eternal faithfulness of God through time to the word that transforms sinners into God's friends. The identity does not reduce all words to one static and eternal word but opens an area in which the oscillation between speech and silence, knowledge and mystical rest, can be found. Its truth grounded in an identity, the *promissio* has the potential to embrace the many spoken words that point to, witness, and convey the *res*.

In this study, the differential between *verbum* and *res* will be explored in order to understand how Luther's insistence on the *promissio* permits a wealth of speech communicating the Trinitarian *res*. Sometimes rich and evocative, sometimes a poor stammering, the words used to describe and define the Trinity are wrapped together, in Luther's thought, with the *promissio* that funds the infinite variety of language. Even the technical terms referring to the naked God (*Deus nudus*) in eternity are infused with the promise of life that is God's own nature. What scholars have spoken about as the new language (*nova lingua*) can be relaxed from its Christological focus and extended into an exploration of the plenitude of words, each communicating one facet of the Trinitarian *res*. The study of the differential composing theological language can also account for the extreme case of demonic temptation in which God and God's word are not to be identified.[131] Between identity and strict separation, Luther's understanding of the Trinitarian mystery is an invitation to study words—words that communicate the God who comes to creation as a story to be told.

A matter for further exploration is how the *promissio* assumes narrative shaping in each of the three theological genres. There is a theological assumption behind this view: if the divine advent, localized in the *promissio*, privileges the present tense as the time of its coming, then there must be a narrative that assigns the past tense to plot the "where from" and the future tense to plot the "where to." The *promissio* concentrates all three modes of

---

131. "... dum nihil distinguit inter Deum praedicatum et absconditum, hoc est, inter verbum Dei et Deum ipsum." WA 18:685.25–27.

time into the present tense of its address.[132] It occupies the middle from which the three modes can be narratively unfolded to tell the story from before to after. Through its narrative extension, the *promissio* reveals the "ontic plus" of God who comes into the world and temporally structures the reality transformed.[133] The narrative potential of the *promissio* is a function of the genre in which it is generated. Each genre articulates the relations of the Trinitarian persons to the essence and to creation according to a narrative plotted to fit the genre-specific subject matter. The eternal Trinitarian discourse of the disputation is theologically governed by the creedal order of Trinitarian presentation; the outer manifestations of the Trinity, in the genres of the hymn and the sermon, are narrated according to the biblical-theological deep structure of Luther's Trinitarian understanding.

For the purpose of exploring the narrative pattern of Luther's understanding of the Trinity, it is more appropriate to speak about discrete narratives, rather than of an ordering of metanarrative. The category of narrative lends itself well to conceptualizing the Trinitarian economy in a way not restrictively temporal. Associated with this category, however, has been the difficulty of relating the atemporal talk of the divine eternity to the narrative talk of the economy. The charge of modalism, directed against a particular and one-sided interpretation of Luther's catechisms, highlights the difficulty in Luther studies. The category might have been used successfully to salvage the integrity of the biblical span from creation to the eschaton. When associated with a hermeneutic of progressive Trinitarian revelation, however, the use of the category makes inroads into the Trinitarian witness of both Testaments and relocates the references to the inner Trinity behind the narrative as the condition for its possibility. The difficulty can be avoided if discrete narratives can be seen to retain genre-specific integrity and to complement or even challenge other narratives. Every narrative is a fragment, localized in discursive spaces. In each life space, the before and after are plotted differently. From the perspective of the divine advent, the narrative is plotted by God's own movement

---

132. Bayer calls the interweaving of all three modes of time that is effected by the present tense of the *promissio*, "die Verschränkung der Zeiten." Oswald Bayer, "Zugesagte Welt in der Verschränkung der Zeiten," ch. 4 in *Schöpfung als Anrede*, 49–50. 57. Childs refers to the "coalescing of time" as the fusion between the "'time of the earthly Jesus' with the 'time of the church'" in the Gospel of Matthew. Childs, *Biblical Theology of the Old and New Testaments*, 272–73.

133. The term "ontic plus" is taken from Jüngel, *Gott als Geheimnis der Welt*, 306.

between the "where from" and the "where to." When the experience of the human "I" is narrated under the impact of the divine advent, the before and after are marked by transformation. Temporally constituted, concretely located, and genre specific, discrete narratives represent the range of theological articulation respective to individual and collective speech, from first-person confession or third-person propositions to remembering the past or anticipating future joy.

The two text-immanent criteria of *promissio* and narrative will be used to guide the investigation of the particular shapes of Luther's Trinitarian understanding in each theological genre and to suggest differences in nuances between the genres. In each genre-language constellation, the play between the two guides is described. Discrete narratives construe the *promissio* in genre-specific ways; the variety of language, shaped by the respective genre, is compelled by the differential between *res* and word. The study's search for the ways in which the relationship between genre and language is constitutive for Trinitarian articulation does betray a material-theological viewpoint. By orienting the study to the categories of narrative and *promissio*, a material dimension is considered bound together with Luther's own understanding of the nature of theological language. Speech about the Trinity is, at some level, constituted by the *promissio* of God—who transforms reality in a way, structuring it according to the three modes of past, present, and future. The stories are in tension with each other, unduplicated while leaving room for others. They challenge theological thinking while extricating it from ultimately conceptualizing the mystery of the Triune God.

THE THREE CHAPTERS:
THE THREE GENRES

In the last years of his life, Luther drew on disputation—a favorite academic genre of his—in writing on the Trinitarian article. The doctoral disputation of Georg Major and Johannes Faber (1544), for which Luther wrote the theses and in which he participated, is studied in chapter two. The representative text is investigated in the textual context of three other Trinitarian disputations that took place in the same period. This chapter studies the way in which the medieval academic genre of the disputation shapes the propositional discourse unfolding a particular grasp of

Trinitarian themes. The category of the inner Trinity sets the stage for conceptualizing Luther's understanding of the Trinitarian economy in later chapters. The Trinitarian subject matter in the disputation is determined as the inner Trinity that is articulated in the proposition: the three *res* are one and the same as one *res*. The discussion of the inner Trinity includes an analysis of the use of reason, which Luther deems fitting to investigate the infinity associated with the Triune God. Luther excludes particular determinations of the concept of infinity while articulating a metaphysics, a semantics, and a logic to the inner Trinitarian proposition.

Luther wrote the hymn "Now Rejoice, Dear Christians" during an eight-month phase between 1523 and 1524 of prodigious hymn composing and translating. In chapter three, the genre of the hymn will be studied, as it shapes the language in which Luther tells a narrative of Trinitarian advent. Figuring crucially into my interpretation of Luther's hymn are a number of psalm genres: the lament and praise psalms and the royal and penitential psalms. By drawing on these biblical genres, I show that Luther's hymn begins with the Spirit's advent. It then moves back into eternity to narrate an inner Trinitarian turn of mercy, and it finally moves forward to tell the story of Christ's incarnation. The hymn suspends the lament in verses two and three as the silence of Christ's death, yet the *promissio*, spoken at distinct sites in the narrative, compels the hearer and singer towards the praise of what God has done.

From the many sermons Luther preached on the Trinitarian article, the Trinity Sunday sermon on Romans 11:33–36 (1537) is a unique interpretation of a biblical text acknowledged to be a classic allusion to the Trinity. In chapter four, the text will be viewed from the twofold perspective in which Luther couches his sermon: the knowledge of God, preached as a narrative of Trinitarian revelation, that converges with the ways in which God is revealed to be "with us." The narrative plots different sites in a gradual movement from the inner to the outer Trinity, and it culminates in the revelation of the Trinitarian essence in the created works. Although the sermon is not untouched by controversy, it stages an incorporation, first of the hearers, into the Trinity's own movement towards creation. It subsequently extends this incorporation into an eschatological movement that reflects the glorification of the Triune God in creation.

The theological genres investigated—the disputation, the hymn, and the sermon—each generate a particular discourse shaping the view of the subject matter. The overall flow, beginning with the specification of the eternity of the Triune God in the disputation, and ending with the eschatological sight of the Trinity in the sermon, intentionally reflects what I have discovered to be the narrative pattern of Luther's Trinitarian understanding. Luther's hymn and sermon move from the inner Trinity to two sites at the outer Trinity; the incarnation, death, and resurrection of Christ; and the Spirit's presence in the church. Doxology embraces even the divine silence in the hymn's song of praise, and the sermon shimmers with yearning for the day when the Triune God will be glorifed in all creation. The most academic genre, the disputation, discloses the narrative extremes—the Triune God whose advent is suspended between eternity and eternity.

2

Luther's Understanding of the Trinity in the Doctoral Disputation of Georg Major and Johannes Faber (Dec. 12, 1544)

In the medieval disputation, Luther found a genre that he valued highly as an academic exercise for training theologians to be ministers of the church. He insisted on its practice to demarcate the boundaries between regions in the academic context, to test the adequacy of diverse tools of reason in studying the subject matter at the center of a region, and to hone the strategy of defense against attacks at the border. In this chapter, by studying how Luther articulates his understanding of the Trinity in the genre of the doctoral disputation, I will show how he relates the elements of narrative and *promissio* to the genre's particular determination of the subject matter to be the infinity of the inner Trinity. The representative text for this chapter is the doctoral disputation of Georg Major and Johannes Faber (1544). Also drawn into the discussion are three other disputations that Luther held, late in his life, on the Trinity: the doctoral disputations of Erasmus Alberus (1543), of Theodor Fabricius (1544), and of Petrus Hegemon (1545). Through the study of the disputation, I aim to show how Luther advocates the use of reason to distinguish, exclude, and define terms used in the debate. The first section introduces the disputation as a form Luther relished using throughout his theological career. Luther's commitment to the genre is related to his view of the way various academic regions made up the medieval university and to the distinct purpose of defending the center of the theological region from heretical attacks at the boundaries. In the second section, I discuss Luther's determination of the inner Trinity as the subject matter of the disputation and the perceived anti-Trinitarian threat prompting Luther's turn to this medieval form. In both heretical attacks against the Trinity and in Aristotle's philosophy, Luther sees a rationalistic reduction of reason to the order of the finite that challenges the concept of infinity associated with the Trinity. By theologically reinscribing the eternity of God in terms of the eternal inner-Trinitarian relations, Luther opens up the theological region to a particular deployment of reason that is fitted to rightly speculate on the inner Trinity. Luther's debate with Aristotle is the theme of the third section. In this debate, Luther demonstrates his use of reason both to exclude particular metaphysical and natural philosophical determinations of the term "infinity" from the theological region. Concluding the chapter is an extended discussion of Luther's use of the tools of metaphysics, semantics, and logic in the theological region for determining the terms of the inner-Trinitarian proposition that three *res* are one and the same as one *res*.

THE DISPUTATION

There is no clearer way to show how Luther regards the positive role of reason in investigating the theological subject matter than by studying his use of the disputation. The genre significantly shaped Luther's theology; it demonstrates his rootedness in a specific trajectory of medieval thought. If an existential-interpretive approach to Luther's theology is often seen as contrasting reason with faith, then the study of the disputation opens up a view of Luther's understanding of the activity of reason that is illuminated by faith. This section will introduce Luther's use of the disputation within the context of the medieval university. I begin with a biographical sketch of the place this genre occupies in Luther's theological career, from his earliest days as a doctor of theology to his last disputation, held in 1545. Turning to the later Trinitarian disputations, I will look at Luther's insistence on the doctoral disputation as a necessary part of training theologians of the church. In the process of examining the doctoral candidate, boundaries are drawn to exclude attacks of heresy, and the theological region is opened up to the use of reason. A discussion of the way Luther conceives the theological region to be one of many regions in the medieval university, and the role of the disputation in demarcating these regions, concludes the section.

LUTHER AND THE DISPUTATION

The disputation was the practice of a medieval genre that Luther valued throughout his career as an academic theologian to sharpen, develop, and clarify central themes of his biblical theology. Luther was a master, as he self-confidently claimed, of this form.[1] As a doctor of theology, Luther made use of the disputation at pivotal occasions in his career.[2] From the Ninety-Five Theses (1517), to his early encounters with the foremost theologians of his time—Cardinal Cajetan (1518) and Johannes Eck (1519)—and to the last doctoral disputation of Petrus Hegemon (1545), Luther relished exercising the disputation to propose reforms, to defend his writings, and to teach his doctoral students. Disputations on the divine majesty as the Triune God[3] did not occupy the center stage of Luther's early years, which were devoted to struggling to articulate the elements associated with the dispensation of Christ's benefits; the Catholic dogma of the Trinity was not up for dispute.[4] The early years served to train Luther in the disputational style of

---

1. "... wens aber disputirens gildt, kum einer in der schul zu mir! Ich wils im scharff genug machen vnd im antworten, er machs, wie krauß er wil." WATr 4:635.19-21 (no. 5047, May 21 to June 11, 1540).

2. Luther's letter to pope Leo X in 1518 claims his right as a doctor of theology to dispute publicly. WA 1:528.27-31 ("Beatissimo Patri Leoni Decimo Pontifici Maximo Frater Martinvs Lvther Avgvstinianvs Aeternam Salvtem," in Resolutiones disputationum de indulgentiarum virtute, 1518).

3. The term, "divine Majesty," is not synonymous, but co-extensive with the terms, "deus absconditus" and "deus nudus." For example, "Deus in maiestate et natura sua," or "Deus absconditus in maiestate" [WA 18:685.14, 21 (De servo arbitrio, 1525)], are formulations referring to the aspect of hiddenness that rises up above the word in the context of demonic temptation (2 Thess 2:4). In introducing sermons held on Trinity Sunday, Luther often speaks of the deus nudus or the deus in maiestate as the Triune God, in eternity, apart from his revelation in the "clothes" of his works. Luther uses the same terms to refer to both the Triune God and that aspect of the divine nature that is the enemy of the demonic attack against the truth of the divine revelation. For a discussion of the naked God as the subject matter of Luther's sermons on the Trinity, see: ch. 4, "Knowledge of God in Luther's Sermons." In ch. 4, "The Hidden God," the theme of the hidden God is treated in relation to the sermon's exhortation.

4. "Und ist solcher artickel im Bapstum und bey den Schultheologen rein blieben, das wir mit jnen daru(e)ber keinen zanck haben." WA 54:64.19-21 (Von den letzten Worten Davids, 1543). In his Schmalcald Articles (1537), Luther concludes his comments on the Trinitarian and Christological articles with, "Diese Artikel sind in keinem Zank noch Streit, weil wir zu beiden Teilen dieselbigen [gläuben und] bekennen." The footnote to this sentence indicates that Luther crossed out the word, "gläuben," retaining, at least, the verb, "bekennen." The confession of faith is common to all Christians. See: BSLK, 415.1-2, 415n1.

his thinking, which appeared in other genres[5] and emerged as significant in articulating his understanding of the Trinity in the last years of his life.

Luther recovered the disputational genre for developing his understanding of the Trinitarian article between 1543 and 1545. The disputations themselves contain remarks on a controversy with various contemporaries, as Luther mentions in the preface to the Major disputation.[6] Perceived in these later years was an anti-Trinitarian threat that Luther addressed from diverse perspectives in a variety of genres. In the ongoing revisions to his translation of the Old Testament into German, Luther took care to adequately represent the divine speech that he understood to distinguish between the three Trinitarian persons.[7] Sections of disputations record more pastoral questions concerning the invocation of the Triune God in prayer[8] and the attribution of the divine essence to each of the three persons in the discourse of praise.[9] With the sense of urgency to pass on true doctrine to a new theological generation, Luther turned to the Trinity as

---

5. Bernhard Lohse suggests that the disputational style is evident in other genres of Luther's writings. Bernhard Lohse, "Luther als Disputator," 250.

6. Servetus and Campanus had noted the lack of biblical evidence, at least historically prior to John the Evangelist, for the Trinitarian dogma. Luther's preface introducing the Major disputation mentions this attack against the Trinitarian article. WA 39,2:290.14–17. See "The Attacks on the Trinity" on the anti-Trinitarian dangers Luther perceives to be articulated by Servetus and Campanus, Cochlaeus and Eck.

7. The exegetical text that will be used in this chapter to discuss Luther's Trinitarian hermeneutic is entitled, *Von den letzten Worten Davids* (1543), in WA 54:28.1–100, 27. This treatise, an exegesis of 2 Sam 23:1–7, was based on a fresh translation of these verses that Luther had previously revised in his Bible revision of 1539–1541. Particularly the translations of verses 2 and 3 show Luther's interest in distinguishing between the three persons of the Trinity: "Der Geist des Herrn" (v. 2a), "der Gott Israel" (v. 3a), and "der Hort Israel" (v. 3b). See: WADB 3:413n1. See also the introduction to *Von den letzten Worten Davids* by F. Cohrs in WA 54:16–24, esp. 19. The final revisions to the Luther Bible were published in 1545.

8. In a polemical section of the Fabricius disputation, Luther argues that the true invocation of the Triune God consists of the certainty that God bestows the forgiveness of sins and eternal life. See: WA 39,2:278.30–279.5 (Fabricius).

9. A part of the Major disputation includes the question of how the divine attributes, such as wisdom, goodness, justice and mercy, are predicated of the divine essence and of the Father. See Major's response in Ibid., 294, 12–13. The logic of predicating infinity of each of the three persons is thematized in the disputations. See "The Logic of the *Totus* and *Solus*" in this chapter. In the hymn, "O lux beata trinitas," Luther converts the disputation's proposition into the first to second person discourse of praise. The Trinity is praised through the attribute of infinity. For the text of the hymn, see: WA 35:473.13–29.

the theme of four doctoral disputations.[10] These later disputations record, in the discourse of the classroom, Luther's understanding of the ineffable subject matter (*res*)[11] in propositions and in concepts handed down in Scripture; the creeds; the early church; the *Sentences* commentaries of William of Ockham (1285-1347), Pierre d'Ailly (c. 1351-1420), and Gabriel Biel (c. 1418-1495);[12] and in his Erfurt education by his teachers, Bartholomaeus

---

10. The records of the disputations include the theses published before the occasion of the actual disputation and the student notes that document the disputation. The 38 theses written by Luther, including an extended debate with Aristotle on the concept of infinity, a small disputational fragment, and Luther's *Quaestio*, spoken at the *Promotionsfeier*, remain of the doctoral disputation of Erasmus Alberus (Aug. 24, 1543) in WA 39,2:253.1-257.37. The theses Melanchthon wrote for the doctoral disputation of Theodor Fabricius and Stanislaus Rapagelanus (May 23, 1544), Luther's *praefatio* as well as fragments of the latter's role as opponent, are recorded in Ibid., 260.1-283.5. The doctoral disputation of Georg Major and Johannes Faber (Dec. 12, 1544) contains, by far, the most material on the Trinitarian subject matter. The records of the *disputatio* include Luther's *praefatio*, his 26 theses on the Trinity for Major and 21 theses on the incarnation and soteriology for Faber, and the *disputatio* that is documented in two variant forms. Ibid., 287.1-320.12. The disputation also includes a nice picture of the preparatory work Major conducted under Melanchthon's supervision. Ibid., 320:13-336.29. Luther's last disputation, the doctoral disputation of Petrus Hegemon (July 3, 1545), includes Luther's short *praefatio* and his 17 theses on the Trinity, as well as an extended record of the disputation on a host of theological themes: the incarnation, original sin, traducianism, and papal authority. There are three variants of the disputation. Ibid., 339.1-401.21. Another disputation of this period, the disputation "De divinitate et humanitate Christi (Feb. 28, 1540)," focuses on the Christological dogma and the *nova vocabula* of theological discourse. Ibid., 93:1-121.22. Thesis 40 refers to the incarnation as the work of the Trinity with an allusion to Bonaventure. Ibid., 95, 19-21. Theses 16-20 of "Die Disputation de sententia: Verbum caro factum est (Joh. 1, 14) (Jan. 11, 1539)," allude to the expository and communal syllogisms discussed in medieval Trinitarian theology. Ibid., 4, 24-33. Copies of student notes in Wolfenbüttel and Munich were discovered by Paul Drews as the basis for his edition printed in the WA. Drews also used additional records of the disputations that were found in Hamburg, Riga, and elsewhere. See the text critical introduction by Heinrich Hermelink in WA 39,1.ix-xii.

11. "Quia rem ineffabilem volebant effari, deinde omnis similitudo claudicat nec unquam (ut dicunt) currit quatuor pedibus." WA 39,2:96.3-4 (De divinitate et humanitate Christi, thesis 50).

12. A picture of Luther's sources can be reconstructed by statements gleaned from Melanchthon and Luther himself, from the curriculum of Luther's arts education at the University of Erfurt, and of his theological education in the Augustinian monastery. Melanchthon attests that Luther could recite portions of Augustine, Biel, and Ailly from memory, that he was familiar with Ockham and Gerson, and that he lectured on Aristotle's dialectics and physics in his early teaching career. See: MO 6:159-160 (Epistolarum Lib. X, 1546). Luther's own account of his education is recorded in WATr 3:563.31-565.9 (no. 3722, Jan. 31 to Feb. 2, 1538). In preparation for his ordination, Luther mentions that he had read Biel's *Canonis Misse Expositio*. Ibid., 564.5. For a study of Luther's sources, see: Otto Scheel, *Martin Luther*, vol. 1, 121-238; vol. 2, 118-42, 190-94, 337-64, 397-410; Walter Mostert, "Luthers Verhältnis zur theologischen und philosophischen Überlieferung," vol. 1, 347-48; footnotes in vol. 2, 839-40.

Arnoldi de Usingen and Joducus Trutfetter.[13] Witnessing to the importance of academic formulation as a theological necessity of disputing not the event of revelation but its truth, the later disputations document Luther's articulation of the Trinitarian subject matter in a genre firmly rooted in the medieval context.

THE DOCTORAL DISPUTATION

Luther valued the academic practice of the disputation. He insisted on its use as a necessary tool to train theologians. Luther disclosed his conviction that the university be the fitting academic context in which theologians be educated by advocating the disputation as the genre to be employed in specific situations. An initial clue for the disputation's occasion is recorded in the first thesis of the Major disputation. Citing Matthew 17:5, Luther writes, "God the Father desired that all disputations concerning the articles of faith should cease, when he said concerning God his Son, 'Listen to him.' "[14] The Father's revelation of the Son, and the Son's speech, when it is heard, should suffice to end all controversy.

Some, however, are not prevented from contesting the Father's imperative or the Son's word. When certain people rise up and question the divine word, then the disputation is used to provide instruction in sound teaching and to defend the latter from the invasion of false doctrine.[15] In view

---

13. Bartholomaeus Arnoldi de Usingen, who taught at Erfurt, was one of the last logicians in the early sixteenth century to write commentaries on both the *Logica vetus* (1514) and the *Logica nova* (1507, 1516). The *Logica vetus* was already known in the twelfth century. It was composed of Aristotle's *Categories* and *De Interpretatione*, together with Porphyry's *Isagoge*. The *Logica nova*, also known during the twelfth century, was composed of Aristotle's *Prior* and *Posterior Analytics*, the *Topics*, and the *Sophistici elenchi*. Johannes Eck, Karlstadt's and Luther's opponent at the Leipzig disputation (1519), and professor at the University of Ingolstadt, published a commentary in 1516-1517 on both parts of the *Organon*. He used Johannes Argyropulos' translation of the *Organon*. Jodocus Trutvetter (Isenachensis) (d. 1519) taught both at Erfurt and Wittenberg and is regarded, along with Usingen and Eck, as one of the last logicians standing in the medieval logical tradition. For a discussion of the medieval reception of Aristotle's *Organon*, see: Sten Ebbesen, "Ancient scholastic logic as the source of medieval scholastic logic," 118-27. For two studies of the shifts taking place from the medieval logical tradition to the study of logic in the sixteenth century, see: E. J. Ashworth, "Traditional logic," 143-72; Lisa Jardine, "Humanistic logic," 173-98.

14. WA 39,2:287.5-6 (Major, thesis 1).

15. The argument is recorded as Major's response to the opponent. "Tota epistola Pauli est disputatio quaedam. Ergo Deus voluit esse exstinctam, et per consequens vestra propositio est falsa. Maior: Disputationes, quae sunt contra verbum Dei, illas voluit Deus esse exstinctas et praecipue argumenta facta ex ratione humana, sed disputationes ex sacris literis sumptas

of the addressees, Luther distinguishes the deployment of the disputation from the use of other genres. When adversaries challenge the divine word, Luther can talk of "resisting them" by disputing with them.[16] In a thesis written for the Major disputation, Luther calls on Christ as the example: "Christ the Lord himself often disputed against the Pharisees on behalf of the weak (who had no need of a disputation)."[17] Christ disputes not with the weak who seek to be comforted but with those who call his word into question. In this thesis, Luther identifies the opponent of the disputation to be those who directly contest the truth of the divine word. Theologians must be trained to recognize their opponents and must learn how to respond to them.[18] For the purpose of training the theologian in her role as respondent, Luther advocates Christ as the example of listening to and of defending the Father's word.

The practice of the disputation is an exercise in both recognizing the opponent's attack and in articulating a fitting response. Luther summarizes the former aim: a theologian must be prepared to "resist the adversary."[19] The term "to resist" alludes to the medieval theory of obligations, the rules governing the execution of the disputation. According to one rule of the doctoral disputation, it is the respondent's task to reply to an opponent's attack by either granting or denying the opponent's argument. The respondent is not required to defend the true thesis under dispute.[20] Often sympathetic to the role of respondent, Luther is not satisfied with merely exposing the error of the opponent but establishes as necessary the practice of learning how to respond with an affirmative. Theologians must learn "to answer and teach others, and truly to hand down the doctrine

---

probat vultque conservari, sicut et Paulus dicit, episcopum debere esse instructum ad docendum et repellendam falsam doctrinam [1 Tim 3:2]." Ibid., 310.22-28 (witness A; Major).

16. "... et resistatur adversario." Ibid., 287.10 (Major, last clause of thesis 3).

17. Ibid., 287.11-12 (Major, thesis 4). With the designation, "Pharisaeos," Luther is alluding to the adversaries of Christ in the New Testament gospels who dispute the truth of Christ as the incarnation of the Second Person of the Trinity. The designation should not be read in light of Luther's anti-Jewish polemic, but should be interpreted as a cipher in biblical terminology for those attacking the truth of the divine revelation.

18. "... ut discamus respondere." Ibid., 266.20 (Fabricius, preface).

19. "... et resistatur adversario." Ibid., 287.10 (Major, last clause of thesis 3).

20. Ashworth, "Traditional logic," 166-67.

of God to posterity."[21] The converse side of resisting the adversary is the demonstration of one's capacity to respond in a way exhibiting a grasp of the true doctrine. Luther claims the perpetual task in the church to be twofold: care for the weak and oppose the adversary with the ministry of the word.[22] The theologian must be trained in the two areas of resistance and care, defense and comfort.

Where each task is practiced is best illustrated by a geographical metaphor that represents the disputation. The disputation covers an area marked by a boundary and enclosing a center. For Luther, the work of the theologian includes the twofold task of defending the borders against the adversary and of articulating the truth at the center. When the heretics attack the articles of faith in such a way as to shatter the certainty of the center, the theologian must be ready to repel the challenges launched from the border and to clarify the central themes under attack.

The work at the center involves more than a conversion of the defense into a positive assertion. Theological fitness is demonstrated by the capacity to articulate what is meant by the articles of faith.[23] It is also exercised when various languages are used to explain the subject matter. Pastoral concerns are threaded through Luther's testing of the doctoral students, requiring them to translate the Latin and Greek terms of technical theological discourse into German "for the sake of the weak and for the purpose of teaching."[24] A fit theologian is bilingual, not only so one can translate classic terminology into a language the laity can grasp, but also so one can match the genre of discourse with a particular audience. The example of Luther's responses to his students discloses his pedagogical intention that differs from the harsh tone in which he addresses heretics.[25] Once

---

21. WA 39,2:266.20–21 (Fabricius, preface).

22. Ibid., 287.9–10 (Major, thesis 3).

23. "... damit dem Teuffel die Thu(e)r auffgesperret sind, hinein zu fu(e)ren, was er wil, So ists nutz und not, das doch ettliche, beide Leien und Gelerten, sonderlich Pfarrherrn, Predigere und Schulmeistere, von solchen no(e)tigen Artickeln unsers Glaubens auch lernen dencken und Deudsch reden," WA 54:59.1–5 (*Von den letzten Worten Davids*).

24. WA 39,2:305.20 (Major).

25. In a Table Talk, Luther compares his disputational style with that of Melanchthon. Melanchthon's critical style displeases Luther, who prefers to gently lead his students up the ladder of learning. "Disputationum usus. Deinde dixerunt de utilitate disputationum circularium, quae magnam utilitatem et exercitium afferrent adolescentiae: Vnd man furet die stoltzen gesellen vnter die ruden, ut experirentur, quales essent. Ideo ego adolescentibus

the propositional discourse of the disputation is mastered and its terms understood, then its content can be articulated in other genres more fitting to comfort consciences in terror. What one learns in the disputation can be converted into genres—such as the hymn or prayer—that are used to assert and to adore the central certainty in the benefits of Christ.[26]

As a genre used to train theologians, the disputation's academic site cannot be regarded as marginal to its purpose. The doctoral disputation, a festive occasion regulated by the university as the final examination required to obtain the doctoral hood,[27] was a medieval form appropriated in the early and late phases of Luther's career as a university professor.[28]

---

laudo argumenta quamvis incomposita, et displicet mihi Philippi Melanchthonis exacta ratio, das er die armen gesellen so bald vberrumpelt; nam oportet per gradus nos ascendere, auff einer treppen zur annder stuffen, nam nemo repente fit summus." WATr 4:104.32-39 (no. 4056, Oct. 11-13, 1538). In some situations, Luther forgets his role as opponent, and further develops the position of the doctoral candidate, the respondent. In this way, Luther goes beyond what is required in the medieval doctoral disputation in order to help prepare his students for the trials and temptations of university and parish life. Ashworth describes the practice of the *disputatio* as follows. The ideal disputation begins with the argument articulated by an opponent who obliges the respondent to defend or attack a proposition initially advanced. The aim of the opponent is to force the respondent to commit errors of logic. During a series of defenses, the logical errors accumulate, and eventually result in a position that is impossible for the respondent to hold. At this point, the *disputatio* ends. In the doctoral disputation, which differs from the obligational disputation, the opponent attacks a thesis presumed to be true. The burden falls on the respondent to grant, deny, or qualify the attack; the respondent is obliged only to show how the argument is invalid and not to argue on behalf of the proposition advanced. Ashworth, "Traditional logic," 166-67. Angelelli discusses two medieval methods of disputing: the question method, favored by medieval logicians, and the argument method. Ignacio Angelelli, "The techniques of disputation in the history of logic," 801.

26. See 46nn8-9.

27. The doctoral disputations are prefaced by a festive speech. See: Luther's prefaces to the Fabricius and Rapagelanus disputation (WA 39,2:266.1-22), the Major and Faber disputation (Ibid., 290.1-21), and the Hegemon disputation (Ibid., 343:1-13[witness A]; 343.1-12[witness B]). Graduation was celebrated on another day. At the ceremony, a doctoral speech was read by an appointed speaker. The *quaestio doctoralis* was delivered to the new doctor by a boy (*puer*). A *quaestio doctoralis*, written by Luther, is recorded at the end of the Alberus disputation (Ibid., 257.1-37). The *quaestio doctoralis* for the Hegemon disputation was delivered to Hegemon by Luther's young son, Johannes (Ibid., 338).

28. Academic disputations were regulated at the University of Wittenberg. The prescriptions for the theological faculty differed from those valid in the Arts faculty. The statutes of 1508 prescribed circular (weekly) disputations for the master during the semester. During vacations, the task fell to the baccalaureats. Also prescribed in the statutes were doctoral disputations for the obtaining of the doctoral degree and the formal disputations ("solemniter") that took place once a year for each master. There are records of twenty Luther disputations until 1521. From 1521 to 1533, the disputations diminished in importance as a pedagogical form. Karlstadt, dean of the theological faculty in 1521, permitted both the circular disputations and the doctoral disputations to take place. However, records of both types disappeared

Luther's love for this form dovetailed easily with its academic purpose in the dialectical pursuit of truth. Text interpretation in the medieval theological faculty took the form of dialectically balancing the reception of authoritative knowledge of Scripture and the academic theological canon that was already established and often appeared to be contradictory. In seeking to understand the truth of the subject matter, the theological material was presented in the literary form of questions and articles, the question,[29] alongside of which the various kinds of disputations emerged as its spoken complement.[30] Rules governed the presentation of the material in a series of questions and articles. Theses were written for the disputation that, through arguments and inferences, would establish a truth persuading one's opponent. With the rise of an interest in particular facets of medieval logic, especially the fallacies and sophistries (*sophismata*), treatises on obligations flourished in the thirteenth century. Obligations—sets of rules for consequences and inferences intended for the disputation—formed the basis for outlining the rules determining the validity of granting or rejecting a logical series of arguments or inferences.[31] When Luther insists

---

between 1525 and 1533. In 1533 with the University reforms, new statutes were proposed by Melanchthon, the *praeceptor Germaniae*, and on May 5, 1536, the Elector Johann Friedrich authorized the program. The doctoral disputations were reinstated, and the circular disputations were required to be held by each master once every three months. These regulations remained in place until Luther's death in 1546, after which the practice of the disputations rapidly declined. For a detailed account of the history of the disputations in the theological faculty at the University of Wittenberg, see: Ernst Wolf, "Zur wissenschaftsgeschichtlichen Bedeutung der Disputationen an der Wittenberger Universität im 16. Jahrhundert," 38–51.

29. Lombard's *Sentences*, a commentary on Paul's Letter to the Romans, is structured by the *quaestio* method. The *quaestio* begins with an initial question or problem. A section follows that consolidates authoritative statements arguing for and against the initial question. Concluding the section is the author's response to the opposing positions that challenge the author's own position. This form of interpreting texts established the structure for the medieval *Summa*.

30. Anthony Kenny and Jan Pinborg, "Medieval philosophical literature," 25. Marenbon stresses that the method and the content of the medieval *quaestio* and the theological *summa* are inextricably linked. John Marenbon, *Later Medieval Philosophy (1150–1350)*, 13–14.

31. A precise understanding of obligation treatises, the function of obligations, their purpose and relation to medieval logic, remain to be clarified. Eleonore Stump, "Obligations: From the beginning to the early fourteenth century," 315. Boethius translated two Aristotelian texts that introduced the founding theory of obligations into Western philosophy. He interpreted Aristotle's *Topics* [VIII (3), 159a 15–24] to mean that the position, rather than the respondent's defense of an impossible proposition, is faulted. A passage in the *Prior Analytics* [I (13), 32a 18–20] stipulates the famous medieval rule that nothing impossible follows from the possible. Stump, "Obligations," 318. The references to Aristotle are in Aristotle, *The Complete Works of Aristotle*, vol. 1, 267 and vol. 1, 51.

on the twofold aim of theological education, he is committed to using the medieval disputation as the genre best suited to achieve his purpose. Luther is convinced that theologians of the church be accomplished in the skill of distinguishing boundary from center and in deploying strategies to articulate responses at both sites. The exercise of the disputational genre trains theologians to dialectically weigh positions and to present them according to practices consistent in all academic regions.

THE REGIONS OF ACADEMIC INQUIRY AND THE DISPUTATION

The way in which scholars have determined the relationship between philosophy and theology has played a crucial role in interpreting the significance of reason in Luther's thought. One way in which Luther has been read assigns weight to Luther's surface polemic. Luther's rhetoric, on the surface at least, leaves an impression that his theology begins and ends with a sharp rejection of any philosophical intrusion into the theological region.[32] If Luther's disputations are studied from the perspective of a strict separation between theology and philosophy, then some interpretations have been proposed that do not wrestle seriously with the issue of reason in theology.

One aspect of the difficulty is concerned with the characteristically modern issue of double truth. Considered relevant to the question of the theology-philosophy relation is inquiry into the possibility of Luther's logic of faith (*logica fidei*).[33] The question whether Luther's logic of faith asserts a theological truth that contradicts a truth claim in philosophy has implications for accusing Luther of a double-truth theory.[34] Although

---

32. The following examples from the later Trinitarian disputations expose Luther's rhetoric that implies the strict separation between theology and philosophy. "13. Excludenda est igitur mathematica et omnis totius creaturae cogitatio in credenda divinitate. ... 17. Quod dialectica arguit haec suis regulis non quadrare, dicendum Mulier taceat in ecclesia [playing on 1 Cor 14:34]." WA 39,2:254.7–8, 15–16 (Alberus, theses 13 and 17); "Error itaque est universa Mathematica, ipsaque fortiter crucifigenda, dum de Deo ipso quaeritur." Ibid., 287.27–28 (Major, thesis 13); "Summa, per rationem et philosophiam de his rebus maiestatis nihil, per fidem vero omnia recte dici et credi possunt." Ibid., 340.12–13 (Hegemon, thesis 17). Many theses of the 1539 disputation on John 1:14 refer to the exclusivity of the theological truth of the incarnation against philosophical invasion. See the theses of this disputation in Ibid., 3:1–5.40.

33. Reijo Työrinoja, "Proprietas Verbi: Luther's Conception of Philosophical and Theological Language in the Disputation," 143–78.

34. In an early phase of research into Luther's understanding of the relation of theology to philosophy, scholars interpreted Luther's position in light of the charge of a double-truth

the charge is anachronistic, the thematization of double truth exposes a conceptual framework that pits two regions, philosophy and theology, against each other. Once theology is seen to be explicitly divorced from philosophy, the claim regarding a distinct type of theological discourse surfaces. In a study of Luther's disputations, Gerber's argument represents the problem of equating the disputation's propositional discourse to a "language of faith" (*Glaubenssprache*).[35] In Gerber's analysis, philosophy is so sealed off from theology that the only window onto theological discourse is that of a "language of faith" as an "existential mode of speech." By determining theological language in this way, the proposition is reduced to a defensive assertion in the event of an attack from philosophy, and it is interpreted solely according to its kerygmatic intention. A similar view is held by Työrinoja. Työrinoja pits the syllogistic form of human reason against the theological proposition that falls "outside" of human reason.[36]

theory. They countered the charge by claiming that, for Luther, the two regions of theology and philosophy are incommensurable realms, a claim that does not necessarily imply a theory of double truth. See: Bengt Hägglund, *Theologie und Philosophie bei Luther und in der occamistischen Tradition*, 87–102; Karl Heim, "Zur Geschichte des Satzes von der doppelten Wahrheit," 1–16; Streiff, "*Novis Linguis Loqui*," 93–114.

35. Gerber's study of Luther's disputations takes, as its starting point, Ebeling's position on "Luther als Sprachereignis" that situates Luther's language and thought entirely within the realm of an existential "Sprachmodus." According to Gerber's interpretation of Ebeling, Luther's understanding of language is based on the distinction between the *deus absconditus*, the God not clothed with the divine word, and the word of God or Christ. Christ is preached as the twofold word: the second use of the law and the comfort of the gospel. By transposing Ebeling's position into a discussion of the *disputatio*, Gerber pits the theological assertion against all philosophical "attacks." "[A]ls 'existentieller Sprachmodus' des Glaubens," the *disputatio* has "ausschließlich theologische Funktion … Sprache, und damit die disputatio, kann nur theologisch, im Streit mit der Philosophie, vom Verbum incarnatum et praedicatum, also vom mündlich ergehenden und gehörten Wort her vollzogen, verstanden, interpretiert werden." Uwe Gerber, *Disputatio als Sprache des Glaubens*, 290. 293. The theological proposition, according to Gerber, is an assertion of faith, asserted in the situation of attack from philosophy. Ibid., 281–82. When the propositional content of the language of faith is reduced to the status of an assertion, Luther's use of the disputational form as a process of distinguishing terms and arriving at definitions in the theological region is misunderstood. By using Ebeling's interpretation of Luther's understanding of language in the genre of the sermon, Gerber limits his reflections on the propositional discourse of the *disputatio* to an assertion, thereby neglecting an in-depth study of the logic, the semantics, and the metaphysics of the proposition.

36. Työrinoja assumes that Luther views theology to be strictly separated from philosophy. "[I]n the case of Trinitarian and Christological formulas a definite position towards the relationships between theology and philosophy … is founded on his [Luther's] view about the essential difference between theological and philosophical language. … When Luther furthermore presupposes that human reason (ratio humana) and its acts essentially have the syllogistic structure and form, it follows that theological propositions also fall outside of

Whether reason has any role to play in determining the theological subject matter is left open by this position.

Whether the possibility of a double-truth theory is explored or Luther's propositional discourse is placed in a theologically exclusive frame of reference, a similar claim is made regarding the connection between theology and philosophy. For these types of inquiry, the separation of theology from philosophy is secured; the language of faith is determined to fight against the language of philosophy.[37] According to White, this reading of Luther is distinctly modern. What White discovers and then rejects is the idealist presupposition of setting philosophy against theology as two monolithic blocks.[38] A characteristically modern conceptuality that pits the logic of abstract reason against the nonrational, existential leap of faith is presupposed. By interpreting Luther's statements of theological exclusivity according to the strict separation between theology and philosophy, the dialectical richness of Luther's thought is collapsed into the surface veneer of his rhetoric. The propositional form as a distinct and complex type of "language of faith" is reduced to an untouchable assertion. Luther's serious wrestling with particular philosophical tools to articulate his understanding of the Trinity is either not even perceived or merely avoided. Against the backdrop of a strict separation between theology and philosophy, Luther is often understood as minimizing the use of reason in theology, a conclusion that misunderstands what his late medieval contemporaries would have considered to be a more reciprocal relationship between the two academic regions.

---

human reason." Työrinoja, "Proprietas Verbi," 169. Työrinoja's claim concerning theological propositions that "fall outside" natural reason remains vague. It could mean: unprovable by natural reason or unintelligible by natural reason. Työrinoja pits Luther against Ailly by assuming that the latter attempts to articulate a logic of Trinitarian faith in the syllogistic form and the former, insisting on the non-epistemic "notion of religious belief," does not only disregard Ailly's understanding of the relation between mystery and reason, but also fails to see the various rational factors informing Luther's regionalism. Ailly would not agree that his articulation of the Trinity is sufficient for the assent of a non-believer. Considered to be an epistemic category, belief, for both Ailly and Luther, embraces and invites the activity of reason to investigate its content. See: Petrus de Ailliaco, *Quaestiones super libros sententiarum cum quibusdam in fine adjunctis*, Book I, q. 5. I would like to thank Marilyn McCord Adams for pointing out the problems in Työrinoja's argument to me.

37. Gerber, *Disputatio als Sprache des Glaubens*, 293.

38. White, *Luther as Nominalist*, 54–55, 82–83.

In order to uncover the dialectic lying underneath Luther's rhetoric, the academic location of his theological activity must be considered. Viewed against the backdrop of the medieval academic context, Luther's polemic loses some of its surface provocation. Some philosophers have recently challenged the typically modern perspective that pits theology against philosophy. They emphasize the link between philosophy and theology in the Middle Ages to be more fluid and interwoven.[39] They expose the fiction of double truth to be a product of positive historical description[40] and argue for the integration of—rather than the separation between—faculties in the medieval university.[41] When the current research into the medieval context of Luther's theological reflection is taken seriously, then a more accurate understanding of his view of philosophy can be perceived.

A precise determination of the role of reason in Luther's theology must represent not only its relation to an academic context but must also locate Luther's thought in a distinct historical trajectory. During the Middle Ages, an increasing rift between philosophy and theology took place that played a role in Luther's own understanding of the type of reason employed in the two regions. Luther's polemic can be seen, at one level, to reflect a gradual separation between theology and philosophy occurring during the historical development of the medieval university.

It began with the introduction of a procedure into the arts faculty that grounded the study of any university curriculum.[42] In the thirteenth century, Aristotle's works and method were adopted at the University of Paris by the philosophical faculty as the foundations for academic study.[43] Rules governing scientific acceptability were determined in the arts faculty and applied to the higher sciences of medicine, law, and theology. According to the model of Aristotelian demonstrative science, the premises on which

---

39. Perler's study involves both a synchronic and a diachronic perspective. He views each philosophical question as a structural chain of interconnecting themes and compares each structure with earlier and later developments. Dominik Perler, *Prädestination, Zeit und Kontingenz*, 3–5.

40. Ludwig Hödl, "'... sie reden, als ob es zwei gegensätzliche Wahrheiten gäbe': Legende und Wirklichkeit der mittelalterlichen Theorie von der doppelten Wahrheit," 226.

41. John E. Murdoch, "From social into intellectual factors: an aspect of the unitary character of late medieval learning," 271–74.

42. Kenny and Pinborg, "Medieval philosophical literature," 14.

43. C. H. Lohr, "The medieval interpretation of Aristotle," 87.

syllogistic inferences were based remained axiomatic for each particular region. Into the fourteenth century, axioms continued to be privileged as the first principles of science. What relaxed between the thirteenth and fourteenth centuries were the strict requirements of the demonstrative scientific model governing the types of inferences that could be made. The belief in the contingency of creation corresponded to a worry about the demonstrability of essences from necessary principles, as stipulated in Aristotle's *Posterior Analytics*. A model of scientific thinking emerged that worked out the plausibility, rather than the certainty, of arguments advanced respective to the subject matter under investigation.[44] In the newer model, the principle of noncontradiction was elevated as the criterion for scientific truth. By orienting scientific arguments to show plausibility rather than strict certainty, the academic regions soon restricted their relations with one another. To each academic region was assigned the task of showing the plausibility of its own inferences, rather than demanding that each region conform to strict demonstrations of certainty that were valid for all regions.

The increased separation between regions, however, did not prohibit the use of the tools of reason, available to all regions, to investigate a subject matter located in a specific region. For example, theologians in the fourteenth century continued to discuss the theological subject matter of the Trinity in relation to medieval logic.[45] What would later surface in Luther's case would be a heightened separation between the theological and philosophical regions that was not entirely determined by a radically new understanding of faith pitted against reason. Rather, Luther's view can be represented according to a more modest claim. He is located in a trajectory

---

44. When a fourteenth-century scholar, such as Pierre d'Ailly, argues for the plausibility, rather than demonstrates the strict certainty of a scientific conclusion, this model of scientific reasoning does not imply conjecture. It represents a late medieval development in scientific argumentation that defines its type of certainty to be formed by an epistemological theory distinguishing between natural light and natural reason. See: Maurice Patronnier de Gandillar, "De l'usage et de la valeur des arguments probables dans les questions du Cardinal Pierre d'Ailly sur le 'Livre des Sentences'," 43–91.

45. For a detailed account relating medieval logic to the doctrine of the Trinity in the fourteenth century, see Alfonso Maierù, "A propos de la doctrine de la supposition en théologie trinitaire au XIVe siècle," 221–38; Idem, "Logique et théologie trinitaire dans le moyen-âge tardif: deux solutions en présence," 185–201; Idem, "Logique et théologie trinitaire: Pierre D'Ailly," 253–68; Johann Auer, "Die aristotelische Logik in der Trinitätslehre der Spätscholastik," 457–96.

that sees the relations between academic regions in terms of a late medieval development in the scientific method defining academic study.

The role that reason plays in Luther's thought is related to his view of the academic context in which various regions are located. By taking into account the more fluid relation between theology and philosophy as well as the historical trajectory of increasing separation between these two regions, a more nuanced judgment of Luther's understanding of reason can be made. In a remark uttered in his Galatians commentary, Luther does not dismiss reason from the theological task. He generously admits the use of "reason illuminated by faith" to investigate the divine will of love.[46] This position sees the activity of reason inquiring into the content of faith no differently from some theologians of the fourteenth century.

Luther's Augustinian view of reason is reproduced on the Aristotelian ground of science that allocates a particular region to a specific object under investigation. Reviewing the regionalism discussed by Aristotle in the Nicomachean Ethics,[47] Luther argues in the disputation on John 1:14 that, in order for a truth claim to be made with respect to a distinct field of scientific research, specific tools of measurement must be employed that are suited to investigate the subject matter.[48] Each region has its distinct subject matter. In order to investigate it accurately, tools must be fitted to use in that specific region.[49] For Luther, the type of reason employed in

---

46. "Ego sum benedictus, humanitate et divinitate, nihil egeo, ... In illam imaginem mus man hinsehen. Qui hoc credit, habet. Non comprehenditur voluntate dilectionis, sed ratione illuminata per fidem." WA 40,2:443.7, 12–13 (In epistolam S. Pauli ad Galatas Commentarius, 1531, published in 1535, to Gal 3:13).

47. Nic. Ethics, I (7), 1098a 20–1098b 8 [vol. 2, 1735–36].

48. Taking his cue from Aristotle's comparison between the carpenter and the mathematician who each employ different tools to measure their respective subject matters, Luther uses the example of the arts and trades ["Ita singula artificia vel potius opera," (WA 39,2:5.31, first clause of thesis 38)] to show that tools employed in the philosophical region are inadequate to measure the truth of the theological subject matter. He concludes, "Quanto minus potest idem esse verum in philosophia et theologia, quarum distinctio in infinitum maior est, quam artium et operum." Ibid., 5.33–34 (thesis 39). For the series of theses discussing this theme, see: Ibid., 5.13–34 (theses 29–39).

49. In De anima, Aristotle discusses the act of thinking. He shows that the thinking part of the soul must be capable of receiving the form of an object of thought without itself being the object. In this way, one can know an object for what it is. See: De anima, III (4–5), 429a 10–430a 26 [vol. 1, 682–84]. I would like to thank Kevin Mongrain for kindly referring this text to me.

the theological region must be obedient to Christ.[50] This view of reason, illuminated by faith and obedient to Christ, initially qualifies the type of reason Luther advocates using in the theological region. Its fit to the subject matter, however, must be tested.

The disputation is the genre in which a type of reason is fitted to a particular subject matter. While the region of theological inquiry shares the terminology and concepts available to other academic regions, the disputation serves to critically receive terms and to define them in view of the subject matter under investigation. The Trinitarian disputations reveal Luther in this light. When the Trinitarian article is contested by attacks from the boundary, Luther uses the disputation in his struggles to articulate a defense as well as an understanding of the central faith. Throughout this process, he advocates and seeks to apply a legitimate use of reason in order to determine the subject matter and to define its terms. Luther regards the doctoral disputation to be the academic form employing reason to draw boundaries between the theological region and other academic regions, as well as to investigate its center in obedience to Christ. In the discussion that follows, Luther's theology will be shown in light of a distinct appreciation for reason to study the Trinitarian mystery.

THE INNER TRINITY AS THE SUBJECT
MATTER OF THE DISPUTATION

The discussions of Luther's regionalist view of the medieval university and of the function of the disputation leave open the question of why Luther used the disputation in the academic context to respond to heresy. In the doctoral disputations, Luther thematizes a particular aspect of the Trinity in his defense against what he considered to be the imposition of temporal categories onto the theological region. Associating a particular use of reason with heresy, Luther's defense of the Trinitarian article focuses on the articulation of the concept of infinity. This section shows how Luther begins to determine the inner Trinity according to the concept of infinity in the context of the later years of Luther's theological career. In these years,

---

50. Luther's Augustinian understanding of the use of reason, employed in the theological region, to shed light on the content of faith is represented in the following thesis from the *disputatio* on John 1:14. "Cum contra Paulus doceat, captivandum esse omnem intellectum (haud dubie et philosophiam) in obsequium Christi [2 Cor 10:5]." WA 39,2:4.6–7 (thesis 8).

Luther observed a rise in attacks against the Trinity and was compelled to respond to what he saw as the demonic and heretical challenges driving apart the Father from the Son.

In order to respond to heresy, Luther demarcated the borders of the theological region in which he was free to articulate the primary distinction shaping his understanding of the Trinity: the distinction between the inner and the outer Trinity. From the perspective established by this distinction, the inner Trinity is related to the concept of infinity. The theological discourse of infinity is of a special type. Concluding the section is a discussion of the "improper" language of infinity and the truth claim that this language makes.

THE ATTACKS ON THE TRINITY IN LUTHER'S LATER YEARS

The last years of Luther's life were marked by a passionate resurgence of the theme of eternity. Some of the most moving sermons preached on the resurrection (1 Cor 15:35–58)[51] and the Trinitarian-doxological tenor of the last hymn he composed[52] unveil Luther's longing for the comfort of eternity in a context of personal tragedy, illness, and frustration.[53] Regarding weak Christians, Luther acknowledges the extent of injury that any challenge to the *promissio* effects. When certainty that the "eternal benefits,"[54] revealed in the Son, is eroded, then the conscience cannot trust the God who forgives sins on account of the Son (*propter Filium*).[55] Counting himself among the

---

51. Luther's sermons on 1 Cor 15:35–58 are found in WA 49:395.4–415.7 (Cantate Sunday, May 11, 1544); Ibid., 422.14–441.10 (Exaudi Sunday, May 25, 1544); Ibid., 761.13–780.13 (Trinity Sunday, May 31, 1545).

52. The last hymn Luther wrote was published without a melody in the 1543 Klug hymnbook. It was a translation of the fifth-century Latin hymn, "O lux beata trinitas." The three stanzas are devoted to the praise of the eternal and Triune God. WA 35:285–86. For the hymn's text, see: Ibid., 473.13–29.

53. Luther's daughter, Magdalena, died in 1542 and Spalatin, Luther's close friend, died in early 1545. Luther writes of his exhaustion in a letter to Anton Auerbach: "... cum sim senex, exhaustus et piger ..., ut in quiete et pace agerem et obdormirem." WABr 10:614.14, 20 (no. 4013, second half of July or August (?), 1544); see also: Ibid., 642.4–10 (no. 4023, Letter to Prince Johann von Anhalt, Aug. 27, 1544,); Martin Brecht, *Martin Luther*, vol. 3, 185–89.

54. "Si habetis filium, Tunc loquor vobiscum, Spiritus sanctus schwebet, et quicquid facit, ist eitel wolgefallen und sonst nichts ... Sed hic loquitur de aeternis bonis, da wir nimer sterben, malam conscientiam haben. Si illum auditis, estis mei filii et beati, nihil nocebit mors etc." WA 49:315.3–4, 5–7 (Sermon on the First Sunday after Epiphany, Jan. 13, 1544).

55. "Nos loquimur de voluntate Dei remittente peccata et iustificante impium propter Filium." WA 39,2:278.23–24 (Fabricius). Fabricius' response indicates that he learned something

weak, Luther is compelled, in these last years, to search for comfort in the themes of eternal life and the eternity of God.

A place at which Luther notices a weakness regarding the articulation of claims of certainty is the relation between Scripture and dogma. At this juncture in his theological career, Luther noticed a crack beginning to develop in the theological unity of Scripture and dogma that, in the seventeenth century, would break the two extremes apart.[56] In 1544, Luther initially observed the rift in the context of discussing the relationship between Scripture and the church's authority. In a role as respondent, Luther disputes a thesis representing both Eck and Johannes Cochlaeus (1479–1552) who, Luther alleges, ground the authority of the Trinitarian dogma in the church and not in Scripture: "Eck and Cochlaeus are asses, who say that the article of the Trinity is established and confirmed, not by Scripture, but by the doctors of the church and the pope. That's a lie."[57] Eck and Cochlaeus represent a position similar to Ailly, who also notices the absence of the Trinitarian article in Scripture, preferring to see it as a matter of the Spirit's special revelation to the church (John 16:12–13).[58] It appears that Luther accuses his opponents of pulling the authority of extrabiblical language apart from its biblical ground. Luther's rhetoric suggests his disagreement with a position claiming the authority of the Trinitarian dogma to rest on an ecclesiological, and not on a biblical, warrant. The problem, as Luther

from his teacher. He links together the Trinitarian nature with the divine will to show mercy. "Cognoscere voluntatem Dei est scire non solum, quod puniat peccatum, sed est credere, Deum ab initio genuisse filium, qui filius sit factus pro nobis homo et mediator. Haec est propria Dei voluntas, ut credatis in eum, quem misit ipse." Ibid., 278.18-21. Complete knowledge of both the triune essence and the divine nature of mercy contrasts with imperfect knowledge of God. Partial knowledge consists of the concept of one God based on the proof by conservation and is articulated in a proposition concerning God's nature to reward good deeds. Luther summarizes this point in the Fabricius disputation. "Gentes vero, die konnen nuhr so hoch, das sie sagen: Deus vult exaudire bonos, non impios, weitter konnen sie nicht." Ibid., 278.24-25.

56. Medieval theologians underline the close relationship between Scripture and the articles of faith by stressing the apostolic origin of the confession of faith, a position Luther also holds. "Das gebet oder bekentnis haben wir nicht gemacht noch erdacht, die vorigen Veter auch nicht, ... also ist dis Symbolum aus der lieben Propheten und Apostel bu(e)chern, das ist: aus der gantzen heiligen Schrifft, fein kurtz zusamen gefasset fu(e)r die kinder und einfeltigen Christen." WA 41:275.29-30, 32-34 (Sermon on Trinity Sunday, May 23, 1535). For a study of the seventeenth-century Socinian criticism of dogma, see: Klaus Scholder, *Ursprünge und Probleme der Bibelkritik im 17. Jahrhundert*, 34-55. For a brief history of "anti-Trinitarians," see: Gustav Adolf Benrath, "Antitrinitarier," 168-74.

57. WA 39,2:305.24-26 (witness A; Major).

58. Ailly, *Sent.* I, q. 5, D, E.

sees it, has to do with the way in which an appeal to the church's authority results in pulling apart Scripture from the articulation of dogma. By
invoking the authority of dogma over Scripture, Luther sees the church's
later doctrinal formulations being privileged over Scripture, a position he
fears errs greatly. The question as to why this rift would present a threat
to the Trinitarian dogma, and thereby compel a disputation to take place,
demands a closer look at what Luther perceives to be the danger.

Looking at another rift detected by Luther paints a fuller picture of what
Luther regards as a threat. For Luther, the issue of a rift presents itself in
the relation between Father and Son. Luther begins the series of theses in
the Major disputation by citing the Father's imperative in Matthew 17:5 as
the reason why disputations should not be held. "God the Father desired
that all disputations concerning the articles of faith should cease, when he
said concerning God his Son, 'Listen to him.' "[59] When the Father is obeyed
by listening to the Son, no defense of the Father's speech is necessary.
Scripture secures the Trinitarian article by virtue of a structure of mutual
revelation in which one person is heard and the other person is obeyed.[60] By
hearing the Son and obeying the Father, both Son and Father are acknowledged to exist in an intimate relation. The relationship between Father and
Son is secured by the dogma that articulates their natural unity.[61] When
Luther claims that the position arguing for the church's confirmation of
the Trinitarian article is a "lie," he is formulating his attack from the perspective shaped by the first thesis of the Major disputation. For Luther,
the dogma cannot be confirmed independently of Scripture by the church.
The church's dogma is placed under the authority of the Father's speech, a

---

59. WA 39,2:287.5-6 (Major, thesis 1). In the genre of the sermon, the Matt 3:13-17 text
plays a significant role in Luther's understanding of a Trinitarian structure of revelation. The
pericope of Christ's baptism was the gospel lesson, prescribed by the late medieval lectionary
Luther used, for the feast of Epiphany. For a discussion of the texts Luther used to preach on
the Trinity, see ch. 4, "The Dogmatic Narrowing."

60. In ch. 4, I discuss what I call the "Trinitarian structure of mutual revelation" as it
is shaped by the genre of the sermon. To summarize, Trinitarian revelation takes place in
a matrix of speech in which one person speaks, revealing another person in relation to the
speaker. Likewise, the Second Person reveals another person by speaking either to that person
directly or about that person. In this matrix of revelation, all three persons are revealed by
revealing each other.

61. Luther contrasts his position with an Arian one. "Non ibi de consensu, sed de unitate
naturae loquitur, id est, Pater et Filius sunt unum natura." WA 39,2:298.3-4 (witness A; Major).

position already implying a Trinitarian theological claim of natural unity between Father and Son.

On the surface, Luther's statement could be interpreted to pit Scripture against the tradition in view of the question of authority. The issue of authority, however, does not turn on the disjunction between privileging either dogma or Scripture as the authoritative ground of the Trinitarian article.[62] For Luther, playing one off against the other does not touch the heart of the issue centering on the authority of extrabiblical language. Luther's position on extrabiblical language offers an insightful clue for discovering the way in which he views the relation between Scripture and dogma.[63] In the Major disputation, Luther refers to two extrabiblical theological terms, *homoousios* (ὁμοούσιος) and "original sin" (*Erbsünde*), and states that although the discrepancy in words might distinguish between the early church and Paul, the different terms refer to the same *res*.[64] With respect to a Trinitarian understanding, what Luther conceptually executes is to orient both Scripture and the church to the relation between Father and Son. In view of the authority of the Father's speech, the Trinitarian

---

62. A claim articulated in the Major disputation reveals, at the surface level, a sympathy for Scripture as the source of the Trinitarian article. "Neque enim crederem vel Augustini vel Magistri scriptis, nisi hunc de trinitate articulum vetus et novum testamentum liquidissime ostenderent." Ibid., 305.10-12 (witness A; Major). This statement must not be isolated from Luther's view of the mutual relation between Scripture and dogma. For Luther, the question of authority is related to the issue of obedience. Obedience to the Father's speech already implies an understanding of the Trinity in terms of hearing both the Son's voice and listening to the Spirit's "grammar." On the Spirit's speech, see "Infinity and the Inner Trinity" and "The Inner Trinity and the Discourse of Infinity" in this chapter.

63. Already in 1521, Luther encounters a difficulty with extrabiblical language. In the response to Latomus (1521), Luther misquotes Jerome and arouses suspicions of Arian leanings. See the introduction to "Rationis Latomianae confutatio (1521)," in WA 8:40. Luther argues, "Nec est, quod mihi 'homousion' illud obiectes adversus Arrianos receptum. Non fuit receptum a multis iisque praeclarissimis, quod et Hieronymus optavit aboleri, adeoque non effugerunt periculum hoc invento vocabulo, ut Hieronymus queratur nescire, quid veneni lateat in syllabis et literis, adeo illud Arriani magis quam scripturas etiam exagitabant." Ibid., 117, 20-25. In the letter to which Luther is referring, Jerome does not address the term, "homoousios," but speaks of the three *hypostases* whose meaning can be interpreted in an Arian fashion. See: Jerome, *Epistula* 15, 3-4 [PL 22:356-57].

64. "Adversarii nostri volunt, articulos nostros non satis esse fundatos in scripturis, suntque vocabulistae, cupiunt enim, vocabulis sibi demonstrari veritatem articuli trinitatis, sicut et Ariani sibi volebant ostendi vocabulum ὁμοούσιον. Et a me Erasmus sibi voluit ostendi vocabulum originale, welches nit sonnderlich lauttet, Erbsundt lauttet besser, wie soll ich im aber thun. Vocabulum quidem non est in Paulo, sed res ipsa et in Paulo et in tota scriptura sacra habetur et exprimitur expressis verbis. Ut igitur res ipsas proprie tradamus, oportet nos uti vocabulis rebus ipsis accomodatis et convenientibus." WA 39,2:305.1-9 (witness A; Major).

claim regarding the natural unity between Father and Son is made, a claim articulated both in the Father's revelation of the Son in Matthew 17:5 (compare Matthew 3:17) and in the extrabiblical Trinitarian language of the church. By orienting the Trinitarian claim to the issue of obedience, Luther succeeds in demarcating the theological region inside which no disputations are necessary. If, on the contrary, the Father's voice is disobeyed, a cloud of suspicion is moved over the Father's natural unity with the Son, and the issue becomes the subject for dispute.

The occasion for the disputation presents itself when attacks are launched from the outside. The intimate relation between Scripture and dogma is threatened by attacks that Luther attributes to the devil. For Luther, the devil's work is constant from Genesis throughout the entire history of the church. Luther does not distinguish historically between attacks against the Father's word in Scripture and in extrabiblical heresies. The demonic challenge from Adam to the Apocalypse consists of questioning the word revealed by the Father—"is it really true?"[65] What the devil calls into question is the unity between the Father and the Father's word. Passages in Scripture are written in its defense.[66] The church's history continues to witness to the defense of the Father's unity with the Son against ancient and recycled heresies.[67] In the early church, the dogma of the substantial unity was formulated by raising the level of discourse from the uncontroversial baptismal formula to the type of eternity associated with the inner-Trinitarian generation of the *logos* (λόγος) in order to combat Arius, one of Luther's favorite heretics.[68] The formulations of the Creed, the decisions of medieval church councils that would be discussed at great length in the medieval *Sentences* commentaries, and Luther's remarks dressing sixteenth-century heresies in the new garb of an old

---

65. WA 49:409.26 (Sermon on Cantate Sunday, May 11, 1544).

66. "… tamen res ipsa defendenda est per scripturas contra Diabolum." WA 39,2:287.15–16 (Major, second clause of thesis 6).

67. "Videmus iam repurgata doctrina verae religionis, quod diabolus non cessat impugnare et confundere articulos fidei, quibuscunque artibus potest." Ibid., 290.5–7 (Major, preface).

68. In an excursus on Col 1:15 and John 17:22, Luther explains that the unity between Father and Son is an inner and natural unity, and he contrasts this unity with the Arian position claiming a unity of consensus or will. Ibid., 297.19–20, 298.1–14, 299.1–13, 300:1–2 (witness A); 297.21–22, 298.15–31, 299.14–29 (witness B; Major).

demonic attack all defend the unity between Father and Son.[69] In Luther's thought, the devil is responsible for both—for disobeying the Father and for denying the truth of the Trinitarian article, a disobedience that erodes both true doctrine and the faith of weak Christians.[70] The disputation, then, becomes a form of speech to demonstrate obedience to the Father in a defense against those who, like the devil, attempt to separate the Father from the Father's word.

The occasional necessity for deploying the disputation is related to what Luther perceives to precipitate the rift. Concerning the rift between Scripture and dogma, Luther detects the erosion of the Trinitarian article as issuing from a particular application of reason. Noted is Luther's explicit mention of an infamous sixteenth-century heretic, Servetus, but exhibited is his fear that a type of reason might be responsible for the attack. Responsibility for eroding the Trinitarian dogma, as suggested by Luther's preface to the Major disputation, is attributed explicitly to Servetus as well as to the Anabaptists and to Campanus.[71] Servetus, famous not only for his anti-Trinitarian position but also for his contributions to the study of geography and medicine,[72] is cited in the same breath with Campanus, whom

---

69. The important Trinitarian definitions were articulated in the following councils: XI. Synod of Toledo (675) in DS *525-41; Fourth Lateran Council (1215) in DS *800; "Cantate Domino" of the Council of Florence (1441 or 1442) in DS *1330-31. For a brief and excellent discussion of the medieval development of the Trinitarian doctrine, see: Jürgen Werbick, "Trinitätslehre," 491-511.

70. "Ideo non solum necesse est, ut nos simus certi de vera Euangelii doctrina, sed etiam ut nostri posteri habeant aliquid veri et certi de religione. Quare haec est causa, cur hi conventus celebrentur, nempe ut defendatur sana doctrina, nos aliique doceamur, et denique ignita tela diaboli deleantur. Es wurde doch nichts Anderst darauß, es muß vmmerdar gefochten sein." WA 39,2:266.11-16 (Fabricius, preface). In a Major thesis, Luther mentions the demonic attack against weak Christians. "Sed hunc doctorem non aequaliter audiunt omnes, et sunt semper aliqui infirmi, quos cribret satan." Ibid., 287.7-8 (Major, thesis 2).

71. "Et hoc quidem hactenus strenue fecit; per Anabaptistas sacramentum baptismi et per alios sacramentum altaris impugnavit. Neque adhuc hodie cessat cribrare articulum iustificationis, et adhuc venient, qui persecuturi sunt articulum de trinitate, et erunt valde sapientes ad cavillandum ... quales fuerunt Servetus et Campanus ..." Ibid., 290.7-11, 15 (Major, preface).

72. Servetus, a Spaniard who had witnessed the forced conversion of the Jews and the persecution of the Moors, wrote two famous books, De Trinitatis Erroribus Libri Septem (1531) and Dialogorum de Trinitate libri duo, de justicia regni Christi, capitula quatuor (1532), for which he was executed by the Genevan magistrates' order in 1553 and posthumously sentenced by the papal court at Vienne. For an exciting biography, see: Roland Bainton, Hunted Heretic: The Life and Death of Michael Servetus 1511-1553.

Luther had met at Torgau in March 1530.[73] In his monograph on Servetus, Bainton shows how Servetus challenged the Trinitarian dogma by placing the biblical text under the scrutiny of reason independent of dogmatic formulation.[74] Although Luther does not mention his exact motivation for referring to Servetus in the context of the later Trinitarian disputations, a relevant clue can be found in the text "A Short Confession concerning the Holy Sacrament" (1544).[75] In this text, Luther insists on the interconnection between what Ockham had defined as the three relations that, in the theological region, are relative and not absolute entities: the relations in the eternal Trinity, the two natures in Christ, and the relation of accidents to substance in the Eucharist.[76] Referring explicitly to these relations, Luther betrays his concern that when one article is eroded, the others will fall as well.[77] The splintering of the dogmatic household is countered by the all-or-none principle, demanding the coherence of the articles of the faith. What Luther could be suggesting is that the danger of erosion is presented when a wedge is driven between two entities in a relation: for example, when a separation is achieved between Father and Son. The problem Luther

---

73. WATr 5:615.17 (no. 6351, Tischreden aus verschiedenen Jahren).

74. Bainton summarizes Servetus' anti-Trinitarian argument that consists of questioning the authority of dogma by comparing it with the earliest biblical layers. Bainton, *Hunted Heretic*, 31. Servetus reveals his knowledge of the canon of Trinitarian doctrine by taking to bat Ockham's followers, Holcot, Rimini, Ailly and John Major (not George!), four theologians who, like Luther, stress the mystery and indemonstrability of the Trinity. Bainton suggests that these names bridge the late medieval critics of a type of scholastic conceptualization of the Trinitarian doctrine and the anti-Trinitarians of the sixteenth century. Ibid., 28–29.

75. The Major preface refers to the Anabaptists ["… per Anabaptistas sacramentum baptismi et per alios sacramentum altaris impugnavit." WA 39,2:290.7–8 (Major, preface)], to whom the "Kurzes Bekenntnis vom heiligen Sakrament" of September 1544 is a lengthy reply. See: WA 54:141.1–167.9.

76. For Ockham, the three relations are theological mysteries that cannot be proven by natural reason and, as relative entities distinct from absolute entities, are to be accepted on the basis of the authorities of Scripture, the sayings of the Saints and the church. See: Marilyn McCord Adams, *William Ockham*, vol. 1, 267–76 and vol. 2, 996–1007.

77. A surprising similarity between Ockham's specification of the three theological relations and Luther's own position is seen in the treatise, "Kurzes Bekenntnis vom heiligen Sakrament (1544)." In this text, Luther argues for the coherence of three articles of faith: the Lord's Supper, the two natures in the one person of Christ, and the Trinity. See: WA 54:157.25–158.6. He concludes with the "all or none" principle. "Darumb heisst's, rund und rein gantz und alles gegleubt, oder nichts gegleubt, Der heilige Geist lesst sich nicht trennen noch teilen, das er ein stu(e)ck solt warhafftig und das ander falsch leren oder gleuben lassen. ... Denn alle Ketzer sind dieser art, das sie erstlich allein an einem Artickel anfahen, darnach mu(e)ssen sie alle hernach, und alle sampt verleugnet sein," Ibid., 158:28–30, 36–159.1.

is addressing seems to be a uniform application of a principle of reason that, if it succeeds in dividing Father from Son, could consequently separate Scripture from dogma.

The particular danger is represented by a distinct group of thinkers. Luther mentions these thinkers in the later Trinitarian disputations, all concerned with the central tenets of the Christian faith. Although some political events in the backdrop can be linked to the motivation for disputing the Trinitarian article, such as fears in Germany of an Ottoman invasion[78] or the increased political measures to exile the Jews from German states,[79] Luther remains almost silent in polemicizing against concepts of God in other religions. Except for one thesis explicitly mentioning the "world's" challenge of Christ's divinity,[80] Luther's references to attacks against the Trinity situate his response against Servetus and Campanus, in connection to the Anabaptists, entirely on the level of an academic intra-Christian debate.[81] Even the remarks on Eck and Cochlaeus serve

---

78. The Ottoman conquest in 1541 at Ofen, Hungary, gave rise to an increasing tension in Germany regarding an impending war with the Turks. In 1542, Luther and Melanchthon wrote introductions to a Latin translation of the Koran that was published secretly in Basel. On Luther's writings regarding this political situation, see: Brecht, *Martin Luther*, vol. 3, 346–51.

79. The forced exile of the Jews from many German states and imperial cities in the fifteenth and sixteenth centuries has been linked to economic and political developments of the rise of early capitalism. In August 1536, the Elector of Saxony, Johann Friedrich, exiled the Jews from his territory. A similar edict was issued on May 6, 1543. See: Ernst Ludwig Ehrlich, "Luther and the Jews," 37; Brecht, *Martin Luther*, vol. 3, 331, 344. During this period of intensified political anti-Jewish measures, Luther published two vitriolic writings that cannot be simply excused as the rantings of an ill man: "Von den Juden und ihren Lügen (1543)" (WA 53:417.1–552.38) and "Vom Schem Hamphoras und vom Geschlecht Christi (1543)" (WA 53:579.1–648.15). In these years, Luther was also involved with completing the revisions to his translation of the Old Testament, finishing his ten-year commentary on Genesis in 1545 (WA 42–44), and publishing commentaries on Isa 9 [WA 40,2:597.1–682.22 (1543–1544/1546)] and Isa 53 [Ibid., 685.1–746.19 (1544/1550)].

80. "Nihil mirum, si Arius, Iudaeus, Mahometh et totus mundus negent Christum esse Deum." WA 39,2:254.17–18 (Alberus, thesis 18).

81. Jansen has found evidence of Luther's suspicion, in 1527, that the Strasbourg theologians propounded a heretical understanding of the Trinity. Jansen, *Studien zu Luthers Trinitätslehre*, 132–34. Luther's increasing conflict with Melanchthon, due to the latter's efforts together with Calvin to seek peace with the Swiss, led up to a confrontation that did not settle the debate. Brecht, *Martin Luther*, vol. 3, 319–27. Bucer sought to alleviate both what he anticipated would be Luther's unkind reception of the decision made in Zurich on August 31, 1543 to publish Zwingli's writings, and to hinder the publication of the "Kurzes Bekenntnis" by writing one letter to Bugenhagen and Melanchthon. In the letter that was never given to Luther, Bucer admits his allegiance to the Wittenberg Concord written by Bucer, and he distances himself from the Zurich theologians. See: Letter from Martin Bucer to Luther in WABr 10:651.1–653.2 (no. 4028, Sept. 9, 1544).

a similar purpose. What unites these thinkers, in Luther's perception, is a particular use of reason that drives a rift between entities in uniquely theological relations.

Related to the demonic disobedience of the Father's word is, for Luther, a special use of reason. When Luther remarks at different junctures in the Major disputation on the threats he perceives to issue from Servetus and Campanus on the one hand and from Eck and Cochlaeus on the other hand, he could be collapsing the two groups into a common front.[82] The early mention of Servetus could serve to preliminarily orient the discussion to the connection between Scripture and dogma. Appearing in the context of the reference to Eck is an explication of this theme; the rift between Scripture and dogma is discussed together with the factors of both the church's authority and the Spirit's dispensation in the church. Luther argues at length against Eck's position, and in doing so, sets the stage for exposing the full force of the anti-Trinitarian attack as the disobedience of the Father's word.

During the course of the Major disputation, Luther forgets himself in his role as opponent and uses the opportunity to dispute Eck's position at length. The debate concentrates on the church's authority in confirming the Trinitarian article of faith and thematizes the problem of how extrabiblical language adequately grasps what is materially contained in Scripture.[83] The difficulty turns on the issue of the Spirit's historical dispensation in the church that Luther isolates to be the common element in Servetus's and Campanus's, Eck's and Cochlaeus's respective positions. A closer look at the historical backdrop to the disputation helps to clarify the issue at stake.

Cochlaeus, Luther's first biographer, argues in his book *Fifth Philippic against Three Books of Philipp Melanchthon* (1543) that Servetus's heresy cannot be combated by Scripture but by the church.[84] Eck, Luther's famous disputation partner on the topic of the church's authority,[85] wrote a book

---

82. Luther refers to Servetus and Campanus in the preface to the Major disputation (WA 39,2.290.15), and mentions the names of Eck and Cochlaeus while disputing the eighth thesis. Ibid., 305.24 (witness A).

83. "Simul nihilominus haec unitas, est trinitas, seu trium personarum distinctarum divinitas." Ibid., 287.19–20 (Major, thesis 8).

84. Ibid., 304n2. The title in Latin is *Philippica Quinta in tres libellos Phil. Melanchthonis.*

85. Johannes Eck, professor at the University of Ingolstadt, began a friendly correspondence with Luther in 1517. Eck's correspondence soon developed into a life-long controversy

directed against Melanchthon, *Enchiridion of Commonplaces*.[86] In this text, Eck links the teaching authority of the church to the Holy Spirit's guidance initiated temporally after Christ's ascension. He charges that "the Lutherans will not observe the Apostles' Creed, the *homoousios* of Athanasius, person in the Godhead."[87] Brushing the polemical formulations aside, Eck and Cochlaeus seem to be arguing on the basis of the Spirit's authority in guiding the church's formulation of dogma, linking the Spirit's authority to its dispensation after the historical moment of Christ's ascension. Church dogma is authoritative, codified under the guidance of the Holy Spirit.[88] Luther, however, sees the position of both Eck and Cochlaeus recurring in the heresy of Servetus and Campanus, "who have said that this article was not treated before John the Baptist and who mock the Scriptures."[89] The discrepancy between dogmatic formulation and biblical subject matter is not linked, for Luther, to the historical sequence distinguishing between biblical language before John the Evangelist and the creedal norm articulated

---

with Luther, that was later extended to include the Swiss reformers, and then to Melanchthon at the Diet of Augsburg (1530). By dismissing Eck merely as one of Luther's opponents, one does not do justice to Eck's learned struggle to preserve the unity of the church. In ch. 1 of the *Enchiridion*, entitled, "On the church and her authority," Eck challenges the objection that "the authority of the Scripture is greater than that of the Church," with a differentiated series of arguments ending with a footnote to Cochlaeus' book: the church is older than Scripture, the church has determined the biblical canon, and validates its authenticity. Johann Eck, *Enchiridion of Commonplaces: Against Luther and Other Enemies of the Church* (1541), 11, 12–17.

86. Melanchthon alludes to Cochlaeus' and Eck's attacks against the faith of the weak. MO 21:601 (Loci praecipui theologici. Nunc denuo cura et diligentia summa recogniti, multisque in locis copiose illustrati, cum appendice disputationis de coniugio, 1559).

87. Eck, *Enchiridion*, 45. Ch. 4, entitled, "That the heretics rashly oppose the Scriptures," begins with the first axiom: "That the heretics wish to receive nothing unless it be expressly proved through the Scriptures." At the end of this chapter, Eck relates Luther's literal reading of Scriptures to Jewish exegesis because he thinks that both types of biblical interpretation challenge the authority of the church. "The Lutherans receive the Scriptures just as the Jews do the Old Testament, because they insist alone on the literal sense, ... to impugn the Church by the Scriptures." Ibid., 49.

88. "Proposition 2: The Church does not err, not only because she always has Christ as her Bridegroom, but also because she is ruled by the teaching authority of the Holy Spirit who never forsakes her." Ibid., 9.

89. WA 39,2:290.16–17 (Major, preface). The note reads that Luther confuses John the Evangelist with John the Baptist. Ibid., 290n2. Although Luther attacked Servetus' 1532 *Dialogues* on the Trinity [See: WATr 1:99.18–21 (no. 237, April 7–15, 1532)], it is more likely that Melanchthon read Servetus' work. See: MO 21:262.9b; 263.10b; 359 (Loci Communes, 1533). The Alberus fragment mentions the debate on the Spirit's dispensation after John. See: WA 39,2:256.11–20. The debate seems to focus on the sending of the Spirit as a historical event connected to the resurrection of Christ. Ibid., 270.29–271.31 (Fabricius).

after the Spirit's sending (Acts 1:8–9; 2:1–13). For Luther, the Spirit's dispensation is the pivot on which the issue of the relationship between Scripture and dogma turns. Luther can accuse Servetus and Campanus, Eck and Cochlaeus of attacking the Trinitarian article because he detects a temporal separation between Scripture and dogma in their positions. The separation between Father and Son is effected from the side of those who limit the Spirit's dispensation to the church. The Father is separated from the Father's word when the voice of the Spirit, who speaks through the prophets, is not heard.

The occasion for the disputations on the Trinity seems to reflect a more general alert for what Luther considers to be the use of a distinct type of reason. For Luther, various manifestations of a temporalizing use of reason are responsible for sequentially eroding the articles of the Christian faith. With the application of this reason, a rift is driven, separating between those entities that are determined to constitute an eternal relation. The Arians, as Luther mentions, attempt to separate the Father from the Son by conceiving the unity as a "unity of will and consensus," not as a "natural" and "substantial" unity.[90] The constant defense of the church against diverse stripes of the Arian heresy is to articulate the eternal relation between Father and Son. With respect to the Scripture-dogma connection, Luther detects a similar activity of temporalizing reason. Luther accuses both Servetus and Eck of invoking the Spirit's dispensation after John the Evangelist for the aim of eroding the Trinitarian dogma. In the case of Servetus, the dogma is eroded when a historical use of reason drives dogma apart from Scripture. In the case of Eck, an inadequate determination of the Spirit's dispensation in Scripture to reveal the Trinitarian article is tied together with an understanding of the Spirit's historical advent in the church, a position Luther also fears results in a separation between Scripture and dogma.

The implications of this rift are far-reaching. Luther never forgets to stress his concern for weak Christians when they are confronted with doubts about the eternal benefits of Christ. If the danger of an illegitimate use of reason succeeds in temporalizing what, in the theological region,

---

90. Ibid., 297.19–20; 298.3, 11–13 (witness A; Major).

are eternal relations, then the disputation becomes the genre in which the right type of reason is tested to determine the concept of infinity.

Luther considers the challenges against the Trinitarian article to provide the occasion for disputation. That Luther locates the Trinitarian disputations in the academic context is, perhaps, surprising to those who consider his theology in light of an existential word-faith correlation. Luther, however, considers urgent the position that historically postpones the Trinitarian article to its formulation in John's Gospel and in the early church creeds. Luther sees the Arian heresy recur in any position that temporalizes the relationship between the Father and the Father's word by historically separating dogma from Scripture for the purpose of either invoking the authority of dogma or criticizing it on rational grounds. For Luther, a common front is represented by the heretics, the theologians, and the philosophers (to be discussed at a later point) who deploy reason to reduce the theological subject matter to the temporal domain. Although the heretics' discourse varies from that of the philosophers, Luther sets up a single strategy to rebuff the rationalist reduction of the Trinitarian article to either a historical dispensation or to a philosophical phenomenon. Luther begins to draw the borders of the theological region in order to open up a space in which the Trinity is discussed in relation to a theologically determined concept of infinity.

INFINITY AND THE INNER TRINITY

Luther draws the boundaries of the theological region by starting to define the categories he considers to be central to the issue at stake. The initial theses of the Major disputation serve to orient the debate around two crucial distinctions in the concept of God that Luther requires in order to relate the concept of infinity to a specific site. In this section, the discussion will concentrate first on the distinction between Creator and creature and then on the second, central distinction in Luther's understanding of the Trinity: the inner and the outer Trinity. Only when these distinctions are in place can the task begin of testing out which determinations of infinity are suited to the inner Trinity.

While Luther is ultimately concerned with the determination of infinity in the theological region, he does not immediately direct his attention to this term. The initial distinction Luther draws is not one distinguishing between time and infinity. Rather, the first distinction Luther sets up is a response to what he perceives to be the challenge launched from the borders of the theological region. What Luther sees as a common front, although diverse with respect to different discourses, is a blurring of the distinction between Creator and creature. The third clause of thesis five in the Major disputation makes a clear distinction between the two extremes: the Triune God is "the sole Creator of all things outside himself."[91] Luther draws the distinction between Creator and creature in terms of a spatial orientation. In fact, a biblical allusion to Isaiah 45:5 serves to locate the Creator in relation to creation that exists on its "outside." With this distinction, Luther intends to ground any resistance to importing particular uses of created reason into a subject matter that transcends the creature's grasp. Discussions in the following sections will show how this primary distinction figures significantly in Luther's understanding of the source of theological language, the relation of the theological region to other academic regions, and the use of the analogy to grasp what ultimately exists outside of the creature and "inside" the Creator.

When the "outside" is assigned to creaturely existence, the question arises how Luther conceives of the relation of the Creator to both its "outer" and "inner" sides. The second distinction Luther draws is a necessary step for the purpose of securing a site at which the concept of infinity is protected from the imposition of reason that is limited to the spatiotemporal domain.

The spatial metaphor feeds into the way Luther conceives of the central distinction in his understanding of the Trinity. In thesis five of the Major disputation, Luther articulates, in most compact fashion, the proposition that can be seen to summarize his conceptual view of the relation between the Trinity and creation. Luther states, "It is an indisputable truth that God, who is one and triune, is the sole Creator of all things outside himself."[92] The terseness of this thesis does not betray the extraordinary length that Lombard dedicates to its unfolding and explaining in his own *Sentences*.[93]

---

91. Ibid., 287.13–14 (Major, third clause of thesis 5).

92. Ibid., 287.13–14 (Major, thesis 5). The first clause of this thesis ("Indisputabilis veritas est …") will be explained in "Tense, Modality" on tense and truth claims of the inner Trinity.

93. This thesis is extremely broad in scope. It covers the first 34 questions of Book I of Lombard's *Sentences* [55–254]. Cf. 105n213.

Luther devotes brevity to what he considers to be indisputable: a thesis, or an article of faith, that conceptually orders the one Creator in relation to creation outside and subsequently orders this Creator-creature relation to the Trinity. By virtue of this move, Luther can then discuss the Trinity according to a distinction he makes between the two sides of God. The Trinity has an "outer" side where the Creator is situated in relation to the creature. By implication, the Trinity has an "inner" side, a side "outside" the creature's grasp.

The term is Luther's own, and it summarizes the theme of the Trinitarian disputations. In the Hegemon disputation, Luther speaks of the inner (*ad intra*) side of God.[94] It is a side that is "turned away from creatures."[95] On the other side and turned "towards us" is the outer Trinity.[96] The inner side is not separated spatially from the outer side. Rather, the terms, "outer" and "inner" are each predicated of a "side" that is either turned towards creation in its works or, as will be discussed shortly, turned to creation in the revelation of the "inside," inaccessible to finite reason and known solely through the action of the Holy Spirit. By first distinguishing the "inner" from the "outer" side of the Trinity, Luther achieves a conceptual privileging of the inner Trinity as the site to which the concept of infinity can be assigned. Only on the "inside" are located the eternal Trinitarian relations that are beyond finite reason.

The fundamental distinction between the inner and outer sides of the Trinity plays an enormous role in Luther's articulation of his Trinitarian understanding in the genre of the disputation. In other genres, such as the hymn and the sermon, the distinction serves to orient the spatial direction necessary for discussing the Trinity as a narrative from the inner to the outer side.[97] The genre of the disputation shapes a theme in more propositional language. Its task is to determine the inner Trinity as the starting point for the stories told in other genres. The task, however, is not possible without the action of the Holy Spirit.

---

94. WA 39,2:398.20 (witness A; Hegemon).

95. Ibid., 296.23 (witness A–B; Major).

96. "Loquitur autem quoad nos seu quoad extra." Ibid., 398.18–19 (witness A; Hegemon).

97. On the narrative of Trinitarian advent, see: ch. 3; on the narrative of Trinitarian revelation, see: ch. 4. It will be shown in these chapters that the inner Trinity is not disregarded, but plotted as the starting point of the respective narrative.

The deployment of the disputation is connected with the appeal to the Third Person of the Trinity. Disputations become necessary as the form in which the defense and articulation of the truth takes place for every generation of theologians.[98] In connection with this aim, Luther notes the significance of the Spirit's work. Luther calls on the Spirit, who alone speaks of what is inaccessible to natural reason.[99] The Spirit, who has spoken through the prophets, speaks of a subject matter that is ultimately a mystery. Luther cites the relevant clause in the Apostles' Creed to make his claim: "No one can know such mysterious things, the Holy Spirit did not reveal them through the prophets."[100] By pointing to the revelation of the inner Trinity, Luther can secure the Spirit's task under the same rubric that accounts for the occasion of disputing. The appropriate attitude of obedience to the Father consists of listening to the Son that, in a situation in which the deployment of the disputation becomes necessary, is redirected to the Spirit. In times of defense, the Spirit's speech is the only source of knowledge concerning a subject matter that exists beyond the bounds of natural reason. Connected to the necessity of disputing against those who disobey the Son is the insistence on listening to the Spirit.

The subject matter of the Spirit's speech is beyond the reaches of natural reason. In a debate with Hegemon on the interpretation of Isaiah 53:8, Luther insists against the error of inferring that those things that are not seen or heard cannot be told.[101] The relation between Father and Son is hidden until the Spirit reveals it through the prophets.[102] Through the Old

---

98. See above, "The Attacks on the Trinity."

99. "... non ex ratione, sed ex verbo." WA 39,2:375.17–18 (witness A; Hegemon).

100. WA 54:48.20–22.

101. "Ergo de his tantis rebus nos adhuc latentibus non est loquendum. Non sequitur." WA 39,2:375.28–29 (witness C; Hegemon). The context of this disputational exchange is prompted by the passage in Isa 53:8, "Generationem eius quis enarrabit." Ibid., 375.2–3 (witness A). Hegemon interprets the passage to refer to the preaching of the church after the resurrection of Christ. In a role as respondent, Luther is more dedicated to correctly interpreting the Isaiah passage than aiming to force his student to make an error. He corrects Hegemon by arguing that the referent of the verse is the inner-Trinitarian generation of the Son. In light of this discussion, Luther states that what is above and beyond creaturely imagination cannot be used an an excuse for silence. Indeed, much theology is concerned with what no eye has seen nor ear has heard, yet it is the task of theology to understand the God located in eternity!

102. The eternal Trinity is not to be identified with the "hidden God," as White assumes. White, *Luther as Nominalist*, 382–83. White is correct in showing Luther's identification of the eternal God with the "naked God," and with what is "outside of time before the world."

Testament prophets and the Psalms, the Spirit speaks of the eternal generation of the Son.[103] Luther does not distinguish logically between the
Spirit's precise act of speaking and the content of the speech. For Luther,
the content of the speech is available through the language of the biblical
prophets, a language that Luther ultimately attributes theologically to the
Spirit. During the disputation, Luther calls on the Spirit in order to provide the language and the knowledge of the inner Trinity. The appeal to
the Spirit does not result in turning the academic formality into a super-
fluous exercise. In the situation of an attack by a united front of temporally restricted reason, Luther clings to the Spirit as the revelatory source
of the inner Trinity.

The aspect of the Trinity that is shaped by the disputation is the inner
Trinity. To be defended and understood as the central determination of
the inner Trinity is the attribute of infinity. In Luther's understanding,
any heretical attack challenges the infinity of the relation between Father
and Son, and his initial appeal in its defense is to the Holy Spirit, who alone
knows and then reveals what no human eye has witnessed. The Holy Spirit's
speech through the prophets, the Psalms, and the church's dogmatic formulations reveals this relation as the eternal generation of the Son from the
Father. When one listens to the Spirit, the Father's word in Matthew 17:5
is heard to point to his Son. Listening to the Son includes the moment of

---

That this *deus nudus* or the divine Majesty is revealed as the three relations in the eternal
essence is, however, not hidden. For Luther, the term, "deus nudus," can refer to the inner
Trinity existing in eternity before the creation of the world in time. "Quia extra illud initium
creaturae nihil est quam nuda essentia divina et nudus Deus. Is autem quia est incomprehensibilis, illud etiam incomprehensibile est, quod fuit ante mundum, quia nihil est nisi
Deus." WA 42:14.28–31 (Lectures on Genesis, 1535–1545, to Gen 1:3). The same term is also used
to refer to the divine Majesty that encounters the devil and the heretics as its enemy. "Ergo
fanaticum est, sine verbo et involucro aliquo de Deo et divina natura disputare, sicut solent
omnes Haeretici; ea securitate de Deo cogitant, qua de porco aut vacca disputant ... Qui autem
extra ista involucra Deum attingere volunt, isti sine scalis (hoc est verbo) nituntur ad coelum
ascendere, ruunt igitur oppressi maiestate, quam nudam conantur amplecti, et pereunt." Ibid.,
11.19–21, 28–30. On the theme of the divine Majesty that encounters the devil as its enemy,
see: ch. 4, "The Hidden God."

103. The Major dispution refers to Ps 2:7, Mic 5:1, Heb 13:8 (WA 39,2:291.6–8 [witness A];
293.9–13 [witness A]; 302.16–18 [witness A]), as biblical texts referring to the eternal generation
of the Son. The Spirit's speech, "qui locutus est per prophetas," is the central focus of Luther's
Trinitarian understanding of 2 Sam 23:2. Citing 2 Pet 1:21 in association with the passage from
2 Sam, Luther writes, "Da her singet man in dem artickel des Glaubens von dem Heiligen
Geist also: 'Der durch die Propheten geredet hat', Also gibt man nu dem Heiligen Geist die
gantze Heilige schrifft und das eusserliche wort und Sacrament, so unser eusserliche ohren
und synne ruren oder bewegen." WA 54:34.38–35.4.

acknowledging his substantial unity with the Father; obeying the Father's imperative involves knowing that the Son exists in an eternal relation with the Father. Luther's claim regarding the infinity of the Trinitarian relations is supported by the appeal to listen to the Spirit, who opens human ears to hear the Son who, in turn, dwells in an eternal unity with the Father. While listening to the three persons, the area of the theological region is drawn by this Trinitarian claim. The theological issue of listening to the Trinity in the theological region must be supplemented by a discussion of the discourse particular to the disputation. Studied in the next section will be the concrete form of the Spirit's language in this genre, how propositional discourse can refer to the inner side of God, and how tense can be understood to make truth claims of infinity.

THE INNER TRINITY AND THE DISCOURSE OF INFINITY

Once the boundaries of the theological region are demarcated, the question arises regarding the type of discourse that refers to the "inner side" of the Trinity. For Luther, the "new language" of theological discourse must account for the way in which terms refer to a subject matter in eternity, lying beyond creaturely grasp. That Luther addresses the question of right speaking about the divine eternity is not to be easily dismissed as marginal to the soteriological focus in genres other than the disputation. Luther's interest in the inner-Trinitarian proposition discloses a soteriological axis, and around this axis pivots the truth claim associated with the eternity of the triune relations. The truth status Luther assigns to the inner-Trinitarian proposition provides the semantic and logical apparatus necessary to understand Luther's great confidence and unshakeable certainty in the *promissio*. The disputation is an indispensable genre in showing how Luther uses reason not to retreat behind an intellectually naive facade of an existential language of faith but to provide arguments for determining the type of infinity associated with the inner Trinity. Such a determination has implications for defining the Trinitarian essence in terms of other attributes, such as mercy, which, in other genres, surface more explicitly in relation to the *promissio*.

This section addresses the issue of the particular discourse fitted and used to refer to the infinity of the inner Trinity. Luther attributes this language and its grammar to the Spirit, who reveals them on the outer-Trinitarian location. For Luther, revelation cannot be seen as excommunicating reason, but rather as providing a space in which reason is invited to articulate what it understands by the Spirit's "improper" speech. In this section, I propose that Luther understands the Spirit's speech according to both Augustine's sign theory and scholastic logic. Particularly the tool of scholastic logic will be discussed to show how "improper" language can refer to an eternal referent and how propositions can make truth claims that are invariably tensed. I conclude by pointing out how Luther envisions the "new language" to refer to both the eternal generation of the Son and the eternity of God.

The "Improper" Language of the Spirit

Luther's interest in what he calls the "new language" (*nova lingua*) first emerges in the Palladius disputation and its preface (1537).[104] The term appears in the disputation on John 1:14 (1539) in a discussion of the intrusion of philosophy into the theological region,[105] and it surfaces again in the Major disputation.[106] The term "new language," not found in either Ockham or Ailly, seems to be associated with the type of discourse Luther advocates using in the theological region. Initially, the term is not specifically limited to either the genre of the disputation or the subject matter of the inner Trinity. As the disputation on John 1:14 suggests, the new language seems to refer to the different types of discourse uttered in the theological region, especially those articulating the theme of Christology: for example, "verbum caro factum est."[107] By virtue of its appearance in the text of the two disputations mentioned above, the term "new language" can neither be prematurely restricted to the genre of the homiletical address, nor can it be too quickly associated with the mediality of the language of

---

104. WA 39,1:231.1-2 (witness AI-II), 231.18-19 (witness AIII-B) (Die Promotionsdisputation von Palladius and Tilemann held on June 1, 1537). In the doctoral speech for Palladius, Luther comments on Luke 21:15, and speaks on the new wisdom and mouth Christ gives to theologians in order that they might speak the *nova lingua*. Ibid., 260.16-17; 261.27-28.

105. WA 39,2:5.36 (John 1:14, thesis 40).

106. For example: "Oportet hic etiam grammaticam totam induere novas voces, cum loqui vult de Deo." Ibid., 303.23-24 (witness A; Major).

107. Ibid., 5.35-36; 39-40.

faith.[108] Pertaining to the various discourses in the theological region, the new language must be specified with respect to the subject matter it articulates in a particular genre.

The new language associated with the inner Trinity is of a specific type. Terms used to refer to the inner Trinity, such as "person" and "trinitas," are, for Luther, "bad" German or Latin, as he states in some sermons.[109] In the genre of the disputation, and in view of its inner-Trinitarian subject matter, Luther tends to refer to the new language as "improper" speech.[110] The focus of the disputation is a proposition that Luther calls "improper," and then refers to a divine speaker. "God speaks here: I accept that God is one and three persons—how that happens, I don't know."[111] If God speaks "improperly," then the speech cannot be understood without the "new grammar" taught by the Spirit.[112] Luther does not hesitate to acknowledge that the inner-Trinitarian language is "improper." It is, however, the only language he knows. Luther admits, "It is true that it is articulated improperly: three things are one thing. ... However, I must speak this way according to the capacity of the weak."[113] By designating this new language to be

108. Streiff pits the "nova lingua" of Luther's discourse against the "closed system of science" represented by "Scholasticism." The conceptuality underlying this opposition looks like the position pitting faith against reason. In order to describe what he means by the "nova lingua" of faith, Streiff uses a distinction found in the contemporary linguistic-literary disciplines. The distinction between instrumental and medial language is appropriated in order to gain an understanding of Luther's particular view of the theological language in the disputations. Showing that Luther's emphasis on the certainty of faith cannot be articulated in the prescriptive or instrumental language of "Scholasticism," Streiff suggests that Luther's understanding of theological language is best described in terms of its mediality. Whereas "instrumental" terms are used when pointing to objects that appear in an already established frame of reference, medial language is used when the terms point to objects that do not appear in a fixed frame of reference. Medial language evokes and shapes a new frame of reference. Streiff, "Novis Linguis Loqui," 241–42.

109. For a list of these terms and Luther's resigned use of them, see: ch. 1, 2n2, and ch. 4, "The Spirit: God Speaks from God."

110. "... quod improprie sit dictum:..." WA 39,2: 305.14 (witness A; Major).

111. WA 39,2:365.1–3 (Hegemon). Similar to: "... Spiritus sanctus ita loquitur." Ibid., 296.16 (witness A–B; Major).

112. Luther relates the *nova vocabula* to the Third Person of the Trinity. In the disputation "De divinitate et humanitate Christi," the respondent attributes to the Holy Spirit the role of providing the grammar for the theological region. Ibid., 104.24–105.3 (witness A).

113. Ibid., 305.14, 16 (witness A; Major). In the Hegemon *disputatio*, Luther makes a similar claim. Regarding the term, "persona," that is constituted by the essence and the relation, Luther states, "Das ist impropriissime geredt, aber wie soll man im thun, natura humana non potest aliter." Ibid., 384.17–19 (witness A; Hegemon). The B version states, "Nos in his rebus

"improper," Luther signals the unlikeness of the proposition's terms to what they might stand for in other academic regions. By stressing distance to other regions, Luther is also marking the special consideration of the nature of inner-Trinitarian language in the theological region. The language is improper because it articulates a subject matter that is above and beyond what creatures can conceive or imagine. The question arises as to how Luther understands this language, although improper, and its capacity to articulate truth claims.

One factor in Luther's understanding of improper language seems to be shaped by the distinction between the inner and the outer Trinity. The inner Trinity is connected to an understanding of eternity that resists any spatiotemporal determination. Any sign that refers to the inner-Trinitarian *res* cannot be understood according to creaturely reason. Luther alludes to Augustine's distinction between *res* and sign when he discusses the outer Trinity's revelation in creation.[114] In his text *On the Last Words of David*, Luther distinguishes between the creature taken absolutely and the creature taken relatively.[115] Taken absolutely, the creature is the *res* itself. The creature, taken relatively, can serve as the sign for the revelation of a particular Trinitarian person. The voice and the dove at Christ's baptism

---

non possumus perfecte loqui, et tamen ita loquendum est." Ibid., 384.20–22 (witness B). The C version states, "Ita loquendum est docendi causa, quamvis sit sermo improprie dictus, tamen sic loquuntur ad explicandum utrumque." Ibid., 384.30–31 (witness C).

114. Augustine's understanding of proper and figurative signs is discussed in *De doctrina christiana* I, 2 (4–6) [CSEL 80:9]. Proper signs point immediately to the thing for which the sign stands, whereas improper or figurative signs are used when the things themselves, that are indicated by proper names, are used to signify something else. Augustine uses the example, "bos." As a proper sign, it points to the thing itself, the ox. As a figurative sign, it points to the ox under which is understood the preacher of the gospel. *De doctr. chr.* II, 10 (32–33) [CSEL 80:42]. According to the metaphorical understanding of theological truth proposed by Jüngel, the metaphor is given the status of improper speech, and its meaning is grasped when the term is transferred from one region to another. "Die Sprache des Glaubens ist durch μεταφορά konstituiert." Jüngel, "Metaphorische Wahrheit," 110. Jüngel's reduction of "improper speech" to the metaphor fails to take into account the analogy as another aspect of theological speech. On the other hand, White has recently argued, on the basis of Luther's disputations, that the transfer of a term from one region to the other effects a change in the term's signification, and not in its supposition. White, *Luther as Nominalist*, 334–38.

115. "Also sihestu, das die Creatur zweierley weise anzusehen ist, ut Res et signum, das sie ettwas fur sich selbs ist, von Gott geschaffen, Und auch gebraucht wird etwas anders zu zeigen oder zu leren, das sie selbs nicht ist." WA 54:62.37–39. Luther reads Augustine according to the distinction between the creature "taken absolutely" and "taken relatively." The terminology of "absolute" and "relative" appears again when Luther discusses the semantics of essence terms, such as "divine essence." See below, "The Semantics of the Inner-Trinitarian Proposition."

in Matthew 3:16–17 are signs for the Father and the Spirit, respectively. What Luther means by the sign as the creature, taken relatively, is what Augustine refers to as a "figurative sign." The creature, taken relatively, is a figurative sign not for itself, but for another *res*; the voice signifies the Father, and the dove signifies the Spirit. With respect to the "improper" inner-Trinitarian proposition, the terms are figurative signs that refer to a *res* outside of any creature. "Improper" speech, such as the term "tres personae," functions as a sign for Father, Son, and Spirit.[116] In the Hegemon disputation, Luther eventually admits that the content of the divine speech, spoken in its outer-Trinitarian location, is "something else" in the inner Trinity. "It is said with respect to us or with respect to the outer, but with respect to the inner, that's another res."[117] For Luther, the central aim of the disputation is to preserve an understanding of this inner-Trinitarian *res* as a distinct kind of *res* outside of the human capacity to grasp it.

Another dimension to Luther's understanding of improper language is related to a medieval discussion of how tensed propositions are understood to refer to the divine infinity. For example, in the Major disputation, Luther mentions different tenses that ultimately refer to the sempeternity of God.[118] There is a specific difficulty respective to the theological region that is concerned with how tensed propositions can refer to the divine infinity in a way that hinders the introduction of multiplicity into the divine essence.[119] Propositions articulate the object of belief that is apprehended in the form of a judgment. Formulating such propositions requires disqualifying any elements introducing diversification into the *res* that is, by definition, immutable.[120] The concern with propositional tense is of tantamount importance for the divine science founded on axioms true for all eternity. From a strictly grammatical perspective, propositional meaning and truth values are altered by modifying the verbs. Aristotle's claim that the verb consignifies time presides over the medieval discussions of grammar and

---

116. Augustine writes, "Personae tres non proprie dictae." *De Trin.*, V, 9 [PL 42:917].

117. WA 39,2:398.18–20 (witness A; Hegemon).

118. "Quare sive futurum sive praesens sive praeteritum accipias, semper est verum, semper nascitur, natus et nascetur." Ibid., 293.23–24 (witness A; Major).

119. An adjacent issue is concerned with how the divine attributes can be predicated of the divine essence without violating its simplicity.

120. M.-D. Chenu, "Contribution à l'Histoire," 124.

logic.[121] In the twelfth century, Abelard defined the proposition (*dictum*) as referring to a state of affairs that is temporally determined.[122] Abelard distinguished between mere predication and a proposition (*dictum*) that articulates the truth value assigned to the state of affairs for which the predication holds. The truth value of a proposition is determined by the duration of time for which the state of affairs is asserted to be the case. In later development, the issue of time emerges as significant to both the disputation's and the written proposition's truth status. For the disputation, the length of time—the required time (*tempus obligationis*)—controls the granting or rejecting of a logical series of propositions.[123] For the written proposition, the truth value can be modified by an impersonal prefix that determines the span of time for which the proposition is held to be true. With the addition of the prefix, the truth value is signaled for the state of affairs articulated by the proposition (*dictum*) or the stated subject matter (*enuntiabile*). Dependent on verb tense and related to the prefix modifier, the modality of the stated subject matter (*enuntiabile*) plays into the later medieval understanding of truth. Specific modal concepts of necessity, possibility, and impossibility qualify the type of extension in time over which a truth claim can be made. The three modes of time are related to the modal qualification of propositions according to the predominant view in which the past is seen as necessary, the present as necessary in a qualified sense, and the future is regarded as contingent.[124] Necessity *per se* is considered to be an eternal truth. Indicated by the qualifier "as of now" (*ut nunc*), possibility is related to a temporal truth that could have been false in the past though not necessarily in the present or future. The impossible is never true at any time.[125] Arousing the curiosity of medieval theologians is the modality of possibility: God's relation to the world as

---

121. Aristotle, *De int.* c. 3, 16b 6–7 [vol. 1, 26].

122. Gabriel Nuchelmans, "The semantics of propositions," 200–201.

123. Angelelli, "The techniques of disputation," 803. Angelelli writes that the *tempus obligationis* functions to "avoid any change of truth value for contingent propositions during the *lapsus* of the time of the obligation."

124. The future, unlike the past and present, is understood by the medievals in general to be contingent. Ailly is the exception. He holds that the necessity of the past is *probabile*, and the contingency of the future is to be held on faith. Calvin Normore, "Future contingents," 358–59, 377.

125. Simo Knuuttila, "Modal logic," 348–49.

discussed in the theme of future contingents. Future contingents relate the modality of possibility to the future tense, while distinguishing human possibility from divine immutability. This distinction preserves, on the one hand, human freedom to act and, on the other hand, the necessity of the divine foreknowledge of the individual as reprobate or predestined. Luther's particular question concerning the modality associated with the inner-Trinitarian proposition is thematized against this backdrop of the medieval discussion of truth and modality.

Tense, Modality, and the Eternal Generation of the Son

In his Trinitarian disputations, Luther gives two examples of how a theologian can construct tensed propositions in such a way as to refer to the eternal generation of the Son. Luther uses the *vel* disjunction to show that two differently tensed propositions refer to the same subject matter. "Some argue, that it can be said either the Father has always begotten or begets the Son; or either the Son has always been begotten or is begotten."[126] In the medieval discussion of tensed propositions, Chenu shows, verbs are understood to refer to a subject that is logically identical, in spite of difference in tense. Three different tenses can be used in propositions signifying infinity, yet the truth value is understood to be unchanging with respect to different modes of time.[127] In Luther's case, the Latin term *vel* accomplishes this aim. In order to preserve the sameness of the object of faith in a complex judgment, a disjunction indicates that all three temporal modes can be used to refer to the eternity that embraces past, present, and future.

Luther gestures to another way in which tense can be understood to refer to the divine infinity. This time, Luther qualifies the present tense, or the *praeteritum*, with the modifier "always" (*semper*). The relevant thesis in the Alberus disputation is formulated as follows: "Others hold to a different way of speaking. They claim that the Son of God should be called 'always born' [*semper natum*], because the perfect tense designates a completed thing, while the present tense designates an uncompleted thing."[128] In this proposition, Luther uses the Latin *semper natum*, a perfect passive

---

126. WA 39,2:254.21–22 (Alberus, thesis 20).

127. M.-D. Chenu, "Grammaire et Théologie," 18–19.

128. WA 39,2:254.23–25 (Alberus, thesis 21).

participle, to denote all three modes of time in the Aristotelian sense. For Aristotle, the knowledge articulated by a proposition is related to the truth claim that depends on the ability of the proposition's tense to function in a way referring to a temporally indefinite content.[129] In the case of accusative-infinitive propositions using the verb "to be" (*esse*), the copula is considered to function atemporally in a way similar to "always" (*semper*). It can be grammatically convertible into the three temporal modes of past, present, and future without changing the unity of the subject encompassing all times. When referring to the eternity of God, an atemporal indicator such as "always" (*semper*) or "to be" (*esse*), is taken to mean not the absence of time or solely one mode of time, but "the fullness and perpetuality of time."[130]

Luther uses another strategy to qualify the eternal referent of tensed propositions. In propositions of two types, Luther conjugates one verb across three tenses. Two theses in the Alberus disputation illustrate this conjugation of two verbs, "to be born" (*nasci*) and "to remain" (*manere*), respective to the subject matter of the Son's relation of origin and of the divine essence.

26. Because the Son is the same from eternity, he has been born, is being born, and will be born in eternity—that is, he is eternal God from God.

27. Thus we can rightly say about God: God remained, remains, and will remain, which signifies nothing other than that God always is or that God is eternal.[131]

In these two theses, the conjugation of verbs is understood to articulate the eternity of the divine essence. Luther summarizes this point at the end of each thesis by mentioning the adjective "eternal" (*aeternus*) or the word that appears in other propositions, "always" (*semper*). In both cases, the verbs are referred to the subject matter from two perspectives. For Luther, the eternity of the divine essence is the same as the infinity of the Son's eternal generation. Luther's conjugation of the verbs, in participles

---

129. Jaakko Hintikka, "Time, Truth, and Knowledge in Aristotle," in *Time & Necessity*, 80–81.

130. WA 39,2:293.11 (witness A; Major).

131. Ibid., 254.35–38 (Alberus, theses 26 and 27).

and in the indicative form, resembles Lombard's discussion of tense in the *Sentences*.[132] Lombard's position grew from the nominalists, who considered grammatically modified verbs to have differing accidental significations, as Chenu shows.[133] The grammatical distinction in tenses accidentally signifies a content that, from the view of the unity of faith, is not compromised by the differing tenses. For Lombard, as well as for Luther, tense does not introduce change into the being of God who remains Triune for all eternity.

For Luther, the variety in tense does not compromise the proposition's truth claim. Regardless of tense, the truth status of propositions referring to the divine eternity eliminates any contingent temporal qualification. When a truth claim is made concerning the eternal nature of God, it is true according to the modality of necessity.[134] In a Major thesis, Luther writes of the "indisputable truth" of the inner Trinity: "It is an indisputable truth that God, who is one and triune, is the sole Creator of all things outside himself."[135] The inner-Trinitarian proposition is necessarily true for all eternity. Luther insists on the pastoral implications of the indisputable truth claim regarding the eternal nature of God. Rather than concerning himself with the modality of possibility that characterizes Ockham's worry about future contingents, Luther is motivated by a soteriological interest in claiming the inner Trinity to be a necessary truth. Weak consciences, terrified by the demonic temptation eroding trust in the benefits

---

132. Lombard articulates the theme of tense regarding the generation of the Son in *Sent.* I, d. 9, c. 4 (32) [106]. The chapter begins, "Utrum debeat dici 'semper gignitur' vel 'semper est genitus Filius'."

133. Chenu, "Contribution à l'histoire," 127-29; Idem, "Grammaire et théologie," 11-13.

134. A related issue is concerned with the proposition on the incarnation. The temporal location in which the proposition is articulated determines the proposition's truth value. For Lombard, the identity of Christ is preserved through time; the faith in Christ of the Old Testament patriarchs is the same as the faith in Christ of Christians. "Sicut antiqui Patres crediderunt Christum nasciturum et moriturum, nos autem credimus eum iam natum et mortuum." Lombard, *Sent.* I, d. 41, c. 3 (183) [293]. The truth value of a proposition articulating faith in Christ who will or who has come is dependent on the temporal location of the statement. If the proposition is articulated with respect to the Old Testament, it is true if the verb, "to come," is in the future tense. In the case of the time after Christ's resurrection, the proposition is true if the verb is in the past tense. In light of this position, Luther's understanding of the unity of faith in both testaments can be related to his harsh polemic against the Jews of the sixteenth century who, in Luther's mind, articulate a false proposition of faith in the Christ who is to come, false because of its location in time after the fact of Christ who has already come.

135. WA 39,2:287.13-14 (Major, thesis 5).

of Christ, are to be comforted by knowing that what God reveals about his nature, his "pure grace and mercy, goodness and faithfulness," is true for all eternity.[136] Faith in the Son includes the knowledge that the divine attributes of mercy and goodness are bound together with the inner side of God.[137] How much more comforting is it to know that these attributes are infinite? In the Fabricius disputation, Luther initially responds that God hears according to the divine attribute of mercy.[138] Later, Luther connects the invocation of the triune name with the divine benefits of the forgiveness of sins and eternal life.[139] There is comfort in knowing that the work of redemption from death, sin, and damnation is attributed to the eternal God and not to a mortal creature.[140] What the eternal God has established is an eternal peace with his creatures, as Luther preaches in a sermon.[141] For Luther, the divine attributes, the divine promise to hear, and the act of redemption are true regardless of the temporal locations of invocation and religious rites. He concludes the relevant section in the Fabricius disputation by using both the present and the perfect tenses to articulate the unity of faith and the object of its belief; "there is and has always been one and the same invocation and faith."[142] For all eternity, God's triune essence

---

136. WA 54:82.29.

137. "Nu aber sollen wirs doch lernen, wie gott sich hie erweiset, Item was Er sey in omnibus suis attributis, wie er sich beweiset, was fur gnade er uns erzeiget, wie freundtlich und gutig. In jenem leben wollen wir sie sehen, nicht in bilden, sondern de facie ad faciem [1 Cor 13:12]. Hie mußen wirs gleuben, quomodo tres sint unus Deus, ein gottlich leben, Das gleuben wir, hinweg vernufft mit ihren gedancken." WA 49:314.31-36 (Sermon on the First Sunday after Epiphany, Jan. 13, 1544, Stoltz version).

138. "Exaudiri per misericordiam est habere benevolum et propitium Deum." WA 39,2:272.29-30 (Fabricius).

139. In this disputation, Luther contrasts a right understanding of invoking the Triune God with the invocation of the "papistae." It seems that Luther links a right invocation with the knowledge that only the Triune God can forgive sins and grant eternal life. See: Ibid., 278.30-279.5.

140. Luther preaches in a sermon, "... nemlich das er 'seligmache nach barmherzigkeit', Der mus gott sein, Das werck ist gottlich, steht keiner Creatur zu selig machen, erlosen vom tod, sunden, verdamnis, das gehort gott zu." WA 49:645.22-25 (Sermon on the First Sunday after Christmas, Dec. 28, 1544, Stoltz version).

141. "Das ist die herrlich schone predigt, quam nemo potuit dare quam pater, nemo afferre quam filius Dei. Non loquitur de pace corporali aut de ea, quam nos habemus fu(e)r den Wolffen, sed pacem praedicat inter nos et Deum et Creaturas. Est aeterna pax." Ibid., 363.15-19 (Sermon on Easter Monday, afternoon, April 14, 1544, Rörer version).

142. "Semper est et fuit una et eadem invocatio et una fides, sed tempora fuerunt dissimilia, alii ritus et caeremoniae fuerunt." WA 39,2:270.1-2 (Fabricius). Luther's statement is

is true. Bound together with an understanding concerning the infinity of the divine nature is the comfort that the attribute of mercy is also true in eternity. This is a truth that Luther sought, fought for, and found in the disputation.

THE INFINITY OF THE INNER TRINITY: CONCLUSION

The doctoral disputation invites reason to demarcate the region in which the inner Trinity can be investigated. In this section, I have described the type of discourse that articulates the inner Trinity. Although "improper," Luther attributes the speech concerning the inner Trinity to the Spirit. Governed by the Spirit's speech, the theological region embraces a particular use of reason to define the infinity linked with the eternal generation of the Son. The particular language available in the theological region requires an account for the way in which it refers to the inner Trinity. The variety of ways in which tensed propositions articulate the divine eternity, whether by a disjunction, an atemporal indicator, or a series of verbs in the past, present, and future tenses, are placed under the rubric of improper language and are taken to refer to the eternity of God. The proposition "God is eternal" makes a truth claim uninterrupted by the modality of possibility associated with the contingency of time. Its truth status is determined to be of the strictest necessity. At this juncture, Luther adds no determination to the divine infinity other than by showing that "improper" language must be understood to refer to the inner side of God. Still lurking at the boundary of the theological region, however, is the danger of a foreign determination of infinity. Luther adds another dimension to what he sees is the anti-Trinitarian disobedience to the Father's word. Luther's debate with Aristotle is the theme of the next section.

---

remarkably similar to a statement found in Lombard's *Sentences*. In the context of discussing the possibility of introducing change into the object of faith by tensed verbs, Lombard writes, "...nec tamen diversa credimus nos et illi, sed eadem. 'Tempora enim, ut ait Augustinus, variata sunt', et ideo verba mutata, 'non fides'." Lombard, *Sent.* I, d. 41, c. 3 (183) [293]. The citation from Augustine is found in the exegesis of John 10:1–10 in the Commentary on John. "Tempora variata sunt, non fides. Quia et ipsa verba pro tempore variantur, cum varie declinantur." *In Joannis Evangelium tractatus*, tr. 45 (9) [PL 35:1722].

LUTHER AND ARISTOTLE ON
THE DIVINE INFINITY

In the medieval academic context, the theological region shares boundaries with other areas—most notably, the various disciplines associated
with philosophy. For Luther, the theological specification of infinity, a term
appearing in both the theological and the philosophical regions, figures
crucially in his understanding of the inner Trinity. A large part of Luther's
disputations on the Trinity is devoted to the process of determining the
term "infinity" by distinguishing between the natural philosophical, the
metaphysical, and the theological definitions. During the course of drawing the borders between the academic regions and defining the type of
infinity respective to each region, it is not surprising that Luther turns to
debate Aristotle.

Aristotle, or more precisely, a medieval version of Aristotelianism, was
engaged in the high Middle Ages as a serious conversation partner on the
terrain of natural philosophy. In the first half of the fourteenth century,
especially in Oxford, the *Physics* was the one work among Aristotle's natural
philosophical corpus that inspired the most commentaries.[143] With the challenge posed to theology's doctrine of creation by Aristotle's understanding
of infinite temporal extension, or the eternity of the world, the discussion
extended beyond the boundaries of the natural philosophical arena to reach
into the discipline of metaphysics. The concepts of time and infinity played
a significant role in medieval theological discussions. These discussions
necessarily distinguished between the eternity of the Creator and creation,
which had a beginning in time.[144] A host of related themes fascinating the
medievals quickly burgeoned. Specific topics became the focus of study,
such as the logic regarding the term "infinite," which was formed by the
distinction between the categorematic and the syncategorematic use of

---

143. John E. Murdoch, "Infinity and continuity," 565.

144. For Aristotle, motion and time have no beginning. The Christian understanding of
the doctrine of creation demands viewing the divine act of creating in time. Aristotle claims
that time, rather than spatial extension, is infinite. On the other hand, the universe provides
the limits of spatial magnitude; spatial extension is neither potentially nor actually infinite.
Phys. III (7), 207b 16–21 [vol. 1, 353].

the term,[145] as well as the paradox of unequal infinites.[146] More theological issues were also addressed, such as the relation of God to the eternal ideas as an "improper infinite"[147] and the relation of the divine infinity to both the actual and the potential infinity.

The theses in the Alberus disputation introduce Aristotle as a respected disputation partner. Luther—who was intimately acquainted since his Erfurt education with at least the *Physics*, the *Metaphysics*, and the *Nicomachean Ethics*—engages Aristotle in a sustained argument distinguishing between a theological and a metaphysical determination of the term "infinity."[148] In this section, by describing Luther's disputation with Aristotle on the subject matter of both the actual and the potential infinity, I will show how Luther excludes these determinations from the theological region. Luther then turns to the term "generation" in order to distinguish its natural philosophical definition from its theological articulation as the "eternal generation of the Son." This section concludes with a discussion of the way in which the disputation shapes Luther's resistance to any analogies that are imposed by natural reason onto the inner-Trinitarian infinity. In the process of excluding the activity of natural reason to define the terms "infinity" and "generation," Luther begins to carve out a theological space for determining his understanding of the inner Trinity.

---

145. The term, "infinite," functions categorematically when it follows the subject term. Its determination of the subject term is numerically adjectival. For example, "homines infiniti currunt," refers to an infinite number of men. The syncategorematic use of the term, recognized if the word, "infinite," precedes the subject term, is taken to mean that its distribution over the subject term is relative to the predicate term. The distinction between the categorematic and syncategorematic uses of the term, "infinite," plays into the metaphysical distinction between the actual and potential infinite. Murdoch, "Infinity and continuity," 567–68.

146. The paradox of the unequal infinites was used as an argument against the existence of the actual infinite. The paradox assumes the existence of some actual infinites. If some exist, then they will be parts of other actual infinites, which is a paradox as all actual infinites are, by definition, equal. Ibid., 569–71.

147. Augustine, *Conf.*, 11, 13 (16) [PL 32:815].

148. Luther's words of appreciation for Aristotle arise in an early Christmas sermon. "Vide quam apte serviat Aristoteles in Philosophia sua Theologiae, si non ut ipse voluit, sed melius intelligitur et applicatur." WA 1:28.19–21 (1514). In "An den christlichen Adel deutscher Nation von des christlichen Standes Besserung (1520)," Luther recommends reading Aristotle without any commentaries or interpretations altogether! "Das mocht ich gerne leyden, das Aristoteles bucher von der Logica, Rhetorica, Poetica behalten, odder sie in ein andere kurtz form bracht nutzlich geleszen wurden, junge leut zuuben, wol reden und predigen, aber die Comment und secten musten abethan, unnd gleich wie Ciceronis Rhetorica on comment und secten, szo auch Aristoteles logica einformig, on solch grosz comment geleszen werden." WA 6:458.26–31.

THE ACTUAL INFINITY

Luther exegetically focuses the debate over the term "infinity" on a passage from Paul's Letter to the Romans that, in the trajectory from Augustine, arises in the context of discussing the knowledge of God.[149] Citing Romans 1:20 in the Alberus disputation, Luther writes, "In Romans 1, St. Paul rightly says: What is known of God has been made known to all people, that is, his eternal power and divinity."[150] This passage in Romans, itself written in a rhetorical disputational style, is acknowledged in the tradition of biblical interpretation as the common proof text (*locus classicus*) concerning the knowledge of God revealed to all humans as divine traces in creation. Augustine refers to this passage in the context of the Platonists' discussion of sense perception and the intelligible Idea.[151] According to Augustine, the Platonists argue that each changing form has its being from what is unchanging and simple. These philosophers, who "surpass all others," conclude that God is known from the traces of the eternal power and divinity in what is created. In his first book of the *Sentences*, Lombard also refers to Romans 1:19–20 in a section devoted to the question of the creature's knowledge of the Creator.[152] With the medieval proofs for the existence of God, the traces of the infinite in creation are interpreted according to the capacity of natural reason to infer, through various sequences, what can be known about God based on aspects of created existence. By alluding to Romans 1:20, Luther acknowledges a tradition of medieval thought that relates the knowledge of God to the metaphysical implications of natural philosophical observations.

The Romans passage overarches the controversy Luther initiates with Aristotle on the possibility of legitimately inferring the infinity of the Creator from the traces of the infinite in creation. After referring to Paul's

---

149. White concludes that the logical structure of Luther's theses cannot be determined by analyzing the logical connectives linking specific consequences that are deduced from a general assertion. Rather, the theses are organized "into successive sections on various theological themes" and possibly, according to "some sort of metatheological principle." White, *Luther as Nominalist*, 120–21. In this section, I suggest that Rom 1:19–20 structures the series of theses. In these theses, Luther aims to distinguish between the theological, the metaphysical, and the natural philosophical regions.

150. WA 39,2:255.15–16 (Alberus, thesis 35).

151. *De Civ. Dei*, 8, 6 [CCL 47:222–24].

152. "Incipit ostendere quomodo per creata potuit cognosci Creator." *Sent.* I, d. 3, c. 1 (9), a. 1 [68].

text, Luther turns to gradually specify the way in which the Jews and then the Greek philosopher determine the concept of infinity. Prior to the allusion to Aristotle, Luther mentions the "sacred tetragrammaton," "Iehova," as the ineffable name by which the Jews refer to God.[153] In this series of theses, Luther perhaps mentions the term "ineffability" in order to build a bridge to what he decides to be the significant focus of his debate. In thesis 30 of the Alberus disputation,[154] Luther gestures to Aristotle's introductory remarks in both the *Physics*[155] and the *Metaphysics* concerning the incomprehensibility of the infinite.[156] Luther uses Aristotle's specification as a springboard in order to launch his own debate on the divine infinite.

The particular type of infinity that Luther intends to engage is the actual infinity. Luther's formulation of thesis 31 in the Alberus disputation makes this point clear. He writes, "In fact, he affirms that infinity or eternity, insofar as it is of this kind, cannot exist and according to reason he seems to speak correctly."[157] Luther refers to a type of infinity whose existence many medieval interpreters of Aristotle considered the philosopher to have denied. The question of whether something infinite can be real—posed by both medieval philosophers and theologians—focuses on Aristotle's rejection of the existence of an actual infinity as a numerical infinity. In the *Physics*, Aristotle denies the existence of an actual infinity,[158] and in the *Metaphysics*, he argues that an infinite number of actual things is impossible.[159] For medieval thinkers, Aristotle's actual infinity is understood to have no highest number in an endless temporal succession. Maier provides the Latin definition, in Aristotelian terminology, of the

153. WA 39,2:255.3-4 (Alberus, thesis 29).

154. "Sensit et Aristoteles, aeternum seu infinitum, in quantum eiusmodi, esse ignotum et incomprehensibile." Ibid., 255.5-6 (Alberus, thesis 30).

155. *Phys.* I (4), 187b 7-35 [vol. 1, 320-21].

156. *Met.* II (2), 994b 21-25 [vol. 2, 1571].

157. WA 39,2:255.7-8 (Alberus, thesis 31).

158. *Phys.* III (6), 206a 20-21 [vol. 1, 351].

159. *Met.* II (2), 994b 20-28 [vol. 2, 1571] denies that one can apprehend infinity. Hintikka argues that Aristotle understood the actual infinity to exist in "the *precise* sense, ... in which the infinite was found to exist potentially." Hintikka uses what Lovejoy has termed Aristotle's principle of plenitude, "according to which no genuine possibility can remain unactualized through an infinity of time" in order to show that the actual infinity exists in the above precise sense. Hintikka, "Aristotelian Infinity," in *Time & Necessity*, 117, 114.

actual infinity: "the infinite is that than which nothing is greater (*infinitum est quo nihil est maius*)."[160] By definition, the actual infinity prevents there being a last number of a series in thought as well as in reality. Although some medieval scholars, such as Robert Holcot (c. 1290–1308), Gregory of Rimini (c. 1300–1358), and William of Ockham,[161] tend toward accepting the existence of the actual infinity in a sophisticated and qualified sense, the predominant denial of its existence is entertained by Luther, who intends to use it in an inference to deny the existence of God.

Luther uses the antecedent premise to construct an inference that shows why he excludes an imposition of natural reason onto the theological determination of infinity. From the denial of the existence of the actual infinity, Luther infers the denial of God's existence. Luther writes, "But he does not see the consequence, or rather, he does not wish to see the consequence, of course, that by reason it follows from this that God does not exist, indeed, cannot exist."[162] The inference Luther draws presents an intriguing conflation of two concepts that, for a medieval thinker such as Scotus, would have been illegitimate.

A concept Luther conflates with the actual infinity is already found in Scotus's work. Scotus makes an inference from the intensive finitude of creation to the intensive infinity of the divine being.[163] For Scotus, the concept

---

160. Anneliese Maier, "Diskussionen über das aktuell Unendliche in der ersten Hälfte des 14. Jahrhunderts," 44. The actual infinity defined analogically to the potential infinity is: "tantum quod non maius," or "tot quod non plures" or, reversing the definition of the potential infinity and considered to be less precise: "infinitum est cuius nihil est extra sumere." Ibid. Maier writes that the question concerning the existence of the actual infinity was posed in the case of the number of the last units of a continuum. The predominant and Aristotelian interpretation considered the continuum to be composed of "semper divisibilia," "d.h. die Anzahl seiner letzten Teile ist potentiell unendlich gross, und ihre Grösse entsprechend potentiell unendlich klein." Ibid., 42n2.

161. Ibid., 43. Maier suggests that Ockham accepted the reality of the actual infinity, not in the sense of a "tantum quod non maius" or "tot quod non plura," but as what lies beyond all finite number and proportions. Ibid., 62. Wolter suggests that, although Scotus "was well aware of the difficulty involved with the very concept of an actual infinite multitude, he personally believed that one could form a constructed or higher level concept of it at least, and if one could, by some flash of 'insight,' conceive this as a whole, it would be a step towards giving some sense to what he regarded as the peak of metaphysical thought, where one reaches the very limits of language and of abstract speculation." Allan B. Wolter, *The Philosophical Theology of John Duns Scotus*, 67.

162. WA 39,2:255.9–10 (Alberus, thesis 32).

163. I would like to thank Marilyn McCord Adams for suggesting Scotus's distinction between extensive and intensive infinity as a way of interpreting Luther's inference from the

of infinity is crucial to his understanding of the relationship between metaphysics and theology. Scotus predicates infinity of the highest being as the
metaphysically determined attribute distinguishing between creature and
Creator.[164] In order to make an inference from the finitude of creatures to
the infinity of the divine being, Scotus distinguishes between extensive
infinity and intensive infinity. Basing his argument on the efficiency of
a first mover that must be infinite, Scotus shows that extensive infinity
does not explain why the power of this first mover is sufficiently infinite
to produce the sum total of an infinite series of effects.[165] Extensive infinity
merely explains how a finite effect is produced over an infinite period of
time. In order to show that the first mover has an infinite power at one and
the same moment to create all creatures simultaneously, Scotus begins his
argument by proving that God's knowledge is infinite. Scotus then argues
from God's infinite knowledge to the infinite power of the divine being.[166]
From the intensive finitude of creatures, Scotus infers the existence of an
intensively infinite being.

Luther locates his own inference in the metaphysical region in order
to show that this inference is entirely incapable of attaining even the existence of the infinite being. Beginning with the antecedent, the denial of
the existence of the actual infinity, Luther forces an equivocation between
the actual infinity and the intensive infinity and infers the denial of the
existence of God. By equivocating two terms that Scotus would have distinguished, Luther's inference ends up denying the very existence of the
being that a metaphysician such as Scotus aims to demonstrate.

Luther imposes an equivocation onto an inference from the denial of
the existence of the actual infinity to the denial of the existence of God in
order to characterize the extent to which natural reason, operating in the
metaphysical region, is restricted. Luther reads Aristotle in such a way as

---

denial of the existence of the actual infinity to the denial of the existence of God.

164. For a detailed presentation of Scotus's understanding of the principle of non-identity
and its relation to the divine attribute of infinity, see: Étienne Gilson, *Jean Duns Scot*, 250–52.

165. Wolter, *The Philosophical Theology of John Duns Scotus*, 270.

166. Wolter summarizes Scotus's argument from the infinite knowledge of God to the
intensive infinity of God's power in ibid., 271.

to force Aristotle into making an inference that he is not able to see.[167] This position is finally attributed to one of Luther's favorite whipping posts, Epicurus, who, according to Luther, denies the existence of God.[168] "For this reason [Aristotle] everywhere disputes so indifferently concerning religion, and Epicurus has been perfected in appearance."[169] Although the historical Epicurus is regarded as having articulated his thoughts in opposition to Aristotle, Luther locates the two Greek philosophers in the same metaphysical region.[170] The use of reason in that region either shies just short of, or is successful in, denying the existence of God. On Luther's terms, the metaphysical region is occupied by some fools (Ps 14:1) who are pious enough to avoid drawing the metaphysical conclusion denying the existence of God.

Luther constructs an inference that he locates in the metaphysical region in order to expose the incapacity of natural reason to attain even the slightest bit of knowledge concerning the infinity that he associates with the Trinity. The equivocation that Luther imposes on the inference he draws shows how he blocks an inference from the metaphysical region to the theological region. With respect to natural reason, Luther argues that it is utterly incapable of inferring the existence of the being that, according to Scotus, would be the intensively infinite being. The metaphysical enterprise threatens to be dismantled entirely when an equivocation results in the denial of both the existence of the actual infinity and the existence of the intensively infinite being.

In his debate with Aristotle, Luther constructs his inference in such a way as to separate the theological region from the metaphysical region.

---

167. "Sed consequentiam non vidit, vel potius videre noluit." WA 39,2:255.9 (Alberus, first half of thesis 32).

168. In the sermon on Rom 11:33–36, Luther identifies the Epicureans as the people who are only interested in filling their bellies. They are not at all interested in the divine justice and commit acts of injustice against others. The Epicureans are not at all the addressees of his sermon. WA 45:95.2–8. See: ch. 4, "The Homiletical Word."

169. WA 39,2:255.11–12 (Alberus, thesis 33).

170. Luther frequently refers to Epicurus as a superficial hedonist. Epicurus' philosophical writings are available as fragments in the works of thinkers who received him, to a large extent in Cicero's *De natura deorum*, a work with which Luther was most likely familiar. Epicurus' philosophical work concentrates on understanding the relation between the unchangeability of the gods and the principles of physics related to the change occurring in the world. A physical explanation underlies Epicurus' understanding of the eternity of the gods. Wolfgang Schmid, "Epikur," esp. 735–36.

An increasing distance between the two regions locates Luther in a trajectory that marks Ockham's criticism of Scotus. From Scotus to Ockham, an increasing separation between the two regions is related to what can be claimed concerning the epistemic accessibility of the theological subject matter. Scotus believes he can prove the existence of the intensively infinite being from the intensive finitude of the creature. Ockham, however, thinks metaphysics can formulate but not prove the infinity of the divine being; he considers the subject matter in the theological region to be less epistemically accessible than his predecessor.[171] Located in the trajectory following Ockham, Luther's inference goes so far as to suggest that the metaphysical project is unsuccessful on its own terms. By showing its incapacity to attain the knowledge of the existence of the infinite divine being, the use of metaphysics for determining the infinity associated with the Triune God is dismissed entirely. For Luther, the concept of infinity and its relation to the divine being are located only in the theological region, the region in which the Trinitarian God is revealed. In his debate with Aristotle, Luther understands the Pauline passage to locate the traces of the eternal power and divinity in the theological region; any traces found in the metaphysical region are rejected as incapable of shedding light on the infinity of the divine being and of the Triune God. The increasing separation in the Scotus-Ockham trajectory between the two regions culminates in Luther's reliance on the revealed word of God to define the divine essence as infinite; the meaning of infinity must be provided by the Spirit in the theological region.

THE POTENTIAL INFINITY

After debating Aristotle on the actual infinity, Luther turns to the second type of infinity that appears in the medieval discussion. The potential infinity is considered by both Aristotle and his medieval interpreters to exist in reality as well as in the mind.[172] Luther introduces the set of theses on the potential infinity by acknowledging Aristotle's position: "He concedes,

---

171. McCord Adams, *Ockham*, vol. 2, 952.

172. Aristotle, *Phys.* III (6), 207a 8–9 [vol. 1, 352]. The medieval Latin, quoted in Murdoch, reads, "Non enim cuius nihil est extra, sed cuius semper aliquid est extra, hoc infinitum est. ... Infinitum quidem igitur hoc est, cuius secundum quantitatem accipientibus, semper est aliquid accipere extra." Murdoch, "Infinity and continuity," 567n6.

however, that potential infinity exists and can be known."[173] In the *Physics*, Aristotle entertains the possibility of conceiving the existence of an infinite temporal sequence by posing the question whether time can be said to have actuality. He asks whether time might exist, at least, "barely, and in the obscure way," when past and future time are regarded as nonexistent, and the present separates the already from the not-yet.[174] Against the backdrop of continuous time as a past that has receded and a future arriving to the present, Aristotle conceives the potential infinity according to two examples. He writes that the way in which the infinite can be said to exist is not to be regarded as a "this," like a person or a house, but in the sense of existing as things whose being consists in a process of coming to be and passing away.[175] Not considered as an object to which one can point, time is understood according to the sense in which a day is or the Olympic Games are. This succession of continuous coming into and going out of existence, of which the totality can never actually exist simultaneously,[176] exists "as an attribute of certain sequences of individual things or individual events—'definite if you like at each stage, yet always different.'"[177] In his *On the Last Words of David*, Luther articulates a position similar to one that Aristotle holds. Creaturely existence can be conceived in the sense of a coming into and a going out of existence.[178] On the issue of an infinite sequence, however, Luther's theological claim differs drastically from that of his opponent.

Luther constructs another inference in order to show how the inference from the potential infinity is incapable of reaching the divine infinity. Even worse, the constructed inference cannot move beyond the eternity of the world. The relevant thesis of the Alberus disputation is articulated

---

173. WA 39,2:255.13 (Alberus, first clause of thesis 34).

174. *Phys.* IV (10), 217b 32–218a 3 [vol. 1, 369–70].

175. *Phys.* III (6), 206a 21–26. 29–34 [vol. 1, 351].

176. The inconceivability of infinity as the unactualizability of the last number in an infinite temporal series, in Met. II (2), 994b 21–28 [vol. 2, 1571], is contrasted with the conceivability of a potential infinite as the existence of finite things coming to be and passing away, as Aristotle states in *Met.* IX (6), 1048b 15–17 [vol. 2, 1655–56].

177. Hintikka, *Time & Necessity*, 116.

178. Contrasting the divine eternal kingdom of 1 Chr 17:14 with an earthly and temporal kingdom, Luther writes, "Auch nicht ein Vergenglich, Zeitlich, Irdisch Reich sein, welchs ein ende hat." WA 54:46.11–12.

as follows: "He concedes, however, that potential infinity exists and can be known, although here again he confuses this with the eternity of the world."[179] Luther qualifies his thesis by accusing Aristotle of confusing the potential infinity with the eternity of the world. Of course, on Aristotle's terms, this inference is legitimate, as Aristotle understands the first mover to move the heavens that exist for all eternity.[180] With his accusation against Aristotle, Luther is also pointing out a bone of contention with Scotus. In medieval theology, a thinker such as Scotus would draw the inference from potential infinity (*infinitum in fieri*) to some knowledge of the divine infinity only by making the necessary distinction between extensive and intensive infinity.[181] Luther does not replicate Scotus's careful distinction. Rather, Luther uses a strategy of collapse in order to expose the captivity of reason to a world-immanent realm. In a manner similar to his inference based on the actual infinity, Luther's inference from the potential infinity is drawn by forcing an equivocation between the potential infinity and the extensive infinity. Luther conflates the potential infinity, as the continuous process of things coming into and going out of existence, with the extensive infinity, which is understood by Scotus in terms of the finite effects of a first cause over an infinite period of time. By equivocating the two terms, Luther constructs an inference that is opposed to the theological claim of creation from nothing (*creatio ex nihilo*). The rhetorical veil of Luther's thesis, however, disguises a traditional medieval theological view of the incompatibility between Aristotle's understanding of an infinite temporal succession and the Christian understanding of a creation in time.

By constructing the inference from the potential infinity to the infinity of the world, Luther follows a strategy similar to the first inference from the actual infinity. Luther aims to expose the incapacity of the metaphysical project to infer beyond the premises of its own region. Natural reason cannot infer from the potential infinity to any type of infinity associated with a divine being. Caught in its own region marked by a sequence of coming into and going out of existence, reason cannot sufficiently

179. WA 39,2:255.13-14 (Alberus, thesis 34).

180. *Met.* XII (8), 1073a 24-33 [vol. 2, 1696].

181. Maier sums up the three medieval definitions of the potential infinity: (a) "infinitum in fieri" as "non tantum quin maius" for infinite magnitudes; (b) "non tot quin plures" for infinite number; (c) the syncategorematic use of the term, "infinite." Maier, *Diskussionen*, 43-44.

transcend its own premises and reach towards the Being that exists beyond all change.[182] Succeeding in his aim to restrict the domain of natural reason to the metaphysical region, Luther shows how this region is entirely separated from the theological region.

Luther's intentional dismantling of the metaphysical task serves his theological aim. It is only in the theological region that the infinity related to the Triune God and the nature of the Triune God to create from nothing (*ex nihilo*) are revealed as articles of faith.[183] In the Hegemon disputation, Luther does acknowledge that natural reason can, at best, draw an inference from the traces of conservation in creation to the knowledge of a divine conserver.[184] With this claim, Luther's position is unveiled to be in continuity with a trajectory in which Ockham is already located.[185] The trajectory marked by the increasing separation between the metaphysical and the theological regions does not turn on the issue of what can be conceived. Scotus, Ockham, and Luther agree on the capacity of natural reason to conceive of the existence of the potential infinity. What can be proved, however, is the subject matter of dispute. Luther follows Ockham by claiming only an incomplete knowledge of the Christian God by natural reason operating in the metaphysical region. Separated from the metaphysical region, the theological region is the only region in which the Trinitarian article is revealed.

Luther's dispute with Aristotle in the Alberus theses is framed by Romans 1:20, cited at the end of the series of theses on the actual and potential infinity. The controversy between the theological and the philosophical

---

182. In a sermon on Gen 1:3, Luther speaks of the structure of language that cannot grasp three things at once. There is no term capturing all three Trinitarian persons together. It is ultimately sight, rather than language, that can apprehend how the three persons are one God. WA 24:31.24–26 (Über das 1. Buch Mose, Predigten, 1527).

183. An intriguing thesis is articulated in the Hegemon disputation. "Tamen articulus de creatione rerum ex nihilo difficilior est creditu quam articulus de incarnatione." WA 39,2:340.21–22 (thesis 21). See Luther's response in ibid., 389.1–390.25 (witnesses A–C).

184. Luther acknowledges that natural reason can, from the traces of the conservation of creation, infer a conserver. However, natural reason cannot know God as Creator. "Verum gubernationem servatis speciebus potest natura videre et cognoscere Deum gubernantem, sed creationem ipsam non intelligit." Ibid., 346.8–11 (witness B; Hegemon). Luther makes a similar argument in the sermon on Rom 11:33–36. See: ch. 4, "The Homiletical Disputation."

185. Ockham permits a qualified use of metaphysical reason concerning the final and efficient causes. For a study of Ockham's arguments concerning the proofs for the existence of God, see: McCord Adams, *Ockham*, vol. 2, 966–79.

determinations of infinity uncovers Luther's intention to show, with Paul, that only from the perspective of the incarnation is the "glory of the divine Majesty" manifest as the trace of infinity in creation.[186] The traces of the infinite power and divinity are revealed not in the metaphysical region but in the theological region. In the Hegemon disputation, Luther interprets the Romans passage at length in order to make a similar claim to the Alberus theses. Luther alludes to a range of philosophers to show that right knowledge of God cannot be inferred from traces of the divine conservation in creation.[187] The incomplete knowledge of a divine conserver in the metaphysical region is regarded, from the vantage point of the theological region, as no knowledge at all of the Triune God as Creator. Natural reason that attempts to move beyond its capacity ends up as either the psalmist's fool or stands under Paul's charge of idolatry.[188] By determining the boundaries between the theological and the philosophical regions in the course of debating Aristotle on the actual and the potential infinity, Luther does not discredit reason as such. Its limits are pointed out in order to make room for a theological use, adequate to study the subject matter of the eternal generation of the Son.

---

186. "Qui scrutando non volet errare, nec a maiestatis gloria opprimi, is fide tangat et apprehendat Filium Dei in carne manifestatum." WA 39,2:255.20f. (Alberus, thesis 37).

187. In the Hegemon disputation, Luther interprets the capacity of reason to infer a God on the basis of the conservation of the world, a God who is "primum movens et summum ens." Ibid., 346.4 (witness A). Luther throws Plato, Aristotle, and Cicero together into one metaphysical soup, stating that the partial knowledge of God on the basis of the *gubernatio* is inadequate to reach both the Trinitarian essence of the Creator and the nature of mercy. Ibid., 345.24-27, 346.1-23 (witness A). The Hegemon debate clarifies Luther's interpretation of Rom 1:20 by distinguishing between two kinds of knowledge of God, "una est ex creaturis visibilibus. ... Deinde est altera cognitio Dei, quae est ex eius verbo ... ex quo solo cognoscimus voluntatem Dei." Ibid., 345.5-6, 12-13, 14-16 (witness A). In Rom 1:19-20, the passage quoted by Luther, Paul picks up a theory of the knowledge of God from the Stoa, as contemporary New Testament scholars claim. See: Ernst Käsemann, *An die Römer*, 78; Schmithals, *Römerbrief*, 78.

188. In a lengthy response recorded in the Hegemon *disputatio*, Luther interprets Rom 1:21, and explains why those people who have an incomplete knowledge of God are charged with idolatry. Although they have some knowledge of God, they do not give God the glory. "Paulus in textu [Rom 1:21] solvit hoc argumentum: Etsi cognoverunt Deum, tamen non glorificaverunt verum Deum. Illa quantulacunque cognitione, quamquam imperfecta, contempto agnito illo Deo ex gubernatione versi sunt ad cultum animalium, quadrupedum, volucrum, et non tribuerunt Deo gloriam. Gentes sciebant, unum esse Deum, sed tamen suas idolatrias non volebant omittere. Haec est causa, cur sint inexcusabiles, quia sciebant, sua idola esse lignea et lapidea, tamen adorabant et divinum honorem illis tribuebant." WA 39,2:347.10-25 (witness A; Hegemon).

NATURAL PHILOSOPHY AND THE GENERATION OF THE SON

The infinity of the inner Trinity is not only distanced from its metaphysical determination. For Luther, the inner-Trinitarian infinity is specified by another term, also found in the region of natural philosophy. The term "generation" is used to refer to the eternal generation of the Son as well as to the generation of finite entities in time and from a source. In this section, I examine how Luther argues for a theological referent to the term "generation" by drawing the boundary between the theological and the natural philosophical regions.

The term "generation" is located by Aristotle and his medieval interpreters in the regions of natural philosophy and biology. Related to the potential infinity, "generation" is defined as the coming and passing away of finite entities; generation is a process of change occurring in the temporal succession of the potential infinite. In the tradition of Aristotelian natural philosophy, the determination of the term includes a discussion of the elements of time and motion that are related to the change occurring when a finite entity comes into and goes out of existence. According to Aristotle's *Physics*, time is defined as the measurement of motion,[189] and motion is the central concern of natural philosophy.[190] The existence of the potential infinite is argued on the basis of the connection between time and motion.[191] In the medieval reception of Aristotle's work, Ockham continues to define time as the number of motion in reference to a before and after[192] and motion as the generation and corruption of entities.[193] The use

189. *Phys.* III (1), 200b 12–25 [vol. 1, 342].

190. *Phys.* III (4), 202b 30 [vol. 1, 345]. Book 7 of the *Physics* deals primarily with the source of motion. See: *Phys.* VII (1–5), 241b 21–250b 8 [vol. 1, 407–418].

191. The capacity of the soul to measure time by motion is related to the time-motion correlation. Perler, *Prädestination, Zeit und Kontingenz*, 226.

192. McCord Adams describes Ockham's understanding of time as "a cosmic clock by means of which we can measure their [temporal events and things] duration." McCord Adams, *Ockham*, vol. 2, 874. Ockham distinguishes between three notions of time, and concludes that time is the number by which one numbers in the sense of the distinct before and after of the first motion. This time is then used to measure other motions. Ibid., 876. There are also three senses in which the term, "time," can be understood when it is related to motion: the first motion, or motion of heavenly bodies that is strictly uniform, and the fastest, inferior motion as the basis of measuring the first motion, and an imagined motion. Ibid., 886.

193. Ockham interprets Aristotle to mean that motion does not exist independently of entities. Ockham, *Quaestiones in libros physicorum Aristotelis*, q. 13 [*OPh* VI, 428–29]; Aristotle, *Phys.* III (4), 202b 30–203a 4 [vol. 1, 345–46]. See: McCord Adams, *Ockham*, vol. 2, 895.

of the term "generation" in the regions of natural philosophy and biology requires Luther to show how the theological determination of the term is related to a concept of eternity that admits no change, either coming to be or passing away.

At junctures in the Major disputation, Luther distinguishes between a theological and a natural philosophical use of the term "generation." When discussing the relationship between Father and Son, Luther identifies the Christological proposition in Colossians 1:15 with the substantial unity between the two persons.[194] In this unity, the concept of eternity is linked to the Father's generation of the Son. When speaking of Christ's "birth," no determinations of past, future, or present can be imposed onto the generation that takes place in eternity.[195] Christ's birth in eternity can in no way be understood as a finite entity coming into existence. In the inner-Trinitarian unity, there is no change of coming to be or passing away because "there is no time here."[196] Any generation from a beginning that is privileged temporally as the origin of its effect is excluded from the determination of the Son's eternal generation.[197] Such an understanding of generation attacks the coeternity between the Son and the Father. Major also repeats his teacher's words. Orienting his response to the term "today" in Psalm 2:7, Major says

194. "In divinis dicitur character et quidem substantiae, id est, ut etiam ingrediatur in substantiam Patris, ut, quod Pater est, sit et Filius. ... Filius est imago huius invisibilis Dei." WA 39,2:296.17-18, 22-23 (witness A–B; Major). Luther is here referring to Melanchthon's commentary on Colossians (Col 1:15). See: MO 15:1223-24; 1237-39 on the *imago dei*. In a polemic against an Arian interpretation of John 17:22, Luther speaks of the natural unity between Father and Son. "Non ibi de consensu, sed de unitate naturae loquitur, id est, Pater et Filius sunt unum natura." WA 39,2:298.3-4 (witness A; Major).

195. "Christus neque in praeterito neque in futuro neque in praesenti dicitur nasci. ... Quare sive futurum sive praesens sive praeteritum accipias, semper est verum, semper nascitur, natus et nascetur; heists in praeterito, so ists in futuro; heists in futuro, so ists in praeterito; heists in praeterito, so ists in praesenti, semper idem est." Ibid., 293.21-22, 23-26 (witness A).

196. Ibid., 293.26 (witness A).

197. "Filius principium non habet temporis, sed principium divinitatis, et Pater cum Filio sunt principium Spiritus sancti. Hic prorsus nullum tempus est. Ideo adhuc firmiter stat, nullum esse Filii principium." Ibid., 293.3-5 (witness A). The syllogism proposed by the opponent is, "Omne, quod natum est, habet principium. Filius est natus. Ergo habet principium." Ibid., 292.20-21 (witness A). Major agrees with his teachers: "In creaturis id, quod generatur, habet principium. Sed alia generatio est in divinitate." Ibid., 302.15-16 (witness A); similar to Major's response: "Respondeo ad maiorem, quae tantum de creaturis loquitur, ubi omne, quod generatur, ab alio generatur." Ibid., 302.8-9 (witness A; Major); similar to Ibid., 315.26-27 (witness A).

that, in the eternity of God, there is no "temporal beginning, middle, or end."[198] For Luther, the type of infinity appearing in the theological region is determined by the Son's inner-Trinitarian generation, which cannot be confused with the generation of finite entities from an origin.

THE INNER TRINITY AND THE ANALOGY

Luther's exclusion of natural reason offers a lens through which his insistent surface polemic against a variety of academic regions can be viewed. For Luther, the inner Trinity exists entirely outside the creature and is beyond creaturely comprehension. The Son is the image of the invisible God, Luther exclaims, "that is already above and beyond all creatures."[199] When responding to the opponent's challenge that there cannot be a unity of three persons, Luther says that the coeternity and coequality of the three persons cannot be understood according to the order of number, of location, and of time.[200] Major articulates a rule that characterizes Luther's exclusion of natural reason from investigating the inner-Trinitarian unity: "It is not valid to argue from creatures to Creator."[201] What is considered to be invalid is the maneuver of taking terms that apply to the creatures in a given sense and then applying them to define the divine infinity in its specific theological sense. For Luther, each science must define and use the terms proper to its own region.[202] With respect to the infinity associated with the inner Trinity, "creaturely" thinking must be excised from the theological region. An imposition of temporalized reason is forbidden from the onset to determine a subject matter that transcends creaturely thought.

---

198. Ibid., 293.11-12 (witness A).

199. Ibid., 296.23 (witness A-B).

200. "... sed hic nullus numeri ordo, loci et temporis est. ... Hic nullus ordo, sed coaeternitas, coaequalitas, imago, natura muß gar neue sein." Ibid., 303.25, 304.1-2 (witness A).

201. Ibid., 308.1 (witness A).

202. "Iam non debet ars artem impedire, sed unaquaeque debet retinere suum quasi cursum et uti suis terminis." WA 42:35.35-36 (Lectures on Genesis, 1535-1545, to Gen 1:14). See also: Ibid., 35:37-42, 36.4-16. Luther writes on the distinction between philosophy and theology with respect to the subject matter. In this citation from a Table Talk, Luther does not, from the onset, exclude the use of philosophical tools in the theological region. Rather, his worry concerns an unreflected confusion between the two regions. "Philosophia non intelligit res sacras, vnd ich hab sorg, man werde sie zu hartt in die theologia vermischen." WATr 5:25.9-10 (no. 5245, Sept. 2-17, 1540). See also the entire talk, as well as an extended German transcription in ibid., 25.8-26.10.

Luther's exclusion of a "creaturely" use of reason can help to shed light on his prohibition of the analogy. In the genre of the disputation, at least, Luther restricts the power of the analogy to explain the inner Trinity.[203] There is no analogical precedent in creation for comprehending the unity between Father and Son.[204] By excluding the analogy that infers from the creature to the Creator, any inference from an academic region into the theological region is blocked. Luther attacks the incapacity of philosophy to grasp the inner-Trinitarian distinctions between persons;[205] he excludes both grammar[206] and mathematics from investigating the inner Trinity.[207] These polemically formulated theses can be interpreted as restrictions to the explanatory power of any analogy, coming from any scientific region, that would attempt to import a temporalized use of reason into the theological region. In this light, the restrictions against analogical thinking can be correctly understood to pertain to the genre of the disputation and its function to use reason in a way testing types of reason as to their fittingness to the object of study.

Luther's initial attitude towards the analogy is complemented by another position. Once the theological region is circumscribed, Luther does permit the use of the analogy inside this region. In the Major disputation, Luther acknowledges that some analogies can be used to explicate the *res*: "Indeed an analogy in nature does not run on all four feet. But they are given to make the *res* known."[208] Even a language that evokes the natural

---

203. In the genre of the sermon, Luther does not shy away from using specific analogies to explain the eternal generation of the Son from the Father, or the term, "person." See: ch. 4, "The Spirit: God Speaks from God."

204. "Non exprimit natura penitus hanc similitudinem. Nulla enim similitudo tollit secum rerum assimilata." WA 39,2:296.21–22 (witness A–B; Major).

205. "Summa, per rationem et philosophiam de his rebus maiestatis [referring to the preceding thesis on the inner-Trinitarian distinctions between persons] nihil, per fidem vero omnia recte dici et credi possunt." Ibid., 340.12–13 (Hegemon, thesis 17).

206. Speaking of the tensed propositions referring to the eternal generation of the Son, Luther responds, "Grammaticum est de futuro et praesenti. Illae autem speculationes non habent locum in divinitate." Ibid., 293.20–21 (witness A; Major).

207. "Excludenda est igitur mathematica et omnis totius creaturae cogitatio in credenda divinitate." Ibid., 254.7–8 (Alberus, thesis 13). For another polemical thesis against mathematics: "Error itaque est universa Mathematica, ipsaque fortiter crucifigenda, dum de Deo ipso quaeritur." Ibid., 287.27–28 (Major, thesis 13).

208. Ibid., 296.13–14 (witness A–B; Major). In the chapter on Luther's sermon (ch. 4, "Doxology as Eschatological Impulse"), it will be shown that Luther sees the analogies of the

philosophical talk of generation is allowed inside the theological region. When responding to the challenge that there is no inner-Trinitarian generation at all because whatever is generated is a subject of a *passio*, Luther says that the type of generation in the inner Trinity is an "inner passion" (*passio interna*).[209] While Luther does admit the possibility of the analogy to shed light on the mystery, its use in the disputational genre is hardly perceptible. The cautious reference to the analogy is related to Luther's view of reason in the disputation. Reason is called upon to establish the boundaries of the theological region. Its function is to exclude foreign determinations rather than to proclaim central words of comfort. In other genres, such as the sermon, reason is located more at the center of the theological region. Its use is to illustrate what is meant by terms for hearers that are not from the onset regarded as heretics but for those seeking God's mercy. On the other hand, the disputation guides reason to investigate the terms of propositions. Articulated is an understanding of the terms that is less evocative and decisively reflecting its location in an academic setting.

THE DIVINE INFINITY: CONCLUSION

On the surface, Luther's rhetoric could suggest a defiant stance against any activity of reason. In the genre of the disputation, however, Luther's rhetoric is formed by his view of reason in distinguishing between regions and in determining the particular application of reason used to fit the study of its respective subject matter. By distinguishing between different senses of terms, reason is tested for its adequacy to study the finite entities with the

---

Trinity to be articulated in the eschatological-doxological language of Rom 11:36.

209. WA 39,2:308.4 (witness A; Major). The challenge of the opponent is: "Quicquid generatur, est subiectum passioni. Deus autem non patitur. Ergo non est generatio in divinis." Ibid., 307.25–26 (witness A). Luther's entire response is, "Dixi in hoc articulo novam esse faciendam grammaticam, et si vultis inferre passionem, inferte internam, non actionem aut passionem externam." Ibid., 308.3–5 (witness A). It remains an adjacent theme as to whether the proposition, "God dies," introduces a temporal change into the Triune eternity. For Luther, the proposition is true without qualifying the divine nature as vulnerable to death. The Christological proposition predicating human attributes *in concreto* to the divine nature, however, is rendered soteriologically harmful when divorced from an understanding of the nature of God as eternal. For soteriological certainty as well as for acknowledging what human salvation "cost God," the discourse of infinity must remain an integral moment in theological reflection. "Daher singen und rhu(e)men wir mit allen freuden, Das Gottes Son, der rechte Einige Gott, mit dem Vater und Heiligem geist, sey fur uns Mensch, Ein knecht, Ein sunder, Ein wurm worden, Gott sey gestorben, Gott trage unser sunde am Creutz, in seinem eigen leibe, Gott hat uns Erlo(e)set durch sein eigen blut." WA 54:92.13–17.

tools of natural philosophy, grammar, metaphysics, or logic, or to study the inner Trinity with the tools of theology. The excluding activity of reason was demonstrated in this section with respect to the concept of infinity. Luther excludes the actual and potential infinity used in the metaphysical region as well as the natural philosophical use of the term "generation." The equivocations Luther forces on the metaphysical region aim to block any impositions of natural reason onto the theological subject matter. Once the inferences drawn by natural reason are prohibited, Luther opens up the theological region and invites reason to understand the glorious mystery of the inner Trinity.

THE INNER TRINITY

By strictly setting the borders between Creator and creature, the center of the theological region is opened up for articulating a right understanding of the eternal Trinitarian relations. Luther's "I do not know" does not relegate the mystery to the silence of adoration, but it provides the starting point for reflecting on the inner Trinity.[210] In this section, I discuss a metaphysics, semantics, and logic that Luther uses to understand the inner Trinitarian proposition. I begin with a description of the discursive form common to structuring any medieval truth claim: the proposition. For Luther, the inner-Trinitarian proposition—that the three *res* are one and the same as the one *res*—serves as the basis for any further study on the theological determination of its terms. The terminology of *res* implies a metaphysical claim that will be analyzed in the second section. The third section isolates the semantic difficulty with how essence terms, such as "essential" and "Deus," are taken to refer to either the distinct *res* as person or the indistinct *res* as the divine essence. I explain how Luther arrives at his position that these essence terms supposit for the distinct *res*. In the fourth section, the discussion focuses on how Luther appeals to the terms *totus* and *solus*—known as "exponibles" in the Middle Ages—in order to explain how the essential attribute, "infinity," can be predicated of each

---

210. "Do muß man still schweigen vnd sprechen: Deus loquitur ibi, audio, esse unum Deum et tres personas, wie Das zugeht, nescio." WA 39,2:364.17, 365.1-3 (witness A; Hegemon); Luther adds the word, "credam," in Ibid., 364.10 (witness B). The C variant is: "Wie es zugehet, hic simpliciter tacendum est et credendum Deo, qui se ita cognoscendum in verbo suo nobis proposuit." Ibid., 364.29, 365.19-20 (witness C).

person.[211] The use of three tools of reason demonstrates the complex contours of the Trinitarian understanding that Luther articulates in conversation with the tradition of Trinitarian reflection before him.

THE INNER-TRINITARIAN PROPOSITION

The discursive backbone of scientific investigation, received from Aristotle's *De Interpretatione* into the medieval disputation, is the proposition.[212] All four of Luther's disputations on the inner Trinity can be seen to be summarized by the proposition: "It is an indisputable truth that God, who is one and Triune, is the sole Creator of all things outside himself."[213] The structure of Luther's proposition is commonplace in later medieval logic.[214] The proposition is composed of a *dictum*, formulated as an accusative plus infinitive, and a mode. The *dictum* signifies a state of affairs, and the mode "modifies" how the subject is related to the predicate. Handled in the section on tense and modality ("The Inner Trinity and the Discourse of Infinity"), the prefix "it is an indisputable truth" functions to denote what is signified by the accusative plus infinitive construction that follows. The mode of "indisputable truth" "modifies" the relation of the one God to the three persons. It denotes what is signified by the three *res* that are one and the same as the one *res* according to the modality of necessity associated with the truth claim that is valid for eternity. This type of mode corresponds to the axiomatic status of the proposition. It is curious that Luther proposes a proposition for dispute that is an axiom in the theological region. Given the situation of attack, Luther employs the disputation in order to defend the proposition as axiomatic in obedience to the Father's word (Matt 17:5).

Unpacking Luther's inner-Trinitarian understanding begins with the terms used in the proposition. In the medieval Arts faculty, the burden

---

211. *Totus* and *solus* are technical terms that have a variety of meanings. *Totus* can be translated as all, completely, or wholly, and *solus* can be translated as only, exclusively.

212. Aristotle summarizes the subject matter of his text, *De Interpretatione*, as the "statement-making sentence," propositions investigated under their grammatical-syntactical and logical-semantic aspects. *De int.* c. 4, 17a 4–5 [vol. 1, 26].

213. WA 39,2:287.13–14 (Major, thesis 5).

214. Nuchelmans discusses various types of propositions, and how they are understood to refer to a particular state of affairs. Represented in his study are: Abelard, Gregory of Rimini, William of Ockham and Robert Holcot. Nuchelmans, "The semantics of propositions," 200–207.

of analyzing propositions was shared between the grammarians and the logicians. The grammarians studied the eight parts of speech in order to arrive at rules of syntax.[215] The logicians studied the significations of terms in propositions.[216] Boethius, who translated Aristotle's *Organon* into Latin, is regarded to have founded the medieval study of logic.[217] His two works on the *Topics* gave medieval logic a foundation by representing Aristotle's topics in a series of axioms that were received into commentaries classifying inferences well into the fourteenth century.[218] The medieval logicians' focus on the way terms signify in propositions—i.e., or their supposition— led to refined statements of truth conditions for propositions of different logical forms. Although Ockham followed William of Sherwood and Peter of Spain in recognizing three kinds of supposition—simple, personal, and material—his nominalist conceptualist view of universals led him to say that terms have simple supposition for concepts.[219] Supposition theory made its way into medieval reflections on the Trinity in order to determine the referents of categorematic terms. Beginning with a debate against Scotus, Luther turns to consider the referent of the categorematic term *res* according to a metaphysical claim.

---

215. The study of grammar in the Middle Ages is considered to have its origins in the Stoa. Medieval grammar was based, to a great extent, on Priscian's sixth-century Latin grammar that was oriented to the work of Apollonius Dyscolus. Ebbesen, "Ancient scholastic logic," 109–11.

216. Ibid., 123.

217. The books of Aristotle's *Organon* were ordered by the third-century commentator, Porphyry, in the latter's *Isagoge*. The *Isagoge* was translated into Latin by Boethius in the late fourth century, and it served as the foundation for medieval logical study. The *Organon* is composed of the *Categories, De Interpretatione, Prior Analytics,* and *Sophistici elenchi* as well as the *Posterior Analytics* and the *Topics* that most medieval logicians placed after the *Prior Analytics.* Ibid., 101–105, 121–23.

218. Aristotle's *Topics* are primarily dialectical strategies of argumentation and principles confirming the strategy. An axiom is a self-evident principle of a demonstrative science from which consequences, governed by laws of inference, are deduced.

219. Philotheus Boehner, *Collected Articles on Ockham,* 233–48; Idem, *Medieval Logic: An Outline of Its Development from 1250 to c. 1400,* 27–36.

THE SCOTUS-OCKHAM TRAJECTORY: THE METAPHYSICAL
CLAIM OF THE INNER-TRINITARIAN *RES*

The determination of the inner-Trinitarian subject matter begins, for Luther as for Scotus and Ockham before him,[220] by ascribing to the terminology stipulated by the Fourth Lateran Council.[221] Using the terminology of *res* found in the records of the Church Council held in 1215, Luther writes two theses in the Alberus disputation.

> 12. For reason cannot comprehend that one indistinct thing is three distinct things. ...
>
> 15. Yet it is truly impossible that one indistinct thing is three most distinct things.[222]

With this gesture acknowledging the terminological authority of the tradition before him, Luther disavows the demonstrability of the inner-Trinitarian proposition, that the one indistinct *res* is one and the same as the three distinct *res*. The inner-Trinitarian proposition is an article of faith and an axiom in the theological region. For the purpose of showing what can be conceived, Luther seizes on one word of the proposition that he will carefully study. He turns to the term, *res*, a metaphysical term. Although Luther wants to distinguish a theological from a metaphysical use, his retention of *res* situates his arguments in a debate fought two centuries before.

Luther works out his understanding of the theological aspect of "three things are one thing" by retracing a trajectory from Scotus to Ockham. With

---

220. Scotus, *Lectura* I, d. 5, q. u, n. 16 [Vaticana XVI, 416]; d. 23, q. u, n. 23-24 [Vaticana XVII, 309]; cf. *Ord.* I, d. 5, p. 1, q. u, n. 8-9 [Vaticana IV, 13-14]; n. 26 [Vaticana IV, 24-25]; Ockham, *Ord.* I, d. 2, q. 11 [*OTh* II, 374].

221. One looks in vain through the records of the Fourth Lateran Council for the proposition, "tres res sunt una res." Rather, the records state that "alia et alia persona sunt una res." The term, "res," refers to the divine essence. "... quia quaelibet trium personarum est illa res, videlicet substantia, essentia seu natura divina." DS *804 (Against Joachim of Fiore); "Licet igitur 'alius sit Pater, alius Filius, alius Spiritus sanctus, non tamen aliud'..." DS *805 (Against Joachim of Fiore). There is no reference to "three res." DS *803-804 (Against Joachim of Fiore); McCord Adams, *Ockham*, vol. 2, 999.

222. WA 39,2:254.5-6, 11-12 (Alberus, theses 12 and 15). In the genre of the sermon, Luther formulates the mystery of the Trinity in this manner: "Und ist ein unbegreifflich ding, quod istae tres distinctae personae unus Deus. Quomodo unus, cum video tres?" WA 49:308.11-12 (Sermon on the First Sunday after Epiphany, Jan. 13, 1544, Rörer version).

a few concise theses, Luther sets up the metaphysical stage on which he forgets the principle of charity and criticizes Scotus's attempt to explain the Trinity by appealing to the latter's notion of formal and real distinctions. Luther begins his criticism: "Scotus and the Scholastics barely and coldly console us with their formal and real distinctions."[223] Extending the attack against both Scotus and the Scholastics for rhetorical force rather than for scientific precision, Luther mounts an attack against the power of the formal and real distinctions to explain the relation of the one indistinct *res* to the three distinct *res*.

The formal and real distinctions form a significant part of Scotus's metaphysics. They are used to explain how an attribute can be predicated of a substance, how attributes are predicated of God, and how the three inner-Trinitarian persons are distinguished from each other as well as how each person is distinguished from the divine essence.[224] According to Scotus's moderate realist view of universals, particulars are metaphysically constituted by a nature common to numerically distinct particulars and an individuating principle or "thisness" (*haeccity*).[225] Although really one and the same *res*, Scotus insists that the nature and the individuating principle are formally distinct.[226] Unlike mere distinctions of reason, formal distinctions are distinctions in reality within one and the same *res* prior to and independent of any act of conceiving of it. With respect to the divine attributes, the attributes are formally distinct from the essence. In terms of the inner Trinity, the person is distinct formally from the essence, and each person is really distinct from the other two persons.

Luther criticizes Scotus on the grounds that reason is incapable of comprehending both the formal and the real distinctions.[227] He is not the first

---

223. WA 39,2:287.29–30 (Major, thesis 14).

224. McCord Adams has isolated two different accounts of Scotus's formal distinction. McCord Adams, *Ockham*, vol. 1, 22–29.

225. *Ord.* II, d. 3, p. 1, q. 1, n. 4 [Vaticana VII, 393]. Unlike Aquinas, Scotus rejects the idea that matter is an individuator or even matter signed by quantity.

226. Ibid., q. 5–6, n. 188 [Vaticana VII, 483–84].

227. "Nam utcunque ista subtiliter dici videantur, ratio tamen non capit distinctionem formalem esse aliam, quam realem seu essentialem." WA 39,2:254.3–4 (Alberus, thesis 11). A similar criticism is found in the Hegemon disputation. "Scotus facit triplicem distinctionem, aliam formalem, aliam realem etc. Ista quidem possunt dici, sed non ratione comprehendi, quia ratio vel animus non potest concipere aliam distinctionem, quam formalem." Ibid., 364.2–8 (witness A); see also: 364.1–6 (witness B); 364.25–27 (witness C; Hegemon).

theologian to criticize Scotus in this regard. In the fourteenth century, Ockham launched a similar criticism against Scotus. From the perspective of his understanding of universals, Ockham rejects the formal distinction and shows how Scotus's position is contradictory even if the formal distinction is granted.[228] Ockham claims that it is impossible for any creature to be formally distinct from another without being really distinct.[229] When Luther attacks Scotus on the issue that reason is incapable of grasping the formal and the real distinctions, his agreement with Ockham is established on the basis of Ockham's metaphysical claims.

When the formal distinction is used to explain the relation between the inner-Trinitarian persons and the essence, Ockham's position changes slightly. For Ockham, and then more radically for Luther, less confidence is placed in the capacity of metaphysical reason to explain or even conceive of the Trinitarian distinctions and their relation to the divine essence. Ockham's position reveals a humility in the face of the incomprehensible Trinitarian mystery. He gives a form of words, but can offer no semantics for it. "There is some sort of nonidentity between the divine nature and the divine supposit. It can be said that in a good sense they are distinct formally, although they are not really distinct."[230] What Scotus can metaphysically assert about the inner-Trinitarian persons, which are formally distinct from the divine essence, Ockham can only modestly veil in a terminology that, for him, is an exception to what unaided natural reason can conceive. Ockham's general rejection of Scotus's formal distinction as a metaphysical description of entities leads to a hesitation within the theological region about using a terminology related to metaphysics.

Luther not only follows Ockham by rejecting the formal and real distinctions to explain the metaphysical composition of particular entities. In the theological region, he goes one step further by rejecting the terminology of the formal distinctions altogether. If reason cannot even grasp the formal and real distinctions in the metaphysical region, then their importation into the theological region to articulate the way in which the Trinitarian

---

228. For a detailed study of Ockham's criticism against Scotus's formal distinction, see: McCord Adams, *Ockham*, vol. 1, 46–59.

229. Ockham, *Ord.* I, d. 2, q. 1 [*OTh* II, 14].

230. Ibid., q. 11 [*OTh* II, 364]; d. 30, q. 4 [*OTh* IV, 366]; quoted in McCord Adams, *Ockham*, vol. 2, 1001.

person is distinguished from the essence must also be rejected.[231] In this regard, Luther's position is similar to one held by Robert Holcot. Holcot, with whom Luther possibly made an acquaintance through Biel's commentary on the *Sentences*, explicitly rejects the formal distinction to articulate the inner-Trinitarian proposition.[232] The argument Holcot advances is one that blocks the formal distinction, articulated in the region of natural philosophy, from conceiving of a subject matter that is governed by faith and "above natural philosophy." Although no evidence is found in the doctoral disputations for a similar argument in Luther's rejection of Scotus on this point, Luther's position agrees with both Ockham and Holcot with respect to differing regions. In the metaphysical region, Luther and Ockham agree that reason cannot grasp the formal and real distinctions, and in the theological region, Luther and Holcot agree that the distinctions cannot even

---

231. A series of theses in the Alberus disputation also shows Luther's attack against Scotus's formal and real distinctions. According to Luther, the distinctions cannot be used to conceive the distinction between person and essence, or the distinction between person and person. The series of theses begins with the difficulty of how the distinction between person and essence is made. Not even the angels, who see the Trinity in eternity, can comprehend how the person is distinguished from the divine essence. "7. Quomodo distinguatur persona a divinitate ipsa, non est rationis inquirere, nec angelis comprehensibile. 8. Imo periculosum et cavendum est ibi, ullam esse putari distinctionem, cum sit quaelibet persona ipsissimus et totus Deus." WA 39,2:253.13-16 (Alberus, theses 7 and 8). Luther follows by rejecting Scotus's formal and real distinctions. "9. Frustranea est cogitatio et nihili Scoti et similium, qui formalem vel aliam distinctionem hic finxerunt. 10. Nesciunt quid loquantur vel affirment, dum talibus sapientiae pharmacis rationem iuvare volunt. 11. Nam utcunque ista subtiliter dici videantur, ratio tamen non capit distinctionem formalem esse aliam, quam realem seu essentialem." Ibid., 253.17-18, 254.1-4 (Alberus, theses 9-11).

232. Holcot writes that no expository syllogism can demonstrate that three *res* are one *res*. "Similiter, non est inconveniens quod logica naturalis deficiat in his quae fidei sunt, et ita sicut fides est supra philosophiam naturalem ponens res produci per creationem, ad quam philosophia naturalis non attingit." Robert Holcot, *Sent*. I, 4 [5. Lyons], *Exploring the Boundaries of Reason*, 26n72. Holcot rejects the various distinctions between essence and relation. For Holcot, to be distinguished means to be distinct. "Ideo ad articulum dico sex: primo quod essentia et relatio in divinis non distinguuntur realiter nec modaliter nec formaliter nec ratione nec convertibiliter nec aliquo alio modo. Ratio est quia sic distingui infert distingui, sequitur enim: distinguuntur ratione, ergo sunt distincta ratione vel secundum rationem, et ultra: ergo sunt aliqua distincta secundum rationem, ergo sunt aliqua, consequens falsum, ergo etc." Holcot, "Utrum cum unitate essentiae divinae," a. 3 in ibid., 102-103, lines 1001-1006. Holcot's criticism of the formal distinction to articulate the relation of the person to the essence is mentioned by Biel in *Sent*. I, d. 2, q. 11, a. 3, dub. 2 (M) in Gabrielis Biel, *Collectorium circa quattuor libros Sententiarum*, vol. 1, 200-201. Biel argues against Holcot's rejection of the formal distinction to even conceive the distinction between person and essence. Biel, needless to say, argues the position that, "[h]aec est similia scientibus logicam et quid dicit distinctio formalis clara sunt." Ibid. [201].

be used to speak of what the angels themselves find incomprehensible.[233] In this regard, Luther finds himself in the company of those who would expel altogether the "violent" terminology of the formal and real distinctions.[234] Luther differs from his student Major who, under the advising of Melanchthon, continues to use Scotus's terminology of the real and formal distinctions to articulate both the formal distinction between person and essence and the real distinction between person and person.[235] If particular terms are rejected, the question then arises as to how Luther articulates what he considers must be defended against attack.

Luther privileges a discourse to articulate the inner Trinity that looks remarkably traditional. Moving beyond both Scotus and Ockham, Luther turns back to a terminology he claims is biblical. It is the language of "person," "hypostasis," and "substance" (*substantia*). In the Hegemon disputation, Luther states, "But since sacred Scripture says that the three persons are distinct hypostases, it would say that nature is three substances. But Scotus does not understand himself. Three hypostases are distinct in such a way that one generates another and they spirate the third."[236] Of course, Luther, as a lifelong translator of Scripture, knows that the technical Trinitarian term "hypostasis" does not appear in the Greek New Testament to stand for what the Latin tradition labels "person" (*persona*). In this excerpt, Luther also reflects terminological inconsistency by claiming the three distinct persons to be three substances (*substantias*). In this matter, Luther is fully aware of the third- and fourth-century terminological confusion in the Greek between οὐσία (*ousia*) and ὑπόστασις (*hypostasis*).[237] Another disputation records Luther's rejection of the term "substance" to stand for "hypostasis" for reasons of terminological

---

233. WA 39,2:253.14 (Alberus, third clause of thesis 7).

234. "Quod autem Scotus dicit, realem aliam esse [quam formalem], violenter dictum est." Ibid., 364.8–10 (witness A; Hegemon); similar to 364.24 (witness C).

235. See Major's preparatory notes in ibid., 333.14–18.

236. Ibid., 364.10–16 (witness A; Hegemon).

237. "Dicunt quidem et illi hypostasim; sed nescio quid volunt interesse inter usiam et hypostasim: ita ut plerique nostri qui haec graeco tractant eloquio, dicere consueverint, υἱαν οὐσιαν, τρεῖς ὑποστάσεις, quod est latine, unam essentiam, tres substantias." Augustine, *De Trin.*, 5, 8 (10) [PL 42:917].

consistency.[238] Although Luther is convinced that the words he is using for the inner Trinity are biblical, he is appealing to extrabiblical sources for a language whose difficulties are known even to Augustine.

Another curious statement illustrates how closely Luther sees the dogmatic terminology to be intertwined with the biblical subject matter. A reference to a biblical passage, 1 John 5:7–8, appears in only the C version of the Hegemon disputation: "We cannot claim this according to reason, but sacred Scripture says in 1 John 5: 'Father, Son, and Holy Spirit, these three are one.'"[239] Luther's reference to 1 John 5:7–8, the three witnesses in heaven and on earth, as a statement in Scripture for the three Trinitarian persons is, on the surface, surprising. In his 1522 translation of Erasmus's Greek New Testament, Luther follows the humanist's early historical-critical lead by rejecting the two verses of the *textus receptus* absent from every known Greek manuscript except four, quoted by none of the Greek Fathers, and first appearing in a Greek version of the Latin records of the Fourth Lateran Council.[240] Erasmus's third edition of his New Testament includes these verses that Luther also interprets in his second commentary on 1 John.[241] Luther excludes the verses from the 1545 publication of his Bible translation, although in the same year he refers to them in the Hegemon disputation. Luther is perhaps alluding to a traditional source that uses the controversial Johannine passage as a biblical warrant for the three persons. In the records of the Fourth Lateran Council, the section on Fiore's anathematization appeals to this verse.[242] Luther's agreement with the renowned church council on a theological rather than on a historical point betrays a position that does not divorce the tradition from Scripture, but rather appreciates the two in harmony.

In articulating the inner-Trinitarian relations, Luther finds the appropriate terminology in Scripture, in the church fathers, and even in the

---

238. "Est una substantia, non tres. Esset quidem non impium, dicere, esse tres substantias, sed tamen nos debemus in docendo docere, esse unam essentiam tantum, ut vitetur amphibologia. Ita etiam nos scriptura docet. Nam in vulgo est una certa regula retinenda de trinitate, quam proponit scriptura, ne perturbentur mentes." WA 39,2:282.10–14 (Fabricius).

239. Ibid., 384.27–29 (witness C; Hegemon). A and B do not refer to this biblical passage.

240. Bruce M. Metzger, *A Textual Commentary on the Greek New Testament*, 715–16.

241. Ezra Abbot, "I. John V. 7 and Luther's German Bible," 459–60.

242. DS *803 (Against Joachim of Fiore).

Fourth Lateran Council. For Luther, the literal mention of technical Trinitarian terms in Scripture is marginal to his primary concern with the capacity of language to refer to the subject matter. Rather than distinguishing historically between biblical and extrabiblical language, a position he concedes to the heretics, Luther opens up the theological region to a flexible terminology that is unified at the level of the *res*, as an extended discussion of this theme in the Major disputation shows.[243] The choice of terminology seems to reflect a privileging of the three persons, a choice most likely based on the Apostles' Creed's confession of faith in the Father, Son, and Spirit. Luther uses terms that pick out the three *res*, whether in the terminology of the Fourth Lateran Council that Luther qualifies with the term "distinct things" (*distinctas*) or in equivalent Greek and Latin terms.[244] With respect to the one "indistinct *res*," Luther's strategy takes the logical form of showing how each person is divine.[245] When Luther rejects the terminology of the formal and real distinctions, he is not, on the surface, battling the philosophy of the Scholastics as such. At the level lying beneath the polemic is a serious engagement with the theological tradition that includes the "Scholastic" church council of Fourth Lateran. Luther's

---

243. In the Major *disputatio*, Luther discusses at length the theme of the relation between extra-biblical Trinitarian terms and the subject matter of Scripture. He disputes the "vocabulistae," who say that only the use of a particular term can demonstrate the truth of the Trinitarian article. "Adversarii nostri volunt, articulos nostros non satis esse fundatos in scripturis, suntque vocabulistae, cupiunt enim, vocabulis sibi demonstrari veritatem articuli trinitatis, sicut et Ariani sibi volebant ostendi vocabulum ὁμοούσιον." WA 39,2:305.1-4 (witness A; Major). Luther claims that, in the case of the extra-biblical term, "Erbsünde," Erasmus is wrong to demand the original term. "Vocabulum quidem non est in Paulo, sed res ipsa et in Paulo et in tota scriptura sacra habetur et exprimitur expressis verbis." Ibid., 305.6-7 (witness A). For Luther, the diversity of terms, in both Scripture and in the Creeds, does not connote a difference at the semantic level of the *res*. Luther can refer to terms, such as "persona," and claim, "[i]ta tres personae et unus Deus in scriptura clarissime probantur." Ibid., 305.9-10 (witness A). Even the terms, "trinitas" or "hypostasis," can be appropriate to articulate the biblical subject matter. "Tres res sunt una res, verum est, etiam ipsum vocabulum trinitatis non esse expressum in sacris scripturis, ich muß aber pro captu infirmorum so reden. Et veritas nostrae fidei loqui ita requirit; ὑπόστασις significat personam Patris, Filii et Spириritus [sic] sancti, wiltu ein ander vocabulum gebrauchen, so thue es, modo ut rei proprietatem serves et exprimas." Ibid., 305.14-19 (witness A). By uniting the terms at the level of the *res*, Luther can then attribute the speech of the prophets, of David, and of the church councils to the Spirit.

244. "… et tres (ut vocant) personas verissime distinctas." Ibid., 253.2-3 (Alberus, second clause of thesis 1). "Simul nihilominus haec unitas, est trinitas, seu trium personarum distinctarum divinitas." Ibid., 287.19-20 (Major, thesis 8).

245. For Luther, the unity of the three persons is articulated in Scripture, particularly in Rom 11:36, as a doxology. See: ch. 4, "Doxology as Eschatological Impulse."

ultimate intention is to stake out the terminological trajectory of a tradition that can be sustained against a rationalist reduction while inviting the
employment of reason to defend the divinity of all three persons.

The terminological stress on the three persons opens up a front at which
Luther must define the term *res*. The term appears twice in the proposition:
as a "distinct *res*" and as an "indistinct *res*." In order to understand what is
meant by the term, Luther turns to the tool of metaphysics and specifies the
way in which the three *res* are metaphysically constituted. The particular
theological concern with the inner-Trinitarian *res* requires thematizing
the ontological status of the relation, an issue Luther addresses in light of
Augustine's concern that accidents cannot be spoken of God.[246] Augustine's
view, intended to avoid the modalism associated with the relation as an
accident, remained normative for any discussion of the ontological status
of the three distinct *res*. The point of controversy in the Hegemon disputation reflects Augustine's contribution but couches his concern in the medieval terminology of relations. Luther airs his worry about the "moderns"
who regard the relation to have minimal ontological status: "A relation in
things does not create the thing, as they say, a relation is of minimal existence and does not subsist *per se*; indeed, according to the Moderns it is
nothing."[247] The terms Luther uses in this thesis are common to a medieval
discussion of the three entities of a relation, the two related things (*relata*)
and the relation obtaining between them, either in reason or in reality. The
moderns who regard the relation as nothing could be the moderns whom
Ockham criticizes in his own work.[248] On the other hand, Ockham himself

---

246. In *De Trinitate*, Book 5, Augustine writes that nothing can be said of God according to
accidents. Accidents impose a change into the thing (*res*). God, by definition, cannot change.
What can be said of God must be said, "according to substance or relation." "Accidens arguit
semper aliquam rei mutationem." *De Trin.*, 5, 4 (5) [PL 42:913]. "In Deo nihil secundum accidens dicitur, sed secundum substantiam aut secundum relationem ... nec tamen omne quod
dicitur, secundum substantiam dicitur." Ibid., 5 (6) [913–14]. In Luther's *disputatio* on John 1:14,
the respondent cites the above passage from Augustine. "Augustinus ait: Omnia, quae sunt
in Deo, sunt substantialia, etiam, quae nobis sunt accidentia, ut loqui, sperare, intelligentia
Dei est substantia. Ita quod apud philosophos est accidens, apud Deum est substantia." WA
39,2:20.5–8 (witness A).

247. Ibid., 340.1–2 (Hegemon, thesis 12).

248. McCord Adams, *Ockham*, vol. 1, 144. McCord Adams writes that the moderns whom
Ockham is criticizing view the metaphysical world as a composite of substances, quantities
and qualities as absolute things. Relations are "respects" or relative things (*res relativae*).
Ibid., 144–46.

could be the "modern" whom Luther challenges. According to Ockham, the relation as really distinct from substance and quality is "nothing"; the claim that relative things are really distinct from absolute things is only marginally intelligible.[249] For unaided natural reason, Ockham maintains that "it is easier to deny than to sustain" that which opposes the authority of Scriptures and the church.[250] Luther is correct in attributing to the "moderns" the position that the relation has an ontological status significantly less than that of the substance. The issue, however, differs when the inner Trinity is considered in the theological region.

Luther formulates the question concerning the person—the distinct *res* as a relation—in the context of determining the priority of either the relation or its related things (*relata*). A thesis in the Hegemon disputation articulates Luther's argument that is curiously couched in both the Augustinian terminology of the relation and in the language of the "distinct things" (*res distinctae*) used by both the Fourth Lateran Council and the late Scholastics. "Relation here [in divine things] does not prove a distinction of things, but distinct things prove that there is a relation."[251] Luther argues that, in view of the inner Trinity, the *relata* have priority over their relations.[252] In this regard, Luther follows Ockham, who finds it is easier to hold that the three really distinct things constituting the three persons are really distinct absolute things.[253] There are no relative things (*res*) in God. Ockham, however, concedes to the authority of the saints, who define the inner-Trinitarian *res* as three relations.[254] Luther agrees with Ockham, although he uses the

---

249. Ibid., 268.

250. Ockham, *Ord.* I, d. 30, q. 1 [*OTh* IV, 306].

251. WA 39,2:340.6-7 (Hegemon, thesis 14).

252. In his commentary on Ps 51, Luther speaks of grace as a relation, rather than as a quality. "Gratia significat favorem ... Pertinet autem ad praedicamentum relationis, quod dixerunt Dialectici minimae entitatis et maximae virtutis esse, Ne putetis esse qualitatem, sicut Sophistae somniarunt." WA 40,2:421.21, 22-24 (Enarratio Psalmi LI, 1532/1538, to v. 12).

253. McCord Adams, *Ockham*, vol. 2, 1003-1004.

254. Ockham writes, "because the authorities of the Saints seem explicitly to posit relations in the Godhead—not merely that some relative concepts are truly predicated about the divine persons the way we say that Socrates is similar or that Socrates is father or son, but that there is there genuine real paternity and filiation, and that they are two simple things, one of which is not the other—therefore I hold with them that the divine persons are constituted and distinguished by relations of origin." *Ord. I*, d. 26, q. 1 [*OTh* IV, 156-57]; quoted in McCord Adams, *Ockham*, vol. 2, 1006. The Trinitarian relations, of which there are four (paternity, filiation, active and passive spiration), show the relations between the three persons to be

term "essential distinction" to indicate three absolute *res*.[255] When defining
the *res* as a relation, Luther, like Ockham, admits that, "in divine matters,"
the relation is the *res*, that is, the "hypostasis et subsistentia."[256]

Once Luther defines the inner-Trinitarian distinct *res* as a relation, he
can then turn to the metaphysical implications of his claim. Using language Ailly or Ockham would never have considered, Luther responds in
the Hegemon disputation that the person is constituted by two *res*. The
relation is one *res*, the essence of the Father is another *res*. The person is
constituted by the two *res*: the one distinct *res* as the relation, and the one
indistinct *res* as the divine essence.[257] Luther recognizes that he is speaking
"improperly."[258] His position, however, does not shy away from making a
metaphysical claim. The language of two *res* that constitute the distinct
person implies that each person is metaphysically constituted by the one
distinct *res* as its distinguishing characteristic, the relation, and the one
indistinct *res* as the essence. The quasicompositional language of Scotus's
own formal distinction appears again when Luther appeals to the terminology of the Fourth Lateran Council. The use of the term *res* forces Luther
to make a claim concerning the person's metaphysical constituents. This

---

identical with the personal properties. The relations are different from the five notions that
are five ways in which we know the Trinitarian persons to be distinguished from one another:
the innascibility of the Father, the active generation of the Father and passive generation of
the Son, the active spiration of both Father and Son and the passive spiration of the Spirit.
From the four relations, one arrives at three persons when active and passive spiration are
conflated in the one person of the Spirit. Werbick, "Trinitätslehre," 504-5.

255. "... sed si qua est essentialis distinctio, sunt tres personae." WA 39,2:364.27 (witness
C; Hegemon).

256. "In divinis relatio est res, id est, hypostasis et subsistentia. nempe idem, quod
ipsa divinitas; tres enim personae, tres hypostases et res subsistentes sunt." Ibid., 340.3-5
(Hegemon, thesis 13). Luther's insistence on the distinct persons as relations cannot be interpreted as a tension between the person and the relation, as Peters suggests. See: Peters, "Die
Trinitätslehre," 570.

257. "Persona constituitur ex relatione et essentia Patris, sic oportet nos loqui, quamvis
non proprie sic loqui possumus, tamen ad res explicandas ita dicendum est: Natura et relatio faciunt personam, relatio est res, essentia est res, et sunt duae res constituentes unam
personam." WA 39,2:384.9-17 (witness A; Hegemon); similar to ibid., 384.9-22 (witness B);
"Persona constituitur ex relatione et ex essentia tamquam ex duabus rebus." Ibid., 384.29-30
(witness C). In contrast to Luther, Major uses the term, "formal distinction," to distinguish
the person from the essence. Major avoids making Luther's metaphysical claim concerning
the two *res* that constitute the person. "Hoc sic intellige: Essentia divina et persona sunt una
res, una essentia divina." Ibid., 333.15-16 (Major's preparatory notes).

258. "Das ist impropriissime geredt, aber wie soll man ihn thun, natura humana non
potest aliter, es heist crede." Ibid., 384.17-20 (witness A; Hegemon).

claim will figure significantly in Luther's determination of the referents of Trinitarian terms.

In order to understand how the three distinct *res* or persons are distinguished from the one indistinct *res* or essence, Luther engages Scotus through the lens of Ockham's rejection of the formal and real distinctions in the metaphysical region. Luther parts ways with Ockham with respect to the term "formal distinction," which Ockham uses hesitantly in the theological region to articulate, rather than to explain, the way in which the person is distinguished from the essence. Located in Ockham's trajectory, marked by an increased distancing of the metaphysical from the theological region, Luther resorts to a distinct terminology to articulate the inner-Trinitarian proposition in various ways. Using a combination of Scripture, Greek, Latin, and Scholastic terms, Luther's terminology reflects a theological privileging that points to the three distinct *res* as persons. Luther follows the authority of the saints, as Ockham does, by defining the persons as relations. Luther then moves beyond Ockham, although he veers remarkably close to Scotus, when he makes a claim in the theological region concerning the metaphysical constituents of the term "distinct *res*." The person, or distinct *res*, is understood to be metaphysically constituted by two *res*: the distinct *res*—that is, the person as relation—plus the indistinct *res*—or the divine essence. Behind Luther's metaphysical claim, however, lurks the danger of positing a quaternity in the inner Trinity. His claim could be interpreted as positing four *res*: three relatives and the essence. The next section explains how Luther possibly detects the quaternity in his own position and resolves it by attributing this problem to the master himself, Peter Lombard.

THE SEMANTICS OF THE INNER-TRINITARIAN PROPOSITION

Consistent with a late medieval debate, Luther is concerned with determining the particular referent of the key term "essence" in propositions of the type, "essence generates essence" and "essence is generated by essence." The aim of this section is to clarify the meaning of the relevant Trinitarian propositions by explaining what entities the terms stand or supposit for in specific propositional contexts. This discussion is motivated by a lengthy debate, recorded in the Major disputation, between Luther and a decision made at the Fourth Lateran Council. In this debate, Luther detects a contradiction in Lombard's position and takes issue against the council's decision that upheld Lombard and anathematized Fiore. The reasons for Luther's attack play a role in showing how Luther understands "essence" to supposit relatively, rather than absolutely, for the Trinitarian persons.

The subject matter for dispute is presented when Luther considers propositions articulating the inner-Trinitarian generation of the Son. An entry into the debate is found in a proposition advanced by the master of the *Sentences*, Peter Lombard, and articulated as a thesis in the Major disputation: "Even the Master of the Sentences did not satisfactorily teach that the divine essence neither generates nor is generated."[259] Luther notes the contradiction when he considers the problem of what "essence" stands for in propositions such as, "essence generates essence" or "essence is generated from essence." The equivocal terminology of essence terms—such as "essence," "God," or "light"—as Luther states during the course of the Major disputation, requires an explanation at the semantic level in order to demonstrate the distinctions of referents in propositions that, at the terminological level, reveal no difference.[260] When the property of generation from an origin used to distinguish between the three persons is eliminated, as in Lombard's proposition, then no distinctions between the persons can be claimed. Luther begins to address this difficulty by turning to a debate between Lombard and Fiore held a few centuries earlier.

Luther is most likely acquainted with the controversy between Lombard and Fiore through Ailly's discussion of the debate in the latter's *Sentences*

---

259. Ibid., 287.31-32 (Major, thesis 15). In the *Sentences*, Lombard's proposition is formulated: "Ad quod, catholicis tractatoribus consentientes, dicimus quod nec Pater genuit divinam essentiam, nec divina essentia genuit Filium, nec divina essentia genuit essentiam." *Sent.* I, d. 5, c. 1 (15) [81]. The Fourth Lateran Council paraphrases Lombard in its decision against Fiore. "Quoniam quaedam summa res est Pater, et Filius, et Spiritus Sanctus, et illa non est generans, neque genita, neque procedens." DS *803 (Against Joachim of Fiore). During the course of the disputation, Luther frequently responds at great length to this thesis. See: WA 39,2:291.19-23, 292.1-2 (witness A); 294.21, 295.1-5 (witness B); 295.13-21 (witness A-B); 313.26-29, 314.1-8 (witness A); 316.16-25 (witness A); 317.6-15 (witness A; Major). During the course of the Major *disputatio*, a vigorous debate erupts between Luther and his colleague, Bugenhagen. Initially siding with Lombard, Bugenhagen is eventually persuaded to accept Luther's proposition. "Pomeranus: Placet mihi solutio: Essentia divina generat essentiam divinam; propterea papa, cum non intelligeret sententiam Ioachimi, non debebat eum damnare." Ibid., 314.9-11 (witness A).

260. "Res ergo ipsa aequivocatur." Ibid., 316.24 (witness A).

commentary. In a series of Major theses, Luther traces the controversy back
to Ailly's disagreement with Lombard.[261] Ailly, who formulates his defense
of Fiore in the pluperfect subjunctive tense,[262] is lauded by Luther as the
"Cardinal of Cambrai, the most learned of the Scholastics."[263] Lombard, who
"defined this abomination standing in the holy place [Dan 7]," is castigated.[264]
Luther is familiar with Fiore's criticism of Lombard and the former's anathematization.[265] Fiore's book, *De unitate trinitate*, lost to theological posterity,
accuses Lombard of positing a quaternity in the inner Trinity. The Fourth
Lateran Council cites Lombard in support of the council's condemnation of
Fiore's position.[266] The theme of the quaternity is what motivates Luther to
seize the opportunity to debate on the referents of essence terms. Luther,
like Ailly, begins the debate by agreeing with Fiore.

There are two possible explanations for Luther's agreement of Fiore's
criticism of Lombard. In a Major thesis, Luther applauds Fiore's charge
that Lombard posits a quaternity in the inner Trinity.[267] From the evidence
in the Major disputation, it is possible to reconstruct how Luther arrives
at the four terms he accuses Lombard of positing. In the fourteenth century, the difficulty of four terms is related to the expository and communal
syllogisms in which four terms are used. Luther explicitly mentions both
syllogisms in the disputation on John 1:14.

---

261. Ibid., 287.31-32, 288.1-22 (witness A; Major, theses 15-26). Luther alludes to the conflict
at the Fourth Lateran Council (1215) in the disputation on John 1:14. "Hic papa vestigatione
monachorum determinavit contra abbatem et damnatam sententiam magistri ... et conclusit
sit papa, quod essentia divina non generat." Ibid., 17.19-20, 21 (John 1:14, 1539).

262. Ailly, known for his sympathies with the conciliar movement, formulates his
defense of Fiore in the more careful pluperfect subjunctive. "Sic igitur ... potuisset respon-
deri Magistro, ante determinationem." Ailly, *Sent.* I, q. 5, E. On Ailly's choice of verb tense,
see: White, *Luther as Nominalist*, 216.

263. WA 39,2:288.21 (Major, thesis 36).

264. Ibid., 288.9-10 (Major, thesis 20).

265. "16. Sed recte ab Ioachim Abbate reprehenditur, quod in divinis quaternitatem
asseruerit. 17. Nec quidquam facit C. Firmiter de Trinitate, probans Magistrum et damnans
Abbatem." Ibid., 288.1-4 (Major, theses 16 and 17).

266. DS *803-808 (Against Joachim of Fiore).

267. WA 39,2:288.1-2 (Major, thesis 16).

16. This expository syllogism is valid: The Father generates in
    divine things. The Father is the divine essence. Therefore the
    divine essence generates. ...

18. This common syllogism is valid: The entire divine essence is
    the Father. The Son is the divine essence. Therefore the Son
    is the Father.[268]

In these syllogisms, four terms, whose referents must be correctly
determined in order for the logic of the syllogism to hold, are used. The
difficulty rests on the referent of the term "essence." If "essence" is taken
to supposit for both the person and the essence, four terms are posited: the
Father, the Son, the Spirit, and the divine essence. The issue of the quaternity turns on the referent of the term "essence." In an exchange in the
Major disputation, Cruciger plays the role of the opponent and argues with
the following syllogism to conclude with Lombard's position: "The essence
of the Son is not really distinct from the essence of the Father, but what
generates is distinct from what is generated. Therefore the essence does
not generate."[269] If the essence is defined as that what neither generates
nor is generated, it appears that the essence is distinguished from the persons, who are defined by their relations of origin. When the essence term,
"essence," is taken to refer to either the divine essence or to the three persons in propositions of the type, "the divine essence generates the divine
essence," a quaternity of terms is posited. The subject, "essence," stands
for the one *res*, and the direct object stands for the person. For Luther, the
quaternity is avoided when the term "essence," in both the subject and
predicate position, is taken to refer to a distinct *res*.

A more likely problem that Luther detects in Lombard's proposition is
the difficulty of positing not a quaternity of terms but at least a binity of
divine substances. This problem seems to arise when an inference from
what applies to creatures in a given sense is applied to theology in another
sense. If "generates" in "the divine essence generates the divine essence"
means the same thing in the theological region as it does in biology, the
subject, "essence," would have to stand for one divine essence, and the

---

268. Ibid., 4.24–25, 28–29 (John 1:14, theses 16 and 18). The syllogisms are discussed at
length in Ailly, *Sent.* I, q. 5, Z–FF.

269. "Filii essentia non est realiter distincta ab essentia Patris, sed generans est quiddam
distinctum a genito. Ergo essentia non generat." WA 39,2:315.24–25 (witness A; Major).

direct object, "essence," would have to stand for another divine essence. By taking both the subject and the object to each stand for one divine substance, the theological absurdity of two divine essences would result. Two essences are posited when both subject and object stand for the one *res* in the proposition "the divine essence generates the divine essence." In the Major disputation, Major responds that this absurdity arises by transferring the argument from biology to theology: "I respond to the major premise, which only speaks about creatures, while everything that is generated is generated by another."[270] Major's response could be what Luther has in mind when the latter accuses Lombard of positing at least a binity of divine substances. In two Major theses, this accusation is summarized.

21. The Master fears (it seems) that two or three essences would be named if one were born from another.

22. At the same time, the following is to be feared: that two or three gods would be made if one is generated from another.[271]

Luther agrees with Major that one must not simply transpose the term "to generate" (*generare*) from biology into theology.

The difficulty Luther addresses has to do with distinguishing, at the semantic level of the proposition, between the distinct *res* as the origin of generating and the indistinct *res* as ungenerated and ungenerating. For Scotus, the formal distinction was supposed to help conceive the distinction between the two *res*. The danger of a quaternity does not figure into the positions of either Scotus or Ockham because the formal distinction serving to distinguish between person and essence is not a real distinction. Luther, who eliminates the terminology of the formal distinction, must find another way to articulate the distinction.

He turns to supposition theory in order to explain the referents of essence terms, such as "essence." For Luther, the term "essence" in propositions of the type "the divine essence generates the divine essence" must

---

270. Ibid., 302.8–9 (witness A). The opponent concludes his syllogism with Lombard's proposition, "Ergo non generat substantia divina." Ibid., 302.6–7 (witness A). Major points out why the opponent's syllogism is invalid. "Non igitur valet ad argumentatio a creaturis ad creatorem." Ibid., 302.10–11 (witness A).

271. Ibid., 288.11–14 (Major, theses 21 and 22).

supposit for the distinct *res* as begetting, begotten, or spirated.[272] Luther supports his view of the semantics of such propositions by appealing to Augustine, Hilary, and the Creed. "Since therefore Lombard, drawing on Hilary and Augustine, took 'light from light' relatively, there was no reason why he could not understand the term 'essence' in the same way, especially since he accepted all other terms relatively, such as the terms 'God,' 'nature,' etc."[273] Luther views the referents of essence terms in propositions of the type "the divine essence generates the divine essence" to be governed by the model "God from God" or "light from light." In the Creed, the rule is stipulated as a semantics signaled by the grammatical distinction between the accusative and the ablative case: "God from God, light from light."[274] The grammar is established by the Creed. It can neither be explained by reason,[275] nor does it follow the rules of predication established in the region of logic.[276] As the rule of faith (*regula fidei*), the Creed dictates the semantics of propositions to show the persons as the referents of the essence term, "essence." Luther concludes by pointing out a blind spot in Lombard's position. Lombard, Luther sympathetically remarks, does refer to the Creed.[277] Therefore, the master should have known better.

---

272. Ockham distinguishes between three kinds of supposition: personal, simple, and material. Boehner, *Collected Articles on Ockham*, 237–41. Boehner defines the three kinds of supposition as follows. "Personal supposition is had when the subject or predicate of a proposition supposits for its significate and has a significative function." Ibid., 237. "Simple supposition is had when a term supposits or stands for an intention of the mind, that is, for a concept or mental term when it has no significative function." Ibid., 238. Boehner uses as an example for simple supposition, "Homo est species." "Material supposition is had when a term does not supposit in its significative function, but supposits either for a spoken or written sign only." Ibid., 239. Boehner's example for material supposition is, "Homo est nomen."

273. WA 39,2:295.16-20 (witness A–B; Major). For other propositions rehearsing this point, see: Ibid., 288.5–6 (Major, thesis 18); 291.19–23 (witness A); 292.1–2 (witness A); 294.21, 295.1–5 (witness A); 295.13–21 (witness A–B); 313.26–314.8 (witness A); 316.16–25 (witness A); 317.6–15 (witness A); 370.21–27 (witness C; Hegemon).

274. Luther cites this portion of the Creed in ibid., 317.13 (witness A; Major). This is similar to: "Filius est lumen de lumine, deradiatio et character substantiae." Ibid., 296.14–15 (witness A–B).

275. "… non potest rationem dicere, quare non et vocabulum essentiae relative acceperit." Ibid., 295.20–21 (witness A–B).

276. "In praedicamento substantiae non docetur, radios claritatis esse de substantia solis, et tamen Spiritus sanctus ita loquitur." Ibid., 296.15–16 (witness A–B). The rule of predication is stated by Major during his doctoral disputation. "Quare tenenda est haec regula: Subiecta debere intelligi, ut concedunt praedicata proprie sumpta." Ibid., 316.11–12 (witness A).

277. "Inde recte dicitur, Deum de Deo, lumen de lumine." Ibid., 317.13 (witness A).

Luther uses semantics to distinguish between "essence," taken to stand for the divine essence, and "essence," taken to stand for the divine person. The distinction is made between the absolute and the relative supposition of the term "essence." Luther summarizes the rule of supposition as follows: "To be God is absolute, but to generate is relative."[278] Lombard could reject the proposition "essence generates essence" by taking the "essence" to have absolute supposition for the one *res*—that is, the "essence."[279] For Luther, on the other hand, the verb "generates" makes the subject and the direct object to have relative supposition for the persons in the same proposition. "That is, it is certain that essence, taken absolutely, does not generate, but taken relatively it generates. When it is said: 'The Father generates,' there, I must say, the article of our faith is rightly articulated."[280] The term "essence" in the proposition under consideration must be taken to supposit for the two persons in order to show that one person, the Father, generates another person, the Son. In view of the relative supposition of the term, "essence," Luther can oppose the decision of the Fourth Lateran Council favoring Lombard,[281] and can even accuse Lombard of proposing a new opinion.[282] The terminology of the distinction Luther makes is flexible. Sometimes he distinguishes between absolute and relative supposition.[283] Other times, he distinguishes between substantial or essential supposition and personal supposition.[284] The variable terminology underlines the one point that "generates" dictates relative supposition.

---

278. Ibid., 316.24–25 (witness A).

279. "Hic quaeritur an Pater genuit divinam essentiam vel ipsa Filium, an essentia genuit essentiam vel ipsa nec genuit nec genita est." Lombard, *Sent.* I, d. 5, c. 1 (15) [80].

280. WA 39,2:316.20–22 (witness A; Major).

281. "Magister ita arguit hoc, quod essentia non generet essentiam, quia vult essentiam retinere absolute, contendit, non sumi relative, ... Iam contra Magistrum et papam dicimus." Ibid., 295.13–14, 15–16 (witness A–B). Lombard cites both Augustine and Hilary to hold the contrary opinion in this debate. *Sent.* I, d. 5, c. 1 (15) [83]. The reference to Augustine is taken from: *De Trin.*, 7, 1 (2) [PL 42:936]; Ibid., 15, 20 (38) [PL 42:1087]. The reference to Hilary is taken from: *De Trin.*, 5, num. 37 [PL 10:155 A].

282. "Una quaeque persona est natura divina et essentia, darumb solt er nicht haben novam opinionem dran gehenckt." WA 39,2:314.6–8 (witness A; Major).

283. Ibid., 291.22 (witness A); 295.14, 16–17, 19–21 (witness A–B); 313.29 (witness A); 314.2–3 (witness A); 316.16, 20, 25 (witness A); 317.12–14 (witness A).

284. Ibid., 316.23 (witness A); 369.1–3 (witness A; Hegemon); 370.10, 13–14 (witness A); 370.10, 15, 17–19 (witness B); 370.21–23, 27 (witness C). Luther's distinctions can function in the same way as Ailly's distinction between mediate and immediate supposition. Ailly, *Sent*

By using semantics, Luther is able to distinguish between the three persons in specific propositions. The only way in which the distinctions between persons can be articulated is by taking essence terms, such as "essence" and "God," to have relative supposition in the context of verbs, such as "generates" and "spirates," "to be generated" and "to be spirated." The source for this semantics is the Creed. For Luther, the proposition "essence generates essence" follows the model dictated by the creedal confession, "God from God" and "light from light." The essence term cannot be taken to stand for the divine essence but must stand for a person according to its relation of origin. Another issue at stake is related to propositions such as the one articulated by Lombard and cited at the Fourth Lateran Council. In this proposition, the verb "to be" might be understood to refer the essence term to the divine essence. This use might be what Lombard has in mind when he writes that the divine essence, as the "three persons in common," neither generates nor is generated.[285] Luther, however, is not prepared to concede to Lombard an absolute supposition for "essence" in the context of discussing "to be generated." The claim of absolute supposition for essence terms does not play into Luther's determination of the inner Trinity. There is another way in which Luther treats essence terms in propositions. In order to predicate attributes, such as infinity, of the divine essence constituting each person, Luther appeals to a type of medieval logic. The logic of the *totus* and *solus* is the final theme to which we will now turn.

I, q. 5. Immediate supposition determines the referent of the term, "essence," to stand for the divine essence. Mediate supposition determines the referent of "essentia" to stand for the person that is constituted by the divine essence. Ibid., M. In ibid., N, Ailly formulates the rule for mediate and immediate supposition. Luther rejects Ailly's terminology in the 1517 "Disputatio contra scholasticam theologiam" [WA 1:226.19-20 (thesis 46)], and again in the disputation on John 1:14 [WA 39,2:4.15-16 (thesis 12)]. A further issue to be explored regards whether Luther rejects Ailly's terminology and replaces what it stands for with the terms, "absolute" versus "relative," or whether Luther entirely rejects Ailly's understanding of "immediate" and "mediate" supposition.

285. "Hic autem nomine 'essentiae' intelligimus divinam naturam, quae communis est tribus personis et tota in singulis." *Sent.* I, d. 5, c. 1 (15) [81].

THE LOGIC OF THE *TOTUS* AND *SOLUS*

The final determination of the inner Trinity reflects Luther's concern with predicating essential attributes, such as "infinity," of the three persons. If infinity can be predicated of the divine essence, the difficulty then arises as to how the same attribute is predicated of the three persons that are distinguished from each other by relations of origin. The theme of predicating essential attributes of each person differs from the above discussion on essence terms that supposit relatively for distinct persons. In this section, I intend to show how Luther determines the distinction between the essence and the person by using two terms commonly identified with the medieval study of logic, *totus* and *solus*. By making use of this logic, Luther can predicate attributes of each person while avoiding the case in which the attribute is predicated of one person to the exclusion of the others.

The question of Trinitarian predication is initially posed by the young Luther. While reading book seven of Augustine's *De Trinitate*, Luther expressed concern over the particular problem of predicating attributes of the three persons, attributes that Augustine predicates substantially of the essence.[286] A question scrawled on the margins is later thematized at length in the Trinitarian disputations. In the Hegemon disputation, Luther mentions the divine attribute he will predicate of the three Trinitarian persons.[287] By definition, "a characteristic proper to God is to exist from himself."[288] For Luther, the divine attribute must be predicated of the essence in such a way as to account for its predication of each Trinitarian person. He turns to the tool of logic in order to accomplish this task.

Luther's reflection on the *totus* and *solus* in inner-Trinitarian propositions takes up an issue that fascinated late medieval logicians. Syncategorematic terms—for example, conjunctions, adverbs, and

---

286. WA 9:20.22–28 to Augustine, *De Trin.*, 7, 1 (1) [PL 42, 931–33]. White discusses in detail Luther's marginal notes to Augustine's *De Trinitate* on the theme of predicating attributes of the essence. White, *Luther as Nominalist*, 196–200.

287. "Deus Pater exsistit a se ipso ab aeterno, Filius exsistit a se ipso ab aeterno, Spiritus sanctus exsistit a se ipso ab aeterno." WA 39,2:398.9–12 (witness A; Hegemon); similar to: Ibid., 398.9–12 (witness A). The variant in ibid., 398.26–27 (witness C), predicates "exsistit a se ipso" of each person while omitting the "ab aeterno." With these propositions, Luther concludes the Hegemon disputation that are his last recorded statements spoken in the disputational genre.

288. Ibid., 397.17–18 (witnesses A–B); 397.31 (witness C).

prepositions—were the primary objects in the medieval consideration of logic.[289] Differing from categorematic terms, syncategorematic terms do not themselves signify or supposit completely as subject or predicate, yet their addition to propositions determines how the categorematic term supposits or stands for things in the proposition and so affects the truth conditions of the proposition. Supposition theory analyzes how syncategorematics affect the distribution of the subject or predicate term with which they are connected. Particularly the modern logic (*logica moderna*) found supposition theory useful in fallacy detection. Words of conjunction—conditionals, disjunctions, inclusions, and exceptives; even verbs technically known as exponibles,[290] and the term, "infinite"—would be strategically placed in a proposition, thereby altering the ability of the categorematic term to pick out a referent.[291] Some terms—such as infinite, *totus*, and *solus*—were taken to function categorematically sometimes and syncategorematically other times, depending on their location in the proposition. For example, Ockham considers the terms *solus* and *totus* to be taken either categorematically or syncategorematically.[292] The question soon arose as to how the exponibles could be used to determine propositions found in the theological region.

In his early days as a student, Luther paid attention to the logic of syncategorematic terms with respect to inner-Trinitarian propositions. White discusses Luther's 1509 marginal notes to Lombard's *Sentences*, in which Luther carefully considers the placement of the term *solus* in the proposition "God is the Father or Creator."[293] Luther's concern reflects a common

---

289. Categorematic terms are either subject or predicate terms, and coincide with groupings defined by medieval grammarians: names (both substantival and adjectival), personal and demonstrative pronouns, and verbs (excluding auxiliary verbs). The verb, "esse," is an exception and can be considered as both a categorematic and a syncategorematic term. Norman Kretzmann, "Syncategoremata, exponibilia, sophismata," 211–12.

290. For example: "differ," "vult," "incipit," "desinit," and "esse." The verb, "esse," is a special case. It can be used categorematically or existentially, as in the proposition, "Socrates est," or syncategorematically or copulatively, as in the proposition, "Socrates est homo." Ibid., 214, 211nn5, 7.

291. See 88n145.

292. For Ockham's treatment of the term, "solus," see: Ockham, *SL* II, c. 17 [*OPh* I, 296]. For his analysis of the term, "totus," see: Ibid., c. 6 [*OPh* I, 296].

293. White, *Luther as Nominalist*, 206–10. White discusses Luther's marginal notes [WA 9:46.23–29; 47.1–2] to Lombard's *Sent.* I, d. 21, c. 2 (88) [175–76]. Lombard's *quaestio* is posed in the following manner: "Utrum possit dici: solus Pater est Deus, solus Filius est Deus, solus Spiritus Sanctus est Deus, vel Pater est solus Deus, Filius est solus Deus, Spiritus Sanctus est solus. Deus." Ibid. [175].

medieval topic of discussion. Also found in Ockham's work, the inner-Trinitarian proposition "only the Father is God" is discussed as to how the term *solus* can be taken either categorematically or syncategorematically and, if taken either way, why the proposition is true or false.[294] The early Luther picks up Ockham's discussion of the semantic alterations taking place when *solus* determines the subject and the predicate term.

Luther's interest surfaces again in the Alberus and Major theses. In the Alberus theses, the distinction between the feminine noun "person" (*persona*) and the masculine noun "God" (*Deus*) makes it grammatically more obvious how the *solus* and *totus* are distributed. *Sola* is distributed to person, and *totus* is distributed to God. Grammatically less perspicuous are the Major theses, in which Luther uses two feminine nouns, person (*persona*) and divinity (*divinitas*), to which the *solus* and *totus* are distributed.[295]

2. Each of these persons is totally God, outside of whom no one else is another God.

3. Nevertheless, it is not possible to say that each person alone is God.

4. For it would be the same to say that God is no one, since each separate person would be wholly God separately, and each person would be separate. ...

6. It is different to say: (a) One person is wholly God, and (b) one person alone is one God.

8. Indeed, it is dangerous and one must avoid supposing that there is any distinction, although each person is totally God and the selfsame God.[296]

Considering thesis two, the term *totus* distributes God in the proposition "is totally God." When *totus* is associated with God in the predicate position, the true proposition [theses 2 and 6a] is articulated: "one person is wholly

294. Ockham discusses the question in *Ord.* I, d. 21, q. u. "Utrum haec sit concedenda de virtute sermonis 'Solus Pater est Deus'?" [*OTh* IV, 40–44].

295. "9. Ut quaelibet persona sit ipsa tota divinitas, ac. si nulla esset alia. 10. Et tamen verum est, Nullam personam esse solam, quasi alia non sit, divinitatem." WA 39,2:287.21–23 (Major, theses 9 and 10).

296. Ibid., 253.4–8, 11–12, 15–16 (Alberus, theses 2, 3, 4, 6 and 8).

God." In this true proposition, *totus* is taken syncategorematically. In the proposition, "is wholly God," *totus* is taken syncategorematically because it distributes for each person that is constituted by the essence.[297] It "does not distribute the term outside itself to which it is added."[298] If it were taken categorematically, *totus* would distribute the God to the God made up of its parts; *totus* would distribute the God to the God as "person plus person plus person."[299] In the inner Trinity, however, three persons are one and the same as the essence. Thus, *totus* cannot be distributed categorematically in the proposition "the whole God is one person." *Totus* must be taken syncategorematically—that is, it distributes the God to each person. In view of the metaphysical claim that "person" is constituted by the indistinct *res* plus the relation, the logic of the *totus*, taken syncategorematically, provides the rule for showing that the entire divinity is distributed to each person.

The exponible, *solus*, is also used in order to make true propositions about the divine persons. The issue is whether or not *solus* is used as an excluding term in propositions such as "the Father alone is God" and "each person is God." Luther considers theses three, four, and six to be false, because *solus* is used in these propositions as an exclusive term. In thesis three, *sola* added to person makes it stand for the included person. Luther considers thesis three to be false and gives his reason in thesis four. *Solus* is an exclusive term because it makes the proposition say that "this person and no other person is God" (thesis four). Luther says if any person is excluded, the whole God is excluded, which is absurd. In thesis six, *sola* is distributed to "person," which is false. Thus, in thesis six, the proposition "one person alone is God" is false.

Luther might have appropriated Ockham's extended discussion of *solus* in order to make his claims. Ockham states that theologians usually understand the *solus* in the proposition "the Father alone is God"[300] to be taken in

---

297. If *totus* is taken syncategorematically, it distributes for all its integral parts. For example, "Totus A est B" is equivalent to "quaelibet pars A est B." See: Ockham, *SL* II, c. 6 [*OPh* I, 268]. I would like to thank Marilyn McCord Adams for these references to Ockham and their explanations in her unpublished notes to this theme.

298. Kretzmann, "Syncategoremata, exponibilia, sophismata," 233.

299. Taken categorematically, *totus* means the same thing as "perfect" or "composed of all its parts." For example, "Totus A est B" signifies the same as "A est B."

300. *Ord.* I, d. 21, q. u. [*OTh* IV, 40–44]. Lombard discusses the question, "Utrum possit dici: solus Pater est Deus." in *Sent.* I, d. 21, c. 2 (88) [175].

the exclusive sense and, therefore, syncategorematically.[301] Taken in this way, *sola* distributes *persona* in the exclusive sense. The proposition "the Father alone is God" signifies that only the Father, to the exclusion of the other two persons, is God. This proposition is absolutely false. Luther's three theses distribute *solus* to person in the exclusive sense and therefore, syncategorematically. Ockham explains why these propositions are false.[302] The proposition "the Father alone is God" signifies that "God" is true of "the Father," and "God" is truly denied of whatever "the Father" is truly denied. In the inner Trinity, the Son is also God, but not the Father. "The Father alone is God" is false when taken exclusively, because "the Son is not the Father, and the Son is God." If, on the other hand, *solus* were taken categorematically, it would not be an exclusive expression. The term *solus* implies that the term to which it is added is solitary.[303] "The Father alone is God" would imply that the Father, who is solitary, is God. This proposition is false. Taken either syncategorematically or categorematically, *sola*, distributed to *persona* in propositions of the type, "one person alone is God," makes the propositions false.

The use of the two exponibles, *solus* and *totus*, forms the way in which Luther understands how attributes are predicated of each Trinitarian person. Luther's inner-Trinitarian logic clarifies his underlying metaphysical claim that each Trinitarian person is constituted by the indistinct *res* and the distinct *res*, or the relation of origin. The logic of *totus* shows that the indistinct *res* is distributed to each person; the logic of *solus* shows that each person—but not to the exclusion of the other persons—is the divine essence. How essential attributes can be predicated of each person, but not of each person alone, is achieved through the syncategorematic function of the term *totus* in a proposition. The distribution of the *sola* to *persona* shows that essential attributes cannot be predicated of one person to the exclusion of their predication of another person. For Luther, each divine attribute can be said to be predicated of the divine essence that is distributed to each

---

301. *Ord.* I, d. 21, q. u. [*OTh* IV, 42]; *SL* II, c. 17 [*OPh* I, 296].

302. The summary of Ockham's argument is taken from Marilyn McCord Adams's unpublished class notes to Ockham, *Ord.* I, d. 21, q. u.

303. Ockham, *SL* II, c. 17 [*OPh* I, 296].

person, although not to each person exclusively.[304] Luther concludes the Hegemon disputation by predicating the attribute "existing from himself from eternity" of each person. "God the Father exists from himself from eternity; the Son exists from himself from eternity; the Holy Spirit exists from himself from eternity."[305] Each term supposits personally for Father, Son, and Spirit, and the essential attribute of "existing from himself from eternity" picks out its referent through the indistinct *res* constituting each person.

THE INNER-TRINITARIAN PROPOSITION: CONCLUSION

In the theological region, Luther sets up an intramural theological discussion in order to determine his understanding of the inner Trinity. The subject matter, articulated in the propositional language shaped by the genre of the disputation, is given an initial contour in a debate situated between Scotus and Ockham. Refusing to use the terminology of the real and formal distinctions to articulate his inner-Trinitarian understanding, Luther draws on other ways to define how the persons are distinguished from the essence and how the persons are distinguished from each other. Luther discusses the metaphysical implications of the terminology of *res* that he receives from the Fourth Lateran Council. Luther claims that the three distinct *res*, one and the same as the one indistinct *res*, are each constituted by the distinct *res* as a relation and the indistinct *res* as the divine essence. The distinct *res* as persons are defined by their relations of origin. Luther turns to the semantics of the inner-Trinitarian proposition in order to show how essence terms can be used to distinguish between the relations of origin in propositions of the type "God from God." The discussion

---

304. Luther's view can be critically compared to Pannenberg's approach who, in receiving Cremer's nineteenth-century text, *Die christliche Lehre von den Eigenschaften Gottes* (1897), distinguishes between the negative attributes of the essence, such as infinity, that serve as preliminary and abstract metaphysical determinations of the concept of God and the concrete attributes derived from Scripture, such as love and mercy. For Pannenberg, the abstract attribute of infinity is determined by a preliminary, or metaphysical knowledge of the divine essence. This attribute is predicated of the unity of the essence. Concrete attributes are not appropriations, but are the one work of God in creation accomplished by the three persons. Pannenberg predicates these concrete attributes of the three persons acting in the essential unity of an economic dispensation. Pannenberg, *Systematische Theologie*, 416–29.

305. WA 39, 2:398.9–12 (witness A; Hegemon); similar to: Ibid., 398.9–12 (witness B). Omitting the "ab aeterno," the C version predicates "exsistit a se ipso" of each person. Ibid., 398.26–27 (witness C).

of the referents of essence terms is staged as a feisty debate, with Luther, Ailly, Fiore, Augustine, and Hilary on one side, Lombard and the Fourth Lateran Council on the other. The outcome, supported by Augustine and Hilary, is the model established by the Creed; essence terms used in propositions distinguish between the persons and are taken relatively rather than absolutely. Based on the metaphysical claim of the two *res* constituting the person and connected to the semantics of essence terms suppositing for distinct persons, the logic of inner-Trinitarian propositions explains why each person is constituted by the relation plus the whole essence. The exponible *totus*, taken syncategorematically, is used in propositions to govern the predication of essential attributes to each Trinitarian person; the exponible *solus*, also taken syncategorematically, hinders this predication to the exclusion of the others. By using the logic of *solus* and *totus* in his determination of the inner-Trinitarian propositions, Luther shows an unhindered transfer of medieval logic into the theological region.

CONCLUSION

In the last years of his life, Luther thematized his understanding of the Trinity in four doctoral disputations. Motivated by his concern to comfort consciences terrified by demonic attacks and to train theologians to articulate the truth of the inner Trinity against the heretics, Luther makes use of the medieval academic genre of the disputation. Below the surface veneer of Luther's theological exclusivity is a sophisticated use of reason that cannot be easily dismissed by pitting philosophy against theology or reason against faith. The study of Luther's Trinitarian disputations has shown how necessary it is to closely view aspects of his Trinitarian understanding in order to gain a balanced and rich picture of his use of reason in the theological region.

Luther's discriminating use of reason has been introduced by the way in which Luther regards the various academic regions in the medieval university. From this regional perspective, we have seen how Luther conceives the attacks from the boundary of the theological region to motivate a defense at the center. At the boundary, heretical attacks threaten to separate the Father from the Father's word, and reason, reduced to the spatiotemporal level, threatens the theological determination of the infinity associated with the eternal generation of the Son. For Luther, the practice

of the disputation aims to demarcate the boundaries from which the attacks
are launched and to articulate a right understanding of the center. The dual
rational discourse of the heretics and the philosophers prompts Luther to
insist on the Spirit's speech as the source of any knowledge of the inner
Trinity. Luther attributes all "improper" language of the inner Trinity,
whether in Scripture or in the church councils, to the Spirit, who alone,
in his outer-Trinitarian location, speaks of the inner-Trinitarian relations.
Once the center has been established, Luther proceeds to hinder a determination of terms, such as "infinity" and "generation," that are used in the
regions of metaphysics, natural philosophy, and biology.

In order to understand a subject matter dependent on the divine speech
for its articulation, Luther resorts to using both biblical and dogmatic language. Luther's terminological repertoire emphasizes the three res as distinct persons. On the basis of this distinctive language, Luther makes use
of some tools of reason in order to articulate how the three res as persons
are one and the same as the indistinct res as the divine essence. By rejecting
the formal and real distinctions, Luther uses metaphysics to show how the
three persons are each constituted by the relation and the divine essence.
Semantics is required to show how essence terms in inner-Trinitarian
propositions supposit for the persons who are distinct from each other by
virtue of their relations of origin. The logic of the totus and solus is used to
explain why essential attributes can be predicated of the divine essence, as
well as of each person, although not to the exclusion of the other persons.

Through the process of the disputation, Luther succeeds in excluding a
determination of the term "infinity," used in the metaphysical region, while
making a claim in the theological region regarding the metaphysical constituents of the Trinitarian person. Luther excludes a natural philosophical determination of the term "infinity" and discusses the term as a divine
attribute that is predicated of each person. A biological determination of
generation is excluded, while semantics is used to determine the referents
of essence terms. Luther's theological exclusivity reflects his conviction
that the inner Trinity is a subject matter revealed only in the theological
region. Nevertheless, the contours of his Trinitarian understanding are
formed by claims of metaphysics, semantics, and logic.

When the form of the proposition is privileged to articulate the eternal relations of the inner Trinity, the category of narrative is excluded

from the discussion. The exclusion of narrative is related to the form in which the subject matter is articulated. In the genres of the hymn and the sermon, the inner Trinity is viewed as the origin of the narratives of outer-Trinitarian advent and revelation. In the disputation, the inner-Trinitarian proposition is understood to refer to an eternal *res* that is outside the creature; even though the verbs are tensed, no narrative movement can be applied to the subject matter. The trace of the *promissio* has been detected in this chapter's discussion of the attacks against weak Christians. When certainty in the eternal benefits of Christ is eroded, the Christian's faith is shattered. One aspect of locating the *promissio* in propositional discourse has to do with the necessary truth claim of the inner-Trinitarian generation of the Son. Bound together with the Son's generation from the Father is the *promissio* that the benefits of Christ are true for eternity. It is, however, only when the outer Trinity is fully explicated as a narrative in the genres of the hymn and the sermon that the inner-Trinitarian location of the *promissio* comes to view.

3

Luther's Understanding of the Trinity in the Hymn, "Now Rejoice, Dear Christians" (1523)

The hymn "Now Rejoice, Dear Christians" offers a presentation of Luther's Trinitarian understanding, conceived in narrative form and articulated in a language generated by the genre of the hymn of praise.[1] The category of narrative is not foreign to many interpretations of Luther's renowned hymn. I focus on its literal beginning—the advent of the Spirit—as well as the genre in which the subsequent narrative is cast. This investigation is guided by the perspective that Luther composed his hymn in the genre of the hymn of praise. By identifying the hymn's genre with the psalm of praise and its language with various types of Psalms, I unfold an approach to the hymn that is then used to view the narrative from the inner to the outer Trinity and the *promissio* as its central plot.

LUTHER AND THE HYMN

The hymn is frequently characterized as a genre particular to Luther's Reformation activity. Luther's hymn compositions were popularized at an early stage in the Reformation and can be regarded as a great contribution to the singing tradition of the church. The hymn Luther wrote in 1523, "Now Rejoice, Dear Christians," betrays both continuity and discontinuity with the medieval tradition of hymnody. The hymn, its text, and its melodies, will first be introduced against the backdrop of Luther's hymn-composing practices. In order to set the stage on which the subsequent interpretation

---

1. The text to "Nun freut euch, lieben Christen gmein" is found in AWA 4:154-57 (cf. WA 35). The first verse will be cited according to "Melodie A" in AWA 4:154. Subsequent verses will be cited according to AWA 4:156-57. The hymn is also found in WA 35:422.22-425.24. Subsequent references to "Nun freut euch" will be given in the text by the verse followed by the line number. A modern German version of Luther's hymn is given by: Martin Brecht, "Erfahrung— Exegese—Dogmatik. Luthers Lied 'Nun freut euch, lieben Christen gmein'," 96–97.

is dramatized, the hymn's genre will be determined to be a song of praise. The second part of this section shows how Luther understands the psalm hymn's text according to its connection with music and as the narrated praise of God's redemptive action in Christ. The psalm hymn as a poetic work based on a particular psalm text is to be distinguished from a use of the term that defines the psalm hymn as a hymn of praise.[2] It is to this latter definition that I will appeal in order to study the hymn under investigation.

TEXT AND MELODY

The hymn "Now Rejoice, Dear Christians" was one of Luther's earliest hymns to rapidly gain widespread popularity. A broad sheet dated inaccurately to 1524 is the only preserved individual copy of what is supposed to have circulated in 1523.[3] The broad sheet was quickly taken up in the three editions of Johann Gutknecht's *Hymnal of Eight (Achtliederbuch)* that were printed in Nürnberg between 1523 and January 1524.[4] "Now Rejoice, Dear Christians" headed the collection that included eight hymns, four written by Luther and four by Paul Speratus.[5] The *Hymnal of Eight (Achtliederbuch)* was soon followed by two larger hymnbooks also including Luther's hymn. These two editions, the Maler and Loersfeld editions, were printed in July 1524 in Erfurt.[6] Since its earliest public appearances, "Now Rejoice, Dear

---

2. I would like to thank Christa Reich for pointing out this distinction to me in a personal conversation on Oct. 5, 1998 in Mainz. I am also grateful to her for corrections to this section that she recommended during this conversation.

3. Philipp Wackernagel, *Bibliographie zur Geschichte des deutschen Kirchenliedes im XVI. Jahrhundert*, 49.

4. Although the title page reads "Wittenberg" as the city of publication, the type of print discloses its Nürnberger origin. See: Ibid. See also the following for an explanation of the inaccurate dating in the three editions of the *Hymnal of Eight (Achtliederbuch)*: Konrad Ameln, "Das Achtliederbuch vom Jahre 1523/24," 90.

5. Only one edition of the *Hymnal of Eight (Achtliederbuch)* assigns the 1523 date to both "Nun freut euch" and to Speratus' hymn "Es ist das Heil uns kommen her." The other three Luther hymns included in the earliest hymnbooks are: "Ach Gott, vom Himmel sieh darein" (Psalm 12) "Es spricht der Unweisen Mund wohl" (Psalm 14) and "Aus tiefer Not schrei ich zu dir" in its four-verse form (Psalm 130). For a list of hymns included in the *Hymnal of Eight (Achtliederbuch)*, see: Johannes Zahn, *Die Melodien*, 2.

6. WA 35:24.

Christians" has retained its status as a classic Luther hymn. It is currently enjoyed by both German[7] and English speaking congregations.[8]

The hymn "Now Rejoice, Dear Christians" sparked a period of prolific composition in this genre. Luther wrote the hymn shortly after the publication of his first song, "We Raise a New Song," which narrated the martyrdom of two Augustinian monks in Brussels on July 1, 1523.[9] In the eight months that followed, Luther wrote an astounding twenty-four out of a total of thirty-six hymns (thirty-seven, if the five verse variant of "Out of the Depths I Cry to You" is included).[10] The rapid circulation of these hymns was due to their reproduction in the popular late medieval medium of pamphlets (*Flugschriften*).[11] Together with hymns written by his colleagues, such as Elizabeth Cruciger and Paul Speratus, Luther's hymns were then compiled in choir books and congregational hymnbooks—for example,

---

7. EKG, no. 239.

8. "Dear Christians, Let Us Now Rejoice," trans. by MacDonald with slight revisions in LW 53:219-20. The translation by Richard Massie, "Dear Christians, One and All," is hymn no. 299 in the LBW.

9. For the text of "Ein neues Lied wir heben an," see: AWA 4:217-20. Luther refers to the event in a letter to Spalatin on July 22 or 23, 1523. "Ceterum, prima Iulii sunt exusti duo fratres nostri Augustinenses e captiuis Anttwerpiensibus, constanterque mortui in Christo, quorum vnus vocatur Iohannes Nesse, nondum triginta annorum." WABr 3:115.9-12 (no. 635). The historical occasion of the monks' martyrdom compelled Luther both to compose the hymn and to write a letter of comfort to the Christians in the Netherlands. The hymn was published towards the end of July or the beginning of August 1523, and the letter is dated to January 19, 1524. See: WA 12:73.1-80.26 for a description of the historical event and Luther's letter.

10. In addition to the psalm-hymns (12, 14, 67, 124, 128, and 130), Luther wrote seven Catechism-hymns ("Dies sind die heilgen Zehn Gebot"; "Mensch, willst du leben seliglich"; "Wir glauben all an einen Gott"; "Nun freut euch, lieben Christen gmein"; "Gott sei gelobet und gebenedeiet"; "Jesus Christus, unser Heiland, der von uns"; and "Mitten wir im Leben sind"), and eight *de tempore* hymns. The three Christmas hymns are, "Nun komm, der Heiden Heiland"; "Gelobet seist du, Jesu Christ"; and "Christum wir sollen loben schon." For Easter, Luther composed "Christ lag in Todes Banden" and "Jesus Christus, unser Heiland, der den Tod überwand," and the three Pentecost hymns, all translations of medieval hymns, are "Nun bitten wir den Heiligen Geist"; "Komm, Heiliger Geist, Herre Gott"; and "Komm, Gott Schöpfer, Heiliger Geist." In a Table Talk, Luther says that the Holy Spirit composed "Veni, sancte Spiritus." WATr 4:409.7-8 (no. 4627, May 26 and 30 and June 1, 1539).

11. Heiko A. Oberman, "Zwischen Agitation und Reformation," 287. *Flugschriften* as the mass communication medium of the late fifteenth and early sixteenth centuries have been the object of recent studies in communications, rhetoric-reception, economics, and poetry-hymnody. See: Rolf Wilhelm Brednich, *Die Liedpublizistik im Flugblatt des 15. bis 17. Jahrhunderts*.

the 1524 Wittenberg choir book, with harmonies composed by the cantor Johann Walter,[12] and the 1529 Wittenberg congregational hymnbook.

Although Luther has the reputation of being the father of Protestant hymnody, he was neither entirely original in his hymn-writing practices nor was he the first person in the 1520s to make use of the genre. The work of Elizabeth Cruciger possibly preceded Luther's compositions. Although controversial, an early dating sometime between 1521 and 1523 has been assigned to Cruciger's famous Epiphany hymn, "Lord Christ, the Only Son of God."[13] In the spring of 1523, Thomas Müntzer published his *German Church Office* before Luther had written his first hymn. Müntzer's groundbreaking liturgical work was a German rendition of the Latin mass that also included translations of ten medieval hymns.[14] While Luther was translating Erasmus's 1519 Greek New Testament in the Wartburg castle, Karlstadt introduced a German mass into the worship service in Wittenberg. Upon his return home, Luther rejected Karlstadt's mass because, according to Luther, it lacked a harmonious connection between text and music.[15] The

---

12. For a published facsimile of Walter's choirbook, see: Johann Walter, *Das geistliche Gesangbüchlein*. See the excellent article on the development of the 1524 Walter choir book in which Blankenburg argues that Luther's contribution is negligible. Walter Blankenburg, "Johann Walters Chorgesangbuch," 65–96.

13. For an example of an early dating, although debateable, of Creutziger's hymn, see: Elisabeth Schneider-Böklen, "Elisabeth Cruciger—die erste Dichterin des Protestantismus," 35. See: Creutziger's hymn in EKG, no. 46. See also: Elisabeth Schneider-Böklen, "Elisabeth Cruciger," ch. 1 in *Der Herr hat großes mir getan*.

14. Thomas Müntzer, *Deutsche Messen und Kirchenämter*. Müntzer's translations of Ambrose's hymn, "Veni redemptor gentium" ("O Herr, Erlöser alles Volks"), of Sedulius' hymn, "A solis ortus cardine" ("Laßt uns von Herzen singen"), and "Veni creator spiritus, mentes" by Rabanus Maurus ("Komm zu uns, Schöpfer") were also translated by Luther in 1523/24. The *Kirchenampt* was published in time for Easter 1523, and the eighteen hymns were ordered *de tempore* for Advent, Christmas, Passion, Easter, and Pentecost. Elliger claims that Müntzer used Luther's Bible translation for the *Kirchenampt*. See: Walter Elliger, *Thomas Müntzer*, 256–91, esp. 256–59. For discussions of Müntzer's translations and theology, see also: Siegfried Bräuer, "Thomas Müntzers Liedschaffen," 45–102; Karl Honemeyer, *Thomas Müntzer und Martin Luther*; and Bernhard Lohse, *Thomas Müntzer in neuer Sicht*.

15. Karlstadt wrote a German mass without also writing hymns for it. On the other hand, Müntzer translated hymns for his own mass. The following excerpt from a treatise written in 1525 discloses Luther's criticism of Karlstadt's mass. "Ich wolt heute gerne eyne deutsche Messe haben, Ich gehe auch damit umbe, Aber ich wolt ja gerne, das sie eyne rechte deutsche art hette, Denn das man den latinischen text verdolmetscht und latinischen don odder noten behellt, las ich geschehen, Aber es laut nicht ertig noch rechtschaffen. Es mus beyde text und notten, accent, weyse und geperde aus rechter mutter sprach und stymme komen, sonst ists alles eyn nachomen, wie die affen tun"; "Wider die himmlischen Propheten, von den Bildern und Sakrament (1525)," WA 18:123.19–24. The notes in ibid., 123 (footnotes 1 and 2)

Latin mass was promptly reinstated until the publication of Luther's own *German Mass* in 1526.[16] Luther's conservative attitude towards the Latin mass was consistent with his own hymn-composing activity. Luther made use of a variety of ways to write his texts. He translated Latin hymns into German, expanded one-verse medieval songs into many-versed hymns, added a Trinitarian doxology to the hymns, and, in view of his own musical compositions, borrowed from secular as well as sacred melodies.[17] Free compositions, without an original text as model, were the exception.

A long-standing debate surrounds the originality of Luther's hymn "Now Rejoice, Dear Christians." The debate is concerned with a few questions: whether Luther used a model or borrowed from various sources, and whether he was entirely original in inventing the hymn's formal structure and writing its material content. On the one hand, Jenny betrays his enthusiasm for what he sees to be "undoubtedly the most original of all of Luther's hymns."[18] The hymn is arranged not as an exegesis of a random set of biblical passages but as a summary of Luther's richly concentrated theology, which reveals Luther's own understanding of the scope of Scripture.[19] The controversy surrounds the original location of the text's central theme, which scholars agree to be the *promissio* in verse seven: "I am yours and

---

clearly refer Luther's criticism to his colleague Karlstadt, not to Müntzer. Both Müntzer and Karlstadt used medieval chanted monophony for their respective masses. Karlstadt justifies his preference for monophony, citing Eph 4:5: "Wenn du also willst, daß der Gesang in der Kirche weiterhin bleibe, so sei es der einstimmige Gesang, auf daß ein Gott sei, eine Taufe, ein Glaube, ein Gesang," quoted as thesis 53 in "De Cantu Gregoriano Disputatio (1522)," in Honemeyer, *Thomas Müntzer und Martin Luther*, 92n6. Luther also used monophony in his *German Mass*, but appreciated polyphonic settings for the choir that sang *alternatim* with the congregation. For two studies on the sixteenth and seventeenth-century practice of singing *alternatim*, see: Christoph Wetzel, "Die Träger des liturgischen Amtes im evangelischen Gottesdienst bei dem Apostel Paulus und bei Martin Luther," esp. 323–24; Walter Blankenburg, "Der gottesdienstliche Liedgesang der Gemeinde," esp. 627–31.

16. Luther's "Deudsche Messe und ordnung Gottis dienstns" was published in 1526. See: WA 19:72.1–113.20.

17. Jenny summarizes the plenitude of forms that Luther used in his hymn compositions: the psalm-hymn, the translation of medieval hymns, the catechism-hymn, the liturgical hymn, children's songs, the "Hofweise," the borrowing of secular and sacred melodies (contrafactures), and free compositions. Markus Jenny, *Luther, Zwingli, Calvin in ihren Liedern*, 15–29.

18. Ibid., 85. Hymns written with either seven or nine lines to each verse are characteristic of Luther's "freie Lieder oder Psalmlieder," tending to be free compositions without an explicit original text. Gerhard Hahn, *Evangelium als literarische Anweisung*, 21.

19. On the biblical texts Luther used in "Nun freut euch," see: Brecht, "Erfahrung—Exegese—Dogmatik," 98–104.

you are mine" (7.5). In early research on the hymn, some scholars claimed that Luther's text is based on a poem by Anna von Köln entitled, "Rejoice, Beloved Christian Community" (*"Ervreuwe dich, lieve Krystengemeyn"*).[20] Dated before Luther's hymn, von Köln's poem thematizes the typical minstrel love formula, the *promissio* appropriated later by Luther. More recently, historians have dated Luther's text before von Köln's and argue that Luther worked creatively without a model (*Vorlage*).[21] On the other hand, the hymn's originality regarding form is also a matter of debate. The hymn's structure discloses a form similar to a popular type of political song among the minstrels.[22] In his literary-linguistic research on Luther's hymns, Hahn reached a different conclusion. He judges that "Now Rejoice, Dear Christians" is an example of the "Luther-verse"—that is, seven lines consisting of two rhymed pairs concluding with an unrhymed line.[23] The debates over the literary and structural originality of the hymn should not detract from interest in investigating one of the most cherished hymns in Luther's repertoire. What the controversy suggests, at most, is that Luther's hymn-composing activity is located somewhere between original approach to the hymn's subject matter and continuity with the medieval tradition.

Four melodies have come to be associated with Luther's hymn in ways that also reflect early sixteenth-century practices. One of the four melodies was taken from a late fourteenth-century Easter processional, "Rejoice, Dear Christendom."[24] This borrowing of a melody from another source, called "sacred parallel-contrafacture," was a common strategy of medieval

---

20. Hans Joachim Moser, "'Nun freut euch, lieben Christen gmein': Die wahrscheinliche Vorgeschichte des Lutherliedes," 137. The love declaration stems from Walther von der Vogelweide: "Dû bist mîn, ich bin dîn." Cited by Paul Gabriel, *Das deutsche evangelische Kirchenlied von Martin Luther bis zur Gegenwart*, 33. The phrase also appears in Paul Gerhardt's hymn, "Warum sollt ich mich denn grämen?" based on Rom 8:35–39: "du bist mein, ich bin dein, niemand kann uns scheiden ... du bist mein, weil ich dich fasse ... da du mich und ich dich leiblich werd umfangen." EKG, no. 297, verses 11–12.

21. Paul Alpers, "'Nun freut euch, lieben Christen gmein' im Liederbuch der Anna von Köln," 133; Alfred Jung, "'Nun freut euch, lieben Christen gmein': Eine theologische Untersuchung des Lutherliedes," 201; Ludwig Wolff, "Zu Luthers Lied 'Nun freut euch, lieben Christen gmein,'" 102.

22. Ernst Sommer, "Die Metrik in Luthers Liedern," 48.

23. Hahn calls the form of Luther's hymn, seven lines to each verse, the "Lutherstrophe." Hahn, *Evangelium als literarische Anweisung*, 21.

24. AWA 4:57.

hymn composing.[25] As Lipphardt suggests, Luther was probably familiar with the German trope of the seven-line Mainz Easter processional,
from which he took the melody.[26] The first line of Luther's hymn "Now
Rejoice, Dear Christians" appeared at the beginning of the processional's
text and also in a fifteenth-century hymn with both a seven-verse and a
three-verse variation.[27] The melody of the processional was first borrowed
to accompany Speratus's hymn "Salvation Has Come Nigh" in the *Hymnal
of Eight (Achtliederbuch)*.[28] In *The Erfurter Manual (Erfurter Enchiridion)*,
published a year later, the same melody was assigned to Luther's hymn,
which appeared with a superscription referring to its original liturgical
site at Easter.[29] The second melody was composed by Johann Walter, the
cantor in Wittenberg.[30] The *cantus firmus*, or tenor, was first printed on the
left-hand side of Walter's 1524 choir book in accordance with the medieval
practice of placing the melody on the left-hand side of the page and the
text on the right-hand side. Walter composed a four-part harmony that he

---

25. The widest definition of a contrafacture is a song composition based on an available
melody (*super* or *contra cantilenam*). A parallel contrafacture is a composition of a sacred song
on a sacred melody. The prefix, "contra," pertains to a specific composition of either a sacred
song composed on a secular melody (sacred contrafacture) or a secular song composed on
a sacred melody (secular contrafacture). A secular parallel-contrafacture is a secular song
composed on a secular melody. See the following for a detailed definition of the term, "contrafacture": Walther Lipphardt, "Über die Begriffe: Kontrafakt, Parodie, Travestie," 104–111.
See also: Werner Braun, "Die evangelische Kontrafaktur," 89–93. Sommer claims that Luther's
reception of the original melody varies little from the metric scheme of the fourteenth-century original. Sommer, "Die Metrik in Luthers Liedern," 49.

26. The fourteenth-century processional entitled, "Fraud uch alle cristenheydt," was
the German trope in the second excerpt from "Regina celi letare alleluia," called "Quia quem
meruisti portare alleluia." Walther Lipphardt, "Ein Mainzer Prozessionale (um 1400) als
Quelle deutscher geistlicher Lieder," 101–104. For a short discussion of the medieval tropes
of the fourteenth-century processional, see: Johannes Janota, *Studien zu Funktion und Typus
des deutschen geistlichen Liedes im Mittelalter*, 194–99.

27. For the texts of these two hymns, see: Philipp Wackernagel, *Das Deutsche Kirchenlied*,
94–95 (no. 137, "Osterlied") and 95 (no. 138, "Ein ald Osterlied").

28. Zahn melody no. 4430 in Johannes Zahn, *Die Melodien*, vol. 3, 70. In the edition of
the *Hymnal of Eight (Achtliederbuch)* found in Zach. Faber, *Luth. Defensionswerck* (17?) in the
archives of the Evangelische Stift in Tübingen, the biblical references to Speratus' hymn
are given.

29. "folget eyn hubsch Euangelisch gesang yn melodey frewt euch yhr frawen vnd yhr
man das Christ ist aufferstanden so man auffs Osterfest zusyngen pflegt die noten aber darzu
synd vber dz Lied Es yst dz heyl vns komen angezeigt," *Das Erfurter Enchiridion (Ferbefaß 1524)
und der Ergänzungsdruck (Erfurt 1525)*, 5.

30. Zahn melody no. 4428 in Zahn, *Die Melodien*, vol. 3, 69.

set in the variant D mode (No. XIII).[31] As the text of the hymn took up one more page in his choir book for verses seven through ten, the tune from the *Hymnal of Eight* (*Achtliederbuch*) was added to the following right-hand page. Walter then composed a three-part harmony, including two descant parts, in the G mode (No. XV) so that Walter's tenor could not be sung with the second harmonization.[32] The third melody assigned to "Now Rejoice, Dear Christians" first appeared in the Klug hymnbook of 1533.[33] Its composer is disputed by some scholars. Jenny attributes the popular melody to Luther,[34] while Blankenburg argues that it is taken from a well-known German folksong, "Awake, Beauty of My Heart."[35] In the most recent edition of the *German Protestant Hymnbook*, however, Luther's name appears as the composer of this melody.[36] There is one melody that scholars agree is Luther's own composition.[37] This fourth melody is the one found in the *Hymnal of Eight* (*Achtliederbuch*). The common thread running through the melodies Luther composed appears to be the influence of medieval love songs and a liturgical sequence that he modified to accompany "Now Rejoice, Dear Christians."

"Now Rejoice, Dear Christians" was written by Luther in a brief period of remarkable productivity in the genre of the hymn. It was included in some of the earliest hymn collections that were published at a time typically associated with the beginning stages of the Reformation. The early success of both the genre and the particular hymn must not be overestimated entirely as a Reformation novelty. In writing poetic texts and assigning melodies to them, Luther's activity reflects the influence of folk songs, love songs, and liturgical sequences, already found in the Middle Ages, that he integrated into his own work. This rootedness in a distinct tradition will be observed more closely when determining the genre of "Now Rejoice, Dear Christians" to be a hymn of praise. The following discussion

---

31. Walter, tenor, nos. XIII & XV.

32. Personal correspondence with Paul Helmer on Dec. 27, 1993.

33. Zahn melody, no. 4429a in *Die Melodien*, vol. 3, 70; *Das Klug'sche Gesangbuch (1533)*, 24–25.

34. AWA 4:57–58.

35. Blankenburg, "Johann Walters Chorgesangbuch," 81.

36. EG(H/N), no. 149. In this hymnbook, the text assigned to this melody is not "Nun freut euch," but "Es ist gewißlich an der Zeit."

37. Zahn melody no. 4427 in *Die Melodien*, vol. 3, 69.

will introduce the issue of genre from its biblical and musical perspectives in order to sharpen the focus onto this particular hymn.

THE GENRE OF THE HYMN

Luther's productive encounter with the genre of the hymn is closely coupled with the theological significance of this form in his thought. The book of Psalms surface as the biblical source for Luther's reflections on hymn composing and singing; Luther regards the psalms to be the model for medieval church hymnody.[38] By understanding the church in terms of its continuity with the tradition of the psalms, Luther can speak of a succession that extends beyond the individual composer's death and into the singing of the church.[39] A pedagogical motivation underlines Luther's theological commitment to placing the genre of the hymn at the center of the church's ongoing life. The hymns of the church are to be learned by the young,[40] in the diverse melodies and languages of the worship service— including German, Latin, Greek, and Hebrew—as Luther suggests in the "Preface to the German Mass."[41] When the church sings its hymns in the

38. "Also wil David seine Psalmen Israels Psalmen, das ist, der Kirchen Psalmen heissen." WA 54:34.23-24 (Von den letzten Worten Davids, 1543).

39. In Von den letzten Worten Davids (1543), Luther thematizes the church's singing in terms of its continuity with David and the composers of the church's hymns. "Und wenn sie sterben, so bleibt die Kirche, die jmer fort jre lieder singet. Also wil David seine Psalmen Israels Psalmen, das ist, der Kirchen Psalmen heissen, welche den selben geist hat, der sie durch David gemachet hat, und die selben jmer fort singet, auch nach Davids tod." Ibid., 34.22-26.

40. Wackernagel writes that the boys in the medieval choir were taught the hymns of the tradition. At the church in Wittenberg, the hymns were arranged in four or five parts by Walter, whereas the congregation would sing the hymns in unison. Philipp Wackernagel, *Martin Luthers geistliche Lieder*, xiv-xvi. The pedagogical intention behind Luther's recommendation to compose harmonies for the hymns in the 1524 choir book was to teach the young [boys] the hymns of the tradition. Luther insists that the youth be taught in the practice of reading the Latin Bible and of singing the psalms in Latin. "Fur die knaben und schuler ynn der Biblia zu uben gehets also zu. Die wochen uber teglich fur der lection singen sie ettliche psalmen latinisch, wie bis her zur metten gewonet, denn, wie gesagt ist, wyr wollen die jugent bey der latinschen sprachen ynn der Biblia behalten und uben." WA 19:80.4-7 (Vorrede zur Deutschen Messe, 1526).

41. Luther recommends teaching the youth the various languages of the tradition of the worship service, basing his insistence on the advent of the Holy Spirit at Pentecost. "..., so solte man eynen sontag umb den andern yn allen vieren sprachen, Deutsch, Latinisch, Kriechisch, Ebreisch messe halten, singen und lesen ... So thet aber der heylige geyst nicht ym anfange. Er harret nicht, bis alle welt gen Jerusalem keme und lernet Ebreisch, sondern gab allerley zungen zum predig ampt, das die Apostel reden kunden, wo sie hyn kamen. Disem exempel wil ich lieber folgen." Ibid., 74.8-9, 16-19.

different languages of its tradition, the same Holy Spirit who composed the hymns through David continues to be present.

Complementing his theological conviction regarding the exemplary status of the psalms for church hymns is Luther's own experience with them. An explicit reference to the psalm hymn is found in a letter Luther wrote to Spalatin in 1523. Luther appeals to the need for poets to compose psalm hymns, especially hymns based on the penitential psalms.[42] In his own role as a hymn composer, Luther can be regarded as the "inventor of the genre of the psalm hymn," as Jenny writes.[43] The novelty of working psalm texts into hymns for congregational singing is, however, rooted in pious ground. Luther's own spiritual formation was steeped in a liturgical tradition whose language and form, as Childs notes, was shaped by psalms.[44] The psalms were chanted daily during the medieval Office of the Hours.[45] In the *Rule*, the basic text of the Brethren of the Common Life, the Psalter was regarded as the only book, common to all, that fostered community.[46] Not a historical accident, it is both an experiential encounter and theological conviction that motivate Luther's choice of the book of Psalms to represent the genre of the hymn.

Luther's concern with the harmony between text and melody points to a connection already explicit in the Bible. The Psalms were originally connected to music. The superscriptions refer to an original context in which the psalms were sung, and they often explicitly mention the instruments

---

42. "Habes autem meos septem psalmos penitentiales & Commentarios [Luther's commentary on the seven penitential Psalms of 1517 in WA 1:158–220], e quibus sensum psalmi capere poteris, Aut si placet assignari Tibi psalmum primum." WABr 3:220.15–17 (no. 698, end of 1523).

43. Jenny writes, "Luther hat als Erfinder des Psalmliedes zu gelten." Jenny, *Luther, Zwingli, Calvin in ihren Liedern*, 18.

44. "In the prayer book, the midrashim, and the rituals of the synagogue the all-encompassing presence of the Hebrew Psalter is visible. Similarly for the Christian church, the New Testament is saturated with citations from the Psalter and such hymns as the 'Magnificat' reflect an unbroken continuity with the praises of Israel. The Psalter provided the decisive impetus in shaping Christian liturgy in all the branches of Christendom both in the early, medieval, and Reformation periods. Even today many of the most enduring hymns of the church are based on Old Testament psalms." Brevard S. Childs, *Introduction to the Old Testament as Scripture*, 508.

45. In a discussion of the seven canonical hours, Biel recommends praying the following psalm verses in preparation for the mass: Pss 83:2; 84:2; 85:1; 115:10; 129:1. Gabrielis Biel, *Canonis Misse Expositio*, vol. 1, 105 (lect 13G).

46. Robert Stupperich, "Devotio moderna und reformatorische Frömmigkeit," 17.

that accompanied the songs.[47] When Luther reflects on the psalms, he recovers their superscriptions as integrally connected to their public rehearsal. The psalms demand that their texts be sung.[48] In Luther's thought, this intimate conjunction between text and music is well known. True psalms and songs are characterized by the tightest connection between music and theology.[49] Luther mentions the examples of the church fathers and the prophets, who wanted to join the word of God to nothing other than music.[50] To the words belong the notes that make the text come alive.[51] Intended to be sung, the biblical texts carry their proclamation into the life of the church.

Luther's insistence on the link between music and speech plays into his understanding of the hymn of praise. Luther refers to both speech and song as gifts from God. Both distinguish humans from animals and are found together when God is praised; "it is necessary to praise God through

---

47. Childs, *Introduction to the Old Testament as Scripture*, 520.

48. There is evidence that hymns were sung much more slowly in the late medieval period than they are sung in churches today. Personal correspondence with Paul Helmer on December 27, 1993.

49. "... sicut fugit ad verbum theologiae. Hinc factum est, ut prophetae nulla sic arte sint usi ut musica, dum suam theologiam non in geometriam, non in arithmeticam, non in astronomiam, sed in musicam digesserunt, ut theologiam et musicam haberent coniunctissimas, veritatem psalmis et canticis dicentes." WABr 5:639.17-21 (no. 1727, letter from Oct. 1 (4?), 1530 to the musician Ludwig Senfl). The art associated with theology is not geometry or mathematics, but music. For example: "Proximum locum do Musicae post Theologiam. Hoc patet exemplo David et omnium prophetarum, qui sua omnia metris et cantibus mandaverunt." WA 30, 2:696.12-13 (Weitere Entwürfe Luthers, "Περὶ τῆς μουσικῆς," 1530). An interesting topic for discussion could be Luther's understanding concerning the relationship between the non-rational element of music and the particular language of the Psalms. For Luther, the language of the Psalms is highly emotive. The Psalms articulate the experience of the heart "mit lebendiger farbe vnd gestalt." WADB 10,1:104.5-6 (Vorrede auf den Psalter, 1528). In his Preface to the Psalter, Luther insists that the Psalms are the exemplary speech of both the saints and the Christian church. By articulating various emotions, the Psalms teach true knowledge of self, of God, and of all creatures. "Denn er leret dich ynn freuden, furcht, hoffnung, traurigkeit, gleich gesinnet sein vnd reden, wie alle heiligen gesinnet vnd geredt haben. Summa, wiltu die heilige Christlichen kirche gemalet sehen, mit lebendiger farbe vnd gestalt, ynn einem kleinen bilde gefasset, so nym den Psalter fur dich, so hastu einen feinen, hellen, reinen spiegel, der dir zeigen wird, was die Christenheit sey, ia du wirst auch dich selbs drinnen, vnd das rechte Gnotiseauton finden, dazu Gott selbs, vnd alle Creaturn." Ibid., 104.3-9.

50. "Vnde non frustra Patres et Prophetae verbo Dei nihil voluerunt esse coniunctius quam Musicam." WA 50:371.14-15 (Praefatio zu den Symphoniae iucundae, 1538).

51. "Musica est optima scientia. Die nothen machen den text lebendig." WATr 2:518.6-7 (no. 2545b, March 1532).

word and song."[52] Luther often comments on the link between the song and the praise of God, an insight conveyed by the Hebrew word for psalms: *tehillim*, or hymns. The song of praise, as Childs remarks, "does accurately reflect the theology of Israel. The psalms have to do with the praise of God."[53] As New Testament scholars have pointed out, the Christological hymns have, as their addressee, God or Christ.[54] In addition to the consideration of praise in song, the content also plays into a determination of Luther's hymn "Now Rejoice, Dear Christians." In Scripture, narrative captures the praise of the mighty acts God has accomplished among God's people. In the opening verse of his hymn, Luther signals the narrative of praise with the invitation to sing of "what God has done for us and of his sweet, wondrous deed" (1.5-6).[55] The subject matter, praise, is introduced, and then followed by nine verses that enclose the captivity of the "I" (verses two and three) in the narrative of what God has accomplished.[56] In an early printed edition of the hymn, the superscription designates the hymn's genre as a song of thanks,[57] a determination with which Burba agrees.[58] Appearing once in the publication history of Luther's hymn, this heading explicitly connects the hymn's narrative to the song of thanks and points to what Luther has recovered from the biblical view of the psalm hymn.

---

52. WA 50:372.3-4.

53. Childs, *Introduction to the Old Testament as Scripture*, 514.

54. "Der Adressat hymnischer Sprache ist Gott oder Christus. Es geht deshalb nicht darum, Mitteilungen zu machen, die dem Adressaten unbekannt wären." Eduard Schweizer, *Der Brief an die Kolosser*, 71.

55. Hahn determines Luther's hymn to be written in the genre of a "Zeitlied[es]" or a "historische[n] Volkslied[es]." Hahn, *Evangelium als literarische Answeisung*, 20-21. Hahn's insight takes seriously the category of narrative to determine the genre of Luther's hymn.

56. The narrative of God's mercy shown in Christ is studied in this chapter from the perspective of a Trinitarian advent. Another perspective for construing the hymn could be an anthropological narrative. This determination is signaled by an early superscription to the hymn: "Ein fein geistlich lied, wie der sunder zur gnade kompt." WA 35:423n1. If, however, the anthropological narrative is investigated, then it must be interpreted in light of the hymn's literal starting point, as I argue in this chapter.

57. "Ein Dancklied für die hochsten wolthaten so uns Gott in Christo erzeigt hat." WA 35:422-23n1.

58. In an early study of Luther's hymns, Burba writes that "Nun freut euch, lieben Christen gmein" is more than a personal recollection of Luther's life in the monastery and that it should be interpreted from the perspective of a "Psalmlied[es]." Klaus Burba, *Die Christologie in Luthers Liedern*, 20.

Another look at the original context in which Luther's hymn is published uncovers the narrative's explicit relation to the Trinity. The question of whether the hymn's narrative structure is to be interpreted in terms of a Trinitarian understanding has, until a recent comment made by Bayer, not been raised.[59] When one looks at the hymnbooks published between 1524 and 1534, it is difficult to imagine why the hymn's relation to the Trinity has been forgotten in subsequent centuries. Luther edited the Wittenberg hymnbooks of 1524 and 1529 and placed his hymn after the German credo "We All Believe in One God," in a section marked off as the catechism hymns.[60] At this site, "Now Rejoice, Dear Christians" functioned as an interpretation hymn (*Deutelied*) of the explicitly three-verse Trinitarian structure of the Credo.[61] Sometime between 1533 and 1534, the hymn was removed from its catechetical context and moved to the section marked "special hymns" at the end of the hymnbooks.[62] Dislocated from its connection with the Creed, the hymn lost its original intention to explicate the hymn that confessed faith in the Triune God. In her book on Luther's hymns, Müller attempts to integrate narrative with dogma. She points out that Luther understood dogma to be a different articulation of the same subject matter narrated in a poetic text.[63] As the location of the hymn in the

---

59. "Dieses Lied ist das sprechendste und zugleich zutreffendste Bekenntnis zu Gott dem dreieinen, das ich kenne." Oswald Bayer, *Aus Glauben Leben*, 60.

60. The order of the catechism-hymns in the Wittenberg hymnbook (1529) are: "Dies sind die heilgen Zehn Gebot"; "Mensch, willst du leben seliglich"; "Mitten wir im Leben sind" [considered to be the *Deutelied* of the two preceding hymns on the Decalogue]; "Wir glauben all an einen Gott"; and "Nun freut euch, lieben Christen gmein." Christhard Mahrenholz, "Auswahl und Einordnung der Katechismus-Lieder in den Wittenberger Gesangsbüchern seit 1529," 125. 129–30.

61. The two hymns, the German Credo and its *Deutelied*, were written against the backdrop of a series of sermons that Luther preached on the catechism. In 1523, Luther began to preach systematically on the three elements of the catechism in the order of their appearance in the Large and Small Catechisms of 1529: Decalogue, Creed, Our Father. The thirteen sermons were held on weekdays beginning on St. Matthias Day, Feb. 24, through to March 10, with the three sermons on the "Symbolum" preached on March 4–6. See: WA 11:31.1–59.30.

62. The Klug hymnbook of 1533 still places "Nun freut euch" after the Credo, whereas the Klug edition of 1534 relegates Luther's hymn to the status of a "special hymn." Mahrenholz attributes the shift in the location of "Nun freut euch" to a narrowed understanding of the liturgical function of the catechism-hymns. Mahrenholz, "Auswahl und Einordnung der Katechismus-Lieder," 130.

63. Christa Müller, a theologian writing in the 1930's on Luther's hymns, observes the connections between dogma, proclamation, and praise. "Luther schied überhaupt Kirchenlied und Dogma nicht als zwei wesensfremde Dinge, sondern beide waren dasselbe

early hymnbooks suggests, narrative is seen as interpreting—not divorced from—the Trinitarian dogma.

A preliminary discussion of Luther's understanding of the hymn has served to situate the particular hymn "Now Rejoice, Dear Christians" in the particular historical and theological context of Luther's writing activity. Luther wrote extensively in a genre that he regarded as integral to the ongoing life of the church. He recovered the biblical source of the hymn, the psalm, and emphasized the hymn text's intimate connection with music. When the psalm of praise is sung, the melody creates time to sing the narrated praise of what God has done. The consideration of Luther's hymn as a psalm hymn in the sense of a hymn of praise and of its original connection between narrative and dogma shapes the perspective from which a study of Luther's Trinitarian understanding begins. The song of praise begins with the advent of the Holy Spirit.

THE HOLY SPIRIT

The question as to where Luther's hymn begins is decisive for interpreting its narrative. Does the hymn's narrative begin with verse two, as many Luther scholars have argued? Or does Luther's hymn begin with its literal starting point in verse one? In this section, I will study Luther's hymn according to its literal beginning and will challenge the view that privileges the human person's captivity in verse two. I suggest that the hymn's literal starting-point, the call to joy, is to be interpreted as the advent of the Holy Spirit. On the surface, the difficulty of this task is related to the fact that nowhere in the opening verse is the Holy Spirit explicitly mentioned. I begin the section by pointing to various clues in the opening verse that suggest the Spirit's arrival. In the second section, the literary connections between this verse and Christ's final words at the end of the hymn are

---

in verschiedener Ausdrucksform: Verkündigung, menschliches Weiterreden der Rede Gottes und darum Lob und Preis der Barmherzigkeit Gottes. ... Wenn hier etwas anstößig ist, so ist es nicht das 'Dogmatische', sondern die Tatsache selbst." Christa Müller, *Luthers Lieder*, 22. Also: "was heute in diesen Liedern 'dogmatisch' anmuten und darum abstoßen mag, das war für Luther gerade das Lebendige und Herrliche an diesen Liedern; das Dogma ist ihm nichts von Gelehrtenköpfen Erdachtes, Weltfremdes, Poesieloses, sondern Dogma ist ihm Gemälde und Gesang der frohen Botschaft, ist Verkündigung, und darum kann das Dogma nicht nur gesungen, es muß gesungen werden." Ibid., 21-22. Müller wrote this book as a decisive political criticism of National Socialism and as a theological contribution to the Confessing Church, interpreting Luther's hymns in light of a resistance to the *Deutsche Christen*. See also: Idem, *Das Lob Gottes bei Luther*.

studied in order to identify the Spirit's advent at the beginning with the fulfillment of Christ's *promissio*. Finally, I turn to Luther's exegesis of Genesis 1 (1523) in order to show that Luther does not limit the Spirit's advent to the Pentecost motif, but considers the Spirit's role to be hidden as the divine pleasure in creation. By arguing that the hymn starts with a contraction between Pentecost and creation, the anthropological narrative from law to gospel is subverted, and the narrative of Trinitarian advent begins.

THE JOYOUS ADVENT OF THE SPIRIT

Narrative has been the popular lens through which Luther scholars have viewed the hymn "Now Rejoice, Dear Christians," yet the category has been used to interpret the hymn in terms of an autobiographical development or a salvation history. In various studies, the hymn is isolated as a representative example of Luther's Reformation insight: the move from sin to grace. Basing his interpretation on Luther's 1545 preface to the Latin writings, Spitta discusses the hymn as "a poetic self-confession."[64] The hymn's poetic narrative from sin to grace mirrors the breakthrough in Luther's own experience. Spitta's lead has been followed by scholars who also argue that the hymn begins with the autobiographical starting point of the sinner and then proceeds to narrate the justification of the "I."[65] Not only restricted to the particular, the "I" is understood to speak for the condition of all human existence; the hymn's beginning is a "diagnosis of the lostness of the human being."[66] When the sinner's autobiography is elevated from its particularity into the concept of human nature, its condition becomes a universal narrative. At this level, the hymn is represented as a "Christologically focused account of salvation history," as Brecht states.[67] Even a study of the individual words in Luther's hymn, as Veit has undertaken, reflects the usual interpretive structure of the move from sin to grace.[68] In this sample of

---

64. Friedrich Spitta, '*Ein feste Burg ist unser Gott*', 225.

65. For example: Jenny, *Luther, Zwingli, Calvin in ihren Liedern*, 85; Jung, "Nun freut euch, lieben Christen gmein," 205; and Martin Rößler, "Ballade vom Ratschluß Gottes zur Erlösung," 446.

66. Brecht, "Erfahrung—Exegese—Dogmatik," 99.

67. Ibid., 96.

68. Veit investigates what he considers to be Luther's Reformation concepts. He studies words, such as sin, justification, and incarnation according to a quantitative semantics, meaning, "der Wortschatz der Lieder wurde nach Häufigkeit des Vorkommens einzelner Wörter

studies, a common hermeneutical problem is detected: When one interprets the hymn according to a personal or universal narrative that begins
with an anthropological starting point in verse two, the significance of the
hymn's literal starting point is overlooked.

Luther's hymn begins before what scholars assume to be its starting
point. The hymn does not begin with verse two, the "I" in captivity. Verse
one announces the hymn's beginning with the call to joy. The opening
line, "Now rejoice, dear Christians" (1.1), echoes the joy associated with
the hymn's liturgical origins in the fourteenth-century Easter processional.[69] Joy is contagious as Christians gather together to sing and dance: "And
let us jump for joy ... sing with delight and love" (1.2, 4). Luther's Advent
hymn "From Heaven Above" contains a similar invitation to leap and sing.[70]
Although Brecht disputes that dancing took place during the mass,[71] there is
evidence that Luther recommends dancing at weddings or during times of

---

und Begriffe untersucht." Patrice Veit, *Das Kirchenlied in der Reformation Martin Luthers*, 6.
It is not surprising that Veit's word-count methodology is unsuccessful in uncovering the
Trinitarian-theological dimension of Luther's hymns. Veit mentions that Luther composed
four Trinitarian hymns ("Gott der Vater wohn uns bei"; "Wir glauben all an einen Gott";
"Erhalt uns, Herr, bei deinem Wort"; and "Der du bist drei in Einigkeit"), and concludes,
"dazu ist zu bemerken, daß der Trinitätslehre im Liedwerk, ganz anders als in den Predigten,
eine relativ unbedeutende Stellung zukommt." Ibid., 81. Veit's conclusion is based on the
assumption that the general tendency of the Reformers, Luther and Calvin, is to underscore
the economic Trinitarian dispensation for an audience of simple folk and children, rather
than to discuss in detail the "metaphysical" and "speculative" dimensions of the doctrine of
the Trinity. In the chapter on the genre of the sermon, ch. 4, I show that Luther does not shy
away from preaching on the "metaphysical" aspect of the Trinity. Veit recognizes Luther's
doxological access to the Trinity by explicitly pointing to Luther's translations of the nine
Latin hymns, each ending with a Trinitarian doxology. For the hymns, "Christum wir sollen
loben schon" and "Komm, Gott Schöpfer, Heiliger Geist," Luther added a Trinitarian doxology
not contained and possibly lost in the original Latin text. Ibid., 82n5. When digging below
the hymns' rhetorical surface or underneath the appearance of Reformation terms specified
in a context other than Luther's, one finds much more Trinitarian material than Veit could
ever detect. An appropriate methodology in Luther research must take into account the use
of words in their depth, rather than on their surface, dimension.

69. Müller classifies this hymn as an Easter hymn by noting the similarities to another
hymn Luther composed for Easter: "Christ lag in Todes Banden." Müller, *Luthers Lieder*, 38.
Müller also points out that Luther never composed a hymn for Good Friday. Ibid., 34. The
eight *de tempore* hymns Luther composed from 1523 to 1524 thematize the divine beginning
in terms of the advent of Christ and the Holy Spirit. For a list of these hymns, see 136n10.

70. "Davon ich alzeit frölich sey, zu springen, singen jmer frey." (14.1–2) in AWA 4:290.
Jenny states that "Vom Himmel hoch" is a contrafacture on a medieval dance song. Ibid.,
109–10.

71. Brecht, "Erfahrung—Exegese—Dogmatik," 97.

demonic trial (*Anfechtung*) to resist the oppressive spirit of sadness.[72] The joy of Easter and the wedding dance, not the despair of the "I," capture the mood at the literal starting point of Luther's hymn.

The call to sing and dance points in the direction of attributing the opening verse to the Holy Spirit. Joy is coupled with the Spirit's advent, which Luther joins to music as the Spirit's special vehicle. The Spirit honors music as "the instrument of his proper office"; music is "the inclination to all virtues."[73] Biblical figures—the prophets and David—are examples of how joyous music accompanying the Spirit's advent is used to combat the attacks of the devil.[74] Luther uses David's example to show how music guides the emotions. When God's word is sung, the Spirit of joy disperses the devil of sadness and dwells among God's people, who sing God's praises.[75] Luther comments on the affective power of music. Music is the "mistress and guide of human emotions,"[76] whose reception is akin to the prophetic word that strikes down and builds up (Luke 1:52).[77] Luther's remarks on the affective force of music resonate with a medieval tradition. Biel and Johannes Tinctoris, a late medieval musicologist, comment at length on the emotive effects of music.[78] Luther's consideration of music as an affective

---

72. WA 17,2:64.23-29 (Fastenpostille on the Second Sunday after Epiphany, 1525); WATr 2:100.6-9 (no. 1434, April 7 to May 1, 1532); WATr 5:36.10-18 (no. 5265, Sept. 18 to 23, 1540); WA 43:315.27-29 (Lectures on Genesis, to Gen 24:5-7, 1535-1545).

73. WA 50:371.9-10, 11.

74. Luther, commenting on 1 Sam 17, writes that a liturgical song, either the *Te Deum laudamus* or the *Benedictus* and accompanied by the "Claves," disperses the devil who tempts one with worries and sorrowful thoughts. WABr 7:105.26-33 (no. 2139, letter to the organist Matthias Weller on Oct. 7, 1534).

75. "Denn dem bo(e)sen geist ist nicht wol dabey, wo man Gottes wort im rechten glauben singet oder predigt. Er ist ein geist der traurigkeit, und kan nicht bleiben, wo ein hertz Geistlich (das ist, in Gott und seinem wort) fro(e)lich ist, Davon auch S. Antonius sagt, das geistliche freude dem Teuffel wehe thue ... Denn es ligt dran, das der hauffe Gottes, oder Gottes volck, ein wort oder lied anneme und fur recht erkenne, weil der geist Gottes in solchem volck sein mus, der in seinem volck wil und sol geehret sein, Also reden wir Christen von unsern Psalmisten." WA 54:34.6-10, 13-16.

76. WA 50:371.2.

77. Using the language of the Magnificat, Luther describes the effects of music. "Siue enim velis tristes erigere, siue laetos terrere, desperantes animare, superbos frangere, amantes sedare, odientes mitigare?" Ibid., 371.5-6.

78. Veit quotes Johannes Tinctoris, a renowned musicologist at the turn of the sixteenth century, who outlined twenty effects of music, including "Musica tristitiam depellit." See: Tinctoris, "Complexus effectum musices," cited in Veit, *Das Kirchenlied in der Reformation Martin Luthers*, 24-25. In the middle of the fifteenth century, Biel also notices the effects

power dovetails with his understanding of praise, which transforms sorrow into joy.

For Luther, the Spirit's advent effects a transformation at the center of the human being. The heart is where the Spirit effects the experience of joy.[79] It is possible that Luther's connection between the heart and the Spirit plays into his earlier discussion of the third article of the Creed in terms of the vivifying rubric.[80] As Theo Bell shows, the early Luther's understanding of the Spirit's work in the human heart is shaped by a reception of Bernard of Clairvaux's sermon on Psalm 84:10, which Bernard preached on the Feast of the Annunciation.[81] Luther's *scholion* to Romans 8:16, a text Bell suggests is pivotal to Luther's insistence on the certainty of faith, refers to Bernard's sermon. Bernard's exegesis connects the psalm verse, concentrated on the word "glory," to both 2 Corinthians 1:12 and Romans 8:16. The glory living

---

music can have. "(Cantus) [e]ffugat etiam accidiam que secundum Gregorium est quedam tristicia circa bona spiritualia et divina, que pro tunc inminent facienda, unde dicitur, IACOB. v [Jas 5:13]: *Tristatur aliquis in vobis? Oret. Equo animo est? Psallat*, ubi GLOSA: *Crebra psalmodie dulcedine nocivam tristiciam depellat.*" Biel, *Canonis Misse Expositio*, vol. 3, 21 (lectio 62B). For details on the medieval tradition relating theology to music, with quotes from Gerson, Boethius, Tinctoris, Biel, and Bonaventure, see: Veit, *Das Kirchenlied in der Reformation Martin Luthers*, 22–26.

79. The Spirit's work in the heart effects distinct changes in the emotions and in physical movement, as these examples from two sermons show. "Solcher glaub machet mich angenem fur gott, da gibt mir Christus denn den heyligen geist yns hertz, der mich lustig und frolich machet zu allem gu(e)ttem. Also werde ich rechtfertig und auff keyn andere weyß. Denn die werck machen dich nur ye mer und mer unlustig, ye lenger du sie treybest. Aber diß werck, ye mer du es treybest und erkennest, ye lustiger machet es deyn hertz. ... Wenn er [der heilige Geist] denn kompt, so muß er das hertz willig, lustig und frolich machen, das es frey hynan gehe und gerne thue alles, was gott gefellet mit frolichem mu(e)tt und leydet was zuleiden ist und auch gerne sterbe." WA 12:547.22–27, 28–30 (Sermon on the Fourth Sunday after Easter, May 3, 1523); "Ja wenns recht inns hertz gieng, wer es nicht wunder, das zu(o) spru(e)ng fur freyden." Ibid., 469.33–34 (Sermon on Palm Sunday, March 29, 1523).

80. In the sermon series on the catechism (1523), Luther stresses the *vivificans* motif of the third article of the Creed. "Spiritui sancto datur honor, quod dicitur spiritus vivificans, quia id quod praedicatur, facit ut vivat in cordibus." WA 11:53.9–11 (Sermon on the Symbolum: the third article of the Creed, March 6, 1523). Later, in the Large Catechism (1529), Luther relates the name, "Holy Spirit" to the verb, "to sanctify" (in German, "Heiliger Geist"; "heiligen"), and interprets the third article of the Creed under the rubric of sanctification. For a summary of this shift in accent, see: Albrecht Peters, *Kommentar zu Luthers Katechismen*, vol. 2, 180.

81. Theo Bell, *Divus Bernhardus*, 91–106. Independently of Bell's work, Helene Werthemann has found Bernard's sermon to be the conceptual backdrop of the "Ratschluß zur Erlösung," a common medieval theme in which the inner Trinity decides for the Second Person to become incarnate in order to redeem humanity. This will be discussed in detail in "Trinitarian Speech" below. Helene Werthemann, *Studien zu den Adventsliedern des 16. und 17. Jahrhunderts*, 53–59. For a demonstration of Luther's reception of Bernard's hymn, see also: Franz Posset, "*Bernardus Redivivus*, 242–44.

in the human heart is, for Bernard, the indwelling of the Spirit.[82] In his scholion, Luther explicitly cites Bernard on the theme of the Spirit's testimony in the heart.[83] The Spirit's work in the heart, a theme received from Bernard, is also evident in Luther's commentary on Hebrews 5:1.[84] A similar understanding of the Spirit's role in transforming the heart appears in sermons Luther preached in 1523.[85] For Luther, the heart is the location of the life-creating transformation effected by the Spirit's advent.

When the heart is transformed, the individual begins to sing in community. The first line of Luther's hymn addresses the Christians together: the first-person plural of the address, "dear Christians altogether" and "all in one" (1.1, 3), is contrasted with the first-person singular, marking the isolation of captivity in subsequent verses.[86] By contrasting the singular and the plural, Luther points out that the work of the Spirit begins by creating community. Luther summarizes the Spirit's particular work in a 1523 sermon on the third article of the Creed: "The proper work of the Holy Spirit is to build the church."[87] The Spirit's address enlivens individuals, liberating the "I" from the isolation of its solitary self and making space for others to live in community. Diversity is gathered into communal unity with the Spirit's advent. In Luther's Pentecost hymn "Come, God Creator Holy Ghost," the Spirit is related to the work of joining the chorus

---

82. Bernard's sermon reads: "… sed cum Spiritus ipse testimonium perhibet spiritui nostro." Bernard of Clairvaux, "In Annuntiatione: Sermo Primus," (1), *S. Bernardi Opera*, vol. 5, *Sermones II*, 13, 9.

83. "Quod testimonium istud sit ipsa fiducia cordis in Deum, preclarissime ostendit B. Bernardus, plenus eodem spiritu, sermone de annunciatione 1. dicens." WA 56:369.27–370.1 (Scholion to Rom 8:16, 1515–1516).

84. WA 57,3:169.10–21 (Commentary on Heb 5:1, 1517). See: Bell, *Divus Bernhardus*, 99–106.

85. "Do schreybt er eyttel fewer flammen yns hertz und macht es lebendig, das es herauß bricht mit fewrigen zungen und thettiger hand und wirtt eyn newer mensch, der do fu(e)let, das er gar eyn andern verstand, gemu(e)t und synn gefasst hab dann vor." WA 12:570.12–15 (Sermon on Pentecost, May 24, 1523); "Gott lesst das wortt, das Evangelium, aussgehen und den samen fallen ynn die hertzen der menschen. Wo nu der ym hertzen hafftet, so ist der heylig geyst da und macht eyn newen menschen, da wirt gar eyn ander mensch, ander gedancken, andere wortt und werck." Ibid., 298.29–32 (to 1 Pet 1:23).

86. "Gmein" is a shortened form of "gemein," meaning together, in common, in community, rather than "Gemeine," meaning congregation. See: Philipp Dietz, *Wörterbuch zu Dr. Martin Luthers Deutschen Schriften*, vol. 2, 72.

87. WA 11:53.32–33 (Sermon on the Symbolum: the third article of the Creed, March 6, 1523).

of voices in the unity of the Father's word.[88] The Spirit joins all believers in the unity of faith: "You have gathered the people from all the languages of the world."[89] The classical biblical text in which the work of uniting is attributed to the Spirit is Ephesians 4:3, a text Luther refers to in a sermon delivered on Palm Sunday in 1523. Expressing his desire that the unity of faith would prevail in a time of schism, Luther preaches that the Spirit, who is the "'bond of peace and unity of the Spirit'," would unite all hearts in the "'unity of the Spirit.' While the outer being [of the church] is diverse, since all hearts are of one mind, the outer possesses a miraculous unity."[90] Hearts are joined together in the room created by the Spirit to enjoy the other in the joy that unites what schism separates.

Luther's hymn does not begin with the solitary "I" in captivity but with the communal joy of praise. Although no explicit mention of the Holy Spirit is made in the opening verse, I have suggested that this silence can be attributed to the Third Person of the Trinity. The call to joy, accompanied by music, are two elements that Luther links to his understanding of the Spirit. With the Spirit's advent, the Spirit transforms the heart to joy and gathers Christians to sing the praise of God together. When the literal introduction is taken as the theological starting point, the facile pressing of Luther's hymn into an autobiographical account of an anthropological shift from sin to grace is corrected. A further corrective is shown when the hymn's end, Christ's *promissio*, is seen in light of its recapitulation at the beginning.

END AT THE BEGINNING: THE *PROMISSIO*

Christ's words, spoken in the final stanzas of the hymn, provide a literary key for attributing the first verse to the advent of the Holy Spirit. Taken from John 14:16, 26, the closing words Christ speaks promise the sending of the Spirit. "I desire to give you the Spirit" (9.4). In this section, the Spirit's advent at the hymn's beginning will be discussed from the perspective shaped by Christ's speech at the end. I will first investigate the content and verb tense of Christ's *promissio* in order to show that Christ's promise to

---

88. "Des vaters wort gibstu gar bald mit zungen ynn alle land" (4.3-4), in Luther's translation of Gregory the Great's hymn ("Veni creator spiritus"): WA 35:446.15-16.

89. "Kom heyliger geyst herre Gott" (1.6-7), in Ibid., 449.2-3.

90. WA 12.468:24-25, 25-27 (Sermon on Palm Sunday, March 29, 1523).

send the Spirit is fulfilled in the first verse. The hymn's end makes visible the opening activity of the Spirit to comfort the community and to lead it in the truth of Christ. A conclusion draws the Trinitarian-theological implications of the *promissio*'s fulfillment, which occurs at the beginning of the hymn.

The fulfillment of Christ's final promise to "give" the Spirit is marked by the literary repetition of the verb "to comfort" at two distinct locations of Luther's hymn. At the end of the hymn, Christ speaks in the future tense: "who shall comfort you in your despair" (9.5). In the opening stanza, Luther repeats the verb "to comfort" in the present tense: "That being comforted, we ..." (1.3). The shift in tense, from the future to the present tense, gives an initial indication that the fulfillment of Christ's words has occurred at the hymn's beginning. Derived from the biblical name for the Spirit in John 14:26, "the Comforter," the verb "to comfort" points to the Spirit's special work. The Spirit is the Trinitarian person who works to comfort "the afflicted, destitute, and despairing hearts."[91] In the midst of trials, anxiety, and possible martyrdom, Christians are comforted by the Spirit.[92] The life of the pilgrim, particularly of the more "advanced" Christian, is characterized by the experience of the comfort and power of the gospel in the midst of suffering, fear, and death.[93] By choosing the verb "to comfort"

---

91. Ibid., 575.34–35 (Sermon on Pentecost, May 24, 1523).

92. After the execution of two Augustinian brothers in Brussels, Luther writes his own letter of comfort to the Christians in the Netherlands. "..., sondern auch die ersten zu seyn, die umb Christus willen itzt schand und schaden, angst und nott, gefengnis und ferlickeyt leyden. ... Darumb, meyn aller liebsten, seyt getrost und frolich ynn Christo." Ibid., 78.3–5, 22 (Ein Brief an die Christen im Niederland, Jan. 19, 1524).

93. Commenting on 1 Pet 4:12, Luther writes about the cross God places on the backs of Christians. God uses this opportunity in order to strengthen the word of power and life in the midst of death. "Wenn der glawb angehet, so lesset es Gott nicht, schickt uns das heylige Creutz auff den rucken, das er uns stercke und den glawben ynn uns krefftig mache. Das heylig Evangelion ist eyn krefftig wortt, darumb kan es nicht zu(o) seynem werck komen on anfechtung, und niemant wird es gewar, das es eyn solche krafft hatt, denn wer es schmeckt. Wo leyden und creutz ist, do kan es seyn krafft beweysen und uben. Es ist eyn wort des lebens, drumb muss es alle seyne krafft ym sterben uben. Wenn denn nicht sterben und todt da ist, so kan es nichts thun, und kan niemant gewar werden, das es solch tugent thut, und stercker ist denn sund und todt." Ibid., 381.19–27 (Epistel S. Petri gepredigt und ausgelegt: Erste Bearbeitung 1523, to 1 Pet 4:12). Luther remarks that God places the cross on the "advanced" Christian. "Das gehet alles dahyn, das man der yhenigen, wilche noch junge Christen sind, yhre zeyt lasse und seuberlich mit yhn fare. Wenn sie nu erwachssen sind, da fu(e)ret sie Gott zum heyligen creutz, lest sie auch sterben, wie die andern Christen, do wirtt denn das bo(e)ckleyn geschlachtet." Ibid., 304, 1–5 (to 1 Pet 2:2). Luther's hymn, "Mitten wir im Leben sind," a translation of an early church antiphon, discloses a similar theme: life in the midst

to capture the Spirit's activity, Luther points to one dimension of Christ's *promissio* that is fulfilled with the Spirit's advent.

Two other biblical passages in Christ's final speech are recapitulated in the hymn's first verse. In his final speech, Christ promises to "give" the Spirit, "who will teach you to fully know me and will guide you in the truth" (9.6–7). Luther uses these words from the addresses in John 16:13–15 and in Luke 24:49 to mark the Spirit's activity. The Spirit works to teach about Christ and nothing but Christ. Luther indicates the Spirit's action by summarizing the hymn's Christological focus: "What God has done for us and his sweet, wondrous deed. It cost him very dearly" (1.5–7).[94] In this summary, God's "sweet, wondrous deed" is introduced in terms of both a turning "toward us" and a great cost. In Christological terms, the turn and the cost of blood are the two crucial elements that the Spirit teaches throughout the hymn. Later in the hymn, the knowledge of Christ will be narrated as the Father's inner-Trinitarian turn to the Son, the Son's incarnation, and the silence of his death. At the beginning, the summary orients the hymn's view to Christ. The knowledge of what God has done is taught by the Spirit when the Spirit comes. In the three hymns he translated for Pentecost, Luther makes a similar point. The Spirit works to teach Christians the right knowledge of the Father and of Jesus Christ.[95] When the right knowledge of Christ is taught, the truth of Christ's promise is revealed. Christ's *promissio* is distinguished by the fact that his word is

---

of death. For Luther's moving text, see: AWA 4:160–61. The antiphon, "Antiphona de morte," was one of the most famous songs in the Middle Ages. WA 35:126.

94. Luther's commentary on 1 Peter, written in 1523, refers to theological themes strikingly similar to the focus of the hymn, "Nun freut euch, lieben Christen gmein." Interpreting 1 Pet 1:18–19, Luther uses a prose that parallels the poetry of verse 1.5–7. "Und sehet, wie so grosse kost Got an euch gewendt hat, und wie groß der schatz sey, damit yhr erkaufft seyt und dahyn bracht, das yhr Gottis kinder wu(e)rdet." WA 12:291.6–8.

95. "Ler uns den vater kennen wol, dazu Jhesu Christ seynen Son, Das wyr des glaubens werden vol, dich beyder geyst zuuersthon" (6.1–4), in "Kom Gott schepfer heyliger geyst." WA 35:447.3–6. "Du werdes liecht gib uns deynen scheyn, lern uns Jhesum Christ kennen alleyn, Das wyr an yhm bleyben dem trewen Heyland, der uns bracht hat zum rechten vaterland" (2.1–4), in "Nu bitten wyr den heyligen geyst." Ibid., 448.1–4. "Und lern uns Gott recht erkennen, von hertzen vater yhn nennen. ... Denn Jhesum mit rechtem glauben und yhm aus gantzer macht vertrawen" (2.3–4, 7–8), in "Kom heyliger geyst herre Gott." Ibid., 449:8–9, 12–13. In a 1523 sermon, Luther preaches on the Spirit who teaches Christ as Lord over sin, death, and all things. "Das kompt daher, das dich der heylig geyst leret erkennen die grosse gu(e)tte unnd gnade Christi, das er die an yhn glewben, zu(o) herren macht, wie er selb ist, uber sund, todt und alle ding." WA 12:577.4–7 (Sermon on Pentecost, May 24, 1523).

the word of truth, as Luther preached in a sermon in 1523.[96] What Christ promises is truly fulfilled with the Spirit's advent.

Luther's hymn begins with the fulfillment of Christ's *promissio*. The shift in verb tense, from the future to the present tense, the literary recapitulation of the verb "to comfort," and the introductory summary of God's "sweet, wondrous deed" are clues suggesting that Luther understands the Spirit's advent in relation to Christ. The Pentecost motif captures Luther's Trinitarian understanding as it has been discussed so far. According to the Trinitarian-theological rubric shaped by the Pentecost motif in John and Luke, the content of Christ's *promissio* is actualized by the giving of the Spirit. The Holy Spirit has no speech other than what Christ speaks; the Spirit's speech is filled with no content other than the Second Person of the Trinity. In his hymn, Luther does not limit the Spirit's advent to the Trinitarian rubric of Pentecost: the Spirit comes to creation in the present.

THE DIVINE PLEASURE IN CREATION

The hymn begins with the Spirit's advent as a summons to joy in the present tense. When the beginning is interpreted in terms of the Pentecost motif of fulfillment, the question arises as to why Luther locates the Spirit's advent not after the final verses of Christ's dismissal but right at the beginning of the hymn. In this section, I will address this difficulty by showing how Luther brings together the Spirit's advent at Pentecost with the Spirit's role in the creation context. Drawing on Luther's printed sermon on Genesis 1 (1523), I suggest that the creation context provides a rubric for understanding the present tense as the time of the Spirit's advent. In the beginning, as Luther understands the relevant passage from Genesis, the Spirit is hidden in creation as God's good pleasure. By uniting the Spirit's hiddenness in creation to the pronouncement of divine pleasure, the hymn's beginning anounces the Spirit's perpetual advent in the community's praise.

The Spirit's hiddenness at the beginning of the hymn dovetails with Luther's understanding of the Spirit's silence at creation. Luther's 1523 "sermon and introduction to Genesis 1" provides an intriguing discussion

---

96. "Darumb soll Christus nicht liegen, so muß seyn wort erfullet seyn worden zu der zeyt, da der heylig geist kam, der muß yhn alles gesagt haben und alles außgericht, das hie der herr sagt und sie freylich geleytet haben ynn alle warheyt." Ibid., 550.33–36 (Sermon on the Fourth Sunday after Easter, May 3, 1523).

of the order of Trinitarian presentation and of the Spirit's hidden presence. According to Luther's interpretation of Genesis 1, the three persons of the Trinity are introduced in a particular order. The order is determined by the way each person participates in the act of creating. For Luther, the grammatical level determines the distinctions between the persons. The verbs "to create, to see, to speak" distinguish between Father, Son, and Spirit while presenting them in the work of creating.[97] Luther detects the Third Person of the Trinity in the words, "God saw that the light was good" (Gen 1:4).[98] To the Spirit is attributed the delight with which God sees what has been created at the end of every day. The pronouncement reveals the divine pleasure, yet the Spirit's presence remains hidden. In his sermon on Genesis, Luther reflects on the Spirit's hiddenness in creation by drawing on two New Testament passages: Luther refers to Ephesians 4:3 and Colossians 3:14 in order to more fully describe the Spirit as the "band" sustaining all creatures and giving them their form, movement, and life.[99] Hidden in creation as its form and life, the Spirit's presence is revealed only in the words of the Father's pleasure. From the perspective offered by Luther's sermon, the opening silence of his hymn can be interpreted in terms of the Spirit's hiddenness. Hidden in the summons to joy, the Spirit is the Father's good pleasure resting on the community.

Another indication at the hymn's beginning can link the Spirit's advent to the creation context. By summarizing God's "wondrous act" as its theme, the hymn looks forward to the narrative of Christ subsequently unfolded in the remaining verses. The hymn's introduction anticipates the incarnation and death of Christ, a perspective typical of the medieval understanding

---

97. "Schopffen, sehen und sprechen haben nocheinnander mußen gehen, und sein doch mittennander geweßen. Ich kan nit zcu gleich sprechen vatter, sohn, heiliger geist." Ibid., 450.36–37, 451, 29 (Ein Sermon und Eingang in das erste Buch Mosi, March 15, 1523).

98. Ibid., 450, 2. The entire passage reads as follows: "Die dritt person aber wird heymlich yn den worten angezeygt, wie wir gesagt haben, da er spricht 'Gott sahe das liecht fur gut ane', das ist, er hat ein wolgefallen darin, dann es ist bey Got ein lust und wolgefallen an dem gewest, das er durch das wort gemacht hat, welchs nit anders ist, dann das Got die creatur erhebt, wie er sye gemacht hatt, und yhn bey stehet." Ibid., 450.1–5.

99. "Das wirt eygentlich dem heyligen geist zugerechnet, das er sey das leben und erhebung aller ding, Darumb die schrifft also von yhm redt, das er sey das band, das da al creaturn halt und allen yr ubung und wirkung geb." Ibid., 450.5–8.

of Old Testament faith.[100] According to this view, the Spirit speaks through the prophets in the Old Testament, witnessing to Christ, who is to come. On the other hand, the dispensation of the Holy Spirit at Pentecost follows Christ's ascension.[101] By beginning the hymn with an anticipation of Christ to come, Luther places the Spirit's dispensation in the creation context. This location does not subvert the Pentecost motif in which the Spirit's sending is integrally tied to Christ's ascension. The creation context serves to unite the distinct moments in a Trinitarian understanding that is embraced by the divine beginning.

The present tense is a superimposition of a looking forward to Christ's incarnation and the fulfillment of the *promissio* that looks back to Christ, who has come. The perpetual advent of the Spirit summons the community to joy anew. For Luther, the present tense characterizes the time of the Spirit's advent. The Spirit's work spans the present to the future resurrection of the dead, as Luther preaches in sermons of this period and writes in the Large Catechism (1529).[102] The way of the pilgrim is a metaphor for the temporal domain of human existence embraced by the ongoing work of the Spirit.[103] Perpetually and in the present tense, the Spirit works to

100. A discussion of temporal propositions in the genre of the *disputatio* concerning the Christ who is to come, and the Christ who has come is found in ch. 2, "Tense, Modality, and the Eternal Generation of the Son."

101. In his Commentary on 1 Peter, Luther discusses the theme of the discontinuity between the two testaments in terms of the distinction between the future and the past tenses. "Zum ersten ist das die unterscheyd unter dem alten und newen Testament, wie wyr ytzt gesagt haben, das das alte hatt gedeuttet auff Christum, das new aber gibt uns nu das, das vor ym alten verheyssen und durch die figuren bedeut ist gewesen." WA 12:275.25–28 (to 1 Pet 1:10). In ibid., 274.24–275.4, Luther refers to the Old Testament as the ground of "our faith," chastizing those who despise the Old Testament and say "es sey nicht mehr von no(e)tten." Ibid., 274.34.

102. A parallel is observed between Luther's sermons in 1523 and the explanation of the Creed in the Large Catechism concerning the theme of the perpetual present tense activity of the Spirit. "Darumb rede ich von dem ampt des heyligen geysts, was er thun soll und ymmer ym schwang gehen lasset, … Denn seyn ampt stehet nicht also, das es schon aussgericht sey, Sondernn das es von tage zu(o) tage ymmer yhe mehr wirckt und weret so lang wyr leben." Ibid., 577.11–12, 18–20 (Sermon on Pentecost, May 24, 1523). A similar passage is found in the same sermon: "Denn wyr predigen nicht also vom heyligen geyst und seynem ampt, als hab ers schon aussgericht und volnbracht, Sondernn also, das es nu hab angefangen unnd itzet ymmer ym schwang gehe, das ers yhe mehr und mehr treybe unnd nicht auffho(e)re." Ibid., 572.28–31. In concluding his explanation to the Creed in the Large Catechism, Luther compares the present tense work of the Spirit to the work of both the Father and the Son that have already been accomplished. See: WA 30,1:191.17–21.

103. The metaphor of the pilgrim to illustrate the Christian life is not new to Luther. "Eyn Christ, wenn er rechtschaffen glewbt, so hat er alle gu(e)tter Gottis und ist Gottis son, wie wyr

"set the gospel in motion."[104] Every time the community is gathered and the praise of God's "sweet" (*süsse*) and wondrous act is sung, the experience of the word is sweetened by the Spirit. In words echoing Psalm 34:9, Luther writes, "For the Word has such grace that the more we interact with it, the sweeter it becomes."[105] In the perpetual advent of the Spirit, the present tense is privileged as the temporal site at which the "sweetness" of God's "wondrous deed" is experienced.

The superimposition of Pentecost onto creation appears to determine the starting point of Luther's hymn. In his work, Luther can assign the Spirit to both sites—Pentecost and creation. In the beginning, God creates many voices of different creatures.[106] When the voices sing out in harmony, they manifest the divine pleasure in creation.[107] On the particular day of Pentecost, the theme of created diversity is rehearsed again. The different languages are given in order to carry the preaching of Christ to all nations.[108] Cast by the Pentecost motif, the Spirit fulfills Christ's *promissio*. Overlaid by the creation rubric, the Spirit's advent announces divine pleasure in what God sees.

---

geho(e)rt haben. Aber die zeyt, die er noch lebt, ist nur eyn pylgerfart." WA 12:290.20-22 (to 1 Pet 1:17). Biel uses the metaphor of the pilgrim when referring to the evident knowledge of theological truths. In the Prologue to his Commentary on the *Sentences*, Biel asks the question, "'Utrum sit possibile' intellectui 'viatoris habere notitiam evidentem de veritatibus' theologicis." Biel, *Collectorium*, vol. 1, *Prologus et Liber primus*, q. 1, A (Prologus) [8].

104. The phrase, "im Schwange gehen," is one of Luther's favorite idioms. He uses it to capture the outward impulse of the gospel as it is proclaimed and sung. For example: "Aber die Summa sey die, das es ia alles geschehe, das das wort ym schwang gehe und nicht widderumb eyn loren und dohnen draus werde, wie bis her gewesen ist." WA 12:37.26-29 (Von Ordnung Gottesdiensts in der Gemeine, 1523). See also 158n102.

105. WA 12:296.19-20 (to 1 Pet 1:22).

106. "... inuenies Musicam esse ab initio mundi inditam seu concreatam creaturis vniuersis, singulis et omnibus. Nihil enim est sine sono." WA 50:368.10, 369.1-2.

107. Luther understands the Spirit in Gen 1 to be the divine pleasure in creation. See: WA 12:450.1-8 (March 15, 1523, on Gen 1). For the citation, see 157nn98-99.

108. "Er [the Holy Spirit] harret nicht, bis alle welt gen Jerusalem keme und lernet Ebreisch, sondern gab allerley zungen zum predig ampt, das die Apostel reden kunden, wo sie hyn kamen." WA 19:74.16-18.

A crucial aspect shaping the approach to Luther's hymn as a narrative of Trinitarian advent is the determination of the beginning. In this section, I have argued that the literal starting point of the hymn is the theological starting point of the Trinitarian narrative. Rather than beginning with an anthropological "I," Luther's hymn begins with the Spirit's advent. Accompanied by music, the Spirit's advent transforms the heart to joy. A second aspect to the Spirit's advent is captured by the Pentecost motif, which fulfills Christ's *promissio*. The rubric of the creation context shapes the present tense advent as the divine good pleasure. The synchronic superimposition of Pentecost and creation at the beginning anticipates the Trinitarian narrative to be unfolded. The Spirit looks back at Christ's *promissio*. Simultaneously, the beginning looks forward to Christ's advent, which will determine the content of the *promissio* in terms of what God has done and for what God is to be praised. By attributing the beginning to the Holy Spirit, Luther's understanding of the Trinitarian narrative begins not with captivity, but with grace. In the verses following the introduction, the Spirit's advent is interrupted by another starting point. How the account of the captive "I" and the corresponding divine silence are to be suspended in the hymn's narrative is the theme of the next section.

THE DIVINE SILENCE

An abrupt break marks the shift from the opening verse of Luther's hymn to the subsequent two verses. It is the poetic depiction of the captivity of the "I" under sin, death, and the devil. Verses two and three articulate an I that is bounded without mediation by what precedes and follows. These verses appear to interrupt the narrative of the Spirit's advent (verse one) and the Father's speech to the Son (verses four and five). God is silent; the "I" sounds out from the abyss of despair.

The radical break presents a moment in Luther's theology that is as intriguing as it is problematic. This interruption has been discussed by scholars as the hymn's theological-anthropological starting point. According to this view, the hymn's narrative moves from law to gospel. When, on the other hand, the hymn is interpreted in light of its literal starting point in verse one, the question arises as to how the interruption is related both to the Spirit's advent and to the Father's speech in eternity.

By looking at the praise and lament psalms as the model for this interpretation, the narrative rupture will be located as a moment in the Spirit's advent and will be viewed from the perspective of the Father's speech as the Christological suspension of silence. The first section begins with a description of the theological-anthropological paradigm that I argue undermines the hymn's narrative of mercy. I then discuss the structure of the lament and praise psalms before turning to the Christological center of the lament. In the genre of the hymn of praise, Luther understands the advents of both the Spirit and of Christ as the two discursive moments in which the lament is suspended as the focus of what God has done: turned the silence of death at the center of the Trinity into speech "for us."

THE LAW-GOSPEL RELATION AND THE DOCTRINE OF GOD

The usual interpretation of Luther's hymn begins not with verse one, but with verse two. When the captivity of the "I" is privileged as the starting point, the hymn's narrative is conceptualized as the move from law to gospel. Scholars draw on Romans 7 as the biblical warrant for the hymn's anthropological beginning—the human under the law.[109] Ebeling summarizes a consensus in Luther research when he defines Luther's understanding of the law according to its accusing function (*usus elenchthicus*).[110] This second sense of the law, driving the "I" to utter despair, is seen as a prelude to the gospel. The difficulty with assigning the law-gospel distinction to Luther's Reformation breakthrough does not have to do with a scholarly fiction. Luther himself asserts the subject matter of theology to be the sinner and the justifying God.[111] The modern problem has to do with the interpretation that views the gospel from a perspective skewed by a theological anthropology. Yeago has pointed out that the distinction between law and gospel, particularly in the tradition stemming from Elert, has been expanded to make an ontology of human existence the interpretive key

---

109. Jung, "Nun freut euch, lieben Christen gmein," 204; Rudolf Köhler, *Die biblischen Quellen der Lieder*, 369, 372.

110. For an exemplary discussion of the relation between law and gospel as the hermeneutical breakthrough of Luther's theology, see: Gerhard Ebeling, "Das rechte Unterscheiden," 219–58; Ebeling, *Luther*, 120–56.

111. "..., ut proprie sit subiectum Theologiae homo reus et perditus et deus iustificans vel salvator." WA 40,2:328.1–2 (Enarratio Psalmi LI, 1532/1534, to v. 2).

to Luther's thought.[112] Yeago's challenge strikes to the heart of a number of Luther scholars who underline the law so much that they undermine the gospel.

In the hymn, the interruption points to the central difficulty of Luther's theology. The challenge is a conceptual one of locating two distinct starting points in a narrative unity. When the law-gospel paradigm is privileged, the doctrine of the Trinity is moved to the margin. Elert, for example, cannot harmonize Luther's reception of the early church's Trinitarian dogma with the evangelical breakthrough.[113] Bayer summarizes other problematic proposals. Scholars attempt to bridge the gap between anthropology and a Trinitarian theology by treating the gospel as a contingent reaction to the law. Or they locate the gospel in the eternal divine will that is subsequently actualized in time, out of necessity, in the incarnation.[114] What Bayer criticizes are Hegelian interpretations of Luther that attempt to conceive the rupture in the text according to a unifying concept of God.[115] Bayer takes seriously the lack of mediation in Luther's text, insisting that the rupture must provide a resistance against conceptual mediation.

Bayer's own interpretation of Luther's hymn exposes the anthropological rupture to the point of its narrative breakdown. The aim of Bayer's study is to spell out the implications of Luther's hymn for the doctrine of the Trinity. Taking Romans 7 as his exegetical point of departure, Bayer notes the absence of mediation between the "I" under the law (Rom 7:24) and the God of the gospel (Rom 7:25a) and interprets the hymn's overall flow as a story composed of two distinct parts.[116] The first part tells the story

---

112. "Thus the law oppresses because it proposes a determinate ordering of our existence and calls for a specified response, and it follows that the gospel liberates because it delivers from determinate order and specified response. The law-gospel distinction thus conceived expands quite naturally into a kind of ontology of human existence, at whose heart is an antagonism, or at least an irresolvable tension, of form and freedom, of order and authenticity." David S. Yeago, "Gnosticism, Antinomianism, and Reformation Theology," 41.

113. Elert criticizes Luther. "Allerdings macht er keinen Versuch, sie von seinem Glaubensverständnis aus zu durchdringen. ... Aber im allgemeinen ist doch die Trinitätslehre in seiner Theologie wie ein erratischer Block stehen geblieben." Elert, *Morphologie*, 191.

114. Oswald Bayer, "Das Sein Jesu Christi im Glauben," 279.

115. Bayer criticizes any representations of Luther that attempt to mediate the two sides by using Hegel's dialectic of self-consciousness. Ibid., 283.

116. "Das Evangelium wird hier wie, freilich schärfer noch, im Lied als eine zweiteilige Geschichte erzählt: als Geschichte einer erhörten Klage, wie sie sich unüberbietbar scharf—wie in einem Brennspiegel—Röm 7,24 und 25a konzentriert. ... Die beiden Teile dieser

of an "ontology of self-justification."[117] Corresponding to this anthropologically determined ontology is an understanding of God as the one who speaks against the "I" in the law.[118] On the other hand, the second part of the story, the ontology of divine justification, corresponds to the God who speaks for the "I" in the gospel. At the level of the doctrine of God, the two parts of Luther's hymn tell the story of a dynamism, a turn from divine wrath to divine mercy.[119] Bayer's effort to take into account the rupture in Luther's doctrine of God, while insisting on the unprecedented act of mercy eluding a final explanation, offers an insightful criticism of theologians who would render harmless the stunning harshness of verses two and three. However, the alleged unbridgeable gap in Bayer's position on the divine nature threatens to dismantle the divine unity altogether. When the law-gospel principle is projected into the nature of God, a wedge symmetrically splits it apart into the two sides of wrath and mercy. The divine conversion to the gospel is experienced as an unprecedented revolution in the divine nature, a turnaround unmediated by conceptual explanation. In a recent clarification of his position, Bayer claims that the first part of the story corresponds to a "'general' doctrine of God or anthropology."[120] Only the second story can be properly defined as a thematization of the doctrine of the Trinity. The result of this clarification is, however, the same. Even when the anthropological level is transposed into some version of a doctrine of God, the "general" view of God is split off from the "specific" Trinitarian story of divine mercy.

Bayer's study of Luther's hymn is a representative example of how the law-gospel relation, when applied to the lack of mediation in the doctrine of God, results in a narrative split. The narrative breakdown tends to eclipse a Trinitarian understanding of the divine mercy by driving it apart from

---

Geschichte sind nach dem Klage—Erhörungsparadigma (Ps 22 usw.) einander zugeordnet—so jedoch, daß kein Übergang vermittelt." Ibid., 277.

117. "So ist diese Ontologie des Selbstseins eine Ontologie der Selbstrechtfertigung." Ibid., 278. [Italics in original text.]

118. "Nicht zu denken ist nicht einmal eine Einheit des Gottes, der—im Gesetz—gegen mich spricht, so daß ich ihn und sein Gericht von ganzem Herzen nur hassen kann (3,3), mit dem Gott, der—im Evangelium—für mich spricht, so daß ich ihn und seinen Sohn von ganzem Herzen nur lieben kann." Ibid.

119. Ibid., 276, 279.

120. Oswald Bayer, "Poetologische Trinitätslehre," 67–79.

the "other" side of God as wrath. An alternative to preserving the lament as an unmediated rupture while allowing for the possibility of conceiving a Trinitarian narrative of mercy will be presented in the next section. The approach is gained by proposing Psalms, not Romans 7, to be the exegetical matrix in which the genre and the language of the hymn—and by extension, Luther's Trinitarian understanding—is born.

THE HYMN OF PRAISE AND THE DIVINE SILENCE

In Luther's hymn of praise, the radical anthropological break (verses two and three) is located narratively after the Spirit's advent as a second starting point. The intention of this section is to argue for a narrative of Trinitarian advent that respects the lament as a rupture. How this aim is achieved is to show that the divine silence characterizing the lament is converted by the divine advent into its own speech. In order to show how the hymn assigns a narrative site to the divine silence, the hymn's sub-genres—praise and lament psalms—are reviewed. Shaped by these genres, the hymn begins with the Spirit's advent, which converts the lament into the confession of sin.

The "I" in Captivity to the Unholy Trinity

The shift from the Spirit's joyful summons to the condition of the "I" could not be more abrupt. Verses two and three interrupt the Spirit's advent with a sharp rupture in subject, mood, and verb tense. The subject is no longer the first person plural, the "we" of the Christian community, but the first person singular.[121] No longer free to enjoy the other in community, the solitary "I" is held captive to what Rößler calls the "unholy trinity."[122] Sin, death, and devil are portrayed as personified forces, actively holding the "I" captive.[123] These terms are situated at the beginning of each line, either in

---

121. "Ich, mein, mich" are repeated throughout verses two and three. I am grateful to Christa Reich for pointing out that the "I" portrayed in verses two and three does not cry out. Rather, the "I" is silent. Personal conversation on Oct. 5, 1998, in Mainz.

122. The phrase, "die unheilige Dreieinigkeit," is coined by Rößler, "Ballade vom Ratschluß Gottes zur Erlösung," 445.

123. The exegetical backdrop to listing the personified forces of sin, death, and devil is 1 Cor 15:55-56, as the following quote from a Trinity Sunday sermon shows: "Denn er [Paulus] alles ungluck zusamen faßet, nennets stachel oder spitzen, damit der todt todtschlecht, ist die sunde, Macht eittel person draus, als seiens drey kriegsknecht, die wider drey hehr spitzen stritten." WA 49:772.10-12 (Sermon on Trinity Sunday, May 31, 1545).

the dative or the nominative case to connote their sheer grip on the "I," who is utterly helpless: for example: "I was imprisoned by the devil" (2.1); "In death I was lost" (2.2); "My sin afflicted me" (2.3); "Sin possessed me" (2.7).

Verbs are joined to the three powers of the unholy trinity in succinct verbal phrases that rivet the "I" to sheer passivity. These verbal phrases are regarded from a literary-linguistic point of view as "the most concise form of figurative speech."[124] In his study of Luther's hymn, Hahn analyzes how the emotive intensification of the poetic discourse is achieved by strategically relating the verbs to the nouns.[125] Verbal phrases mark the passivity of the "I": "I was imprisoned by the devil" (2.1); "I was annihilated by death" (2.2); "Sin completely possessed me" (2.7); "that nothing but death remained with me" (3.6). Other verbal phrases indicate an active torturing of the "I": "My sin afflicted me night and day" (2.3); "Fear brought me to despair" (3.5). The captivity of the "I" is further dramatized by verbs connected to it: "In [sin], I was born" (2.4); "I also fell ever deeper into it" (2.5); "My good works did not count; they were tainted by [sin]" (3.1–2); "The free will hated God's judgment; it was dead to the good" (3.3–4); "To hell, I must descend" (3.7). Taking the "I" as their subject, these verbal phrases qualify the passivity of the "I" by connoting an incapacity to extricate itself from captivity. This incapacity is attributed to the "free will" that is incapable of doing any good: "My good works did not count; ... it [the free will] was dead to the good" (3.1, 4). The fiction of the free will is exposed as a bondage to death; the anticipated merit of good works is revealed as a hopeless illusion. With the poetic summary of two aspects to the "I," its captivity to the unholy trinity and its death to the good, Luther captures the central insight of his theological anthropology. The human is "guilty and ruined."[126] Its space is hell; its time is limited by death. There is no crying out for God but the silence of the terrified conscience.

Luther correlates the "I" with a distinct picture of God. The "I" does not perceive God as the Trinitarian essence of mercy. The judgment of God is determined by the "I" as the object of hate. The captivity of the "I" to free will's hatred is told: "The good will hated God's judgment" (3.3).

---

124. Hahn, *Evangelium als literarische Answeisung*, 116.

125. Ibid., 113.

126. See 161n11.

The only place where the word "God" is mentioned in these two verses, as a genitive of judgment, indicates a specific knowledge of God. Without mentioning the word "law," Luther resorts to the free will motif in order to point out that the will is only free to be at enmity with the divine judgment. In a 1523 sermon, Luther preaches on a similar theme: "We lay there in the muck, completely hating the almighty and eternal God and harsh Judge."[127] Elsewhere, Luther draws out the devastating implications of the "I's" hatred: all creation becomes the source of terror.[128] The "I" cries out from a place where God is not its only enemy; all creation becomes the source of terror.

The poetic compendium of verses two and three presents the disconcerting depth of Luther's theological anthropology. Death encloses the "I," pressing in from all sides. An interpretation that privileges the captivity of the "I" as the hymn's starting point would continue with the narrative move to the gospel. A narrative of Trinitarian advent, however, plots the lament of the "I" as an interruption. It is to the issue of genre that I will turn in order to show how an interruption does not split the narrative into two unmediated parts. Rather, the lament is suspended at the center of the triune mystery.

The Plot of "Before" and "After" as a Function of Genre

The issue of genre is the crucial factor in locating the interruption within the narrative of Luther's hymn. Luther shares the insight of modern biblical scholars when he divides Psalms into two basic types. The genre of praise or thanks and the genre of the lament are the elementary forms in the "little Bible," as Luther calls the Psalter.[129] The biblical scholar Hermann

---

127. WA 12:470.24-25 (Sermon on Palm Sunday, March 29, 1523).

128. "Dann syntemal Gott widder yhn ist, so mussen auch alle ding wider yhn sein." Ibid., 443.10-11 (Ein Sermon und Eingang in das erste Buch Mosi, March 15, 1523). Luther continues with this familiar and vivid picture of experiencing the world as an ominous and terrifying place: "... so gehet es dann, wie Moses schreibt Leviti. xxvi. [Lev 26:36], Das die gotlosen auch ein rauschents blatt, das vom bawm fellt, erschreckt, da kan das hertz nit so viel muß kriegen, das es eyn manheyt fasset wider ein so(e)lch gering rauschent blatt." Ibid., 443.11-14.

129. In his "Vorrede auf den Psalter (1528)," Luther summarizes the two genres found in the Psalter: the praise or thank Psalms and the lament Psalms. "Wo findet man feiner wort von freuden, denn die lob Psalmen odder danck Psalmen haben? ... Widderumb wo findestu tieffer, kleglicher, iemerlicher wort, von traurigkeit, denn die klage Psalmen haben?" WADB 10,1:102.8-9, 12-13. Luther describes the Psalter as "ein kleine Biblia" in ibid., 98.22. On the lament psalms, see: Ibid., 102.12-15.

Gunkel also notes, "The lament songs in particular form the essential foundation of the Psalms."[130] In an insightful study on the themes of life and death in Psalms, Christoph Barth explores the relationship between songs of praise and lament.[131] Psalms of lament illustrate in the present tense the experience of the limit that threatens human beings. From the boundaries, images of death diffuse into the space of life. In lament psalms, "The individual often finds himself in the immediate vicinity of Sheol. The individual stands within its gates, right at the border; but the individual is not entirely gripped by hell."[132] Barth discusses the psalmist's understanding of death's invasion into the present tense of the living as a power not to be identified with YHWH, whose unambiguous will is the covenant with Israel.[133] Not occupying a definite geographical site, the realm of death is seen as a prison in which the possibilities of room to live in community and in relation to God are cut off.[134] The prisoners of death are sinners, divorced from living in the divine presence.[135] Barth shows that a shift in perspective takes place when the lament is integrated into the song of praise. When the lament appears in a song of praise, its original present tense is converted into the past tense. From the present tense perspective of life, the song of thanksgiving assigns the song of lament to the past tense.

Luther's hymn represents the two basic genres of the Psalter in a manner that dovetails with Barth's insight. A quick glance at the verb tenses of Luther's hymn discloses the difference between praise and lament. Luther draws on all three German past tenses—the perfect, the imperfect, and the pluperfect—to paint the poetic picture of the captivity of the "I" to the powers of the unholy trinity: "lay imprisoned; was lost; afflicted, was born, was possessed by" (2.1-5, 7). Enclosing the past tense lament is the present tense praise: "Now rejoice." (1.1). The genre of the

---

130. Hermann Gunkel, *Einleitung in die Psalmen*, 173.

131. Christoph Barth, *Die Errettung vom Tode: Leben und Tod in den Klage- und Dankliedern des Alten Testaments.*

132. Ibid., 91.

133. Ibid., 57.

134. "Dem Verlust der Aktionsfreiheit im Tode entspricht die Bezeichnung und Beschreibung des Totenreiches als *Gefängnis*—ein Zug, der sich in den Unterweltsvorstellungen fast aller Völker findet." Ibid., 61. Death as a prison is a theme in many lament psalms, as Barth indicates. Ibid., 80.

135. Ibid., 86-94.

hymn of praise structures the narrative by situating the moment of lament from the standpoint of communal singing and rejoicing. Formally, Luther's hymn is structured by the lament-praise distinction that Barth discusses. With respect to content, it remains to be shown how the lament is plotted by the narrative as the conversion of silence into the particular language of the confession of sin.

The Pneumatological Conversion of Silence into Speech

The Spirit's advent and the lament's interruption are two narrative moments in Luther's hymn. Narratively prior to the lament is the Spirit's advent. From the perspective of the hymn's narrative starting point, the lament is assigned a temporal location in the past tense. The starting point becomes the "after" in relation to which the "before" is plotted. In the narrative flow, the "after" becomes the perspective from which the "before" is viewed. What has already been shown is how Luther attributes the narrative starting point to the Spirit. The question now emerges as to how the plot of "after" in relation to the "before" is understood in terms of the Spirit's advent. Luther incorporates the "before" into the narrative in a way that correlates the site with an aspect of the divine advent that is not erased from memory but rendered in a distinct type of speech.

The lament correlates the "before" with a particular knowledge of God. Articulated in the lament is the hatred of the "I" for the divine judgment. This insight is not only generated by the genre of the hymn. In sermons, especially those preached in 1523, Luther consistently thematizes the specific experience of hating the divine judgment. In one sermon, Luther discusses what reason knows about God without faith. For those in this group, the conscience experiences God as enemy.[136] Enmity or hatred are, for Luther, human experiences that correspond to an understanding of the divine nature in terms of judgment. In his hymn, the lament becomes the site at which the experience of hating the divine judgment is articulated.

The hatred of the "I" corresponds to an aspect of the divine advent that Luther locates under the Third Person of the Trinity. In his hymn

---

136. "Die es aber mit vernunfft one den glauben fassen und fulens, das yhn das gewissenn sagt, das yhn Gott feindt ist, die ko(e)nnen wider rwe noch freude haben. Die andern aber, die nicht solchen verstand fassen oder fulen, konnen nit meer, dann das sye sagen 'got hat himmel unnd erden geschaffen', kumbt aber nicht yns hertz, Sunder behalten die wort nur auff der zungen." WA 12:443.25, 444.1-4 (Gen 1).

and in sermons held in 1523, Luther consistently locates the divine judgment under the rubric of the Spirit's advent.[137] Preaching on the key text of John 16:5–15, Luther speaks of the "before" in terms of the Spirit's advent as judge.[138] Christ promises to send the Spirit, who will accuse the world on account of righteousness. When the Spirit comes as judge, the Spirit exposes human captivity to sin and the complete incapacity for the good.[139] In his commentary on Psalm 51:6, Luther attributes the knowledge of sin to the work of the Spirit.[140] Luther can articulate the Spirit's advent as judge in terms of the preaching of the law. "When God wants to call us to account," the law uncovers the knowledge of guilt.[141] The law, although incompetent in transforming the heart, prepares one to accept the comfort of the gospel.[142] The Spirit's advent as judge is a moment in Luther's theology that he captures in the hymn of praise. Luther does not metaphysically divide

---

137. An interesting point for further investigation concerns the distinction between the eschatological advent of Christ as judge and the perpetual present tense advent of the Spirit that includes the dimension of judgment.

138. The description of the Spirit's advent as judge is evident in this sermon. "Drumb wenn der heylig geist kompt, straffet er die leut und spricht 'Die werck die du than hast und auch die du noch thust, sind nur eytel sunde: drumb ists verloren, das du dich untersteihist mitt deynem vermugen fur die sund genugthun'." WA 12:546.10–13 (Sermon on the Fourth Sunday after Easter, May 3, 1523).

139. In the hymn: "Mein gu(o)te werk die golten nicht" (3.1).

140. "Non enim agitur hic de peccato metaphysice nec historice, sed Theologice et in spiritu agitur de illa cognitione, ut pronunciemus et iudicemus nos esse peccatores, Deum autem esse iustum." WA 40,2:369.19–21 (Enarratio Psalmi LI, 1532 (1538), to verse 6). See also: Ibid., 326.34–37 (to verse 2); 369.27–32 (to verse 6); 422.27–31 (to verse 12).

141. "Denn also gehet es auch zu zwyschen Gott und uns. Wenn Gott rechnung will halten, so lesset er aussgehen die predigt von seynem gesetz, durch wilchs wyr lernen erkennen, was wyr schuldig sind." WA 12:677.24–26 (Sermon on the Twenty-second Sunday after Trinity, Nov. 1, 1523).

142. Luther frequently sharpens the "before" to its radical edge, pointing out that the gospel impacts those best who are entirely crushed by despair. A delightful comment on Luke 1:53 portrays the move from law to gospel under the rubric of pastoral care. "Die schmeckens aber am besten, die ynn tods no(e)ten ligen, odder die das bo(e)ß gewissen druckt, da ist der hunger eyn gu(o)tter koch, wie man spricht, der macht, das die speyß wol schmecket." Ibid., 304.23–26 (to 1 Pet 2:2). In another genre, Luther writes of the despair driving the human to doubt in one's own capacity to fulfill the demands of the law. Out of a desperate situation marked by doubt and fear, emerges the hope in a "great help." "Das ist, sie entpfynden die schweryn und last des gesatzs, das es von ynen erfordert die ding, die sie auß iren krefften nit vermo(e)gen zu(o)thu(o)n. Darumb fallen sie nit daruff mit iren natürlichen vermo(e) gen, das sie es allein hylten, Sunder in irer angst und unvermügligkeit erwarten sie einer grossen hilff, damit sie es auß hertzen volbringen mo(e)gen." Ibid., 462.12–16 (Predigt am Tage der Verkündigung unser lieben Frauen, March 25, 1523).

the aspect of the divine nature as judgment from the advent as the summons to joy. Rather, he assigns the two aspects to two narrative moments under the rubric of the Spirit's advent. The narrative distinction between "before" and "after" is plotted by the Spirit's present tense advent. The emerging picture reveals the Spirit's present tense advent, which plots its own moment of judgment in the past tense.

With the Spirit's advent, a discursive conversion from silence into speech is effected. Under the rubric of the divine judgment, the lament articulates a speech that, on the surface, is crushed by the divine silence. There is no divine response to the hatred of the "I" for the divine judgment. When this lament is viewed from the perspective shaped by the genre of the hymn of praise, it is transformed into a speech effected by the Spirit's advent. The lament is articulated as a confession of sin. Confession recalls the "before" as captivity to the unholy trinity and as the incapacity for good. From the perspective of the "after," the preceding enmity with the law is acknowledged and confessed.[143] With the conversion of the lament to confession, a narrative asymmetry between judgment and joy is achieved. The Holy Spirit plots the advent as judge "before" its own advent as the transformation to joy.[144] Luther does not import the divine judgment symmetrically with joy into the doctrine of God. Rather, he assigns the two moments to two narrative locations that end up converting the "before" of judgment into the "after" of confessional discourse.

The genre of the hymn and its particular language cannot be underestimated when showing how Luther articulates his understanding of the Trinity as a narrative of Trinitarian advent. Barth's study on the lament and praise psalms provides the key to locating the lament under the rubric of

---

143. "..., wann man gleich gottis gesetz treybt, so pleybt dannoch das hertz ungefurt und ungetriben; dann inwendig ist das hertz dem gesetz feind." Ibid., 464.19–21 (Sermon on Palm Sunday, March 29, 1523). In his "Vorrede auf den Psalter (1528)," Luther writes that the lament psalms provide the language articulating the experience of the divine wrath. "Da sihestu abermal allen heiligen yns hertz, wie ynn den tod, ia wie ynn die helle, wie finster vnd tunckel ists da von allerley betru(e)btem anblick des zorn Gottes." WADB 10,1:102.13–15.

144. In the genre of the sermon, a similar content is thematized. "Do sihet das hertz Gott nymmer mit schelen augen an, dencket nicht, er werd yhn ynn die hell werfen, wie vorhyn, ehe der heylig geyst kam, do es keyn gu(o)tt, keyn liebe noch trewe, sondern nichts denn zorn und ungnad Gottis fulet, Sondern die weyl der heylig geyst solichs yns hertz drucket, das yhm Gott so freundlich und gnedig sey, so dunckt es yhn, das Gott nicht mehr zornen kunde und wirt so lu(e)stig unnd unerschrocken, das er umb Gottis willen alles thutt und leydet, was zu(o) thun unnd zu(o) leyden ist." WA 12:571.33–572.5 (Sermon on Pentecost, May 24, 1523).

the Spirit's advent in the hymn of praise. Initially viewed as a suspension of the past tense in present tense praise, the lament interrupts the Spirit's advent in such a way as to expose the "before" as the divine silence in the face of the divine judgment as one aspect of the Spirit's advent. The narrative plotting correlates the "before" with the aspect of the divine advent as judgment. Yet the "after" provides the occasion for its articulation in the language of the confession of sin. Only from the Spirit's advent in the present tense is the articulation of the past tense rendered as a confession. According to this interpretation, Luther neither reduces the divine judgment to a subjective projection nor isolates it as an independent dimension of the divine nature viewed apart from the Trinity. The theological starting point suspends the anthropological starting point as both the divine silence in the past tense that, at the moment of its advent in the present tense, overcomes its own silence and becomes the speech of the community's confession of sin.

From the perspective of the first plot in the Trinitarian narrative, the Spirit is conceived in relation to distinct types of speech: praise, and lament as the confession of sin. For Luther, the church's singing and the Spirit's speech remain undistinguished. In a later section, I will discuss why Luther, at this juncture in his theological thinking, does not consider the Spirit as speaker in the same way as he understands the Father's voice in eternity or the Son's address in time. Suffice it to say that, in his hymn, the speech of the Spirit is intimately bound up with the hymns of the church.

The narrative is not arrested under the rubric of the Spirit. With the Spirit's advent is promised the fulfillment of teaching the community and leading it in the knowledge and truth of Christ. The Spirit knows no other content of speech than Christ. It is to the Christological focus of the lament that I will now turn. The speech of Christ in the lament is captured by yet another subgenre of the psalms. In the language of the penitential psalms, the lament articulates the totality of the experience of death and points to the Christological mediation of the silence of death into the speech of life.

THE CHRISTOLOGICAL TRANSFORMATION
OF SILENCE INTO SPEECH

The Spirit's advent converts the lament into the language of confession and assigns it to the liturgical site of the confession of sin. The lament remains the focal point of present tense praise, but the impact of its unmediated status continues to interrupt the narrative. In this section, I argue that the lament is mediated by the second advent in Luther's narrative, the advent of Christ. Access to the Christological mediation of the lament is initially gained by looking at its content as an exegesis of the penitential psalms. It will be argued that the lament articulates the totality of Christ's death in the language of the penitential psalms by suspending this speech in the hymn of praise. Two narrative sites further gain access to the lament in an anticipatory mode. The outer-Trinitarian advent of the Spirit and the inner-Trinitarian speech of the Father suspend the lament's content in view of a Christological mediation. What is mediated in speech, however, is the silence of Christ's death.

The Christological Mediation of the Penitential Psalms

The issue of genre plays a significant role in shaping the relationship between praise and lament. Christoph Barth asks precisely this question as to how the lament can be mediated in the hymn of praise. He notes the discourse of the lament psalm independently of its suspension in the praise psalm. The lament's *pars pro toto* speech recalls the brush with death, not a total annihilation, from the perspective of deliverance.[145] When the lament is situated within the hymn of praise, its language articulates the total experience of death. Barth's insight dovetails with Luther's hymn. Suspended in the hymn of praise, verses two and three are observed to articulate a totality; the condition of the "I" is narrated from the depths of ultimate godforsakenness.[146] The question Barth poses at the end of his discussion can be seen to sharpen the focus of Luther's hymn. Barth asks, "Who is the individual involved, who knows that he is under God's wrath

145. The lament's suspension in the hymn of praise does not mean "von einem totalen Aufgehen in der Wirklichkeit des Todes," but "[m]it dem Wachsen der Not nähert sich der Einzelne dem totalen Aufgehen in der Wirklichkeit des Todes." Christoph Barth, *Die Errettung vom Tode*, 93.

146. "Dagegen zeigt das Danklied eine fast formelhafte Darstellung des Todeserlebnisses: in der Regel ist hier—im Rückblick auf den Zustand der Bedrängnis—von einem totalen Aufgehen in der Wirklichkeit des Todes die Rede." Ibid.

and forsaken by God—who now appears as one saved before God's coun-tenance?"[147] The individual, an Israelite representing the collective, is one who has endured more than a partial encounter with death. From the per-spective of the Israelite who has experienced total godforsakenness and in the name of this one standing for all, the present tense of the song of praise suspends the full impact of the past tense lament.[148] Barth's question can be asked of Luther's hymn: Who is the individual who has endured the full impact of death, hell, and devil in such a way as to suspend it as the lament of a totality in a hymn of praise?

When the poetic text of the lament is observed, one notes that Luther uses the discourse of a particular genre of psalm. The literary surface of Luther's hymn draws explicitly on the language of the penitential psalms. Luther's hymn echoes the scope spanned by these biblical passages: "fear" (3.5 in Ps 32:7); "sin" (2.3, 7 in Pss 38:19; 51:4, 5, 11); "Into [sin], I was born" (2.4 in Ps 51:7); "to die" (3.6 in Pss 102:4, 12; 143:7); "lay imprisoned" (2.1 in Ps 102:21); "deeper" (2.5 in Ps 130:1); "judgment" (3.3 in Ps 143:2); "devil" (2.1 as "the enemy" in Ps 143:3); "To hell I must descend" (3.7 as "to descend into the grave" in Ps 143:7). Luther was well acquainted with the penitential psalms, having published a commentary in 1517 and again in 1525.[149] In his well-known 1523 letter, Luther asked Spalatin to assign to poets and musicians the task of composing on the penitential psalms for congregational sing-ing.[150] The backdrop of Luther's acquaintance with the penitential psalms emerges at the forefront of the hymn's discourse; the lament appears to be an exegesis of the penitential psalms. Once the connection between the genres of the lament and penitence is noted, the answer to Barth's question can be sought in the exegetical tradition of the penitential psalms.

The Christological interpretation of the penitential psalms arose in the church's tradition at their liturgical site. Prayed during the seasons of Advent, Lent, and at the burial of the dead, the liturgical function of the

---

147. Ibid., 94.

148. Barth concludes that the Psalms do not anwer his question. The New Testament names the individual, "David," who is the "Platzhalter" of the "king of the Jews." Ibid., 96.

149. For the 1517 publication of Luther's commentary on the penitential psalms, see : WA 1:158.1–220.23. Luther published a revision of the 1517 "Die sieben Bußpsalmen" in 1525. See: WA 18:479.1–530.10.

150. Five of the seven penitential psalms are explicitly mentioned in the letter to Spalatin: 6, 32, 51, 130, 143, and excluded are 38 and 102. See: WABr 3:220.15–23 (no. 698, end of 1523).

penitential psalms was to prepare for the divine advent.[151] Preparation for the divine advent at Christmas, Easter, and the resurrection from the dead demanded an attitude of repentance. The model for true repentance was provided by the penitential psalms, understood as the speech of Christ. The association between confession and the cross seems to have emerged from the New Testament itself. Psalm passages are spoken by Christ on the cross (e.g., Matt 27:46; cf. Ps 22:2) or are used to interpret the event of Christ's passion (e.g., John 19:24; cf Ps 22:19). In the exegetical tradition following Augustine, Aquinas placed the penitential psalms in the mouth of Christ both as the head of the church and as the individual penitent preparing for absolution.[152] In various commentaries on these psalms, the psalms were understood to be Christ's prayer before the Father, pleading that the Father might show mercy to those for whom Christ died. The psalms were also considered to be Christ's speech to Christians, teaching the appropriate language and content for the church's confession of sin. Both the Christological and tropological interpretations were received by Luther in his 1517 commentary on the penitential psalms.[153] For Luther, the penitential psalms taught true repentance and the most certain absolution.[154]

---

151. For a commentary on the penitential psalms summarizing the history of their interpretation, see: J. M. Neale and R. F. Littledale, *A Commentary On the Psalms from Primitive and Mediaeval Writers*, vols. 1–4.

152. In Neale and Littledale, *Commentary on the Psalms* as follows: Ps 6 in vol. 1, 124; Ps 32 in vol. 1, 496; Ps 38 in vol. 1, 609; Ps 51 in vol. 2, 183; Ps 102 in vol. 3, 285; Ps 130 (the voice of the church represented by Peter) in vol. 4, 228; Ps 143 in vol. 4, 357.

153. "Dißen psalmen betet Christus yn seynem leyden und puß, die er vor unser sund than hat. ja das ist die rechte regel. wer all psalmen horet, gleych als auß Christus mund geredet, unnd alßo ym nach redet wie ein kynd seym vater nach betet, kan ym aber nit nach beten, er sey ym dan gleychformig yn der puß unnd leyden. darumb malet disser psalm auffs aller klerest die weyß, wort, werck, gedancken und berden eyns waren rewigen hertzen." WA 1:175.17–22 (Die sieben Bußpsalmen, 1517).

154. The penitential psalms teach true repentance that is constituted by two types of knowledge: knowledge of sin and knowledge of grace. "Proponitur hic doctrina de vera Poenitentia. Sunt autem in vera Poenitentia duo, cognitio peccati et cognitio gratiae, seu, ut notioribus appellationibus utamur, timor Dei et fiducia misericordiae ... Sic plane apparet Prophetam singulari consilio in hoc Psalmo voluisse relinquere veram sapientiam religionis divinae, explicatae sanis verbis et sano sensu, ut, quid peccatum, quid gratia, quid tota poenitentia esset, disceremus. Ac sunt huius generis alii quoque Psalmi, sicut Psalmus: 'Beati, quorum remissae', Item: 'De profundis clamavi.'" WA 40,2:317.34–37, 318.17–21 (Enarratio Psalmi LI, 1532 (1538), introduction). Luther preaches on the pronouncement of the absolution that is attributed to the Holy Spirit; the absolution is spoken by God. "Das ander stuck, welchs auch hieher gehoret, ist, das du mit rechtem glawben die Absolution horist unnd nicht zweyfelst, das die wort, so der spricht, dem du beychtist, Got selbs rede, denn Got hat sich also demuetigt

In his early struggles against the fear of reprobation, Luther discovered comfort in the Christological mediation of the penitential psalms.[155] By linking the confession of sin articulated in the "Pauline Psalms" with the divine mercy mediated by the wounds of Christ,[156] the horror of the pre-destining divine majesty was stilled.

At the surface of Luther's hymn, the penitental discourse of the lament drives in the direction of answering Barth's question. The question Barth asks—the identity of the one who has experienced the totality of death and divine judgment in such a way as to mediate its full impact in the hymn of praise—is answered. The most central mystery of the Christian faith is concentrated on the one who endures the silence of God to its extreme and then mediates this experience in speech: the cross and resurrection of Jesus Christ.[157] The lament articulating the totality of an experience ter-minating in death and in the descent to hell is placed in the mouth of an

---

unnd herunder gelassen, das er seyn heylig gottlich wort dem menschen ynn mund legt, das er gantz nit soll zweyffeln, das ers selb sage." WA 12:493.3-7 (Sermon on Maundy Thursday, April 2, 1523, text II).

155. It seems that Luther's terrified conscience arose in connection with the locus of predestination associated with Rom 9:16. Commenting on predestination in 1517, Staupitz, Luther's spiritual advisor and the vicar-general of the Augustinian Observantist congre-gations in Germany since 1503 redirected Luther's focus from the fear of reprobation to the divine mercy. The wounds of Christ were to be viewed as the source of the divine mercy. In the Middle Ages, the wounds were allegorically interpreted from the rock clefts found both in Exod 33:22 and in the Song 2:13-14 ("amica mea in foraminibus petrae"). It was Bernard of Clairvaux, preaching on the Song of Songs in sermons 61 and 62, who interpreted the "amica mea" as a metaphor for the soul. The soul finds a place in the wounds of Christ and there, the eyes of the heart are cleansed. "Et revera ubi tuta firmaque infirmis requies, nisi in vulneribus Salvatoris?" Bernard of Clairvaux, "Sermo LXI," (3), *S. Bernardi Opera*, vol. 2, *Sermones super Cantica Canticorum (36-86)*, 150, 7-8; "Quid enim tam efficax ad curanda conscientiae vulnera, necnon ad purgandam mentis aciem, quam Christi vulnerum sedula meditatio?" Ibid., "Sermo LXII," (7), 159, 24-26. In sermon 62, Bernard interprets the rock clefts in conjunction with Col 2:3, Eccl 24:30, and Ps 54:7. He then preaches on the church's place in the rock clefts. "Ecclesia ergo in foraminibus petrae, per quam introspicit, et videt gloriam Sponsi sui." Ibid., "Sermo LXII," (4), 157, 29-30. For a detailed study of the relation between Luther, Bernard, and Staupitz on the wounds of Christ and the assurance of election, see: Bell, *Divus Bernhardus*, 250-57.

156. In his introduction to the Psalms, Bonhoeffer attributes the term, "Pauline Psalms," to Luther. "Die sogenannten 7 Bußpsalmen ... aber nicht nur sie ... führen uns in die ganze Tiefe der Sündenerkenntnis vor Gott, sie helfen uns zum Bekenntnis der Schuld, sie lenken unser ganzes Vertrauen auf die vergebende Gnade Gottes, so daß Luther sie mit Recht 'paulinische Psalmen' genannt hat." Dietrich Bonhoefffer, "Das Gebetbuch der Bibel: Eine Einführung in die Psalmen (1940)," 391.

157. "Denn von der Vernachlässigung der Klage ist nicht weniger als das innerste Geheimnis des christlichen Glaubens betroffen: Kreuz und Auferweckung Jesu Christi." Oswald Bayer, *Leibliches Wort*, 335.

individual who alone can speak when God is silent. It is Christ who alone experiences the totality of death and mediates its silence into the lament. Articulated in the language of the penitential psalms, the lament mediates Christ's silence by suspending it in the past tense. The Christological mediation does not smooth over the lament's discontinuity by elevating it into a narrative unity. Access to the silence is achieved through the speech that mediates the "where-to" of Christ's advent and anticipates the salvation Christ accomplishes.

The Christological Mediation of the Lament

Access to the lament's Christological mediation is not solely determined by its literary proximity to the penitential psalms. In Luther's texts, textual indices surround the rupture in such a way as to suggest the Trinitarian matrix in which the lament is suspended. In verses four and five, the Father's speech to the Son recapitulates elements of the lament "in eternity" (4.1). The lines "And helps him out of the affliction of sin. Strangles bitter death for him" (5.5–6) allude to the phrases found in verse two, "In death, I was lost. My sin afflicted me night and day" (2.2–3), as well as in verse three, "That nothing but death remained with me" (3.6). In speaking to the Son, the Father relocates the lament's discourse of sin and death in the imperatives that anticipate Christ's act of saving those captive to the unholy trinity. Christ is destined to be "the salvation of the poor" (5.4), as the Father commands; Christ "shall become my brother" (6.4), assuming "my desperate form" (6.6) that is identified with the content of the preceding lament. Recasting the descent of the "I" in verses two and three is the narrative introduction to Christ's descent to earth. The lines "I also fell ever deeper into [sin]" (2.5) and "To hell I must descend" (3.7) are recapitulated in verse six, "He came to me on earth" (6.2). Literary markers signal the lament's content that is similar to both the imperatives in eternity and the narrated introduction to the incarnation. These markers point to the Christological mediation of the lament by anticipating Christ's advent.

The lament is Christologically mediated in an anticipatory mode at two sites in the narrative. Privileged as the hymn's starting point is the Spirit's advent, which determines the narrative site of the lament as a "before." As "before" suspended in its totality, the speech is converted into the confession of sin in preparation for absolution. By superimposing the suspension of totality with the figure of liturgical preparation, the Spirit's advent anticipates the Christological mediation of the lament. The Spirit leads the community to the site at which the knowledge and truth of Christ is obtained: to Christ's advent. The Christological mediation of the lament is not only limited to a pneumatologically inspired preparation. Already prepared in eternity is another narrative privileging of a starting point prior to the lament. In the inner-Trinitarian speech of the Father, the totality of death is recapitulated under the promise of life: "And let him live with you" (5.7). Here, the Father's speech anticipates the mediation of the totality by suspending it in the imperative of life.

The anticipatory mode of the lament's suspension at this juncture in the narrative in no way devastates the status of the lament as a rupture. From the standpoint of the Father's speech, the lament is retained as a rupture in an inner-Trinitarian decision. This motif is known in the Middle Ages as the Trinitarian "decision for salvation" (*Ratschluß zur Erlösung*).[158] Not novel to Luther, the theme of an inner-Trinitarian location for the decision towards showing mercy appears in late medieval spiritual poetry,[159] in a popular thirteenth-century poem entitled "Redemption,"[160] and in art.[161] Bernard of Clairvaux's sermon on Psalm 84:10–11 set the dramatic stage for its reception. In his sermon, four women—personified as mercy, truth, righteousness, and peace—plead before the throne of God to be reunited in harmony.[162] Luther cites Bernard's sermon at the beginning in verse five.

---

158. The motif of the "Ratschluß zur Erlösung" differs from the "Ratschluß zur Schöpfung." In the latter, the three persons decide in eternity to create the world. The former portrays the decision in eternity to save the world. Both motifs are represented in early church and medieval art. See: Wolfgang Braunfels, *Die Heilige Dreifaltigkeit*, xxv.

159. Werthemann, *Studien zu den Adventsliedern des 16. und 17. Jahrhunderts*, 55.

160. On the historical background and a summary of the poem, "Erlösung," see: Hermann Paul, ed., *Grundriss der Germanischen Philologie*, vol. II/1, 280–81. A detailed introduction to the poem and a copy of the poem's text, written in *Mittelhochdeutsch*, is found in Friedrich Maurer, *Die Erlösung: Eine geistliche Dichtung des 14. Jahrhunderts*. There exists another poem, well-known in the late Middle Ages, that narrates the inner-Trinitarian decision to redeem. The poem is the record, in late thirteenth or early fourteenth-century German, of a vision seen by a woman, Mechthild of Magdeburg. See the poem's text in P. Gall Morel, ed., *Offenbarungen der Schwester Mechthild*.

161. Braunfels, *Die Heilige Dreifaltigkeit*, xxv; Peter Grassl, "Der Ratschluss der Erlösung (Phil 2, 5–8)," 121–28.

162. Bernard quotes the biblical passage at the beginning of his sermon. "Ut inhabitet gloria in terra nostra, misericordia et veritas obviaverunt sibi, justitia et pax osculatae sunt." Bernard of Clairvaux, "Sermo I," (1), 13, 4–5.

The Father speaks to his Son in eternity, "Now is the time to show mercy and compassion" (5.2).[163] A temporal qualifier determines the beginning of an inner-Trinitarian decision that extends into its outer-Trinitarian actualization. By marking the Father's speech as a decision, Luther is able to locate the lament in relation to its Christological mediation without harmonizing it with the eternal nature.

The inner-Trinitarian decision to show mercy remains the access to the lament as it is suspended in the Spirit's and Father's speech. Not erased from memory or harmonized by the narrative form, access to the lament is created on one side by its conversion into the confession of sin and, on the other side, in the Father's speech as the *promissio* of life. In spite of this discursive access, the lament points to the mystery lying at the center of the Trinitarian relations. The silence of God is mediated by speech on either side. The divine silence is the site at which the totality of the experience articulated by the lament is located, and this silence, which takes upon itself death, points to the mystery rupturing the heart of the Trinity. To Christ is attributed the speech articulating the totality of the divine silence, a death whose silence is mediated in the promise of salvation. For the community that sings the hymn of praise, the silence of God is accessible only in the language of confession and the Father's promise of life in Christ. The mystery of death at the center of the relation between Christ and the Father remains silent.

TRINITARIAN SPEECH AND SILENCE: CONCLUSION

Appearing as a radical break in Luther's hymn, "Now Rejoice, Dear Christians," the silence of God points to the Christological center of Luther's understanding of the Trinity. Rather than isolating the lament as the anthropological starting point of a narrative from law to gospel, the lament has been discussed in this section according to its location within a narrative of Trinitarian advent. The lament's placement in the hymn as the focus of praise and its penitential language becomes the perspective from which Luther's understanding of the Spirit's advent, the Father's speech in eternity, and the anticipation of Christ's incarnation are viewed.

---

163. Bernard's sermon places the speech in the mouth of the virtue, mercy, who speaks, "'Eget miseratione creatura rationalis,' ait Misericordia, 'quoniam misera facta est et miserabilis valde. Venit tempus miserendi eius, quia jam praeteriit tempus.'" Ibid., (10), 24, 6–8.

As the focus of the Trinity's central mystery, the silence of Christ's death and its suspension as a lament in the hymn of praise are worked out as the speech of three Trinitarian persons. By assigning the lament to the past tense, the Spirit's advent converts it into the language of the confession of sin and allocates to it the liturgical space of preparation for Christ's advent. Literary and narrative elements of the lament are recapitulated on the other side, in the Father's speech to the Son, which also anticipates the incarnation. That the lament is accessible as speech points to the Christological mediation of silence in the particular language of the penitential psalms. Barth's question concerning the lament's mediation into the praise hymn is answered by the person who can properly articulate the totality of captivity and godforsakenness. The hymn of praise cannot capture the inner-Trinitarian silence of the beloved Son's death, but its speech as lament remains the focus of praise.

THE INNER-TRINITARIAN TURN AND
THE OUTER-TRINITARIAN ADVENT

An abrupt shift from the lament's hell to eternity precipitates the question regarding the narrative in relation to Luther's Trinitarian understanding. The Spirit's advent suspends the lament as a confession of sin. When considering the other side, the Father's speech seems to interrupt the lament. The intention of this section is to interpret the remaining verses of Luther's hymn as a narrative from the inner to the outer Trinity in which the lament is suspended Christologically. I will discuss the two Trinitarian sites, the inner and the outer Trinity, each in terms of a particular person who speaks the *promissio*. The focus of the first section is the inner Trinity in eternity. Luther identifies this Trinitarian location with the divine essence of mercy and narrates an inner-Trinitarian turn preceding the outer-Trinitarian dispensation. In the second section, the Father will be discussed according to the way Luther understands the term "person" to be a subject of speech. By drawing on the ancient tradition of prosopographic exegesis—which is itself based on yet another psalm genre, the royal psalm—I will show how Luther locates the *promissio* in the Father's inner-Trinitarian speech. In the third section, the outer-Trinitarian advent of Christ will be discussed as the *promissio* in Christ's speech that Luther represents to be constituted by Christ's incarnation, from his birth to his death, and finally, to his ascension to the Father. From the mercy seat in eternity, a full picture of Luther's understanding of the Trinity is gained; the divine essence of mercy, plotted as the *promissio* in the speech of Father and Son, is accessible through the Spirit for all eternity.

THE INNER-TRINITARIAN ESSENCE:
THE DIVINE PASSION AND MERCY

Luther begins to articulate his understanding of the inner Trinity in verse four of the hymn. Located "in eternity" (4.1), the inner Trinity is marked by one attribute, the divine mercy, which appears in the hymn as it is shaped by the narrative of an inner-Trinitarian turn. In this section, I trace the moments in the inner-Trinitarian narrative in order to show how the attribute of mercy grounds a turn that precedes the turn towards the outer Trinity. The movement unfolds from the lament, heard by God in eternity, to the heartfelt compassion compelling God to remember God's mercy and desire to help. By showing that an inner-Trinitarian turn precedes Christ's advent, I challenge the interpretation that locates the turn from wrath to mercy in the inner Trinity. This discussion of the inner Trinity has, as its focus, the Christological pivot around which the inner-Trinitarian turn turns towards the outer-Trinitarian gain of salvation.

The radical shift from hell to heaven could not more stunningly capture the divine passion in eternity. Rapidly following the third verse's terminal point of sinking down into hell, the fourth verse swiftly transports the hymn's narrator into eternity. What is found there is beyond anticipation: "There in eternity God laments my exceeding misery" (4.1–2). Luther's intriguing glimpse into eternity unexpectedly finds not a wrathful God, but a God deeply affected by "my distress and misery." Not appearing as the divine judge expected by the preceding lament, God is introduced as the dative object of the verb "lament" (4.1). At this site, Luther begins to unfold what was introduced in the opening verse as the divine cost.[164] In an eternity preceding an action, God begins to experience the passion of being intimately tied to humanity.

The words chosen to introduce the divine pain could not be more evocative of their biblical echoes. Luther characteristically uses the terms "to

---

164. "Gar theür hat ers erworben" (1.7).

lament" and "misery" to speak of the plight of human captivity. Often found in Luther's writings of this period, the nouns "lamentable" and "misery" appear as predicates of humanity.[165] The term "misery" is used according to its original meaning as the German translation of the Latin "exile," or exile in a foreign land, as well as according to its later meaning in a translation from the Latin, "misery."[166] In Luther's explanation to the second article of the Creed in the Large Catechism, the two nouns appear in the context of Christ's incarnation. The language of the lament identifies the "where-to" of the incarnation to be "our grief and misery."[167] As a verb, "to lament" or "to grieve" (*jammern*) appears to be Luther's translation of the Greek verb σπλαγχνίζομαι. Found frequently in the Synoptics, the verb is translated by Luther with a phrase attributed to Jesus: "It grieved him." Jesus is moved by the plight of individuals or the masses, and this disposition compels him to heal, forgive, feed, and raise from the dead (Matt 9:36; 14:14; 15:32; 20:34; Mark 1:41; 6:34; 8:2; Luke 7:13). In New Testament parables, the king is moved by pity to forgive the slave's debt (Matt 18:27), the Good Samaritan cares for the victim (Luke 10:33), and the Father welcomes the prodigal Son (Luke 15:20).[168] Luther does not limit the phrase "it grieved him" to the life of Jesus in time. By appearing in the hymn, the phrase captures the essential determination of the divine nature in eternity.

When Luther predicates "my misery" (4.2) of the "lament" (4.1) affecting God, a communication of attributes appears. Dislocated from its usual anthropological context, the lament is now identified with the inner Trinity in eternity. The divine essence is characterized by the deepest identification of God with human exile and misery. In a 1523 sermon on the first article of the Apostles' Creed, Luther alludes to Romans 8:31–32 as the scriptural backdrop for the Father's "great care for us," the Father who "so decisively takes upon himself what is yours as much as if it were his own."[169] Luther

---

165. For example: WA 12:680.11 (Sermon on the Twenty-second Sunday after Trinity, Nov. 1, 1523).

166. "anderes, fremdes land"; "für fremde, ausland, zumal land der verbannung, exilium." Dietz, *Wörterbuch zu Dr. Martin Luthers Deutschen Schriften*, vol. 1, 526.

167. WA 30,1:186.21.

168. Judg 2:18 is one of the rare examples of this phrase appearing in Luther's translation of the Old Testament.

169. "Er hat grosser sorg gegen uns quam pater carnalis, es sein ernstlich wort, et pauci perpendunt, er nimbt sich dein so hart an als seyn selbst, quicquid tibi fit, ipsi fit." WA

does not limit the identification between human despair and the divine essence to the outer-Trinitarian *promissio* addressed by Christ in verse seven. Already in the inner Trinity, the claim of reciprocity, "For I am yours and you are mine" (7.5), communicates the lament to the divine essence.

The inner Trinity's identification with the lament is explicated by a divine attribute that is mentioned only once in the hymn. In the narrative introduction to the inner-Trinitarian turn, Luther explicitly refers to the divine mercy in the phrase, "He remembered the divine mercy" (4.3). By appearing once in the hymn at this site, the term "mercy" signals the center of Luther's understanding of the divine nature.[170] It is a noun, related to the verb "to have mercy on," that "penetrates to the biblical subject matter" from various viewpoints.[171] Particularly in Luther's translation of Psalms and the prophets, the verb "to have mercy on" is attributed to the Lord who has mercy on his people particularly after a time of wrath (Pss 102:14; 103:13; 109:12; Isa 14:1; 30:18; 54:8; 55:7; 60:10; Jer 12:15; 15:5; 30:18; 31:20).[172] From the perspective of the Synoptics, the verb "to have mercy on" (ἐλεέω) is usually found in the imperative mood as the cry of those in need of healing (Matt 9:27; 15:22; 17:15; 20:30–31; Mark 9:22; 10:47–48; Luke 16:24; 17:13; 18:38, 39). As a divine attribute, Luther translates both Greek nouns ὁ οἰκτιρμός ("pity, compassion") and τό ἔλεος ("mercy") with *Barmherzigkeit* ("compassion" or "mercy"; Luke 6:36; Rom 15:9; 2 Cor 1:3; Eph 2:4; 1 Pet 1:3).[173] When the noun τά σπλάγχνα ("compassion") occurs together with either τό ἔλεος ("mercy") or ὁ οἰκτιρμός ("pity"), the wonderful doubled use of the word "heart" results in the German: "through the heartfelt compassion of

---

11:49.32–34 (Sermon on the Symbolum: first article of the Creed, March 4, 1523).

170. Commenting on Luther's hymn, Karl Barth locates the attribute of mercy in the immanent Trinity as the central divine attribute determining God's freedom and power. "Die Freiheit und Kraft seiner Barmherzigkeit ist also gerade nicht erst (so noch H. Cremer in seinem Lexikon-Art. ἔλεος), die eines 'heilsökonomischen Verhaltens', sondern echt und recht die Freiheit und Kraft seiner ewigen Gottheit. Gott der Vater, der Sohn und der Heilige Geist ist in sich selber barmherzig." KD II/1, *Die Lehre von Gott*, 418.

171. For this phrase, I am indebted to Childs, *Biblical Theology of the Old and New Testaments*, 522.

172. WADB 10,1:432, 436, 472; WADB 11,1:58, 96, 158, 160, 172, 234, 242, 290, 294. Luther translates "erbarmen" together with "Elend" in Isa 49:13. See: WADB 11,1:146. The references to the Psalms and the prophets are taken from Luther's Bible translation of 1528.

173. WADB 6:238; WADB 7:74, 140, 194, 300. All references to the New Testament are taken from Luther's 1522 translation.

our God" (Luke 1:78); "from the bottom of the heart of Jesus Christ" (Phil 1:8); "heartfelt love and compassion" (Phil 2:1), and "heartfelt compassion" (Col 3:12).[174] The verbal form appearing in the hymn, "He remembers his compassion" (4.3), is entirely characteristic of particular psalms (Pss 25:6; 51:3; 69:17)[175] and the Magnificat (Luke 1:54, 72).[176] From Luther's translation of passages in Psalms, Isaiah, Jeremiah, and the Synoptics, the verb "to have mercy" and the noun "mercy" point to a central moment in Luther's understanding of the divine nature. Divine mercy is shown towards those held captive to sin, sickness, and death.[177] The sinner crying out to God in the Psalms, the people repenting of their idolatry, and the individuals begging Jesus for healing all appeal to the attribute of the divine mercy by which God remembers and acts. It is this attribute that ultimately grounds the communication of the lament into the divine nature. Mercy is designated as the ground of the inner-Trinitarian passion.

The divine attribute of mercy marks the origin of the inner-Trinitarian turn from passion to action with two crucial verbs. Both words appear in the tense characteristic of the narrative form—the first in the active mode of the imperfect tense, the second, in its passive mode. "He remembered then his mercy, he desired to help me" (4.3-4). Narrated by two verbs, the turn from passion to action arises as an unmistakeable allusion to the Augustinian tradition of Trinitarian reflection. Familiar with the De Trinitate at least since 1509, Luther strategically alludes to the same verbs that Augustine uses to define the inner-Trinitarian relations.[178] In book 14, Augustine conceives of the inner Trinity as the self-reflection of the divine essence according to memory-intellect-will.[179] From the unity

---

174. WADB 6:214; WADB 7:212, 216, 232.

175. WADB 10,1:174, 262, 320.

176. WADB 6:212, 214.

177. In a manner similar to "Nun freut euch," Luther strategically places the divine attribute of mercy as the object of "jammern" in the hymn, "Mitten wir im Leben sind." "Es yamert deyn barmhertzigkeyt unser klag und grosses leyd." (2.6-7) in AWA 4:161. In his explanation to the second article of the Creed in the Large Catechism, Luther speaks of the groundless mercy that grounds the turn to help. "... bis das sich dieser einige und ewige Gottes son unsers iamers und elends aus grundloser gu(e)te erbarmete und von hymel kam uns zuhelffen." WA 30,1:186.20-22.

178. Luther's marginal notes to Augustine, De Trinitate are found in WA 9:16.1-23, 42.

179. Augustine, De Trin., 14, 7 (10) [PL 42:1043-1044].

of self-reflection emerge the two moments of thinking itself and willing itself. These two moments apprehend the two infinite processions from the Father, who thinks his own essence and wills it. Self-knowledge according to the intellect generates the Second Person of the Trinity. The Third Person proceeds from the self-willing according to the will.[180] In his hymn, Luther alludes to the two verbs "thinking" and "willing" in order to orient them to the divine attribute of mercy. By this connection, the two terms imply a movement towards the outer Trinity.[181] For Luther, mercy conveys an impulse outward, towards the active showing of "friendship, love and goodness."[182] In the context of explicating the divine mercy, the two verbs refer to the two inner-Trinitarian processions as they narrate a turn outwards. The inner-Trinitarian relations are not sealed off from their economy. The eternal processions of Son and Spirit are conceived in view of their turn towards their respective advents.

Narrated as the final moment of the inner-Trinitarian turn is God's turn to the Son. The turn concludes with a poetic allusion to the inner-Trinitarian relation between Father and Son. "He turned the Father's heart to me" (4.5). In the Middle Ages, the term "Father's heart" was taken to refer to the eternal generation of the Son. The title of a fourth-century hymn by Prudentius explicitly mentions this procession, "Born from the Father's Heart"—usually translated "Of the Father's Love Begotten."[183] The term "Father's heart" also appears literally in Bernard of Clairvaux's popular sermon on Psalm 84:10. It refers to the location at which the four virtues

180. Werbick discusses Augustine's Trinitarian understanding in terms of the "monosubjective" model. See: Werbick, "Trinitätslehre," 538.

181. The literary constellation of "Jammer und Elend," "erbarmen," and "helfen" also appears in Luther's explanation to the second article of the Creed in the Large Catechism. See 183n177.

182. Luther defines the term "mercy" in his Preface to the Psalms (1528). "Denn ḥeseḍ, das sie barmhertzickeyt, vnd ich guete habe verdeutscht, heysst eygentlich, das, wenn man yemand freundschafft, liebe odder wolthat erzeygt, wie es Christus Matt 12. [Matt 12:7] aus Hosea [Hos 6:6] selbs deutet vnd spricht." WADB 10,1:94.17–19 (Vorrede auf den Psalter, 1528). Luther continues with Christ's quote in Matthew from Hosea. "Ich habe lust an der barmhertzikeyt vnd nicht am opffer, das ist, Ich will das man freundschafft, liebe, vnd wolthat beweyse, lieber denn opffern." Ibid., 94.19–21.

183. The opening lines of Cruciger's hymn are often understood by scholars to allude to Prudentius' hymn: "Herr Christ, der einig Gotts Sohn Vaters in Ewigkeit, aus seim Herzen entsprossen, gleichwie geschrieben steht." See: EKG, no. 46. A matter for further study is whether "natus" is to be distinguished from "entsprossen," as Christa Reich suggested in a personal conversation on Oct. 5, 1998 in Mainz.

beg the Father to be reunited.[184] By mentioning the Father's turn to the Son
as his heart, Luther does not limit the turn to an inner-Trinitarian procession. Luther explicitly couples the inner-Trinitarian turn with an allusion
to the divine pain and opens up the inner Trinity to its outer-Trinitarian
direction. The divine cost, introduced at the hymn's beginning, is already
situated in the inner Trinity. "His sweet, wondrous deed" (1.6) that costs
God "greatly" (1.7) is recapitulated in the final two lines of verse four: "It
was indeed for him no joke. It cost him his most precious possession" (4.6,
7). By introducing the Second Person of the Trinity, the "Father's heart"
(4.5) in terms of the divine cost, the outer-Trinitarian moment of Christ's
death is anticipated. The Christological center of the inner Trinity is not
divorced from an extension into the outer Trinity, but becomes the pivot
around which the inner Trinity turns.

Luther articulates the inner-Trinitarian turn of the divine mercy in a
narrative form that is not external to the subject matter. Accessible in this
form, the turn is given no reason other than the divine attribute itself. No
ultimate explanation is offered—neither for the divine capacity to suffer,
nor for the turn towards the Son—other than the inexplicable ground of the
divine nature itself. The hymn's narrative of mercy dovetails with Luther's
conception of the divine essence in other genres. In sermons preached in
1523 and in the Small Catechism (1529), Luther grounds the Father's giving
of all good things in the divine nature of mercy.[185] Mercy is the groundless
ground of the divine turn towards creation. When God gives out of mercy,
"without my worth or merit," no payment is required.[186] Remarkably absent

---

184. Bernard mentions the "cor patris" at the juncture in the sermon when the four
virtues, truth, righteousness, peace, and mercy return in a state of turmoil and dishar-
mony. At the heart of the Father, they ask him if he has forgotten his mercy by quoting Ps
76:8, 10: "Numquid in aeternum proiciet Deus? aut non apponet ut complacitior sit adhuc?
Numquid obliviscetur misereri Deus, aut continebit in ira sua misericordias suas?" Bernard
of Clairvaux, "Sermo I," (9), 22, ll. 23, 1-2.

185. "Item das uns alle gu(e)tter durch den vatter geschenckt sind, on unßern verdienst,
auß lauter barmhertzickeyt." WA 12, 265, 25-26 (introduction to 1 Pet 1:3-9); "... vnd das alles
ausz lauter veterlicher go(e)tlicher gu(e)tte vnd barmhertzigkeyt on alle mein verdienst vnd
wirdigkeyt." WA 30,1:248.9-12 (Small Catechism, 1529).

186. In a sermon Luther preached around the time he composed his hymn, he mentions
the divine turn towards compassion as a direct consequence of the divine essence of mercy.
"So folget nu auss der barmhertzickeyt, syntemal sich Gott jamern lesset des elends. ... Thut
er dir aber barmhertzickeyt, so bezalistu nicht." WA 12:681.6-7, 21 (Sermon on the Twenty-
second Sunday after Trinity, Nov. 1, 1523). This sermon on Matt 18:23-35, the parable of the
wicked servant, can be read as a literary and theological parallel to Luther's hymn. "Darumb

from Luther's account of the divine nature is the terminology of wrath. Not a turn from wrath to love, the inner-Trinitarian turn is told as the narrative of the attribute of mercy. Following the narrative of mercy is a further extension of the inner-Trinitarian turn. The speech of the Father to the Son in verse five offers an intimate glimpse into the divine nature as a conversation of love.

THE INNER-TRINITARIAN SPEECH OF THE FATHER

The Father's turn captures Luther's understanding of the term "person." Introduced by the phrase, "He spoke to his beloved Son" (5.1), the fifth verse thematizes a central element in Luther's understanding of the Trinitarian person as a speaker of a distinct type of speech. In this section, the Father's address to the Son is discussed as the speech filling the eternity of the inner Trinity with a conversation of love. The speech's content anticipates the soteriologically determined inclusion of those in despair. In order to show that Luther's understanding of the inner-Trinitarian conversation does not imply a "naive tritheism," I will study the tradition of prosopographic exegesis in which the speech of a distinct speaker becomes the basis for an interpersonal model of the Trinity. Luther conceives the Father's speech according to the prosopographic model of the royal psalms and shifts the content of these psalms to include the *promissio*. The section ends by explaining that the silence of the Holy Spirit in the hymn is shaped by Luther's exegetical strategy.

In his hymn, Luther uses the form of direct speech to identify a Trinitarian person as a distinct subject of speech. Forming a dialogical understanding of the inner Trinity is Luther's recovery of an exegetical tool that can be traced back to Tertullian's reception of an early church method of Christological interpretation. In arguing against the predominant view proposed by von Harnack,[187] Carl Andresen suggests that

---

kumpt nu der Herr und erbarmet sich des jamers, weyl der knecht also da gefangen ligt und bestrickt ynn seynen sunden und dazu eyn solcher narr ist, das er yhm selbs herauss will helffen, sihet noch keyne barmhertzickeyt, weyss von keyner gnade zu sagen, sondern fulet nichts denn die sunde die yhn ubel drucket, und weyss niemant der yhm helffe. Da erbarmet sich der Herr uber yhn und lesset yhn loss. Da ist uns nu abgemalet, was das Euangelion und seyn art ist und wie Gott mit uns handlet." Ibid., 680.11-17. Luther adds the central verse of the penitential psalm, Ps 51:19, to the above interpretation of the king's mercy shown to the servant. Ibid., 680.27-681.5.

187. A. von Harnack, *Lehrbuch der Dogmengeschichte*, vol. 2, 299n1.

Tertullian's terminology of "three persons–one substance" is not borrowed from the legal realm. Rather, the concepts are determined by a distinctly biblical type of exegesis used by Justin Martyr, Theophilus of Antioch, and Irenaeus.[188] Tertullian, as Andresen claims, made the decisive move from an earlier Christological exegesis of Genesis 1:26; 3:22; and Psalms to a Trinitarian interpretation of these biblical texts.[189] According to this type of Trinitarian exegesis, the person is seen as a speaker, introduced by formulas of address such as ἐκ προσώπου, that stem from the literature of late antiquity.[190] Tertullian's reception of prosopographic exegesis for conceiving the dialogical character of the Trinity dovetails with his intention to stress the oral nature of the word in his translation of the Greek term "word" (λόγος) with the Latin "speech" (sermo).[191] When Luther includes direct speech in the inner Trinity, he is not to be interpreted as tending toward a "naive tritheism."[192] Rather, Luther borrows from the tradition of prosopographic exegesis that uses the form of direct speech to expose an understanding of "person" as subject of speech.

Luther advances an interpersonal model of the inner Trinity by appealing to a particular type of prosopographic exegesis. The royal psalms provide the form for assigning direct speech to the First Person of the Trinity. In these psalms, Psalms 2 and 110, the Father addresses the Son directly; the content of the speech is independent of speaker and hearer. Luther reproduces the form of the royal psalms in his hymn.[193] The Father is introduced

---

188. Carl Andresen, "Zur Entstehung und Geschichte des trinitarischen Personbegriffes," 1–11.

189. Ibid., 11–12. See Tertullian's interpretation of Gen 1:26 and 3:22 in *Adv. Prax.* 12, 3 [CSEL 47:245]; Pss 44:2; 2:7; 109:3, in ibid., 11, 4 [CSEL 47:243]; Isa 45:14 in ibid., 13, 2 [CSEL 47:247].

190. Andresen researches the literature of late Antiquity, from Homer to Plato to a fourth-century Neo-Platonist, in order to show how the understanding of person developed in relation to the distinct speakers in Plato's dialogues and on the stage of the Greek theater. Andresen, "Zur Entstehung," 14–18.

191. *Adv. Prax.* 12, 6. 7 [CSEL 47:246].

192. Peters, "Die Trinitätslehre in der reformatorischen Christenheit," 564.

193. In a 1523 sermon held on the Feast of Ascension, Luther preached on both Ps 2:7 and Ps 110:1. In these psalm verses, the Father speaks to the Son. The speech's content is the power of the ascended Christ over sin, death, and devil. Luther refers to Ps 2:7 in order to strengthen his hearer's confidence and certainty in Christ as Lord over all the earth. "Da sehet yhr aber, das Christus eyn herr ist ubir alle wellt von got gesetzt. Wenn er denn meyn freundt ist und ich gewiß dafur halte, das er fur mich gestorben ist, und hatt mir alles geben, wer wil mir denn thun? oder ßo man mir etwas thut, was wil mirs schaden?" WA 12:563.33–34, 564.1–2

as speaker with the formula, "He spoke to his beloved Son" (5.1). His speech discloses his royal regard for the Son with a phrase stemming from medieval secular poetry: "my heart's valuable crown."[194] Luther's use of the formula to introduce the Father as speaker points to the interpersonal model of the inner Trinity associated with Richard of St. Victor.[195] The Father addresses a distinct speech to the Son, who hears. In contrast, a Trinitarian conversation that is modeled after Genesis 1 or John's prologue collapses the content of the speech with the Second Person of the Trinity. This latter type of exegesis offers the warrant for the intersubjective model. In the Augustinian tradition associated with this model, the inner-Trinitarian word, translated with the Latin *verbum* ("word"), is identical with the eternal generation of the Son. Both Trinitarian models, either based on the royal psalms or Genesis 1, locate the Father's word in the inner Trinity, and in his hymn, Luther follows suit.[196] The interpersonal model, however, proves to more adequately construe the hymn's content than the intersubjective model. Luther uses the occasion of the Father's address to fill eternity with a particular content that is distinct from the Son.

What is spoken in eternity is minimally a declaration of love for the Son that maximally embraces the *promissio*. After the simple address to "the

---

(Sermon on Ascension, May 14, 1523). In the same sermon, Luther refers to Ps 110:1, 5–6 (Ibid., 564.5–6) and Ps 68:19. "Das er nit alleyn alle creatur regiere und erfulle (denn damit ist noch nit meynem glawben geholffen noch die sunde hynwegk genommen) ßonder hat auch das gefengniß widder gefangen gefurt." Ibid., 564.25–27. A favorite image for Luther is portrayed in his translation of Ps 68:19: Christ imprisoned the prison [that held the prisoner captive]. "Du bist ynn die ho(e)he gefaren vnd hast das gefengnis gefangen." WADB 10,1:312 (1528).

194.   Wolff, "Zu Luthers Lied," 100. In the hymn: "meyns hertzen werde kron" (5.3).

195.   Werbick summarizes the Victorine's Trinitarian model as an "interpersonal" one. The Victorine had articulated a Trinitarian understanding on the basis of book 7 of Augustine's *De Trinitate* that went beyond Augustine's monosubjective model. Richard of St. Victor used Augustine's distinction between the lover and the beloved, and defined the Spirit as the *condilectus* of overflowing love to avoid the binitarian tendency of Augustine's understanding of the Spirit as the *vinculum amoris*. See: Werbick, "Trinitätslehre," 508–11. According to the "intersubjective" model of the Trinity associated with Augustine, the inner-Trinitarian word is not conceived as the Father's direct speech to the Son. Rather, the word, "logos," that Augustine translates with the Latin *verbum* is generated eternally by the Father as the *verbum internum*.

196.   The inner-Trinitarian site at which the Father speaks contrasts with the outer-Trinitarian location of the Father's speech to the Son at his baptism (Matt 3:17). In the medieval lectionary Luther used for his sermons, the gospel for the feast of Epiphany was Matthew 3:13–17, the baptism of Jesus. The voice of the Father is located in the outer Trinity. The Father speaks, "diß ist meyn lieber son, ynn wilchem ich eyn wolgefallen habe" (Matt 3:17). WADB 6:22 (1522). This verse significantly shapes Luther's understanding of a Trinitarian structure of mutual revelation that is shaped by the genre of the sermon. See: chapter 4.

crown of his heart," the Father speaks to the Son in the imperative mood. A series of imperatives literally recapitulates sin and death in the inner Trinity in such a way as to relate them to the Father's *promissio*. The Father's speech locates the sin that "afflicts me night and day" (2.3) in the context of the desire to help: "And helps him out of sin's affliction" (5.5). Death, described as the terminal point of wretchedness (3.6), is now suspended in the Father's imperative: "Strangles bitter death for him" (5.6). The imperatives to the Son surround the lament with the promise to help. Suspended in eternity is the totality of the lament as it is viewed in anticipation of its Christological mediation. The theme of the "heard and answered lament" is captured in the inner-Trinitarian speech of the Father;[197] the answer to "my misery" (4.2) is already heard, and answered, in eternity: "And be the salvation of the poor" (5.4). In the string of imperatives to the Son, the Father speaks and thereby locates the *promissio* in the inner Trinity.

The final determination to the *promissio* is manifest in the last imperative. At this site is disclosed the Christological pivot around which the inner-Trinitarian turn to the Son turns to the outer Trinity. Wrapping up the Father's speech is an imperative in the passive form. "And let him live with you" (5.7). Omitted during the narrative of Christ's death and life (verses six to ten), the only reference to the resurrection in the entire hymn is located here in the inner Trinity. In his speech, the Father anticipates the Christological mediation of Christ's total experience of death. From the perspective of victory characteristic of the royal psalms, the Father's speech surrounds death with the *promissio* of life. The anticipatory mode of the inner-Trinitarian *promissio*, however, is not identical with its actualization. Only Christ can articulate the *promissio* in such a way as to communicate

---

197. See Bayer's article on this theme in "Erhörte Klage," *Leibliches Wort*, 334–48. Brecht criticizes Bayer by pointing out that "die Klage nicht zur Anrufung Gottes wird." Brecht, "Erfahrung—Exegese—Dogmatik," 99. Brecht is correct in showing that, on the anthropological level, the lament of verses two and three is without an addressee. When considering the lament according to the full force of its reception in the genre of *Danklied*, the *Erhörung* is understood to be already answered in eternity. The "erhörte Klage" appears in the genre of the sermon as well. "Nu hat Gott dißem ubel eynen radt erfunden und also beschlossen, das er Christum seynen son wolt ynn die welt senden, das er seyn blu(o)t vergosse und sturbe, da mit er fur die sund gnug thete und sie hynweg neme und das denn der heylig geyst ynns hertz keme, der solche leut die mit unlust und zwang ynn des gesetzs wercken daher gehen, willig machet, das sie on zwang und mit frolichem gemuet Gottis gebot hielten. Sonst mocht durch keyn ander mittel dem jamer geholfen werden." WA 12:544.22–28 (Sermon on the Fourth Sunday after Easter, May 3, 1523).

his life, mediating the totality of his death, to liberate the captive: "You have now become saved" (8.7).[198] The lament's suspension in the *promissio* accompanies the outer-Trinitarian advent of the second Trinitarian person, as will be described in the following section. At its location in the inner Trinity, the *promissio* articulates the Father's desire for the life of those held captive and anticipates the actualization of this desire.

At this juncture, the *promissio* emerges clearly as the central plot of the hymn's narrative. Both sides of the narrative surround the lament and converge towards its Christological mediation. At the outer-Trinitarian site of the Spirit's advent, the anticipation of Christ's advent coincides with the fulfillment of Christ's *promissio*. That Luther gives no other voice to the Spirit except the singing of what Christ has done is integral to Luther's understanding of the Spirit's relation to Christ. Christ's *promissio* is matched with the Spirit's work by the way in which the latter is sent by the former to lead the community in the knowledge and truth of Christ. In the inner Trinity, the Father's *promissio* of life is bound together with the Son's advent. The Father addresses the Son as the person who will both suspend the totality of the lament in his death and communicate the victory of life to the captive. At both points, the Spirit's outer-Trinitarian advent and the Father's inner-Trinitarian speech, the Son's incarnation is anticipated by defining its "where-to" and by surrounding it with the Christologically defined *promissio*. The plots differ with respect to the locations at which they respectively anticipate Christ's advent. The Spirit is identified with the outer Trinity and the Father with the inner Trinity; the outer-Trinitarian site links the Spirit's work to the singing community, and the inner Trinity is marked by the Father's speech to the Son alone.

What Luther achieves by suspending the lament in the *promissio* at the two points is to construct a narrative of Trinitarian advent in view of its Christological center. The *promissio*'s central plot is used to conjugate the Trinitarian relations through a narrative that is accompanied by direct speech. The persons of Spirit and Father anticipate the Christological mediation of the lament's suspension by each plotting the *promissio* in a way defining their respective personal characteristics. In view of the

---

198. The perfect tense of Christ's *promissio*, "du bist geworden," is converted into the third person singular of the confession of faith. "Ich gleube, das Jhesus Christus, warhafftiger Gottes son, sey mein HErr worden." WA 30,1:186.10–11 (Large Catechism, 1529).

outer-Trinitarian ecclesiological context, the Spirit summons the community to prepare for Christ's advent. In the inner Trinity, the Father hears the despair of the "I" and turns to the Son. The Father's love makes room in the Son for the life of the world.

Luther's use of the interpersonal model of the Trinity leaves open the question concerning the Holy Spirit's placement in the inner-Trinitarian conversation. The difficulty in assigning a role to the Holy Spirit is related to the lack of an explicit textual warrant in the biblical passages associated with a prosopographic interpretation. Andresen has pointed out that the difficulty resulted from the Eastern church's efforts to extend the concept of the *homoousios* to the Holy Spirit. This process led to the decline of the adequacy of prosopographic exegesis to warrant a Nicene understanding of the Trinitarian doctrine.[199] Due to both a Sabellian reception of prosopographic exegesis and the lack of biblical passages warranting the Holy Spirit's speech, this exegetical tool lost its impact in the tradition of biblical interpretation soon after Hilary of Poitiers wrote his *De Trinitate*.[200] A particular uncertainty in Luther's own Trinitarian understanding is detected in the years around 1523 that might explain the difficulty. Luther's discussion of the Holy Spirit in the sermons of 1523 is limited to the Spirit's outer-Trinitarian role in "creating the church"[201] and in dispensing the forgiveness of sins.[202] The problem with the Spirit's inner-Trinitarian posture is later resolved in an interpretation of John 1 in 1528. In this sermon, Luther moves beyond the difficulty arising in the hymn by placing the Spirit as the hearer of the Father's word. Luther further understands the Spirit's role as hearer to be the way by which the Spirit receives the essence from both the Father and the Son.[203] By the time Luther wrote his 1543

---

199. Andresen, "Zur Entstehung," 34.

200. Ibid., 28–39.

201. See 152n87.

202. "Remissio peccatorum comprendit baptismum, panem, confessionem." WA 11:54.6–7 (Sermon on the Symbolum: the third article of the Creed, March 6, 1523). "Christus remittit peccatum et pater, pater vult, filius meruit, spiritus sanctus der richtets auß." Ibid., 54.2–3.

203. "Eben auff die weis loquitur de spiritu sancto, quod est spiritus sanctus deus non a se ipso sed er horts. Ubi? ynn der gotheit, quod ist ein horen, da durch er sein wesen hat, ut dicimus, Christum esse verbum dei, id est perfecta divinitas. Hoc verbum audit aliquis, qui est spiritus sanctus. ... Ostensum ergo, quod spiritus sanctus a seipso non habet dz wesen sed a patre et filio." WA 28:51.34–38; 52.2–3 (Wochenpredigten über Joh. 16–20, 1528–1529, June 27, 1528, to John 16:12–14). In the chapter on the sermon, the role of the Spirit as listener of the

treatise on 2 Samuel 23:1–7, *On the Last Words of David*, he firmly grounded the divinity of the Spirit in the Spirit's role as hearer of the inner-Trinitarian conversation and, in the outer Trinity, the Spirit speaks through the prophets what is heard in the inner Trinity.[204] In his 1523 hymn, however, Luther's emphasis on the outer-Trinitarian work of the Spirit tends towards neglecting an explicit discussion of the Spirit's participation in the inner-Trinitarian conversation.

THE OUTER AND INNER TRINITY: THE ADVENT OF CHRIST

Luther dedicates the second half of his hymn, verses six to ten, to the advent of the Second Person of the Trinity. Christ's advent mediates the *promissio* "for us." The Son's descent to earth and ascent to the Father locate the *promissio* in God's eternal life. The mercy seat is the climax of the hymn's narrative. At this site, Christ prays the penitential psalms on behalf of those for whom he died. Here, the Father's promise of life is accessible in the Son, and the Spirit is sent to fulfill Christ's promise to comfort, guide, and lead the community.

With a seamless transition, Luther introduces the hymn's Christological plot. The short introduction to the incarnation in verse six narrates Christ's change of place from the inner to the outer Trinity in terms of his obedience to the Father: "The Son was obedient to the Father" (6.1). The immediacy of the Son's obedience admits no rupture that would separate the divine decision for showing mercy from its full actualization at an outer-Trinitarian extreme. Immediately transferred into Christ's advent through his obedience to the Father is the divine essence of mercy that is moved into the incarnate space of the outer Trinity.

Luther uses the Son's obedience as the pivot around which the inner-Trinitarian mercy is turned to its outer-Trinitarian advent. The outer-Trinitarian extension narrates Christ's descent towards the lament as the terminal point of his advent. Guided by the paradigm of descent in Philippians 2:6–11, Luther signals the "where-to" of Christ's incarnation

---

inner-Trinitarian conversation is related to the Spirit's role as revealer of the inner Trinity. See: ch. 4, "The Holy Spirit."

204. "So ist der Heilige Geist auch da, als der rechte einige Gott, der durch David und alle Propheten mit uns Menschen redet, und alle warheit von der Gottheit uns offenbaret und leret." WA 54:51.24–27.

with literary clues echoing the preceding lament. As "my brother," Christ
assumes "my desperate form" (6.6) "to earth" (6.2).[205] Indicated by the terms
"my brother" and "my desperate form," the terminal point of Christ's outer-Trinitarian descent is situated by the lament's content. The narrated
portion ends with a phrase capturing the final moment of the "where-to"
in terms of a particular power in the unholy trinity. The phrase "He wanted
to capture the devil" (6.7) anticipates the Christological mediation of the
captivity of the "I" by the devil in verse two.[206] It is Christ's encounter with
the devil that Luther uses to dramatize the amplitude of Christ's descent
from heaven to earth and to describe the terminal point as a battle between
death and life, a battle that takes time to be fought and won.

The narrated introduction is quickly succeeded by the remaining verses
in which Christ speaks "to me." Constitutive of Luther's narrative of advent
is the prosopographic display of Christ as speaker at his outer-Trinitarian
location. Parallel to the formula introducing the Father as speaker in the
inner Trinity is the anticipation of Christ's speech: "He spoke to me" (7.1).
By introducing Christ's direct speech with this formula, Luther identifies
the person of Christ with the subject matter of his speech. Christ's person
is constituted by the speech that communicates the stages of the battle
with the unholy trinity. A literal reprise captures Christ's outer-Trinitarian
encounter with the powers previously narrated in the lament. Christ confronts the three powers: the enemy (7.7), death (8.5), and sin (8.6).[207] Luther
uses a mixture of verb tenses to paint the intensity of the confrontation.
In the future tense, Christ predicts the silence of his own death: "He will
shed my blood" (8.1). The direct face with death is told in the present tense:
"Death devours my life" (8.5). What Christ communicates in the present and

---

205. In a 1523 sermon on the gospel text Luke 19:29–34, Luther includes an interpretation
of the epistle text, Phil 2:6–11. Luther concentrates his reflections on the final moment in
the movement of descent. Christ has truly become the "least" of all humans. "Also ist nun
Christus gewest, hatt sich so tieff herunter gelassen, das kain mensch so gering hat sein
mu(o)gen, mit dem er nicht gern zu(o) schaffen hab gehabt und dem er nicht hett gedienet,
Also das er warhafftig der aller untterst mensch ist wordenn." WA 12:469.27–30 (Sermon on
Palm Sunday, March 29, 1523).

206. "Dem Teüffel ich gefangen lag" (2.1).

207. "Da will ich für dich ringen" (7.4). Luther mentions the powers of death and sin
in verse eight. "Den todt verschlingt das leben mein; Mein unschuld tregt die sünde dein"
(8.5–6). The explicit reference to the devil is found at the end of verse seven ["Uns soll der
feynd nicht schayden" (7.7)] and at the beginning of verse eight ["Vergiessen wirt er mir
mein blu(o)tt" (8.1)].

future tenses is the definition of his person as the one who mediates the content of the lament's totality. The lament's content, as we have seen in the section on the lament psalms, is properly attributed to the one person who alone mediates the total experience of death. Only when this lament is suspended in the memory of collective rehearsal of what God has done can the present and future tenses of the one person's narrative be converted into the past tense of communal praise.

Luther appeals to the strategy of prosopographic autobiography in order to focus the hymn's soteriological lens. Christ defines his person entirely in terms of the stages of the battle and communicates these stages "to benefit you" (8.3). With this phrase, Luther summarizes his central insight concerning Christ's advent: Christ communicates "to you" the battle, each stage of which mediates an element of the lament's content through the person of Christ. The definition of Christ's person is a self-definition that surrounds the lament with the *promissio*. When Christ speaks, "I suffer all to benefit you" (8.3), and the powers of the unholy trinity are mediated by Christ, who suffers them in order to take them captive. Luther mentions the power of sin together with the *promissio* of forgiveness. "My innocence carries your sin" (8.6). The attempt of the devil to separate the "I" from God is prevented by the *promissio*: "The enemy shall not separate us" (7.7). Death, the final enemy experienced by Christ, is overcome by the life promised in the inner Trinity. "Death devours my life" (8.5) is attached to the Father's promise, "And let him live with you" (5.7). Luther's insight regarding the identity between the person of Christ and the narrated *promissio* in the hymn also remains the focus of the explanation to the second article of the Creed in the Large Catechism. In this work, Luther subsumes each subarticle under the rubric of Christ as Lord, identifying each stage in Christ's life with the redemption Christ accomplishes "for me" (*pro me*).[208] In the

---

208. For Luther, each stage of Christ's life is constituted by the *promissio*. In a sermon on the second article of the Creed as well as in his explanation to the Large Catechism, Luther discusses each subarticle in terms of the confession of faith of the "I." Each stage of Christ's life is confessed in the context determined by Christ as "my Lord," and each stage discloses the exchange of Christ's victory with "my" captivity. "Heri dixi: si dico 'Credo in deum' hoc est: credo eum esse meum. Ita hic: credo Christum esse dominum meum, me eius esse, hae-reditatem quam possidebit, trutz allen qui adversantur Christo, quia mei curam habet, quia iuvare vult illud quod suum est." WA 11:52.9–12 (Sermon on the Symbolum: the second article of the Creed, March 5, 1523). "Die stu(e)cke aber, so nacheinander ynn diesem artikel folgen, thuen nichts anders, denn das sie solche erlo(e)sung verkleren und ausdru(e)cken, wie und wodurch sie geschehen sey, das ist was yhn gestanden und was er daran gewendet und gewagt

hymn, the use of direct speech accentuates the point more clearly than the first-person speech of the confession of faith. By casting Christ's self-definition in a prosopographic autobiography, Luther identifies the *promissio* of salvation with the person of Christ.

At the climax of the battle, Christ speaks what scholars have understood to be the summarizing *promissio*, a declaration of indivisible love. In the language reminiscent of sacred medieval bride mysticism,[209] Christ articulates the *promissio*: "For I am yours and you are mine" (7.5). Luther's use of this love formula in the genre of the hymn links a chain from the minstrels to two early seventeenth-century hymns.[210] The same phrase appears consistently in Luther's works of the early Reformation period. It serves as the theological key to his famous *The Freedom of a Christian* (1520)[211] and is woven frequently into sermons preached around 1523.[212] It is a formula Luther uses in his translation of certain New Testament passages:

---

hat, das er uns gewo(e)nne und zu seiner hyrschafft brechte. ... Und dis alles daru(e)mb, das er mein HERR wu(e)rde." WA 30,1:186.32–36; 187.4–5 (Large Catechism, 1529). In a 1523 sermon, Luther sees the entire life and person of Christ in terms of "serving us." "Wo mitt? da mitt, das er sein leben und alles was er vermocht an seiner gantzen person do hin gewent hatt, das er uns dinet; und das sind solche wortt, die kains menschen hertz aussprechen noch begreyffen kan." WA 12:469.31–33. In the same sermon, Luther interprets the incarnation to be the way in which Christ, as servant, wins salvation *pro me*. "Dann ist das nicht ein groß ding, das die ho(e)chst majestet sich also tieff herunter wirfft und sich nicht wil fur ein herren haben gehallten, sonder dienet mir verzweyffeltem bu(o)ben, so ich doch so vil wider in gethan hab, und trytt fur mich und lest sich umb meintwillen to(e)dten und fryst also mein sund wegk und erwirbt mir so groß reichlich gnad. Diß ist alles so groß, das man sich davor entsetzenn mu(o)ß, groß ist die person, die sich herab lesset, groß ist auch der dienst, das er mir erwirbt ewig gerechtigkait und seligkait und alles was got hatt, Nympt von mir das gro(e)st u(o)bell und armu(o)tt, die hell und den tod. Das ist recht das euangelium außgelegt, das man sihet, warumb es uns fur gelegt ist." Ibid., 469.35–470.2.

209. Wolff, "Zu Luthers Lied," 100.

210. The phrase occurs in verse 11 of Paul Gerhardt's hymn, "Warum sollt ich mich denn grämen?": "du bist mein, ich bin dein, niemand kann uns scheiden." EKG, no. 297. Verse 2 in "Mein schönste Zier und Kleinod bist" (Leipzig 1597) alludes to the same Romans passage, "Drum soll nicht Tod, nicht Angst, nicht Not von deiner Lieb mich trennen" and continues in verse 3: "Du bist nun mein und ich bin dein." EKG, no. 358.

211. WA 7:55.32–33.

212. For example: "Das heysst aber 'geschmeckt', wenn ich mit dem hertzen glewb, das sich Christus myr geschenckt hat und meyn eygen ist worden, und meyn sund und unglu(e)ck sein sind, und nu seyn leben meyn ist." WA 12:304.18–20 (to 1 Pet 2:2–3); "Denn syntemal Christus der brewtigam ist, und wyr die braut sind, so hatt die braut alles, was der breutigam hatt, auch seynen eygenen leyb." Ibid., 307.23–25 (to 1 Pet 2:5); in Roth's Postille: "Dem man geho(e)re ich an, Ich byn sein, er ist mein, Unnd wo er bleibet, da bleibe ich auch." WA 17,2:293.3–4 (to John 20:24–29).

the speech of the bride in the Song of Songs 2:16,[213] the Father's speech
to the elder brother in the parable of the prodigal son (Luke 15:31),[214] and
Christ's reference to the Father in John 17:10.[215] Not a peripheral remark,
the love declaration appears in Luther's hymn, as it does in his theology of
the 1520s, in order to summarize the central mystery of Christ's advent.
This is the mystery of the divine mercy that is turned from the inner to
the outer Trinity, binding the ties of love so tightly that no unholy power
can prevent or separate Christ from those to whom he declares his love.
When the two lines following the address of love are taken into account,
the summary *promissio* can be interpreted in the context of Romans 8:28–
29: "And where I dwell, there shall you be. The enemy shall never separate
us" (7.6–7). The passage in Romans, already seen as the overarching rubric
of the Father's passion, also governs the validity of the outer-Trinitarian
love formula.[216] Seamlessly transferred into the outer-Trinitarian extension of the inner-Trinitarian decision of mercy is the *promissio*, mediated
by Christ, who directly communicates the Father's love "to you."

With the *promissio* Christ speaks at the outer-Trinitarian periphery, the
last word is not yet spoken in the hymn. A final moment concludes with
Christ's ascension to the inner Trinity. Christ introduces his ascension into
heaven by mentioning the place of his return—his Father: "Toward heaven
to my Father" (9.1). A shift in the subject of the pronoun "my" distinguishes
between the outer-Trinitarian "where-to" of the lament and the life in the
Father's presence. After having mediated the lament as "my brother" (6.4),
Christ ascends to "my Father" (9.1). If Christ's person is constituted by the
promissio, then the ascension marks the final stage in the communication
of salvation. Christ's departure from "this life" is not a loss that annuls the
effect of his direct speech.[217] It is the final word concerning Christ's reign.
With his return, Christ incorporates the lament that he has mediated in
"this life" into the reign of the inner-Trinitarian life. In the presence of

---

213. The bride speaks to the beloved, "Meyn freund ist meyn vnd ich byn seyn." WADB
10,2:136 (1524).

214. "Er aber sprach zu yhm, Meyn son, du bist alltzeyt bey myr, vnd alles was meyn ist,
das ist deyn." WADB 6:284 (1522).

215. "... vnd alles was meyn ist das ist deyn, vnd was deyn ist das ist meyn." Ibid., 394.

216. See 181–82n169.

217. "Far ich von disem leben" (9.2).

the Father who has spoken to the Son, "And let him live with you" (5.7), Christ communicates the fulfillment of his advent as resurrected Lord and ascended master: "There I want to be your master" (9.3). Christ's reign from his inner-Trinitarian location before the Father fulfills the final word marking the narrative. It is the word of mercy that Christ speaks and by which he rules from the mercy seat.

Although implicit in Luther's hymn, the inner-Trinitarian picture of the mercy seat fittingly captures what Luther elsewhere explicitly articulates as his Trinitarian understanding of the divine mercy. Luther coined the term "mercy seat" (*Gnadenstuhl*) when translating distinct passages in the Old and New Testaments.[218] Bernard's sermon on Psalm 84:10 once again painted the backdrop of Luther's translation of the Vulgate, "throne of grace," as "mercy seat." Bell has linked Bernard's sermon to Luther's early glosses on Hebrews 4:16 and Hebrews 5:1.[219] In these glosses, Luther retained the Latin term "to the throne of grace" (*ad thronum gratiae*) while stressing the content to be the awesome throne that one can approach without fear.[220] In his 1522 translation of the New Testament, Luther translated the Greek word τό ἱλαστήριον in Romans 3:25 (in the Vulgate, *propitiatio*) and the phrase τῷ θρόνῳ τῆς χάριτος in Hebrews 4:16 ("throne of grace") with the same German term, "mercy seat" (*Gnadenstuhl*).[221] Luther also connected the New Testament term to the Hebrew term, כַּפֹּרֶת (*kapōret*) in Exodus 25:17, 20, 22 (in the Vulgate, *propitiatorium*). The mercy seat recovers the meaning of the Hebrew term as the cover of the ark of the covenant.[222] For Luther, both the New and the Old Testaments converge in the same image of the mercy seat as the place where the divine mercy is accessible on account of a blood sacrifice.

---

218. Jacob and Wilhelm Grimm, *Deutsches Wörterbuch*, vol. 4,1:5 (Leipzig, 1958), 591f.

219. Bell, *Divus Bernhardus*, 100.

220. In the Vulgate, Heb 4:16 reads, "adeamus ergo cum fiducia ad thronum gratiae." Heb 5:1 reads, "pro hominibus constituitur."

221. Rom 3:25: "wilchen gott hat furgestellet zu eynem gnade stuel, durch den glawben ynn seynem blut." WADB 7:38 (1522). Heb 4:16: "Darumb last vns hyntzu tretten, mit freydickeyt zu dem gnaden stuel, auff das wyr barmhertzigkeyt empfahen vnnd gnade finden auff die zeyt, wenn vns hulffe nott seyn wirt." WADB 7:354 (1522).

222. Exod 25:17, 21: "Du solt auch eyn Gnaden stuel machen von lautterm golt, ... Vnd solt den Gnaden stuel oben vber die lade thun." WADB 8:278 (1523).

The blood of Christ marks the inner-Trinitarian change that has taken place at the mercy seat after the divine essence of mercy has been conjugated through the narrative of Christ's advent. In an interpretation of 1 Peter 1:2 (1523), Luther draws together the covenant at Sinai in Exodus 24 with a penitential psalm verse in order to expose the change in the inner-Trinitarian speech that occurs with Christ's blood sacrifice. Luther alludes to Exodus 24:5–8, the passage in which Moses sprinkles blood on the ark of the covenant and on the people as a sign of the covenant. In the Trinitarian context of the mercy seat, Luther converts the Psalmist's plea in Psalm 51:9 into Christ's direct speech to the Father.

> To sprinkle however means to preach that Christ has shed his blood and stands for us before his Father and says: "Dear Father, there you see my blood that I have shed for this sinner." As you believe, so you have been sprinkled [with Christ's blood].[223]

This excerpt from Luther's commentary on 1 Peter represents his Christological understanding of the penitential psalms as the speech of the ascended Christ. At this narrative location, it is Christ, not the Father, who speaks. Christ presents his wounds, his cross, his death to the Father, importing his blood into the heart of the inner Trinity itself.[224] For Luther, the cross at the heart of the Trinity is the inner-Trinitarian mercy seat. The blood mediates the totality of the lament through Christ's speech, which assures the forgiveness of sins as well as the victory over the powers of the unholy trinity.[225] Appearing consistently in many other texts written

223. WA 12:264.9–12 (to 1 Pet 1:2).

224. In an interpretation of John 10:15, Luther alludes to the Father's address of love, not as it is located in the inner Trinity prior to the incarnation, but during Christ's passion. "Also wirt mich die wellt ansehen und erkennen, aber meyn vatter wirt also sagen 'das ist meyn lieber son, meyn ku(e)nig, meyn heyland', Er sihet nicht auff meyn elend, nicht auff meyn wunden, auff meyn creutz und todt, sondern auff die person die ich bin: Darumb wenn ich gleych mitten ynn der hellen und dem teuffel ym rachen were, so musz ich dennoch widder herfur, denn der vatter wirt mich nicht lassen." Ibid., 539.16–22 (Sermon on the Second Sunday after Easter, April 19, 1523).

225. "Das ist nun die gewalt die er lest predigen, das alle die an yhn glawben, von der gefengniß loß sind, Denn ich glawb an den, der sund, todt und allis was uns anficht, gefangen hat. Es ist eyn liebliche und trostliche rede, wenn man predigt, das der todt alßo hynweg genummen und erwurgt ist, das man yhn nit mer fu(o)let odder entpfindet, aber nur denen, die das glawben. ... Und darumb wer der sund wil loß seyn und erredtet vom teuffel und todt, der muß da hyn kommen, da er ist. Wo ist er aber? Hie bey uns ist er und darumb ynn hymel gesessen, das er nahe bey uns sey, ßo sind wir bey yhm da oben und er bey uns hie unten:

by Luther in 1523 is this theme of Christ speaking from the inner-Trinitarian mercy seat that has been sprinkled with his blood.[226] Imported into the relation between the Father and the Son is Christ's blood, which has become the *promissio* of mercy.

Luther's hymn ends with the reign of the ascended Christ at the mercy seat. From this culminating perspective shaped by the entire narrative, the lament in verses two and three can be placed in Christ's mouth. These verses cannot be limited to the human "I" without damaging the integrity of the Trinitarian narrative. By preserving the lament in its past tense totality, Luther succeeds in sharpening the Christological focus of the narrative of mercy. The lament in its totality can only be spoken by Christ before the Father.[227] Its presence in the hymn is not eradicated when Christ ascends

---

durch die predig kompt er herab, ßo kommen wir durch den glawben hynauff." Ibid., 565.9-13, 17-21 (Sermon on Ascension, May 14, 1523).

226. "Denn gleych wie die Sonn nicht deste weniger scheynet und leuchtet, ob ich schon die augen zu thue: Also stehet dieser gnaden stuel odder vergebung der sunde ymmer dar, ob ich schon falle." Ibid., 688, 24-27 (Sermon on the Twenty-second Sunday after Trinity, Nov. 1, 1523). In an exegesis of Ps 102:20, Luther writes on the mercy seat that exists for all eternity. The penitential psalm (102) is cross-referenced with Rom 3:25. "Der heylige hohe tempel gottis ist der gebenedeyte mensch Jhesus Christus, yn dem der ewige gott leybhafftig gantzlich wonet. derselb tempell ist unß gegeben tzu eym propitiatorio, Ro. iij. das ist, tzu eynem throne der gnaden [Rom 3:25], vor wilchem wer do sich beuget, der hat vorgebung aller sunde unnd alle gnade." WA 1:203.11-14 (Die sieben Bußpsalmen, 1517). The link between the mercy seat and Rom 3:25 is a theme also evident in 1532. In a sermon preached in this year, Luther distinguishes between two chairs, the "Rechtstuhl" and the "mercy seat" that Luther states is "Christ himself." "Denn so leret mich die schrifft, das Gott den menschen zween Stule gestellet habe, Einen Rechtstul fur die, so noch sicher und stoltz sind und jre sunde nicht erkennen noch bekennen wollen, Und Einen Gnaden stul fur die armen, bloden gewissen, die jre sunde fulen und bekennen, fur seinem gericht verzagen und gerne gnade hetten, Dieser Gnaden stul ist nu Christus selbs, sagt S. Paulus Rom. 3., den Gott uns gestellet hat, das wir dazu zuflucht haben sollen, wo wir fur Gott durch uns selbs nicht konnen bestehen. ... Welcher heisst GNADE und VERGEBUNG DER SUNDEN." WA 36:367.1-7, 13 (Sermon on Nov. 24, 1532). In a sermon preached in 1523, Luther refers to Christ's blood as the great price God paid in order to establish the mercy seat. "War ist, das der bloß glaub selig mach und uns nicht kost. Aber dennoch hat es Gott etwas gekostet, und also vil, das er hat mu(e)ssen mensch werden unnd uns erlo(e)sen. Darumb mu(o)ß man also in gott glauben durch das blu(o)t Christi, wie Paulus sagt ad Rom iij., 'Sy seind alle sünder und haben den preyß nicht den sy got sollen geben'. Sy werden aber frumm durch die kost und erlo(e)sung Christi, den gott gestellet hat zu(o) ainem gnadenthron, durch welchs blu(o)t wir angenem werden durch den glauben. Also mu(o)ß ich meinen glauben richten, das ich ja nit one mitel zu(o) got kumme und die kost auß dem weg stoß." WA 12:582.20-29 (Sermon on Corpus Christi, June 4, 1523).

227. Among contemporary theologians, Bonhoeffer's view of the Psalms as a book of prayer is a compelling interpretation of how Jesus teaches Christians the right way to pray before God. Bonhoeffer writes, "... daß wir das rechte Beten allein von Jesus Christus lernen konnen, daß es also das Wort des Sohnes Gottes, der mit uns Menschen lebt, an Gott den

to the mercy seat. At this juncture, the lament illustrates in a poetic text what late-medieval art pictorially represents. Paintings and sculptures portray the cross at the heart of the Trinity; the Father holds the cross on which Christ is dead, and the Spirit as a dove hovers nearby.[228] As long as the lament remains the content of Christ's speech, it is mediated by Christ in the *promissio* spoken in eternity, as Luther defines in a sermon.[229] Captured by the image of the mercy seat, the reign of Christ determines the inner Trinity to be the suspension of the lament in the eternal essence of mercy.

The final two verses of Luther's hymn close the narrative circle with the occasion for the Spirit's advent. Christ parts with the words identifying his rule with the "giving" of the Spirit: "There I want to be your master. The Spirit I will give to you" (9.3-4). The rule of Christ complements the access to the inner-Trinitarian mercy with the outer-Trinitarian fulfillment of the promise to send the Spirit, a fulfillment that circles back to its initial advent. Participating in Christ's reign, the Spirit has no other task than to comfort, lead, and guide the community in the knowledge and truth of Christ. In his 1 Peter commentary, Luther extends the mercy seat motif to include the Spirit, "through whom one can come to the Father."[230] Through

---

Vater ist, der in der Ewigkeit lebt. Jesus Christus hat alle Not, alle Freude, allen Dank und alle Hoffnung der Menschen vor Gott gebracht." Bonhoeffer, "Das Gebetbuch der Bibel," 375.

228.   "Man kann ihn *die* mittelalterliche Form für die Darstellung der Heiligen Dreifaltigkeit nennen." Braunfels, *Die Heilige Dreifaltigkeit*, xxxv. [Italics in original text.] The tour guide at the St. Andreas church in Eisleben, the town in which Luther was born and in which he died, claimed that late medieval paintings or sculptures of the mercy seat were rare in the middle-German area and more popular in southern Germany. It is surprising to find a sculpture of the mercy seat dated to 1500 in the St. Andreas church, the church in which Luther held the last sermons of his life. The sculpture, the Father holding the cross on which Christ is dead, was part of the altar for the Feast of Corpus Christi, one of fourteen altars in this church. Personal conversation with the tour guide at the St. Andreas church in Eisleben on Aug. 24, 1996.

229.   Luther clearly stresses that the kingdom of grace will never cease. "Denn er hat ein solch reich angefangen und auffgericht, darynn eyttel gnade ist, die da nymmer mehr auffho(e)ren soll, da dyr alles soll vergeben werden, wie offt du sundigist, syntemal er das Euangelium hatt ausgehen lassen, das da keyne straffe, sondern eyttel gnade verkundigt. Weyl nu das regiment stehet, so kanstu nymmerdar widder auff stehen, wie tieff und offt du davon fellist. Denn ob du gleych fellest, so bleybt doch das Euangelion und dieser gnaden stuel ymmerdar stehen." WA 12:676.17-24 (Sermon on the Twenty-second Sunday after Trinity, Nov. 1, 1523).

230.   Luther's understanding of prayer is shaped by the locations of the three persons of the Trinity in relation to the person praying. Christ, at the right hand of the Father, sends the Holy Spirit who brings us before the Father in the name of Christ who speaks on our behalf. This picture's narrative site follows Christ's ascension. "Aber das alles nicht anders, denn

the Spirit, the sinner is led to Christ, who alone prays a prayer that is well pleasing to the Father.

In Luther's hymn, Christ's final words are spoken under the rubric of the anticipated advent of the Spirit. Exhortational themes, similar to those of the pastorals, are the content of Christ's parting address.[231] The "kingdom of God" (10.3) is to be characterized by obedience to do and teach what Christ has done and taught: "What I have done and taught, that you shall also do and teach" (10.1-2). Christ's address of love becomes the central commandment in the kingdom of God when the Spirit comes and opens up the individual to love.[232] The Spirit effects a tropological conversion not only of the lament into the confession of sin ("The Pneumatological Conversion"), but also of the life of service to neighbor. Ruled by the Spirit of Christ, Christians are free to show grace and mercy to others.[233] The

---

durch die aufferstehung Christi, darumb das er erstanden und gen hymel gefaren ist, und sitzet zur rechten hand Gottis. Denn darumb ist er hynauff gefaren, das er uns seynen geyst gebe, auff das wyr new geporn werden, und nu durch yhn durfften zum vatter komen und sprechen: 'Sihe ich kome fur dich und bitte, nicht also, das ich mich auff mein gebete verlasse, sondern darumb, das meyn herr Christus fur mich tritt und meyn fursprecher ist.' ... Darauß kan man aber urteylen, was eyn rechtschaffen Christlich leere odder predig sey. Denn wenn man wil das Evangelium predigen, so muß es kurtz umb sein von der aufferstehung Christi." Ibid., 268.9-16, 18-20 (to 1 Pet 1:3).

231. "Das laß ich dir zu(o) letze" (10.7). "Das Märtyrerlied und das Danklied nehmen uns wie Luthers Osterlieder 'zur Letze', zur Stärkung auf unserm Wege, in die tägliche Pflicht der Dankbarkeit, die das, was uns gegeben und was uns damit verheißen ist, umspannt und uns zu Trägern einer lebendigen Hoffnung macht: 'Der das hat angefangen, der wird es auch vollenden.'" Gabriel, *Das deutsche evangelische Kirchenlied*, 34.

232. Luther discusses Phil 2:6-11 in view of Christ as "example" and "picture" of "the great love shown to us." "Das ist nun das aller ho(e)chst werck der lieb, das man also eins sey. Und da setzt S. Paul den herrn Christum zum exempell und zum bild, das wir uns die grosse liebe, die er gegen uns gethan hatt, auch lassen erwaichen." WA 12:469.1-3 (Sermon on Palm Sunday, March 29, 1523).

233. Luther discusses the freedom of the Christian in tropological terms. "Denn die Christen mu(e)ssen alleyn ym geyst gefurt und regirt werden, also, das sie wissen, das sie durch den glawben schon alles haben, da durch sie selig werden, und keynes dings mehr dazu durffen, und fort hyn nichts mehr schuldig sind zu(o) thun, denn das sie dem nehisten dienen und helffen mit allem das sie haben, wie yhn Christus geholffen hatt, und das also alle werck, so sie thun, on zwang und frey daher gehen und fliessen auss lu(e)stigem und fro(e)lichem hertzen, das Gotte danckt, lobt und preyst umb der gu(e)tter willen, die es von yhn entpfangen hatt. Also schreybt S. Paulus 1. Timo: 1. [v. 9] Das den gerechten keyn gesetz geben ist, denn sie thun alles frey von yhn selbs und ungeheyssen, was Gott haben will." Ibid., 332.1-10 (to 1 Pet 2:16). For Luther, Christ's government is characterized by sheer grace and mercy. We, who are set free by Christ, are to show mercy to those "die yhr yamer und elendt fu(e)len und gerne herauss weren." Ibid., 534.17 (Sermon on the Second Sunday after Easter, April 19, 1523). For examples of Luther's understanding of the freedom and grace shown by Christ that compels to mercy towards neighbor, see: Ibid., 294.28-30 (to 1 Pet 1:22); Ibid.,

theme of the Spirit's role in converting Christians to serve their neighbors appears frequently in Luther's tropological exegesis of Philippians 2:6–11, from *The Freedom of a Christian* (1520)[234] to other writings in 1523.[235] Christ's final warning is severe. He commands the community, "Be on your guard against human laws, thereby is the precious treasure spoiled" (10.5–6). For Luther, the "human law," meaning "law" in 1 Peter 1:18, is contrasted with the "precious treasure" of Galatians 2:21 and 2 Peter 2:1.[236] The precious treasure, which has cost God his blood, is not to be compromised by any human law. The sweet act of wonder, accomplished in Christ and taught by the Spirit, becomes the focus of the community who sings "to his praise and honor" (10.4). Luther's hymn ends where it has begun: with the thanks to God effected by the Spirit who transforms individuals to praise God in singing Luther's hymn.

Luther's hymn culminates with Christ's reign from the mercy seat, a fitting conclusion to the narrative that has conjugated the divine attribute of mercy through the three persons of the Trinity. From this terminal point, the hymn's starting point—the Spirit's advent—can be seen in light of the

---

333.5–7 (to 1 Pet 2:16); Ibid., 356.24–26 (to 1 Pet 3:12); Ibid., 530.20–23 (Sermon on the Second Sunday after Easter, April 19, 1523).

234. WA 7:65.10–25; similar in the German version: Ibid., 35.12–19 (Von der Freiheit eines Christenmenschen, 1520).

235. The theme of the treatise on freedom is the tropological conversion of the Christian that is effected by Christ's word. The freedom of faith in the inner person converts the outer person to love one's neighbor. In the sermon on Palm Sunday, March 29, 1523, Luther interprets Phil 2:6 tropologically. "Bistu nun ein christen, so mu(o)stu nicht dein gu(o)t, dein nutz, dein eer suchen, Sonder dich verzeyhen und das alles faren lassen und heruntter fallen, das du nu(o)r andern dienest, wie dir Christus gethan hatt, welcher gleiche gotthait hatt mit dem vatter." WA 12:470.41–471.2.

236. The "Schatz verachten" is mentioned in Luther's sermon on Matt 18:23–35, the parable of the wicked servant. Luther preaches at length on Christ's government of "sheer grace," the "gospel" and the "mercy seat" that "ymmerdar stehen." Ibid., 676.21, 23, 24 (Sermon on the Twenty-second Sunday after Trinity, Nov. 1, 1523). Luther then turns to the unworthy servant who demands payment from another slave. The king's pardon has not touched the heart of the wicked servant. In this context, Luther explains that the servant, who rejects the treasure, must be relegated to the charge of the worldly government. "Denn es ist wol eyn feynis ko(e)nigreych und gnedigs regiment, weyl darynne eyttel vergebung der sund predigt wirt, es gehet aber nicht yederman zu hertzen. Darumb sind viel rauchlose leut die des Euangelii missbrauchen, frey dahynn leben und thun was sie wollen, meynen, niemant soll sie straffen, weyl das Euangelium eyttel vergebung der sund predigt. Denen ist das Euangelion nicht gepredigt, die den hohen schatz also verachten und leychtfertig damit umbgehen. Darumb geho(e)ren sie nicht ynn das ko(e)nigreych, sondern yns welltlich regiment, das man yhn were, das sie nicht alles thun was sie lustet." Ibid., 677.2–10.

genre of the hymn of praise. Under the rubric of the Spirit, the lament's discourse is converted into the confession of sin. At the same time, its past tense is oriented towards anticipating the Christological mediation through the narrative of Christ's advent. In this section, the lament's suspension in the hymn of praise has been discussed in terms of its completed mediation in Christ's outer-Trinitarian incarnation and death. The lament's silence points to the Son's death as the mystery at the heart of the Trinity, yet it is accessible as the penitential psalms that Christ speaks before the Father. The lament's Christological mediation is indicated by the change of inner-Trinitarian speaker from the Father to the Son and also by the "giving" of the Spirit, sent to transform individual lives into a tropological exegesis of Christ's own life. In the hymn of praise, the lament remains the focus in eternity of what the divine mercy has accomplished; the divine mercy alone becomes the object of praise. As Luther states, the appeal to mercy is what funds every single hymn of praise. "Here there is nothing to praise but sheer compassion."[237] The word of mercy, issued from the inner-Trinitarian mercy seat, is the word of God for eternity.

TRINITARIAN NARRATIVE AS INTERPRETATION OF DOGMA

The location of Luther's hymn in the hymnbooks printed from 1524 to 1535 signifies its originally intended function as an interpretation of the German credo. What soon became erased in the hymnbooks, at least, was the complementarity of two discourses witnessing to the same subject matter. Dogma, in the form of the confession of faith, was dislocated from its narrative explanation; narrative was loosened from its moorings in the confession of a truth that transcends every rational effort to conceptualize it. I have reconnected the Trinitarian article of faith with the narrative in the hymn, "Now Rejoice, Dear Christians." As a summary, I limn the contours that shape Luther's narrative explanation of the Trinitarian article.

Luther understands the attribute of mercy to be the significant determination of the divine essence. The divine mercy is privileged as the attribute affected by human plight and despair and moved to show itself in Christ's

---

237. Ibid., 266.17 (to 1 Pet 1:3–9). Also: "Der rhum geho(e)rt niemant denn Gott alleyn, Gott hatt es uns on alle unser verdienst verheyssen und auch offinbart oder kund than das, das er von ewickeit versehen und verordnet hatt, ehe die welt geschaffen ist." Ibid., 292.29–31 (to 1 Pet 1:20).

advent. It is the inexplicable ground for the Father's inner-Trinitarian turn to the Son, for Christ's outer-Trinitarian incarnation and death, and for the Son's transformation of the inner Trinity into the eternal mercy seat. Each plot in the narrative of Trinitarian advent becomes the place where a distinct person comes to the fore, showing the divine mercy through the characteristic of its personhood. At these locations, each person makes visible its own personhood by connecting speech with its own particular construal of the *promissio*.

The Trinity is assigned three locations of advent that do not easily fit into the conceptual distinction between the immanent and the economic Trinity. In Luther's hymn, the speech of a particular person marks the Trinitarian side with which that person is identified. The Father emerges only in the inner Trinity. Here, a prosopographic formula determines the subject of speech to be the Father and the addressee to be his Son. At the outer Trinity, the Son is introduced as the person who speaks the *promissio* of love to a distinct addressee, "to me." From another outer-Trinitarian position, the Spirit's speech converges with the community's singing. The addressee of the community's praise is the Triune God.

At each location of Trinitarian advent, the *promissio* is spoken as part of the prosopographic self-identification of the person. In his inner-Trinitarian speech to the Son, the Father reveals himself to be the Father of the beloved Son and continues to speak the *promissio* on behalf of the human "I." The Father fills the inner Trinity with his spoken promise of life: "And let him live with you" (5.7). Christ's outer-Trinitarian incarnation is unfolded at every stage of battle by his personal address of love. Christ defines himself in the narrative of his outer-Trinitarian life and identifies each stage with the *promissio* of salvation.[238] With the advent of the Spirit, Christ's address becomes the object of praise; without the Spirit, there would be no knowledge of what God has turned to humanity in Christ.

The movement between the three Trinitarian locations is grasped narratively as it is compelled by the attribute of mercy. In eternity, the inner Trinity is moved to compassion by human misery. Known as the "decision for redemption," this movement is narrated as an inner-Trinitarian turn preceding the Son's incarnation. The Son's obedience to the Father

---

238. "Da bistu sälig worden" (8.7).

guarantees the continuity from the inner to the outer Trinity. The immediate shift in the *promissio* from the passive imperative in the Father's speech to the Son's obedience indicates an inner-Trinitarian openness to its subsequent turn to the outer Trinity. What Luther accomplishes by this shift is to show that the entire divine essence of mercy is moved from its inner- to its outer-Trinitarian location. The Son's advent, then, becomes the arena in which the *promissio* is unfolded as the prosopographic narrative of Christ's life. The narrative continues to be unbroken by the sending of the Spirit. When Christ has ascended to his Father, he fulfills his promise to "give" the Spirit. Christ's *promissio* at the end is fulfilled by the Spirit's advent at the beginning. Also fulfilled upon his ascension is the Father's *promissio* of life. At the inner-Trinitarian mercy seat, Christ prays the penitential psalms before the Father, moving the Father to show mercy to those for whom he died.

Luther's ingenuous weave between narrative and speech does not erase the central focus on the rupture. In Luther scholarship, the rupture has been privileged as the anthropological starting point of Luther's hymn and his theology. Beginning with the human under the law, the problem of describing the divine turn from wrath to mercy has been interpreted in terms of a revolution in the divine essence. In contrast to this position, I have shown how Luther's understanding of the Trinity begins and ends by underlining the divine mercy as the unexpected ground of the inner-Trinitarian turn to the outer Trinity. Luther begins his hymn with the Spirit's advent, and he introduces the rupture as "before" from the perspective of the "after." Even the "before" is preceded by the divine passion in eternity. Mercy is underscored as the essential divine attribute motivating the origin of the inner-Trinitarian turn to the outer Trinity. In assuming a narrative framework privileging the divine mercy, the status of the rupture is not inevitably compromised. Rather, the rupture is suspended Christologically in the inner Trinity as the silence of the cross; as silence, it strikes at the heart of the Trinitarian relation between Father and Son. With the advents of the Spirit and of Christ, the divine silence is transformed into speech. The Spirit converts the lament into the confession of sin; Christ communicates the *promissio* of his life, won in the battle with death. The rupture is also retained in a narrative understanding of the Trinity in order to block an unrestrained speculative access to the inner Trinity. Narrative access to the inner Trinity is achieved Christologically, both as the suspension of the lament into the past tense of the hymn of praise and as the speech of the ascended Christ before the Father. The rupture is strategically located in the hymn at a juncture preceding a narrative entry into the inner Trinity; the inner Trinity is accessible at no other place than at the cross of Christ.

CONCLUSION

In this chapter, Luther's understanding of the Trinity was studied according to the genre and the language of the hymn, "Now Rejoice, Dear Christians." The subject matter of praise was determined to be the divine essence of mercy, unfolded in a narrative of Trinitarian advent. Each plot in the narrative was seen to be constituted by a particular manifestation of the *promissio*. When the voice of a Trinitarian person was heard, the *promissio* was spoken in a way disclosing the person and its location at either an inner-Trinitarian site or at its outer-Trinitarian extreme. The narrative began with the advent of the Spirit to the outer Trinity. Following Christ's ascension at the end, the Spirit's advent fulfilled Christ's *promissio* and converted the lament into the discourse of the confession of sin. Placed after the Spirit's advent, the lament continued to remain the focus through which the narrative was oriented, at its different sites, to the lament's Christological mediation. The Father's voice identified the first moment of the inner Trinity to be the divine decision for redemption. In eternity, the divine essence of mercy was narrated as the Father's inner-Trinitarian turn to the Son that terminated in transferring the Father's *promissio* of life to the Son. At its outer-Trinitarian extreme, Christ's advent was narrated in the interweave between a prosopographic interpretation of his person and his assumption of the lament's totality. Christ spoke the *promissio* in a direct address. He communicated the *promissio* of mercy through the stages of his battle that mediated the lament through the victory he won with his blood. The Trinitarian picture of the mercy seat concluded the narrative. It showed the Trinitarian essence in eternity to be constituted by Christ's mediation of the lament in the penitential psalms spoken before the Father as well as by his "giving" of the Spirit. At the center of the eternal relation between Father and Son, the silence of the cross has become accessible in the speech of the *promissio* of mercy.

4

Luther's Understanding of the Trinity in the Two Sermons on Romans 11:33-36 Preached on Trinity Sunday (May 27, 1537) and the First Sunday after Trinity (June 3, 1537)

The sermon and Paul's Letter to the Romans can be considered to be the genre and biblical text most closely related to the theme of Luther and the Reformation. In this chapter, a unique sermon on Romans 11:33-36 is chosen from Luther's vast homiletical repertoire in order to study Luther's preaching on the Trinity. The chapter's focus is a two-part sermon Luther preached on this text from Romans, held on Trinity Sunday, May 27, 1537, and on the first Sunday after Trinity, June 3, 1537.[1] In his sermon, Luther takes into exegetical account the text's relation to both the theme of the entire book of Romans, the knowledge of God (Rom 1:18-20), and to its immediate surrounding in Romans 9-11, three chapters noted for their concentration of citations from the Old Testament and for their status in

---

1. The sermon is published in two editions, the Rörer macaronic version of 1537 and the 1544 German text of Cruciger's *Sommerpostille.* Considered by Luther scholarship to be closer to the original spoken sermon, the Rörer text will be used as the primary text for this chapter. The Rörer text is found in WA 45:89.16-93.33 (Sermon on Trinity Sunday, May 27, 1537); Ibid., 94.1-98.8 (Sermon on the First Sunday after Trinity, June 3, 1537). At points of difference, the Cruciger text will be considered. The Cruciger text is found in WA 21:508.1-522.23 (Cruciger's Sommerpostille, 1544). Luther held Cruciger's redaction in high esteem. Concerning Cruciger's printed version of a sermon Luther preached on 1 Tim 1, Luther exclaims in a Table Talk: "Ich halte, er hats besser gemacht, dan ichs geprediget habe; do ich die predigt that, waren nicht tzehen pauren in der kirchen ohne die drey fursten vnd hoffgesinde." WATr 3:42.30-32 (no. 2869b, Jan. 2, 1533). Another Table Talk records Luther's enthusiasm for Cruciger's version of a sermon on Matt 5-7: "Iam studeo in sermone Christi [1532 sermons on Matt 5-7], vnd ich hab kein besser buch gemacht; zwar ich habs nicht gemachtt, sondern Creutziger. Sermo in monte ist auch gutt, aber dis ist das best." WATr 5:41.5-7 (no. 5275, Sept. 23-Oct. 3, 1540). For the purpose of simplifying the pronouns in this chapter, the two sermons will be referred to in the singular.

the theological tradition as the classic prooftext on predestination.[2] How Luther interprets the theme of the knowledge of the divine wisdom in light of a Trinitarian doxology remains to be explored.

The intention of this chapter is to show how Luther conceives the Trinity in the genre of the sermon as a narrative of Trinitarian revelation. Luther plots three primary sites, and at each site, the *promissio* is determined according to a convergence between the revelation of a Trinitarian person and the particular way in which that person is "with us." The narrative unfolds through a movement from the inner to the outer Trinity, until it culminates in the revelation of the triune essence in the works of creation.[3] Before the discrete sites are investigated, I discuss the predominant approach to Luther's sermons by scholars. The "word-event" approach will be reviewed and then challenged in light of the doctrinal component evident in sermons Luther preached on both the inner and the outer Trinity. The narrative of Trinitarian revelation will then be studied in the subsequent three sections. The first discussion displays Luther's understanding of the Holy Spirit, who reveals the Trinity to Christians from the "inside out," and then turns to Luther's point of contrast, the "people" (*gentes*; Rom 1:18) who attempt to know God from the "outside in." I propose an alternative to the "instrumental" notion of homiletical speech by describing the Spirit's way with the church as one that incorporates hearers into a "right speaking" of the inner Trinity. The next site discloses the content of the Spirit's revelation to be a sermon that the Father preaches in eternity.

---

2. In his sermon, Luther alludes to the theme of predestination as a possible interpretation of Rom 11:33. "Ideo Paulus: 'O profunditatem' [Rom 11:33]. Non wil furen text auff die versehung, ut gedeutet." WA 45:92.33–35.

3. The sermon is based on Luther's own 1530 translation of the passage in which he modified the final preposition in Rom 11:36 from his 1522 translation, "zu," to "in." The later revision agrees with the Greek preposition in Erasmus's Greek New Testament, "εἰς αὐτὸν," as well as with the Vulgate's "in ipso." Erasmus's annotations mention Origen's translation of this passage and document the Vulgate's translation: "quod perfectio omnium et finis in ipso erit." WADB 7:569. The biblical passage from "Das Neue Testament (1522)" reads: "O wilche eyn tieffe des reychtumbs, beyde der weyßheyt vnnd der erkentnis Gottis, wie gar vnbegreyfflich sind seyne gericht, vnd vnerforschlich seyne wege. Denn wer hat des hern synn erkand? odder wer ist seyn radgebe gewesen? odder wer hat yhm was zuuor geben, das yhm werde widder vergolten? Denn von yhm vnnd durch yhn, vnd zu yhm sind alle ding, yhm sey preyß ynn ewickeyt Amen." Ibid., 66.6–11. The modified verse reads as follows in Luther's 1546 edition: "Denn von jm, vnd durch jn, vnd in jm, sind alle ding, Jm sey Ehre in ewigkeit, AMEN." Ibid., 67.10–11.

At this location, the *promissio* is seen to be the soteriological focus of the inner Trinity's Christological center. The final narrated site is the way of God "to us" in Christ, the way of revelation in Christ that is to be distinguished from the God hidden from view. The chapter—and by extension, this study—concludes by showing how Luther uses the Trinitarian structure of the doxology in Romans 11:36 as a grammar for reading the revelation of the Triune essence in the created works and as an eschatological vision of the day when all creation will be incorporated into the glorification of the Triune God.

LUTHER AND THE SERMON

If Luther could be associated with only one genre, that genre would be the sermon. The intention of this section is to introduce Luther's extensive preaching activity and to argue that he regarded the Trinity as an important homiletical theme. I begin by observing the common elements in studies of Luther's homiletical theory in order to show why the Trinity has often gone unnoticed. Fixed on the sermon as a Christological concentration of the twofold word of law and gospel, scholars have generally conceived the preached word according to a relational ontology and have determined the act of preaching to be an event justifying the hearer. This understanding of Luther and the sermon has, in my estimation, contributed to a dogmatic narrowing in view of the sermon's homiletical content. In the second section, I show, in a preliminary fashion, that Luther did preach on the inner Trinity on specific feast days of the church year and on the outer Trinity in the catechetical sermons. The third section focuses on the Romans 11:33–36 sermon and discusses its doctrinal content or scope to be the Trinity, a stress that demonstrates Luther's homiletical interest in doctrine. It is to the genre of the sermon, Luther's lifelong passion, that I now turn.

THE SERMON AS "WORD-EVENT" IN
CONTEMPORARY LUTHER SCHOLARSHIP

In research on Luther, the genre that has been considered to be clearly privileged in connection with the theme of Luther's theology of the word is the sermon. In terms of daunting quantity, more than 2,000 sermons document thirty-five years of preaching activity, beginning with the conferral of Luther's doctoral degree.[4] The impressive record of preaching up to four times a week[5] veils the fear Luther felt, even as an old and experienced preacher, each time he ascended the pulpit, an activity he performed out of sheer obedience to God.[6] The year in which he preached the sermon investigated in this chapter, 1537, was also marked by extraordinary preaching activity.[7] Against a tense historical backdrop, clouded with the fear of his

---

4. It is estimated that Luther preached over four thousand sermons during the course of his theological career. Approximately two thousand three hundred of these sermons are preserved, and only thirty of these were preached on a passage from Romans. Fred W. Meuser, *Luther the Preacher*, 18. Upon Staupitz's recommendation, Luther began preaching regularly in the Augustinian monastery in Wittenberg, most likely from 1510 or 1511 on. In 1514, he was asked by the city council to become the substitute for the sick Simon Heinz at the Wittenberg city church and, after Bugenhagen had become the church's preacher, Luther often preached during the latter's absence. Alfred Niebergall, "Die Geschichte der christlichen Predigt,"70–71.

5. On average, Luther preached between two and three sermons each week. One hundred and fifty sermons are preserved from the year 1528. It has been estimated that Luther preached about four times a week during this year.

6. "Neque enim me in officio verbi retinet, nisi alienae, immo divinae voluntatis obedientia, mea voluntate, sicut semper abhorrui, ita nunquam in hanc usque horam accessi." WA 5:20.10–13 (Operationes in Psalmos, 1519–1521); "Tantum hoc mihi credite humanum opus non esse praedicationem, et ne audax sitis, sed Deum timens praedicator. Ego enim antiquus et exercitatus praedicator usque hodie timeo praedicaturus." WATr 2:539.28–30 (no. 2606a, early 1532); "Es ist mir auch gewest. Ich habe mich wol ßo seer gefurcht furm predigstul als yhr, noch must ich fort." WATr 3:187.6–7 (no. 3143a, May 1532). On Jan. 1, 1530, Luther announced to his Wittenberg congregation that he would withdraw from his preaching activity. He complained of the pittance that was paid to the preachers, was frustrated with the congregation that did not show love towards neighbor, and spoke of his preaching that accomplished not even the least effects of civil discipline. Until Sept. 15, Luther preached only a few sermons in neighboring towns. An example of Luther's frustration is: "Ich bins wol so mu(e)de, der grossen undanckbarkeit halben jm volck, aber viel mehr der untreglichen beschwerung halben, so mir der Teuffel und die welt zu messen." WA 30,2:340.31–33 (Vermahnung an die Geistlichen, 1530). For the story of Luther's sermon strike, see: WA 32:xvii–xxii, and Martin Brecht, *Martin Luther*, vol. 2, 280–85, 415–16.

7. "Luthers Predigttätigkeit war auch in diesem Jahre eine außerordentlich reiche." Karl Drescher and Oskar Brenner, General Introduction to the sermons of 1537 in WA 45:xi.

imminent death,[8] and injected with the hope for a papal council,[9] Luther ascended the chancel up to three times a week, preaching three *lectio continua* series, and often replacing his colleague, Bugenhagen.[10] By choosing to preach a sermon on Romans 11:33-36, rather than on the gospel lesson prescribed for Trinity Sunday, John 3:1-15, Luther shows a readiness after 1530 to extend his preaching to epistle lessons.[11] Luther's vast number of sermons does not only represent his productivity in a genre closely linked to his practical-theological commitment. They also capture a form many scholars deem to be representative of the Reformation itself.

In addition to their number, Luther's sermons have become the focus of attention for scholars interested in determining the central theological insight of the Reformation. Luther scholarship increasingly agrees that there is an intimate relation between Luther's theology and the genre of the

---

8. Luther's health had deteriorated considerably by the end of 1536. The elector Johann Friedrich had asked Luther to summarize a faith statement for the Catholic General Council that could also be used as Luther's testament for Protestant pastors and preachers in Electoral Saxony. Intended as a document replacing his "Vom Abendmahl Christi. Bekenntnis (1528)," Luther wrote the Schmalcald articles in December 1536, an unofficial document signed by only a few theologians. In early 1537, during the meeting of the Schmalcald League, Luther became so ill that he feared the worst and asked to be transported out of Schmalcald into Electoral Saxony in order to die there. On the tortuous journey, he suddenly became well again and returned to Wittenberg on March 14. See: Reinhard Schwarz, *Luther*, 206-207; Brecht, *Martin Luther*, vol. 3, 179-85.

9. On June 2, 1536, Pope Paul III issued the bull "Ad dominici gregis curam," a recommendation for a council to be held on May 23, 1537, in the papal territory of Mantua. At the Protestant assembly of the Schmalcald League in January and February of 1537, from which Luther left early due to serious health problems, the League rejected the papal offer. Luther, who had, in 1535, met with the papal nuntius, regretted the League's decision. See: Schwarz, *Luther*, 203-6.

10. During Bugenhagen's absence, Luther preached regularly on Sundays and on feast days in the Wittenberg city church. In addition to these sermons, Luther preached three *lectio continua* series. One of these series was based on Matt 18-24. Between Easter and Pentecost, Luther preached a special series on John 14-16. Beginning in July 1537 with Bugenhagen's absence, Luther was also responsible for the Saturday evening sermons, customarily held on the Gospel of John. As Luther did not know at which passage Bugenhagen had left off, Luther started preaching from the beginning and continued through to chapter four.

11. The medieval lectionary readings prescribed for the first Sunday after Trinity were: 1 John 4:16-31 for the epistle and Luke 16:19-31 for the gospel. Luther appropriated, with very few modifications, the medieval lectionary tradition, as indicated in his 1522 translation of the New Testament. For the lectionary Luther used, see: Ferd. Cohrs, "Register der Episteln und Evangelien," in WADB 7:529-44. For Trinity Sunday, the Protestant church retained the gospel pericope (John 3:1-15) from the medieval lectionary. In the *Missale Romanum*, the Roman Catholic Church replaced the Johannine passage with Matt 28:16-20. See: J. Beckmann, "Trinitatisfest," 1041.

sermon.[12] The unique status attributed to the genre's association with the Reformation cannot be uncoupled from the sermon's liturgical significance in the late medieval period. Noted in the late Middle Ages is a tendency to separate the sermon from the celebration of the mass.[13] Although this dissociation might have contributed to Luther's claim regarding the centrality of the preached word, other developments demonstrate Luther's continuity within a distinct medieval trajectory. The late medieval sermons of mendicants and of the German mystics, as well as the fourteenth-century development of the office of preachers apart from the priesthood, evidence the importance of the sermon historically prior to Luther's appropriation of this genre.[14] When viewed against this historical backdrop, Luther's high estimation of the sermon can be appreciated.

Luther's rhetoric betrays his conviction that the preached word is the unique vehicle for communicating divine benefits. Indeed, for Luther, the sermon contains nothing less than the divine word of power to raise the dead.[15] Preaching is an office that concentrates all the divine benefits given by God to the church and dispensed in it. In many texts, Luther claims that the sermon is the "biggest" and "best" "service to God."[16] It is the first of the four "marks" of the church, the liturgically distinct offices that communicate the forgiveness of sins: preaching, baptism, the Lord's Supper,

---

12. Asendorf summarizes a consensus in Luther scholarship by stating, "daß Luthers Theologie wesentlich Predigt ist." Ulrich Asendorf, "Die Bedeutung der Predigt für Luthers Theologie," 98.

13. In the high Middle Ages, the sermon was moved from its prior location in the altar-room to the chancel. In the altar-room, the sermon was set apart from the celebration of the mass, and a liturgy emerged in relative independence from the mass liturgy. Elements of the sermon liturgy were: the confession of sins, the absolution and the three catechetical elements, the Apostles' Creed, the Our Father, and the Decalogue that was added to the catechism in the thirteenth century. See: Niebergall, "Die Geschichte der christlichen Predigt," 248–56; Eberhard Weismann, "Der Predigtgottesdienst und die verwandten Formen," 20–25.

14. In the *Formula missae* (1523), Luther reflects late medieval practice by placing the sermon before the Introit to the mass. WA 12:211.6–8. When Luther preached in the Wittenberg city church, he placed the sermon after the recitation of the Creed, a site he recommended in the *Deutsche Messe* (1526). See: Ibid., 211n2, and WA 19:95.3.

15. WA 30, 2:555.3–4 (Eine Predigt, daß man Kinder zur Schulen halten solle, 1530).

16. WA 36:237.29–30 (Zwo Predigt uber der Leiche des Kurfürsten Hertzog Johans zu Sachsen, Aug. 18, 1532). See also: WA 40,1:361.29 (In epistolam S. Pauli ad Galatas Commentarius, 1531/1535, to Gal 3:6); WA 45:682.22–23 (Sermons and Commentary on John 14–15, 1538, to John 15:8). In German, *Gottesdienst* is also the technical term for church or worship service.

and the office of the keys.[17] Not restricting the activity to the ordained ministry, Luther advocates preaching as a demonstration of love towards one's neighbor.[18] Luther tightly links the preaching office to the divine will. God the Father instituted the office on account of the blood of Christ.[19] Yet, what constitutes the power of the preached word is the promised presence, "without ceasing," of the resurrected Christ, victorious over sin, death, and devil.[20] Although the Christological focus is often stressed, Luther does not fail to emphasize the Trinitarian dimension of the preached word. In a text representing his praise of the preaching office, Luther describes the contribution of each Trinitarian person to the sermon's power.[21] The sermon localizes the revelation of God's will that sinners might live; in it, the right knowledge of God in the person of Christ, the gifts and the power of the Holy Spirit, and recommendations on the right way to discipline soul and body are available. In light of this office, ordained by God and communicating Christ's life-giving work, Luther could say, "Thus says the Lord," after every sermon he preached.[22] To God is attributed the word's power and more. God himself is the speaker of the preached word.

17. WA 50:628.30; 630.22; 631.7; 631.37 (Von den Konziliis und Kirchen, 1539).

18. WA 34,2:178.1-20 (Sermon on the Thirteenth Sunday after Trinity, afternoon, Sept. 3, 1531, on Luke 10:27-37). Prenter interprets Luther to distinguish between the office of the priesthood that includes all Christians and the representative function of the spiritual office. The offices are co-extensive by virtue of their being both ordained by God. All Christians are called to preach the word of comfort as a deed of love towards neighbor, and an individual can, in circumstances in which no representative is available, fill the function of the spiritual office. See: Regin Prenter, "Die göttliche Einsetzung des Predigtamtes und das allgemeine Priestertum bei Luther," 329-30.

19. "Ich hoffe ia das die gleubigen vnd was Christen heissen wil, fast wol wissen, das der geistliche stand sey von Gott eingesetzt vnd gestifftet nicht mit gold noch silber, sondern mit dem theüren blüte vnd bittern tode seines einigen sons vnsers herrn Jhesu Christi [1 Pet 1:18-19]." WA 30,2:526.17, 527.1-4.

20. "Denn weil Gotts wort vnd ampt, wo es recht gehet mus on vnterlas, grosse ding thun, vnd eitel wunder werck treiben." Ibid., 533.17-18.

21. "Denn durch sein ampt vnd wort wird erhalten, das reich Gottes, ynn der welt, die ehre, der name, vnd rhum Gottes, die recht erkentnis Gottes, der recht glaube vnd verstand Christi, die frucht des leidens vnd bluts vnd sterbens Christi, die gaben werck, vnd krafft des heiligen geists, der recht selige brauch, der tauffe vnd sacrament, die rechtschaffen reine lere des Euangelii, die rechte weise den leib zu zuchtigen vnd creutzigen Vnd der gleichen viel." Ibid., 539.7-13.

22. WA 51:517.9 (Wider Hans Worst, 1541). The quote from "Wider Hans Worst" is frequently found in the secondary literature on Luther's sermons. In this passage, Luther attributes the preached word to God and, for this reason, no forgiveness is required for a bad sermon! "Denn Ein prediger. ... müs mit Jeremia (Jer 17:16) sagen vnd rhümen Herr du weissest das was aus

In various reconstructions of Luther's homiletical theory, the object of interest has become the link Luther makes between the word of God and the preached word, a link that is then studied according to a theological determination of the word's nature.[23] Research on Luther's sermons has appealed to a claim of identity between the divine word and the preached word in order to explain how Luther understands God to be the subject of the speech.[24] The question arising in these studies seems to be concerned with the kind of identity Luther establishes in order to claim that God is the speaker of a word that truly has the power to raise the dead. In order

---

meinem munde gangen ist, das ist recht vnd dir gefellig, Ja mit Sanct Paulo vnd allen Aposteln vnd propheten trotzlich sagen. Hec dixit Dominus Das hat Gott selbs gesagt Et iterum Ich bin ein Apostel vnd prophet Jesu Christi gewest ynn dieser predigt Hie ist nicht not, ia nicht gut vergebung der sunde zu bitten, als were es vnrecht geleret, Denn es ist Gottes vnd nicht mein wort, das mir Gott nicht vergeben sol noch kan. ... Wer solchs nicht rhumen kan von seiner predigt, der lasse das predigen anstehen, Denn er leugt gewislich vnd lestert Gott." Ibid., 517.5, 7–13, 15–16. In order to combat a false sense of attributing the preached word to God, Luther qualifies the identity between the preached word and the divine word by appealing to the Old Testament prophets. Only those prophets who were sent by God were given the divine word; those prophets who were not sent did not speak the word of God. See: WA 47:191.25–196.40 (The Fourty-Seventh Sermon, Commentary on John 3–4, 1538–1540, to John 3:34).

23. Luther did not write a treatise on preaching. Scholars have reconstructed Luther's homiletical theory from his references to the word of God, particularly from references to the divine word as preached. The predominant texts used for these reconstructions are Luther's remarks concerning the preached word that are sprinkled throughout his sermons, theological treatises such as "De servo arbitrio (1525)" and "Wider Hans Worst (1541)," as well as the anecdotal material recorded in his Table Talks. Hirsch offers a delightful collection of these remarks in Emanuel Hirsch, ed., "Selbstzeugnis," 1–38. Rare in the secondary literature on Luther's sermons is a study devoted exclusively to one discrete text. Bayer's meditation on Luther's sermon preached on Mark 7:31–37 [WA 46:493–495 (Twelfth Sunday after Trinity, Sept. 8, 1538)] is an example of how Luther's preaching on the miracle story effects the "opening of one's eyes" to see creation. Bayer relates the sermon to Luther's understanding of justification. See: Oswald Bayer, "Tu dich auf! Verbum sanans et salvificans und das Problem der 'natürlichen' Theologie," Schöpfung als Anrede, 62–79.

24. Beutel, In dem Anfang war das Wort, 459; Karl-Heinrich Bieritz, "Verbum facit fidem," 486; Martin Doerne, "Predigtamt und Prediger bei Luther," 44–45; Emanuel Hirsch, "Luthers Predigtweise," 19; Alfred Niebergall, "Luthers Auffassung von der Predigt nach 'De Servo Arbitrio'," 103; Hans Thimme, "Martin Luther als Prediger," 37; Eberhard Winkler, Impulse Luthers für die heutige Gemeindepraxis, 74; Idem, "Luther als Seelsorger und Prediger," 236. Among these scholars, Meinhold represents the exception. "So ist die Predigt nicht unmittelbar 'Wort Gottes', aber sie ist die persönliche Applikation des göttlichen Wortes und des ewigen Sinnes, den Gott mit dem Werke Christi verbunden hat." For Meinhold, the word of God is eternal, and is to be distinguished from the human word that is temporal. The sermon functions as a hermeneutical bridge between the eternal word of God and the temporal word of the preacher. The preached word cannot be directly attributed to God. Meinhold's claim would be disputed by the majority of Luther scholars who claim that Luther identifies the eternal with the temporal word. See: Peter Meinhold, "Luther und die Predigt," 118.

to approach the question, a crucial distinction in Luther's doctrine of God must first be addressed.

Luther's attribution of the preached word to God is not a naive or general identification of all words with a divine speaker. In his famous response to Erasmus, Luther draws a distinction that many scholars have evaluated to be a key passage in their studies of Luther's homiletics. God, as the speaker who reveals the divine will, is to be distinguished from the silence of the hidden God and his inscrutable will.[25] There is a distinction "between the preached God and the hidden God, that is, between the Word of God and God himself."[26] The identity between God and the word is founded on a prior distinction between these two extremes.[27] Grounded in the doctrine of God, the distinction between God himself as hidden and the divine word as revealed feeds immediately into Luther's understanding of the preached word, which he underlines with the certainty of eternal salvation. Once the distinction is made between the hidden and revealed God, the identity between God and the preached word can be secured. This identity secures the identity of the speaker, who has the power to raise the dead.

The distinction Luther draws is not intended to be a formal criterion for predicating the preached word of God. For Luther, the distinction is a material one, pointing to the identity of the preached God, who is Jesus Christ: "Nothing except Christ is to be preached."[28] Only when Christ is preached can the communicated will of God be certain, the *promissio* that

---

25. A distinction between God and the Scriptures of God is drawn in the introductory section of "De servo arbitrio." "Duae res sunt Deus et Scriptura Dei." WA 18:606.11. Later in the text, this distinction is explained in terms of the distinction between the hidden and revealed God. "Aliter de Deo vel voluntate Dei nobis praedicata, revelata, oblata, culta, Et aliter de Deo non praedicato, non revelato, non oblato, non culto disputandum est." Ibid., 685.3-5.

26. Ibid., 685.25-27.

27. For examples of scholars who reconstruct Luther's homiletical theory on the distinction between the preached God and the God who is not preached, see: Horst Beintker, "Luthers theologische Begründung der Wortverkündigung," 21-24; Gerhard O. Forde, *Theology is for Proclamation*, 23-27; Niebergall, "Luthers Auffassung von der Predigt nach 'De Servo Arbitrio,'" 91-97; Max Schoch, *Verbi Divini Ministerium*, 33.

28. WA 16:113.7-8 (Predigten über das 2. Buch Mose, Dec. 11, 1524, to Exod 7:3). Examples of scholars citing this text in view of preaching are: Hans-Martin Barth, "Luthers Predigt von der Predigt," 482; Bieritz, "Verbum facit fidem," 487; and Winkler, "Luther als Seelsorger und Prediger," 234.

the sinner would live.[29] Luther defines the subject of speech, God, to be in a material identity with the word that is spoken, Jesus Christ. The preached word is integrally connected to a Trinitarian understanding in which the Christological scope, localizing the communication of the Father's will, is identical with effecting the content of what is spoken.

From this understanding of the word follows the discussion of preaching as a soteriological event. The material content of the preached word is Christ, yet the content of what is communicated is justification. There is astounding consensus in Luther scholarship regarding the sermon to be the location of the "event of justification."[30] Claimed to be the center of his Reformation breakthrough, Luther's understanding of justification by faith alone is used to determine the sermon to be an event in which God is entirely active in justifying the sinner, who is wholly passive in receiving the justification.[31] The preached word localizes justification as an event through the "asymmetric constituting context"[32] between the God who acts by justifying and the sinner who passively appropriates this divine action. In Bayer's terminology, the *promissio*, the pronouncement of forgiveness, funds every sermon in such a way as to effect its content in a recipient.[33] When God speaks, the content of the speech is communicated, with all its benefits, to the hearer.

The event character of the sermon is a central motif in Luther's word-oriented breakthrough when the latter is viewed through the lens

---

29. The revealed will of God is, for Luther, the certainty that God desires not the death of the sinner, but life (Ezek 18:31–32). "Et quid est ferme plus quam dimidium sacrae scripturae quam merae promissiones gratiae, quibus offertur a Deo misericordia, vita, pax, salus hominibus? Quid autem aliud sonant promissionis verba quam illud: Nolo mortem peccatoris?" WA 18:683.17–20.

30. "Für ihn [Luther] stand das Predigtgeschehen in einem unlösbaren *Zusammenhang mit dem Ereignis der Rechtfertigung*, und gerade diese Verbindung verschaffte der Predigt die Geltung, die sie in der Reformation erhalten hat." Niebergall, "Luthers Auffassung von der Predigt nach 'De Servo Arbitrio'," 84. [Italics in original text.]

31. The English phrase, "Luther's understanding of justification by faith," is often rendered in the German as "Luthers Rechtfertigungsglauben." For example: Prenter, "Die göttliche Einsetzung des Predigtamtes und das allgemeine Priestertum bei Luther," 330.

32. This is Herms's terminology in Eilert Herms, "Das Evangelium für das Volk," 27.

33. According to Bayer, Luther's Reformation breakthrough consists of seeing the mutual relation between the sermon and the Lord's Supper. The sermon is the interpretation of the "gift-word" (*Gabewort*), and the Lord's Supper is the occasion for the preaching of the sermon. Bayer, *Promissio*, 248.

of relational ontology. Proposed by Luther scholars in Germany, a relational ontology is constructed on particular identities that constitute the "word-event."[34] The objective pole is determined to be the preached word in an identity with the divine word that, in turn, is identified with the divine activity of justifying. On the subjective pole, the passive reception of justification is considered in an identity with faith that is created by God. The resulting relationship between the active word and its passive appropriation is discussed as a word-faith correlation,[35] or as the word's invitation to faith,[36] or as the word's intention to awaken faith in God and love towards neighbor.[37] Constituted by the relation between the objective and the subjective extremes, the correlation gains its status as an event when the move from unbelief to faith is effected in the human recipient.[38] The sinner is justified by faith each time the word is preached.

But, then, what are the implications for understanding the content of preaching to be the Trinitarian doctrine when the preached word is taken narrowly as a justification event?

THE DOGMATIC NARROWING AS AN IMPLICATION OF THE WORD-EVENT APPROACH TO LUTHER'S SERMONS

Viewed within the conceptual framework of a relational ontology, the sermon tends to be characterized as a word event. Particularly evident in this approach is the emphasis on the kerygmatic concentration of the preached word. In the following section, the kerygmatic moment of Luther's sermons will be discussed in terms portrayed by an existential

---

34. The term, "word-event," in German, "Wortgeschehen" or "Sprachereignis," characterizes Ebeling's "hermeneutic-homiletics." See: Ebeling, *Evangelische Evangelienauslegung*, 487; Idem, *Wort und Glaube*, vol. 1, 348.

35. Herms, "Das Evangelium für das Volk," 28; Meinhold, "Luther und die Predigt," 117.

36. Winkler, "Luther als Seelsorger und Prediger," 234.

37. Herms, "Das Evangelium für das Volk," 37; Detlef Lehmann, "Luther als Prediger," 13-14.

38. "Diese Absicht des Textes [zum wahren Glauben zu bringen und vom Unglauben abzubringen], identisch mit der Absicht der Wundertat selbst, wiederholt sich in der Absicht seiner Predigt durch Luther. ... Analysiert man Luthers Predigt, so stellt man leicht fest, daß sie von ihrem Anfang bis zu ihrem Ende, daß sie durch und durch vom 'Dualismus' von Glaube und Unglaube, von Selbstverschlossenheit und Offenheit, Taubheit und Hören, Blindheit und Sehen bestimmt ist." Bayer, "Tu dich auf!" *Schöpfung als Anrede*, 62-63. In a study of Luther's homiletics, Rössler argues that Luther intends the sermon to affect the conscience. The reception of the preached word in the conscience includes an experiential dimension to the move from law to gospel. Dietrich Rössler, "Beispiel und Erfahrung: Zu Luthers Homiletik," 206-8.

interpretation. This vantage point is set up in order that I might point out some reasons as to why the doctrinal content in Luther's sermons has remained undetected. This neglect will be preliminarily corrected by reviewing the sermons Luther preached on the Trinity; this section will lay the groundwork for discussing the knowledge of God as the central theme of Luther's 1537 sermon on Romans 11:33–36.

The relational ontology proposed by Luther scholars provides the conceptual framework necessary for showing how Luther conceives the move from law to gospel. When the word is preached, two extremes, considered by Luther to be the subject matter of theology, are brought into a relation: the justifying God and the sinful human being.[39] At one extreme is the word of Christ, which is designated to be the twofold word, the word of law and the word of gospel.[40] At the other extreme is the sinful human. When the relation between the two poles is constituted by the preached word, a dynamic shift is actualized in the sinner: the shift from law to gospel. Justification takes place when the word effects an anthropological displacement from law to gospel. It is a kerygmatic moment, an existential transfer that occurs. Preceding the imputation of the gospel is the word of law that sets the conditions for the event of justification but does not by itself contribute to the gospel's efficacy. The anthropological transfer from unbelief to faith, from law to gospel, occurs when the power of the resurrection, which has overcome death on the cross, effects this victory in the living heart of the believer.[41] The gospel justifies the sinner each time it is preached, and the word anticipates the ultimate eschatological demonstration of the gospel's power to raise from the dead.

---

39. "... subiectum Theologiae homo reus et perditus et deus iustificans vel salvator." WA 40,2:328.1–2 (Enarratio Psalmi LI, 1532/1538, to Ps 51:2).

40. There is a relative consensus in research on Luther's sermons that the preached word, in an identity with the Second Person of the Trinity, is constituted by the twofold word of law and gospel. See: Doerne, "Predigtamt und Prediger bei Luther," 49; Emanuel Hirsch, "Gesetz und Evangelium in Luthers Predigten," 54–56.

41. In his article on the function of narrative in Luther's sermons, Lischer argues that Luther re-tells the biblical stories in order to provoke the hearer's participation in a particular story. The theological depth dimension of "story" narrates the anthropological transition from human wretchedness to redemption. An anthropology informed by the idea of the pilgrim in process is synchronized with Luther's eschatological impulse that preaches the God who accomplishes the final redemption of creation. Lischer's reading of narrative in Luther's sermons correctly distinguishes between "story" as "medium salutis" and God, not "story," who redeems. Richard Lischer, "Die Funktion des Narrativen in Luthers Predigt," 313, 318, 328–29.

The event must ever be temporally rehearsed anew. Every preaching situation constitutes the relation between the justifying God and the sinful human. Each time the word is preached, the two extremes are brought into a relation that justifies the sinner. When the word is viewed in terms of constituting the relation, then its content can be conflated into a kerygmatic pivot around which the move from law to gospel turns.

Once the preached word is understood to stage an existential justification event, its content can be emptied of a dogmatic emphasis without detracting from its efficacy. A few observations in studies of Luther's homiletical theory expose a thinning in the doctrinal content of the sermons. When the sermon is reduced to a kerygmatic intention, the location of reception in the hearer tends to be privileged over the objective extreme of the word's content. The subjective moment is upheld as the location at which the word-faith correlation is constituted.[42] Reception can be accompanied by abstraction from the word's content without reducing its effect. In an extreme case, Ebeling intellectualizes the distinction between law and gospel in the hearer's reception of the word, suggesting that justification is the capacity to draw this distinction.[43] Another understanding of justification that seems to be removed from the word's content is Elert's reduction of the event to a relation between God and faith. Elert collapses any substantial content Luther might give to the justifying word into a "mathematical point ... without extension" and elevates justification to the level of the transcendental "I."[44] If justification is understood in terms of

---

42. In the context of discussing Luther's understanding of art in terms of a reception aesthetics, Beutel concludes that the subjective element in the "word-faith" correlation is decisive in determining the content of what is received. "Der Rezipient entscheidet darüber, was das Rezipierte für ihn ist: So etwa ließe sich die Grundstruktur der zentralen reformatorischen Relation von Wort und Glaube bestimmen. ... Auch seine homiletische Theorie ist von dieser Auffassung durchdrungen." Beutel, "Offene Predigt," 524–25.

43. "Denn der Ort des Unterscheidens [zwischen Gesetz und Evangelium] auch unter dem Wort der Verkündigung ist der Hörer selbst." Ebeling, "Das rechte Unterscheiden," 252.

44. The extreme case of reducing the human subject to a transcendental I in the event of justification is represented by Elert. "Die Gerechtigkeit, die uns zuteil wird, hat keinerlei Ausdehnung, sie ist niemals in dem Sinne etwas Empirisches, daß sie an den Inhalten unseres Bewußtseins aufgezeigt werden könnte... Dann ist aber auch hier das Ich, das die justitia empfängt, als 'mathematischer Punkt', das transzendentale." "Der evangelische Ansatz hat, theologisch verstanden, seinen Ort im Einzelnen. ... Aber diese Einsamkeit ist transzendentaler, nicht empirischer, Art. Das Zwiegespräch zwischen dem Glauben und Gott wird von Gottes Seite durch Vermittlung des 'Wortes' geführt. Damit tritt der Einzelne sofort in eine neue, wenngleich ganz andersartige überindividuelle Einheit ein." Elert, Morphologie, 72, 280–81.

a relation, mediated by the word whose empirical status is questionable, then the efficacy of the transcendental event does not require a doctrinal determination to the word's content. What suffices is the discrete instantiation of the preached word, which constitutes a relation between God and the transcendental "I."

Another serious reduction in the doctrinal dimension of the word is observed as an implication of the law-gospel scheme for the doctrine of God. When law and gospel are viewed as the symmetric elements constituting the twofold word, their projection into the eternal nature of God is either erased or the implications for a doctrine of God are not explicitly drawn.[45] According to this orientation, the exclusive focus on Christ leaves little room for the Spirit, who is given no more than a hermeneutical status in bridging the individual's reception of the shift from law to gospel.[46] When law and gospel are further confused with the distinction between the hidden and the revealed God, a conceptual hindrance blocks a serious investigation into the Trinity, identified as the object of worship,

---

45. Ebeling locates the distinction between law and gospel entirely in the hearer. Beutel, Herms, and Niebergall gesture towards an asymmetry between law and gospel at the level of the preached word, but do not draw out the implications of this view in the doctrine of God. Beutel draws a distinction between the law as the "verbum ad nos" and the gospel as the "verbum in nos." See: Beutel, *In dem Anfang war das Wort*, 381. Herms writes that, for Luther, "[d]ie Predigt ist selbst das Evangelium," but qualifies this statement by indicating the constitutive function of the law for the gospel. "Für den *Inhalt* des Evangeliums ist der Inhalt des Gesetzes konstitutiv." Herms, "Das Evangelium für das Volk," 42, 31. [Italics in the original text.] Niebergall claims that the gospel is properly the word of God. The law does not accomplish what the gospel does: the sinner's justification. Niebergall, "Luthers Auffassung der Predigt nach 'De Servo Arbitrio,'" 98–99.

46. For Ebeling, the Spirit becomes necessary for the hearer's capacity to distinguish between law and gospel. "Im Leben damit recht umzugehen, daß das Gesetz nie zum Bestehen vor Gott dient, aber auch auf keinen Fall dem Evangelium zuwider daran hindern darf, dazu braucht es den heiligen Geist." Ebeling, "Das rechte Unterscheiden," 252–53. An alternative way of conceiving the Holy Spirit and its relation to the word has been advanced by Sylvia Hell. Rather than reducing a discussion of the Holy Spirit to the transition from law to gospel in the "invisible" heart of the believer, Hell locates the word in the church, the visible community of faith. With this starting point, she identifies the Spirit as the subject of the external word by which God reveals himself and by which God works. The Spirit makes present the soteriological event of the cross to the church through the *verbum externum*, the preached word and the sacraments, and, as the *verbum internum*, works the reception of faith that is identified with "sanctification." Rather than exclusively focusing on an identification between the word and the Second Person of the Trinity, Hell's contribution consists of showing the relation of the Spirit to the preached word. By considering the Spirit as the medium between God and humans that cannot be abstracted from the two *relata*, Hell's view is still conceived within the relational ontological framework that characterizes studies of Luther's sermons. Sylvia Hell, *Die Dialektik des Wortes bei Martin Luther*, 144–55.

not speculation.[47] The distinction Luther draws in *The Bondage of the Will* (1525) is interpreted by shrinking the sermon's content to the narrative of Christ and by avoiding any speculation on soteriological claims made with respect to the inner-Trinitarian nature.

The content and movement in Luther's sermons on the Trinity open up a perspective to viewing the Triune essence in a way that challenges the adequacy of a relational ontology to conceive the sermon. If the content of the preached God is the incarnate Christ, as Luther claims by citing Colossians 2:3 in *The Bondage of the Will*,[48] then the proclamation of the gospel demands to be considered in light of the Trinitarian relation between the divine nature—that is, the treasure of wisdom and knowledge—and the incarnate Christ. A Trinitarian understanding of the divine majesty is obviated by the Christological center of the preached God, particularly to locate the *promissio* in the inner-Trinitarian essence as the origin of its power. In his homiletical practice, Luther does just that. He does not dismiss the divine majesty as the subject matter of speculation, but preaches in detail on the revelation and the knowledge of the inner-Trinitarian side of God.[49] His hearers are invited to look into the realm of the eternal, where the "abyss"

---

47. An opinion in Luther scholarship identifies any form of speculation with philosophy and dismisses it as "dangerous." "Wie es um Gott an sich bestellt ist, die spekulative Frage der Philosophen wird von Luther ausdrücklich als abwegig und gefährlich abgewiesen." Thimme, "Martin Luther als Prediger," 28. In "The Hidden God," I will show that only a certain kind of speculation by a particular audience is guilty of "wrong speculation." Inner-Trinitarian "right speculation" is considered not only to be theologically legitimate, but is also a necessary part of what must be known for salvation.

48. The Colossians passage is cited in both the sermon on Rom 11:33–36 and in "De servo arbitrio." "Inspice Christum, quid loquatur et faciat, et tum habes eum, in quo omnes thesauri." WA 45:96.15–16. "Occupet vero sese cum Deo incarnato seu (ut Paulus loquitur) cum Ihesu crucifixo, in quo sunt omnes thesauri sapientiae et scientiae, sed absconditi; per hunc enim abunde habet, quid scire et non scire debeat." WA 18:689.22–25.

49. When Luther discusses his understanding of the Trinity, he is not simply rejecting any speculation on the divine Majesty, as this quote from "De servo arbitrio" might suggest. "Relinquendus est igitur Deus in maiestate et natura sua, sic enim nihil nos cum illo habemus agere, nec sic voluit a nobis agi cum eo." Ibid., 685.14–15. The difficulty emerges with Luther's terminological inconsistency. The term, "divine Majesty," can stand for either the hidden God or the revealed God and is not to be exclusively identified with the God that is not preached. In a Table Talk, Luther reflects on the fear he experiences while preaching on the divine Majesty. "Ich hab mich nie entsatzt, das ich nicht wol predigen kan, aber daruon hab ich mich oft entsetzt vnd geforcht, das ich vor Gottes angesicht also hab vnd soll mussen reden von der grossen majestet vnd von dem gottlichen wesen. Drumb seit nur starckh vnd bettet!" WATr 2:144.17–20 (no. 1590, May 20 to 27, 1532).

of the divine essence is one and the same as the three persons.[50] Luther's sermons reflect a conviction that the Trinitarian doctrine is to be understood and preached, not only adored in silence.

The sermons that Luther preached on the Trinity during his lifetime challenge the narrowed existential conclusions drawn by the word-event approach. A preliminary survey of Luther's sermons shows that he regarded the doctrinal subject matter to be of importance in the pulpit. Luther preached regularly on the theme of the Trinity, from an early sermon on the birth of Christ that has emerged as the focus of recent Finnish research on Luther's Trinitarian understanding,[51] to one of his last sermons in which he relates the mystery of the Trinity to baptism, to the blood of Jesus Christ, and to the bread and wine.[52] Most of Luther's sermons explicitly devoted to the Trinity are concentrated on two feast days of the church year. On the feast of Epiphany, Luther preached on the revelation of the Father, Son, and Spirit at the baptism of Jesus in Matthew 3:13-17.[53] The same text

50. Similar to the term "divine Majesty," the term "Abgrund" can refer to both the revealed and the hidden God. When discussing the Trinity, Cruciger's text emphasizes the groundlessness of the divine essence with the phrase, "tieffen abgrund" (WA 21:516.1). Rörer's transcription of Luther's sermon speaks of the "gru(e)ndlichen wesen[s]" (WA 45:89.26), as well as of God "in seim gottlichen, abgrundlichen wesen" (Ibid., 90.1-2). At this juncture, Cruciger's version reads, "unergru(e)ndlichen wesen" (WA 21:509.5). In his explanation to the Creed in the Large Catechism, Luther writes of the deepest "Abgrund" of the divine essence that is revealed. "Sihe, da hastu das gantze Go(e)ttliche wesen, willen und werck mit gantz kurtzen und doch reichen worten auffs allerfeineste abgemalet. ... Denn da hat er selbs offenbaret und auffgethan den tieffsten abgrund seines veterlichen hertzens und eitel unaussprechlicher liebe yn allen dreyen artickeln." WA 30,1:191.28-29, 34-35. When discussing the fall of Satan in the sermon on Rom 11:33-36, Luther can refer to the "Abgrund" of the divine essence into which Satan falls. "Sicut Satan suam sapientiam, quid deus sit, ideo in abgrund." WA 45:96.9-10.

51. WA 1:20.1-29.31 (Sermo Lutheri In Natali Christi, Dec. 25, 1514). See: Tuomo Mannermaa, "Grundlagenforschung der Theologie Martin Luthers und die Ökumene," 26-29; Idem, "Hat Luther eine trinitarische Ontologie?," 43-60.

52. WA 51:129.11-17 (Sermon on the Second Sunday after Epiphany, Jan. 17, 1546). Luther died in Eisleben on Feb. 18, 1546.

53. According to the lectionary, the gospel lesson for Epiphany is Matthew 2:1-12 and the epistle, Isaiah 60:1-6 (WADB 7:537). Luther explains his preference for substituting the story of the three kings at Epiphany with the baptism of Jesus. "Istud festum mecht wol heissen 'ein feiertag unsers herrn tauff', plus quam quod gentes ex Arabia venerunt adoraturi puerum, ... Si non hies 'der iij konig tag', vellemus vocare 'des Christi tauffe tag', ut ostertag. Sed schadet deinem glauben nicht, quod dicitur '3 regum dies'." WA 49:202.6-7, 10-12 (Epiphany, 1541). In a Trinity Sunday sermon, Luther mentions that the Matthew 3:13-17 text prescribed for Trinity Sunday is more appropriate than the prescribed John 3:1-15 gospel lesson. See: WA 46:433.8-11 (1538). Other Epiphany sermons preached on the Matt 3 text are: WA 20:217.1-232.12 (1526); WA 27:13.1-16.38 (1528); WA 47:640.6-646.10 (1539); WA 49:201.1-205.26 (1541); WA 51:107.1-117.42 (1546); WA 52:98.8-104.11 (Hauspostille, 1544); WA 49:308.1-317.30 (First Sunday after Epiphany,

that had provided Augustine with the occasion for speaking on both the inner-Trinitarian side of God and the divine outer-Trinitarian work of baptism was considered by Luther to be one of the most wonderful revelations of the three persons in Scripture.[54] The gospel pericope for Trinity Sunday was the story of Nicodemus and Christ in John 3:1–15, a text Luther once questioned as to its relation to the article of the Trinity.[55] In spite of his early puzzlement, Luther often linked the passage to a discussion of the Trinity.[56] He eventually concluded that the Trinity was the subject matter of the entire chapter of John 3 that showed, "in the most beautiful and friendly way," the way in which the three persons of the Trinity work to make "us poor humans" righteous.[57] Luther preached frequently on the Trinity, sometimes in contexts other than the feasts of Epiphany and Trinity and sometimes on texts other than the prescribed lessons for these feasts: in the three famous Torgau sermons on the second article of the Creed,[58] in Christmas sermons,[59] in a Trinity Sunday sermon based

---

Jan. 13, 1544); on the baptism of Jesus in Mark 1:4–11: WA 49:675.1–681.22 (Sermon on the First Sunday after Epiphany, Jan. 11, 1545).

54. "[D]as gros wunderwerck, ... Das mag ein Offenbarung heissen." Ibid., 308, 5. 8–9; Augustine, *Sermon* LII [PL 38:354–64].

55. "Non video, cur hoc Euangelium hodie legerint de S. Trinitate, cum nihil." WA 36:184.15–16 (Trinity Sunday, May 26, 1532). Luther's puzzlement reflects the historical introduction of John 3:1–15 as the gospel lesson for the Sunday after Pentecost into the seventh-century lectionary, seven centuries before the institution of Trinity Sunday. Gerhard Kunze, "Die gottesdienstliche Zeit," 525.

56. The following sermons on John 3:1–15 were preached on Trinity Sunday: WA 15:567.1–570.36 (May 22, 1524); WA 17,1:278.1–284.13 (June 11, 1525); WA 20:413.1–432.39 (May 27, 1526); WA 27:186.30–194.13 (June 7, 1528, morning); WA 27:194.14–195.38 (June 7, 1528, afternoon); WA 29:384.25–387.38 (May 23, 1529, morning); WA 36:184.15–187.16 (May 26, 1532); WA 37:87.10–88.34 (June 8, 1533); WA 37:414.11–419.14 (May 31, 1534); WA 41:608.21–612.40 (June 11, 1536); WA 45:446.16–447.29 (Conciunculae quaedam D. Mart. Lutheri amico cuidam praescriptae, 1537); WA 52:335.6–345.27 (Hauspostille, 1544); WA 52:345.28–356.33 (Hauspostille, 1544).

57. Ibid., 346.17 (Hauspostille, 1544). "Es scheinet aber, man habe es darumb eben auff diß Fest von der heyligen Dryfaltigkeyt gelegt, das so sein und eygentlich die unterschid der personen ist angezeigt in dem ho(e)chsten und gro(e)sten werck, das Gott mit uns armen menschen handlet, das er uns gerecht und selig machet." Ibid., 345.31–35. Referring to John 3:16, Luther speaks of the Father's love for creation, of the Father's sending of his Son, and of the Holy Spirit who, through the waters of baptism, inflames the heart to have faith. Ibid., 345.35–346.6.

58. WA 37:35.25–72.12 (April 16 and 17 (?), 1533).

59. WA 46:531.1–537.23 (First Sunday after Christmas, Dec. 29, 1538, on John 1:1–3, including Ps 2:7 and Titus 3:5); WA 47:634.1–640.5 (Sermon on the Day before Epiphany, Jan. 5, 1539 on John 1:3–16).

on a Pentecost text,[60] and most notably, in sermons handling an arrangement of biblical texts.[61] Many sermons shape the subject matter towards the outer-Trinitarian works, particularly the sermons on the catechism[62] and on baptism.[63] One pattern characterizing Luther's Trinitarian sermons thematizes an outer-Trinitarian work as the occasion for discussing the Trinity. A second pattern begins with the Trinitarian article that is subsequently described in terms of either the inner-Trinitarian relations of origin or as their outer-Trinitarian manifestations. It is this latter pattern that the sermon on Romans 11:33–36 reproduces. Luther draws his hearers deep into eternity and unfolds the Trinitarian nature of God as the sermon's doctrinal content. It remains to be shown how Luther regards the knowledge concerning the inner side of the Trinity.

KNOWLEDGE OF GOD IN LUTHER'S SERMONS ON THE TRINITY

The knowledge of God emerges as a central theme in Luther's preaching. For the sermon on Romans 11:33–36, as well as for others on the Trinity, the frequent appeal to doctrine is characteristic of a preaching style appropriated from the rhetorical tradition. Luther is committed to preaching on the revealed God because God desires to be known. Luther refers to two

---

60. WA 49:464.25–470.2 (Trinity Sunday, June 8, 1544, on Acts 2:17).

61. Ebeling claims that only a small portion of Luther's sermons are based on an *ad hoc* arrangements of texts. Ebeling, *Evangelische Evangelienauslegung*, 21. The *ad hoc* Trinitarian sermons are: WA 17,1:98.1–37 (Sermons on Matthew, March 15, 1525, with a section on Matt 28:19); WA 17,2:237.12–245.30 (Sermon on Palm Sunday, Fastenpostille, 1525, on Phil 2:5–12); WA 24:16.1–59.2 (Sermons on Gen 1, 1527); WA 34,1:498.14–504.33 (Trinity Sunday, June 4, 1531, including Deut 6:4, Rom 8:11, and Isa 42:8); WA 41:79 (Sermon on Ps 110, May 8, 1535); WA 41:270.1–279.38 (Trinity Sunday, afternoon, May 23, 1535, including Col 1:15, Acts 20:28, Matt 28:19, and John 14:9); WA 45:11.1–24.24 (Eine Hauspredigt von den Artikeln des Glaubens, in Schmalkalden gehalten, Feb. 11, 1537); WA 46:433.7–439.27 (Trinity Sunday, June 16, 1538, on texts including 2 Thess 2:4 and Rom 11:36); WA 47:779.24–784.34 (Trinity Sunday, June 1, 1539, on 1 Pet 4:9 and various texts); WA 49:761.13–780.13 (Trinity Sunday, May 31, 1545, on 1 Cor 15:54–56).

62. These sermons will be discussed in "Knowledge of God."

63. In 1528, Luther held a series of five sermons on baptism in which he also preached on the Trinity. All of the following sermons are found in WA 46. See WA 46:124.1–151.10 (Jan. 20); 151.11–155.39 (Jan. 27); 167.1–173.29 (Feb. 10); 174.1–178.30 (Feb. 17); 179.1–185.29 (Feb. 24); 194.14–201.23 (March 3). Other sermons preached on the theme of the Trinity and baptism are: WA 29:388.1–390.23 (Trinity Sunday, afternoon, May 23, 1529); WA 45:181.1–185.21 (Predigt am Gallustage in der Schloßkirche, Oct. 16, 1537, on Titus 3:5–8); WA 49:645.1–651.40 (Sunday after Christmas, Dec. 28, 1544, Titus 3:4–8).

sites of revelation: the outer Trinity, which is the special nuance in the catechetical sermons, and the naked God (*deus nudus*), the place at which the Christological heart is exposed in eternity.

The relation between the knowledge of God and faith in God forms the conceptual matrix in which Luther conceives his sermon on Romans 11:33–36. In a short *exordium* that is characteristic of his preaching style,[64] Luther announces the main concept of his sermon (*status*) to be the article of the Trinity.[65] Luther preaches "in order that this chief article of the Christian church might be known and remain by faith."[66] Luther immediately draws an intimate connection between faith and knowledge, which are the two ways by which the Trinitarian article is preserved in the church. Luther uses this coupling as a launching pad for the remainder of his sermon. He seeks to show how faith is tied to a growth in knowledge regarding a

---

64. Luther's sermons tend to begin with a short introduction, mentioning the feast day and the pericope on which the sermon is to be held. Luther's introductions differ from the extended *exordium* appearing in many late medieval sermons. In these latter sermons, the *exordium* includes the reading of the text in both Latin and German, the response of the congregation with a silent Ave Maria or Our Father, and a singing of the Antiphon, "Veni sancte spiritus." See: Weismann, "Der Predigtgottesdienst," 22. Althaus and Hirsch have contrasted Luther's apparent lack of an *exordium* with the *exordia* of medieval sermons. Althaus speaks of Luther's "Formlosigkeit" as a function of prophetic speech, and Hirsch writes on Luther's new development of a "schriftauslegende[n] Predigt" in which only a loose ordering between text elements is established at the expense of an introduction and a conclusion. This research must be revised in light of Luther's own commitment to preaching on one main theme in each sermon. In this chapter, I show that Luther's sermon is structured by a narrative of Trinitarian revelation that tightly weaves points of contrast into the main theme. See: Paul Althaus, "Luther auf der Kanzel," 17; Hirsch, "Luthers Predigtweise," 2.

65. The term *status* is defined by Melanchthon in his 1519 book on rhetoric. "Nulla pars artis magis necessaria est, quam praecepta de statibus, in quibus hoc primum ac praecipuum est, ut in omni negocio, seu controversia diligenter consideremus, quis sit status, hoc est, quae sit principalis quaestio, seu propositio, quae continet summam negocii, ad quam omnia argumenta referenda sunt, velut ad principalem conclusionem." MO 13:429 (*De Elementis Rhetorices*, Book 1). In a Table Talk, Luther describes his intention to preach on one "status" in every sermon. He admits, "Brevitatem et perspicuitatem khan ich nit also zwsamen bringen sicut Philippus et Amsdorffius. Ich vleisse mich in meinen predigen, das ich einen spruch für mich neme, vnd da bleib ich, vnd das ich den wol anzeige, das sie khunnen sagen: Das ist die predig gewesen, id est, in statu semper maneo." WATr 3:210.8–12 (no. 3173b, June 1532). Luther's conscious effort to expound one main concept does not result in what Johann Gerhard characterizes to be "heroic disorder." Cited in Althaus, "Luther auf der Kanzel," 17. In a Table Talk, Luther states that the sermon's concept is a gift of God; the preacher is God himself. "Conceptus praedicandi est Dei donum. Vnser Hergoth wil alein prediger sein. ... Es ist mir offt widerfaren, das mir mein bester concept zu ronnen ist. ... Martinus Lutherus dixit se saepius in somno vexatum esse, quasi praedicare debuisset et nullum habuisset conceptum." WATr 3:357.15–16, 17–18; 358.1–2 (no. 3494, Oct. 27 to Dec. 4, 1536).

66. WA 45:89.18–19.

subject matter found only in the church. When Luther, during the course of his sermon, interprets the right knowledge of the Triune God from the Trinitarian doxology in Romans 11:33–36, he will appeal again to this intimate link between faith and knowledge.

At the beginning of the sermon, the emphasis on the knowledge of God does not expose an uninvited lapse into doctrinal discourse. Luther's dogmatic privileging of the Trinitarian article dovetails with recent studies on Luther's sermons that show how the sermon is formed by two aspects of the rhetorical tradition, doctrine and exhortation.[67] In the early sixteenth century, the element of doctrine figured centrally in homiletical theory. Erasmus had recovered the ancient *genus deliberativum* for his understanding of the sermon, a *genus* that is associated with Quintilian's *contio*, meaning deliberative speech used in public addresses.[68] As O'Malley has studied, this genre was privileged over other forms in the middle of the sixteenth century.[69] At this time, Melanchthon was developing his own homiletical

---

67. Luther's words show his reception of the rhetorical and biblical traditions. "Dialectica docet, rhetorica movet. Illa ad intellectum pertinet, haec ad voluntatem. Quas utrasque Paulus complexus est Rom 12. [Rom 12:7–8], quando dixit: Qui docet in doctrina, qui exhortatur in exhortando. Et haec duo conficiunt modum praedicandi." WATr 2:359.18–21 (no. 2199a, Aug. 18 to Dec. 26, 1531). Luther speaks of the two liberal arts, dialectics and rhetoric, as integral aspects of preaching in Ibid., 2:368.23–28 (no. 2216, Aug. 18 to Dec. 26, 1531). A preacher must be trained in dialectics because, in Scripture, "[e]s ist gar viel mehr in doctrina quam exhortatione gelegen." WATr 4:307.29–30 (no. 4426, March 20, 1539). Luther outlines the different parts of dialectics that are used to describe the subject matter and shows that rhetoric "decorates" the description. Ibid., 647.6–649.6 (no. 5082b, June 11–19, 1540). In his monograph on Luther's sermons, Nembach argues that Luther understands the sermon to be shaped primarily by *doctrina* and *exhortatio*. Nembach relates Quintilian's genre of the "Volksberatungsrede" to the doctrinal and exhortational moods of Luther's sermons. Ulrich Nembach, *Predigt des Evangeliums*, 117. 139. Junghans has pointed out the one-sided tendency of Nembach's emphasis on Quintilian as Luther's only source in the rhetorical tradition. Junghans also suggests that Nembach's emphasis on the pedagogical dimension of the "verbum externum" tends to neglect essential aspects of the "verbum internum": for example, that the preached word is the word of mercy and forgiveness, enlivening the heart and turning sorrow into joy. Helmar Junghans, "Luther und die Welt der Reformation," 149–50.

68. Erasmus, O'Malley suggests, constructed five preaching *genera*, four of which can be reduced to the *genus deliberativum*. John W. O'Malley, "Content and Rhetorical Forms in Sixteenth-Century Treatises on Preaching," *Religious Culture in the Sixteenth Century*, 242–44. In an article on Luther's sermons, O'Malley refers to Birgit Stolt's study of Luther's "Predigt, dass man Kinder zur Schulen halten solle (1530)." In writing this sermon, which was not intended for the church chancel, Luther appropriated both the *genus deliberativum* and Quintilian's *contio*. O'Malley, "Luther the Preacher," *Religious Culture in the Sixteenth Century*, 10. Luther explicitly refers to the term "contio" in WATr 3:357.19 (no. 3494, Oct. 27 to Dec. 4, 1536).

69. O'Malley, "Content and Rhetorical Forms," 242–44.

theory, based on the *genus didascalium*.[70] This genre, which Melanchthon had transferred from dialectics to sacred rhetoric, had, as its function, to teach true doctrine in a propositional and argumentative manner. By borrowing from these genres that each shape doctrine in particular ways, Luther's sermons exude a doctrinal air. This dogmatic privileging would later lead scholars to observe the lack of a clear distinction between chancel and lectern.[71] If no perspicuous distinction in genre can be detected, it remains a curiosity as to why Luther's sermons are often investigated as existential discourses intended to awaken faith rather than as objects of doctrinal richness.

Luther's sermon does not solely proclaim a doctrine as the object of knowledge. Rather, the sermon's opening sentences penetrate deep into the mystery of God's own desire. Luther extends the initial connection between faith and knowledge into the divine will. He preaches "in order that this chief article of the Christian church might be known and remain by faith, that we might know God as he desires to be known."[72] The Trinitarian

---

70. O'Malley writes that Melanchthon rejected the classic *genus demonstrativum* for preaching, and developed a new, fourth genus, the *genus didascalium*. O'Malley, "Content and Rhetorical Forms," 242–44.

71. Ebeling writes, "[d]as Katheder wechselte Luther ständig mit der Kanzel." Ebeling, *Luther*, 48. See also: Lehmann, "Luther als Prediger," 11; Meuser, *Luther the Preacher*, 38–39; O'Malley, "Luther the Preacher," 8. The similarities between the two genres rest on the teaching component that determines the lecture and, to a large extent, the sermon, as well as on the line-by-line biblical exegesis structuring both lecture and sermon. O'Malley locates the exegetical structure of Luther's sermons in the trajectory of the patristic and monastic homilies that deviates from the thematic sermons of the medieval *artes*. O'Malley, "Luther the Preacher," 4. The genres of the lecture and the sermon can be distinguished in terms of the difference in audience, as Ebeling points out. Ebeling, *Luther*, 48. However, the addressees of both genres do tend to overlap, as Luther himself admits in a Table Talk. "Ich wil Doctorem Pommeranum, Jonam, Philippum in meyner predigt nicht wissen, den sie wissens vorhin baß den ich. Ich predige ihnen auch nicht, sondern meinem Henslein vnd Elslein; illos observo." WATr 3:310.9–12 (no. 3421, Tischreden aus verschiedenen Jahren). Luther's qualification of the sermon's audience to be children could suggest a rhetorical difference between the two genres. The picture-language, use of idioms and popular expressions, the dramatic staging of various characters on the homiletical stage, and a distinct dialogical style are rhetorical strategies deployed in Luther's preaching. The structural difference between the lecture and the sermon can be detected in Luther's use of the *contio*, or main concept, that shapes the line-by-line exegesis in the sermon. The main concept is stated in the sermon's *exordium* and remains the central focus of each wave of exegetical unfolding. More importantly, the difference could also be related to Luther's high estimation of the homiletical word as the communication of the divine word. Radically anti-Donatist in his view, Luther insists that the preached word requires no forgiveness. It is ordained by God as the way by which God is active in communicating the divine will to forgive. The power of the preached word is given a status that is not shared by its academic theological counterpart.

72. WA 45:89.18–19.

article is announced as the way God desires to be known.[73] Already in this programmatic sentence, Luther steers his sermon in view of the passage heading Paul's Letter to the Romans. Luther's sermon on Romans 11:33–36 introduces the Trinitarian subject matter in a way that is guided by the passage framing the entire book of Romans: Romans 1:18–20, the knowledge of God.[74] The knowledge of God, knowledge of both the Triune essence and of God's will, is the focus of the sermon's text, Romans 11:33–36. In light of the Trinitarian doxology, the theme of the knowledge of God in the created works (Rom 1:18–20) will gradually be read. Luther sets up the subsequent movement of the sermon by linking the Trinitarian revelation to the way of the divine desire. His sermon will follow a narrative of revelation that unfolds the Trinitarian essence by plotting, at different sites, the desire of each person to be with creation in a particular way.

As the subject matter of preaching, the Trinity is available in a particular location. Luther insists that the church is the location in which the knowledge of the Triune God is preserved.[75] The Trinity is the highest article of "our faith" and of the "holy, Christian church."[76] It is the subject matter of sermons preached for a feast day that was instituted at a relatively late date, in 1334, into the church calendar by Pope John XXII.[77]

---

73. In his sermon, Luther conflates the knowledge of God as Triune with the knowledge that God desires to be known in this way. This theological conflation avoids the error that Jüngel points out, of limiting the sermon to the *docere evangelium*. "Dennoch wäre es verfehlt, diese informierende und katechisierende Tendenz der evangelischen Anrede gegen deren befreiende Wirkung geltend zu machen, die als solche zur Feier der Gegenwart Gottes und der in ihr sich einstellenden unmittelbaren Gegenwart des ganzen ungeteilten Daseins drängt." Eberhard Jüngel, "Der evangelisch verstandene Gottesdienst," 298.

74. I am indebted to Brevard S. Childs's canonical-approach to biblical interpretation that has provided me with a canonical perspective in studying Luther's sermon. The theme of the knowledge of God in creation, a theme shaping the entire book of Romans, is woven into Luther's sermon on Rom 11:33–36.

75. "Ista Epistola ordinata in hunc diem, quod dicitur festum S. Trinitatis, ut iste articulus capitularis in Christiana Ecclesia." WA 45:89.17–18.

76. WA 41:270.10. Rörer's transcript speaks of "iste articulus capitularis in Christiana Ecclesia." WA 45:89.18. Cruciger's text refers to "der erste, hohe, unbegreiffliche Heuptartickel." WA 21:508.13. In another sermon, Luther calls the Trinitarian article "der hochste und erste artickel." WA 46:436.6 (Trinity Sunday, 1538). In yet another sermon, Luther preaches that one should know something about "den ho(e)chsten Artickel unsers glaubens." WA 52:335.10–11 (Trinity Sunday, Hauspostille, 1544).

77. In 1334, Pope John XXII instituted the Feast of Holy Trinity into the church calendar on the Sunday after Pentecost. The relatively late institution of Trinity Sunday into the church year is preceded by an early *missa de trinitate* for which no particular day was specified. In the

Although few Christians have any degree of sophisticated knowledge about the Trinity,[78] and not even Augustine who named it the highest article[79] understood it,[80] the Triune essence, the "divine Majesty" itself, is the focus of some of Luther's sermons.[81] The precise content is propositional, as Luther states at the beginning of the Romans 11 sermon. "Today we must preach and reflect on this article: that the true God is three persons in one divine essence."[82] The article remains in the church in its propositional form, the indisputable truth of which is acknowledged in the genre of the confession of faith.[83] Luther refers to the content of the article as the naked God (*deus nudus*), revealed to be naked in its eternal nature.[84] Not to be confused with the naked God (*deus nudus*) apart from the word,[85] the naked God (*deus nudus*) is identified with the divine nature that is revealed in the preached word without the clothing of works by which God

ninth-century sacramentary of Senlis, the mass was designated between Pentecost and the Sunday after Pentecost and, in the eleventh century, the octave of Pentecost was celebrated at Cluny to commemorate the Holy Trinity. At the Third Lateran Council (1179), Pope Alexander III declared that no particular Feast Day dedicated to the Trinity was necessary, since every mass included the "Gloria patri." Trinity Sunday was celebrated throughout the late medieval period. See: Beckmann, "Trinitatisfest," 1041. Kunze suggests that the demand for a feast dedicated to the Trinity is coupled with the introduction of the credo into the liturgy in 1014. See: Kunze, "Die gottesdienstliche Zeit," 525. The Protestant church appropriated the feast day and named the following Sundays, the Sundays after Trinity. The Roman Catholic Church named them the Sundays after Pentecost. See: Beckmann, "Trinitatisfest," 1041.

78. WA 27:187.10-11 (Trinity Sunday, 1528).

79. Ibid., 187.14-15.

80. Ibid., 186.31.

81. WA 45:181.8 (Predigt am Gallustage in der Schloßkirche, 1537). Luther identifies "wesen" with "maiestet" in the Torgau sermon: WA 37:38.11 (1533).

82. WA 45:89.22-23.

83. Luther speaks of the "nude words" of the simple confession that refer to the naked God. "Die weyßheyt gotis hat yr geselschafft myt den eynfeltigen qui verbo nudo adherent, Nicht myt den narren vor der welt, sed cum simplicibus fidei. ... Bleybet bey dem simbolo et simplicissime interroganti responde Unum deum, tres personas." WA 29:385.12-14, 25-27 (Trinity Sunday, 1529).

84. "Aber diss fest heut ist, wer Er an jm selbs sey ausser allen kleidern oder wercken, blos an seinem Go(e)ttlichen wesen." WA 41:270.18-20 (Trinity Sunday, 1535).

85. One aspect of the *deus nudus* is the extreme hiddenness apart from the word. "Relinquendus est igitur Deus in maiestate et natura sua, sic enim nihil nos cum illo habemus agere, nec sic voluit a nobis agi cum eo. Sed quatenus indutus et proditus est verbo suo, quo nobis sese obtulit, cum eo agimus, quod est decor et gloria eius, quo Psalmista eum celebrat indutum [Ps 21:6]." WA 18:685.14-17. Cf. 221n49.

encounters creation.[86] This is the God who precedes creation, the Triune essence in eternity.

After transporting his hearers to view the naked God (*deus nudus*), Luther sets up a crucial distinction that will play out during the remainder of the sermon. Luther distinguishes between the knowledge of the inner side of God and the knowledge of God from the divine works in creation. This serves to privilege one side of God as the subject matter of Trinitarian revelation and to demonstrate that another side, the outer side, encounters creation as a unity. It is the one God, Luther preaches by alluding to Isaiah 45:5, who works what is found on the outer side: "Christians know and God reveals that God is one, a single divine essence, and that beside and outside of God there is no God, not even the devil cannot be more than one."[87] The divine essence encounters what exists on the outside in the unity of the work.[88] Only on the inner side can the distinctions between the three persons be detected: "On the inside they are distinguished."[89] Only when the inner Trinity is revealed is the subject matter available concerning that "where no creature exists or can exist."[90] By thematizing the naked God (*deus nudus*) in his sermons on the Trinity, Luther makes a crucial theological claim that privileges the inner-Trinitarian revelation as the sole way by which the Trinity can be known in creation that it encounters as a unity.

There are other sermons on the Trinity that, on the surface, appear to marginalize the dogmatic priority Luther assigns to the inner Trinity, particularly those delivered between 1524 and 1535. These sermons are oriented to the divine economy in three works that are appropriated respectively to

---

86.   In the following two sermons, Luther speaks of the works in which God is clothed. "Und so fort an, das alle andere fest von unserem Herrn Gott so predigen, wie er gekleidet ist etwan mit einem werck." WA 41:270.17–18 (Trinity Sunday, 1535); "Darumb gleich wie die andern Fest im Jar unsern Herrn Gott kleyden und einwickeln in seine werck, die er thun hat, das man dabey sein hertz und willen gegen uns erkennen soll." WA 52:335.15–17 (Trinity Sunday, Hauspostille, 1544).

87.   WA 45:89.23–25.

88.   "... quae alle drey 1 werck an uns thun." WA 45:181.25–26 (Gallustag, 1537).

89.   Ibid., 181, 26. The distinction between "intus" and "outside" parallels a distinction Luther draws in 1525 between God "qui pro se dominus est" and God "qui pro te datus." WA 16:309.4 (Trinity Sunday, 1525, text on Exod 16:15–16).

90.   "... da gar keine Creatur nicht ist noch sein kan." WA 46:59.37–38 (Commentary on John 16, 1536, to John 16:13).

the Trinitarian person effecting the work. Catechetical in their emphasis, these sermons explicate the outer-Trinitarian relation of God to creation as it is determined by the Creed. The catechetical focus of these sermons seems to promote a view that the Trinitarian differentiation is situated at the outer side, the side encountering creation. It remains to be clarified as to how the Trinitarian understanding of the catechetical sermons coheres with what I have represented as Luther's view regarding both the inner side as the site at which the Trinity is distinguished into three persons and the outer-Trinitarian encounter with creation in the unity of the one, divine nature.

Luther's earlier Trinitarian sermons are catechetical in their focus. In them, Luther preached on the confession of faith as the textual source for articulating his understanding of the Trinity, especially in the phase leading up to the writing of the Large and Small Catechisms in 1529.[91] The practice of preaching on the Creed was not novel to the sixteenth century. The Creed was an element of the medieval sermon liturgy, and Luther followed medieval precedent by preaching on the catechism during distinct times of the church year.[92] In these sermons, Luther's Trinitarian understanding is, on the whole, consistent with the material insights and tripartite structure that are represented in the explanation to the Creed in the Large Catechism.[93] Each article of the Creed is explained as the appropriation of

---

91. Luther preached an early series of sermons on the catechism in 1523 and, in 1528, he prepared for the writing of his Large and Small Catechisms by preaching three individual series on the catechism. The early sermons on the three articles of the Creed are found in WA 11:48.16–54.36 (March 4, 5, 6, 1523). Three sermons, each on all three articles of the Apostles' Creed, are in WA 30,1:9.14–11.7 (May 23, 1528); 43:27–46.6 (Sept. 21, 1528); 86.1–94.29 (Dec. 10, 1528). The genre of the catechism, as Strauss writes, plays a crucial role in the pedagogical aim of the Reformation. Gerald Strauss, *Luther's House of Learning*, 156. In his book, Strauss aims to show the pedagogical contribution of the Reformation, the sources of pedagogical reform in the sixteenth century, as well as the reception of these reforms in the period following the Reformation.

92. Weismann, "Der Predigtgottesdienst," 21. Sermons on the catechism were preached four times a year, for two weeks at a stretch, with four sermons per week. The total number of sermons preached each year on the catechism would be thirty-two sermons. Other sermons prescribed throughout the week would be: three sermons on Sunday (5am on the epistle; 10am on the gospel, and evening sermons on either the gospel or an Old Testament lesson or the catechism); Monday and Tuesday on the catechism; Wednesday on Matthew; Thursday and Friday on the Apostolic Letters; and Saturday evening on John. See: Meuser, *Luther the Preacher*, 37–38.

93. The only significant difference between the early sermons and the Large Catechism is detected in Luther's understanding of the third article of the Creed. In the early sermons,

a work to a Trinitarian person.[94] The works of creation, redemption, and sanctification are appropriated respectively to the persons of Father, Son, and Spirit.

The catechetical sermons have left Luther scholars with the conceptual problem of interpreting the relation between the effects of the divine economy and the Trinitarian persons as causes of these effects. A metaphysics of effects has emerged as the common framework in which the economy of works is privileged as the order of knowing (*ordo cognoscendi*), which is then related back to the immanent Trinitarian essence.[95] Haunting this way of interpreting the divine economy as a narrative plotting of works is the suspicion of modalism.[96] The charge of the modalist heresy, however, reflects more the difficulty with the economy of works as a distinctly modern theological starting point than a negative judgment on Luther's Trinitarian understanding. If the sermons on the outer Trinity can be viewed according to the speculative theological starting point with which Luther himself begins, then another model for conceiving the relation between the Trinitarian persons and their respective works can be

Luther explains the Holy Spirit under the rubric of *vivificans*, whereas the explanation to the Creed in the Large Catechism (1529) marks the third article decisively under the rubric of *sanctificans*. For a discussion of this development, see: Peters, *Kommentar zu Luthers Katechismen*, vol. 2, 176–81.

94. The three appropriations of creation, redemption, and sanctification are used to orient the focus of each article. "Also das der erste artikel von Gott dem vater verklere die Schepffung, der ander von den Son die erlo(e)sung, Der dritte von dem Heiligen Geist die heiligung." WA 30,1:183.5-7. One Trinity Sunday sermon thematizes the confession of faith. "Tu autem cum dicis: Credo in deum, in filium, in spiritum sanctum, hic in unum deum credis, quamvis tres personae diversis operibus proponentur et profiteantur." WA 29:385.19-21, (Trinity Sunday, 1529).

95. Jansen interprets Luther's doctrine of the Trinity according to the contemporary systematic theological move of an "Analogieschluß" from the economic to the immanent Trinity. His conclusion is distinctly modern in its perspective privileging the revelation of the Trinity in the history of salvation. "Dieser Abschnitt zeigt deutlich, woher die Aussagen über die immanente Trinitat stammen: aus einem Analogieschluß von der Offenbarung Gottes auf sein Wesen. Von der biblisch bezeugten Heilsgeschichte in der Welt, wird zurückgeschlossen auf Gottes ewiges Wesen." Jansen, *Studien zu Luthers Trinitätslehre*, 203.

96. "In einem anderen Kontext würde ich die offensichtlich modalistische Form, die Luther für diese Anordnung gibt, beklagen. 'Schöpfer, Versöhner und Heiligmacher' ist natürlich kein Äquivalent für 'Vater, Sohn und Geist', wie Lutheraner weithin denken, es aus Luthers Katechismen gelernt zu haben." Jenson, "Die trinitarishce Grundlegung," 15n12. Asendorf mistranslates the English term, "Redeemer" with the German, "Versöhner." According to Luther's Large Catechism, the Second Person of the Trinity is named, "Herr" and "Erlöser." "Das sey nu die Summa dieses Artickels, das das wortlin HERRE auffs einfeltigste soviel heisse als ein Erloser." WA 30,1:186.29-30.

proposed. The question arising from the consideration of Luther's catechetical sermons concerns the conceptual framework in which Luther understands the Trinity. Which side of the Trinity does Luther privilege as the starting point for reading the revelation of the triune essence in the works?

According to a metaphysics of effects, the conceptual starting point is the effect that is subsequently appropriated to one of the three persons. Although this method privileges the economy as its point of departure, Luther insists that the knowledge of the Trinitarian essence of God is not available as an inference from the outer-Trinitarian works to the inner-Trinitarian persons but must be the content of revelation. In the sermon on Romans 11:33–36, Luther stresses this point with unambiguous clarity. "But according to revelation, this one divinity is three; there are three persons inside the essence."[97] On their outer side, the three persons work in consort, as Luther claims by appealing to the rule attributed to Augustine: the external works of the Trinity are indivisible (*opera trinitatis ad extra sunt indivisa*).[98] When God encounters creation, the divine essence is clothed with the works that reveal the unity of the nature.[99] The inference from effect to cause is only valid under the qualification of a prior revelation. Even the key passage in the Large Catechism that can be conceptually skewed towards a metaphysics of effects can be seen, upon closer look, to privilege the revelation of the inner Trinity as the source of the knowledge of God. In the explanation to the Creed, Luther uses the term "transfigure" (*verkleren*) to suggest that the revelation of the person sheds light on the work that is subsequently appropriated to that person.[100]

---

97. WA 45:90.28–29. Luther continues to emphasize the distinction between the inner and the outer Trinity. "Deus non solum sein euserlich regiment, sed sein innerlich, Gottlich wesen." Ibid., 90.30.

98. The rule is explicitly stated in the treatise, *Von den letzten Worten Davids.* "Hie her geho(e)rt die Regel S. Augustini: Opera Trinitatis ad Extra sunt indivisa. Die Werck, so von Gott auswendig der Gottheit gemacht, sind nicht zeteilen, Das ist, man sol die Personen nicht teilen in die Werck einer jglicher von aussen jr unterschiedlich Werck zu eigen, Sondern die Person sol man inwendig der Gottheit unterscheiden, und doch allen dreyen auswendig ein jglich Werck on unterscheid zu eigen." WA 54:57.35–58.3 (1543).

99. Luther identifies the clothes with the divine works in WA 41:270.18 (Trinity Sunday, 1535).

100. In Luther's explanation to the Creed, the revelation of the three persons serves as the starting point for reflecting on the three appropriations. "Aber das mans auffs leichteste und einfeltigste fassen ku(e)nde, wie es fur die kinder zu leren ist, wo(e)llen wir den gantzen Glauben ku(e)rtzlich fassen ynn drey heuptartikel nach den dreyen personen der Gottheit,

In another sermon on Titus 3:5-6, which treats baptism together with the Trinity, Luther appropriates three works to the three persons on the basis of Romans 11:36.[101] The direction of interpretation begins with the revelation of the three persons and then proceeds to appropriate the works in ways denoted by the prepositions in the biblical text.

The dogmatic privileging of the inner-Trinitarian revelation is not divorced from a soteriological claim. "If this distinction did not exist," Luther preaches in a sermon, then "it could not be said that salvation is by the Father, through the Son, and in the Holy Spirit."[102] In this citation, Luther exposes his understanding concerning the divine work in creation, specifically in baptism, in terms of its soteriological efficacy. By associating the knowledge of the inner Trinity with a soteriological claim, Luther reveals an insight that emerges at the center of his sermon on Romans 11:33-36. The soteriological dimension to the knowledge of God is not reductionistically tied to an outer-Trinitarian dispensation. It arises in Luther's sermon as constitutive of the inner-Trinitarian revelation itself. It is this soteriological center that accompanies the movement in Luther's sermon. The whole sermon proceeds along the way of revealing the inner Trinity, and at each site, it unfolds yet another dimension to the divine desire to be known as the Triune God in eternity: as the inner Trinity, who desires the life of the world.

KNOWLEDGE OF THE TRIUNE GOD: CONCLUSION

The theme of the knowledge of God has been shown in this section to figure significantly in many sermons Luther preached. Luther's sermon on Romans 11:33-36 represents his conviction that doctrine is a central

---

dahin alles was wir gleuben gerichtet ist, Also das der erste artikel von Gott dem vater verklere die Schepffung, der ander von dem Son die erlo(e)sung, Der dritte von dem Heiligen Geist die heiligung." WA 30,1:183.1-7 (Large Catechism, 1529). According to medieval logic, only a *suppositum* is capable of acting. The relation between this medieval logical claim and the three works that Luther appropriates to the three persons of the Trinity in his explanation to the Creed in the Large Catechism is a possible topic for further study.

101.   In the Gallus Day sermon, Luther appropriates three segments of one work to the three persons of the Trinity. Regeneration is appropriated to the Spirit, the effects of baptism to the Son, and the Father is the source of the entire action. WA 45:181.18-19 (1537). The rule for this type of appropriation is based on Romans 11:36. "Von, durch, in im ist alles. ... Ibi pater, von dem alle, filius, per quem, spiritus sanctus, in quo omnia creata et tamen creatio unum opus. Sic redemptio, nisi quod 3 person da sein." Ibid., 181.20-21, 22-24.

102.   Ibid., 181.28-30.

component of the sermon's content. By pointing out a dogmatic emphasis in Luther's preaching activity, the blind spot of the word-event approach to Luther's sermons has also been located. According to this approach, the preached word is understood to constitute a relation justifying the sinner, and its content is determined less by doctrine, more by a kerygmatic moment that must be rehearsed continuously. When preaching on Romans 11:33–36, Luther is not satisfied to thin the Trinity to a Christological narrative but unapologetically announces the status of the Trinity Sunday sermon to be the knowledge of the Triune God, known by faith and preserved in the church. It is the knowledge of God without the clothes of the divine works, the inner Trinity existing "outside" of the creature. In the compact *exordium*, Luther gestures to the subsequent exegetical direction of his sermon. He will use the epistle lesson, Romans 11:33–36, to interpret Romans 1:18–20 as the knowledge of the Trinity in the created works. In order to arrive at this goal, Luther must unfold a narrative that gradually moves from the inner Trinity to the outer Trinity and then to the Trinitarian essence in creation. To the first site in this narrative we will now turn.

THE HOLY SPIRIT

Luther begins to unfold the sermon's Trinitarian theme by plotting the first site in the narrative. At this site, the Holy Spirit comes "from heaven" to reveal the inner side of God. The Spirit, as will be discussed in this section, is the Trinitarian person whom Luther identifies as the agent of revelation. Particularly in the church's ongoing preaching, the Spirit reveals God's inner side to Christians on God's outer side. The relation between the preached word and the divine word is conceived in the framework of a narrative of revelation that I propose as an alternative to the word-event approach.

THE SPIRIT: GOD SPEAKS FROM GOD

The theme that Luther unfolds early in his sermon concerns both the knowledge of God and the source of its revelation. An initial gaze serves to orient the hearers to "heaven," from which the divine wisdom is revealed.[103]

---

103. "Hoc Christianis revelatum e celo." Ibid., 89.26–27.

A further New Testament passage adds the precise determination of the revelation's source. Alluding to 1 Corinthians 2:9–11, Luther presents the first site in his sermon. "God reveals" the divine wisdom "to us" through the Holy Spirit.[104] Initially captured by an assertion, the subject of revelation is shown in light of a movement, illustrated by an analogy from 1 Corinthians 2:11. Luther demonstrates his characteristic freedom in citing Scripture by modifying the verse that Paul formulates in the third person to the first-person singular. "I see and touch you. And you see and touch me. But you do not know what I have in my mind unless I reveal it."[105] The Spirit reveals on the outside the inner thoughts of God not accessible by sight or touch.[106] On the outer side of God, the Holy Spirit reveals what is found on the inner side—that is, the divine wisdom. At this early stage in the sermon, Luther focuses on the Spirit in order to begin interpreting Romans 11:33, the divine wisdom in relation to the Trinity.

The sermon already offers an answer to the question in Romans 11:34. In his sermon, Luther cites the text: "Who has been his counselor?"[107] Paul's question, itself a citation from Isaiah 40:13–14, infuses this section of the sermon with its doxological tenor.[108] Doxology embraces the assertion answering the question. "We have [the Spirit], Paul says, and Paul asks who knows what is in God except the Spirit, who sees the inmost things of God, who has revealed God to us?"[109] Luther rehearses the doxological impulse of the text in a question that he answers by pointing to the Spirit. The answer to the question in Romans 11:34 is God the Spirit, who alone knows the divine wisdom and then reveals it. Posed as a question, the doxology

---

104. "Nobis per spiritum sanctum deus revelavit." Ibid., 90.8–9.

105. Ibid., 90.10–11.

106. Luther asserts that the knowledge of the depths of God is revealed by the Spirit. The Spirit, "qui greifft in die tieff dei," reveals the inner side of the Trinity to Christians. Ibid., 90.12.

107. Ibid., 91.23–24. The entire passage reads, "Non praedicamus rationem, sed sapientiam, quae non potest comprehendi, sed so tieff, ut dicat: 'Quis eius consiliarius?' [Rom 11:34] praedicamus sapientiam revelatam a Deo e celo, foris revelatur per verbum, intus revelat in corde." Ibid., 91.22–25.

108. Luther's 1528 translation of Isa 40:13–14 is: "Wer vnterricht den geist des HERRN, vnd welcher radgeber vnterweiset yhn? Wen fragt er vmb rad, der yhm verstand gebe vnd lere yhn den weg des rechts? vnd lere yhn die erkentnis, vnd vnterweise yhn den weg des verstandes?" WADB 11,1:120, 122.

109. WA 45:90.18–19.

intends to awaken initial wonder at the Spirit, who reveals what can only be disclosed by God. At the very onset, Luther gestures to what he will unfold in his sermon. The divine wisdom (Rom 11:33) is the point of convergence between the Spirit and the divine desire to be known as Triune.

Plotted by the Spirit is the divine desire to be known through a particular language. Conceived in the church, the Trinitarian article is described in the language of the church's dogmatic formulations.[110] Its formulations emerge from the church's struggle, in a situation of "great desperation," to define the Triune essence in the context of heresy.[111] Even the feast of Trinity Sunday was instituted by the church in order to uphold the Trinity as its principle article and to prevent the church from falling prey to heresy.[112] In his earlier catechetical Trinitarian sermons that concentrate on the divine economy, Luther tends to shy away from using classic Trinitarian language. However, other sermons throughout this early period are permeated with the language of the eternal distinctions, and, especially after 1535, they continue in their insistence upon using the terms "person" and "substance."[113] The inner-Trinitarian proposition Luther provides in the

---

110. "Pueri confitentes Symbolum etiam non intelligunt, sed tamen, ut Augustinus inquit, Gestantur in sinu matris Ecclesiae sanctae." WA 46:433.27-29 (Trinity Sunday, 1538).

111. "... auß grosser noth und ursach," WA 34,1:498.25 (Trinity Sunday, 1531); "Ursach haben darzu geben Arianer und Macedonianer," WA 27:187.4 (Trinity Sunday, 1528).

112. WA 29:384.30-31; 385.4-5 (Trinity Sunday, 1529); WA 34,1:498.24-25 (Trinity Sunday, 1531). In an interpretation of John 16:13, Luther exhorts his hearers to fight for the preservation of the articles of faith that confess Christ's victory over sin, death, devil, and hell. "... so lasst uns doch zuvor kempffen und erbeiten, bis wir diese no(e)tige stu(e)ck haben, Erhaltung der reinen Lere, des Glawbens und Siegs wider sund, tod, Teuffel und Helle." WA 46:56.34-36 (Commentary on John 16, 1538).

113. In various sermons, Luther uses technical Trinitarian language. He speaks of the eternal generation of the Son in WA 17,1:279.4-5 (Trinity Sunday, 1525); WA 37:41.16 (Torgau, 1533). In 1538, Luther defines the term "person" by using the legal analogy. "Person heisst ein gestalt, ut dicitur: Ein Jurist fu(e)ret ein person des verklagten, Das etwas sonderlichs und eigens ist. ... So hat man das wort auff die Gotheit gezogen, ut macht damit discrimen. Persona est pater, patris offitium, opus, eigenschafft, der da gebirt und zeuget, non zeuget. Filii eigenschafft, quod a patre nascitur. ... Person, wenn man ein ding sein eigens zuschreibet, quod alteri non competit. Da kan man kein gleichnis fu(e)ren." WA 46:536.15-17, 19-21, 22-23 (First Sunday after Christmas, Dec. 29, 1538). The terms, "wesen" and "substantia," are found in WA 37:38.9 (Torgau, 1533). Jansen notes a shift in the language Luther uses. According to Jansen, the sermons delivered in the 1520s are addressed to a congregation composed primarily of children and are characterized by an emphasis on the economic Trinity. During the controversy with the anti-Trinitarians in the 1530s, Luther's theological concern is to preach on the unity of God to an adult congregation. The language Luther uses is theologically oriented to the axiom *opera trinitatis ad extra sunt indivisa*. Jansen, *Studien zu Luthers Trinitätslehre*, 207-10. Jansen is correct in observing discursive nuancing to be a function of audience. However,

sermon on Romans 11:33-36 reflects a consistency in many other sermons to use the technical and propositional language of the church councils—as in, for example: "He has revealed and permits us to preach this article, that there are three persons in the deity."[114] Even the classic terminology of the relations of origin is unapologetically preached from the chancel.[115] Luther neither rejects thematizing the inner Trinity nor does he use a language for its articulation other than the technical language adopted by the church.

The words of the church's conciliar decisions, Luther never fails to emphasize in the homiletical genre, are not elegant German but a crass stammering in every language. The term "'Three-foldedness' [*Dreifaltigkeit*] is indeed not an accurate term."[116] It is "really bad German."[117] For the Latin *trinitas*, that Luther considers to be a "crass term,"[118] the alternative, "Call it a triad," is proposed.[119] Even the term "person," which Luther translates with either the Greek "hypostasis" or the German "Wesen oder Substanz" (essence or substance) is used only because the church fathers found no other word.[120] Luther's minimalist use of the early church's terms to artic-ulate the inner Trinity does not imply a rejection of scholastic Trinitarian

---

he fails to see that Luther's catechetical sermons are not only directed to children. These sermons are also shaped by the texts on which they are based. As sermons on the confession of faith, they tend towards explaining the outer-Trinitarian clothes in which God is dressed. The other sermons that are based on the relevant Trinitarian texts prescribed for either the feast of Epiphany or Trinity Sunday are consistent in at least mentioning, if not explaining in detail, the inner-Trinitarian terms denoting the distinction between the persons. These sermons are not limited to the theme of the natural unity.

114. WA 45:90.12-13.

115. For example: "Verus deus tantum unus, sed in ista vera deitate est persona, quae dicitur pater, a quo genitus filius et ex utroque processit spiritus sanctus." Ibid., 90.14-15; "Und dennoch der Son ein ander person sey jnn dem selbigen einigen wesen und maiestet, also das der Son sey vom Vater jnn ewigkeit geborn, nicht der Vater von dem Son." WA 37:38.10-12 (Torgau, 1533).

116. WA 41:270.6 (Trinity Sunday, 1535).

117. WA 46:436.7 (Trinity Sunday, 1538).

118. WA 27:187.3 (Trinity Sunday, 1528).

119. WA 46;436.12 (Trinity Sunday, 1538). "Gedritt" as a singular noun used in the six-teenth century means, "aus dreien bestehend," and was later shortened to "ein Dritte." Grimm, "Gedritt," *Deutsches Wörterbuch*, vol. 4/1, 2039-2040.

120. "Wir haben das wo(e)rtlin 'Person' mu(e)ssen gebrauchen, wie es denn die Veter auch gebraucht haben, denn wir haben kein anders, und heisset nichts anders denn ein Hypostasis, ein Wesen oder Substantz, das fur sich ist und das Gott ist." WA 46:550.16-19 (Commentary on John 1-2 in sermons from 1537 and 1538, to John 1:2). Luther is familiar with Augustine's confusion between *ousia* and *hypostasis*. See: ch. 2, "The Inner Trinity."

theology.[121] The Greek and Latin terms sufficiently denote what is defined by a distinction characteristic of the disputation's discourse: the distinction between the three *res* and the one *res*. By limiting his use of terms to a few Greek, Latin, and German words, Luther restricts his speculation on the Trinity to a view guided by the church's language.

The terminological minimum witnesses to a content that is ultimately ineffable. On the extreme side, Luther restricts the use of the analogy to illustrate the meaning of the technical terms. The depths of the divine majesty are referred to in terms that know of no analogy in creation.[122] Luther attributes the difficulty to the extension of terms referring to the three *res*, whose unity cannot be grasped in one word.[123] In his exegesis of Genesis 1, Luther states that the structure of language is incapable of grasping two things at once.[124] Luther emphasizes the ineffability of the inner Trinity because he intends the sermon to bring the hearers to believe the simple words of the confession of faith. The reason Luther gives for the prohibition of the analogy can be compared to a similar strategy deployed in the disputation.[125] On the other hand, Luther can also advocate the use of the analogy. For example, Luther illustrates how language can refer to a subject matter that is "above human language." An analogy is drawn between the way a father stammers with his son and the way God reveals the inner-Trinitarian essence. "Just as a father stammers and uses bad German with his son,

---

121. Ch. 2, "The Scotus-Ockham Trajectory" discusses Luther's reception of Ockham in a dispute with Scotus on the formal and real distinctions.

122. "Unum deum habemus, sed der in seiner natur so seltzam ist und wunderlich, ut non possit ausgesprochen. Non possum vobis dare similitudines, sed volo, ut credatis, ut verba sonant." WA 27:188.13–16 (Trinity Sunday, 1528).

123. "Germanicum verbum non est commodum, quia summa est simplicitas in divinitate." WA 46:436.28–29 (Trinity Sunday, 1538).

124. Luther attributes the three verbs in Gen 1:3, "create, speak, and see," to Father, Son, and Spirit. No one word can capture all three verbs. "Wie wol nu die drey zugleich gewesen sind, so must ers dennoch nacheinander schreiben, denn er kund es nicht zu gleich mit eim wort fassen." WA 24:31.24–26 (Über das 1. Buch Mose, Predigten, 1527).

125. One function of the disputation is to gain practice in the use of reason to draw the borders of the theological region. Through this procedure, the imposition of natural reason is blocked from the determination of the subject matter found exclusively in the theological region. At this juncture, the exclusion of the analogy is stressed. Once the borders of the theological region are sufficiently drawn, a more sympathetic evaluation of the analogy is permitted. See: ch. 2, "The Inner Trinity and the Analogy."

so too God stammers with us."[126] Luther also uses analogies to illustrate the eternal generation of the Son or to describe the term "person."[127] He permits the analogy on account of "our weakness" but limits its explanatory power by ceaselessly insisting that the subject matter can only be believed, not exhausted by the understanding.[128] Ultimately sight, not language, can grasp the three *res* in one moment. The eschatological impulse is implied by the Trinitarian article that, in creation, admits few analogies but that, in eternity, joins understanding to the sight of the three persons in the divine essence.[129] Trinitarian terms are necessary, and they must be understood in light of faith. One day, however, the divine light will shine so dramatically that all will see how three persons are one God.

In this life, the reliance on the church's formulation, although poor, of the inner-Trinitarian subject matter is not a contingent stipulation. For Luther, the reliance on the church's language is warranted by the revelation of the Holy Spirit, who alone comprehends the mystery of the divine

126. WA 45:89.21; "... ist zu hoch uber menschlich sprach." Ibid., 89.20. Cruciger's text differs from Rörer's on this point. Where Rörer appeals to an analogy to describe the stammering language God uses to speak with us, Cruciger writes about the stammering and "baby-talk" of those who speak when their faith is pure. "Aber weil mans nicht besser hat, mu(e)ssen wir reden, wie wir ko(e)nnen. Denn (wie ich gesagt habe) dieser Artickel ist so hoch uber menschlich verstand und Sprache, das Gott als ein Vater seinen Kindern mus zu gut halten, das wir stammeln und lallen, so gut wir ko(e)nnen, so nur der Glaube rein und recht ist." WA 21:508.28–32.

127. Luther uses the analogy of human birth to describe the Son's eternal generation. "Ich pflege ein grob, einfeltig Gleichnis zugeben zur anleitung diese geburt des Sons Gottes vom ewigen Vater etlicher massen zuverstehen, nemlich diese: wie ein Leiblicher Son fleisch und blut und sein wesen vom Vater hat, also hab auch der Son Gottes, vom Vater geborn, sein Go(e)ttlich wesen und natur vom Vater von ewigkeit." WA 46:541.21–25 (Commentary on John 1–2 in sermons from 1537 and 1538, to John 1:1–3).

128. "Und werden also fu(e)rgebildet durch gleichnis oder bilde der natu(e)rlichen ding, das wir sie nach unser schwacheit fassen und davon reden ko(e)nnen, Aber nicht ausforschen noch begreiffen, sondern allein mit dem glauben an diesen worten (wie wir ho(e)ren, das Christus selbs davon redet) halten und dabey bleiben sollen." Ibid., 60.19–23 (Commentary on John 16, 1538, to John 16:12).

129. The eschatological impulse sometimes arises when Luther reflects on the sight of the three persons. "Intus sunt unterschieden. Quomodo sind, non intelligo, sed debeo credere, usque dum videbo." WA 45:181.26–27 (Gallustag, 1537); "Wie aber solches zuge [how the Holy Spirit is given the divine nature from both the Father and Son], das kan ich dir nit sagen, es ist unbegreyfflich uber alle Engel und Creatur. Darumb kan man weyter und mer davon nicht gedencken noch haben, denn die schrifft uns vorsagt, Der selben wort mo(e)gen wir uns brauchen, Aber das wesen verstehen, geho(e)rt nit in das leben hie, sonder in das ewige leben." WA 52:342.31–35 (Trinity Sunday, Hauspostille, 1544).

majesty.[130] What is believed is what God speaks concerning the inner-Trinitarian essence.[131] It is God who speaks for God, an assertion from Hilary's *De Trinitate* that Luther often cites. "According to Hilary, who asks: who is better able to speak about God than God himself?"[132] Luther can claim that the Spirit speaks "from God" by appealing to the Pentecost story. At Pentecost, the Father pours out the Spirit, who then reproduces at the outer Trinity the Father's nature to speak.[133] In another sermon, Luther couples the outpouring of the Spirit with a reverse movement. The Spirit, poured out in the church, invites Christians to "leave behind the creature, to fly to heaven and hear what God himself speaks concerning his essence."[134] For Luther, any speech in the church concerning the inner-Trinitarian essence is to be attributed to the Holy Spirit. Whether the speech be the technical stammering of the conciliar decisions or the ongoing preaching in the church, it is the way by which the Spirit continues to reveal the inner Trinity "to us."[135] By attributing the church's language to the Spirit, Luther posits the church in a relation of confession. The church confesses that the Spirit, who alone knows the depths of the incomprehensible essence, is the source of revelatory discourse.

---

130. The Spirit who reveals the inner-Trinitarian essence is no insignificant, human spirit, but the Spirit of God. "Das es nicht menschlich noch eines geringen Geists ist, solch hohe, unbegriffliche und unausgru(e)ndliche geheimnis der Go(e)ttlichen Maiestet, so im Euangelio solt offenbaret werden." WA 41:80.32, 81.10-11 (Sermon on Psalm 110, May 8, 1535).

131. What God speaks concerning the divine nature must be believed. "Ideo ei credendum, cum de se loquatur." WA 45:182.10 (Gallustag, 1537).

132. WA 34,1:500.9-10 (Trinity Sunday, 1531). Luther often alludes to this sentence from Hilary's *De Trinitate*: "A Deo discendum est, quid de Deo intelligendum sit." Hilary of Poitiers, *De Trinitate*, 5 (21) [PL 10:143 = NPNF, vol. 9, 91].

133. The term Luther prefers to use when describing the sending of the Spirit is found in Acts 2:17: "to pour out." In a Trinity Sunday sermon, Luther preaches on the Father's pouring out of the Spirit. "1. sic dicit Ioel [Joel 3:1], quem inducit Petrus: 'Ego effundam'. Ibi inducit personam, quae vult effundere Spiritum sanctum." WA 49:465.3-4 (1544). Luther then connects the Father's speech with the property of the divine nature to speak from itself. "Deus de se ita loquitur, de me i. e. de meipso." Ibid., 465.18.

134. Luther's equivalent to my paraphrase reads, "[d]a mus man hoch uber alle Engel und alle himel komen und alle Creatur hie niden lassen und sich hinauff schwingen und allein ho(e)ren, was Gott von sich selbs sagt und von seinem jnnerlichen wesen, sonst werden wir es nicht erfaren." WA 41:270.20-23 (Trinity Sunday, 1535).

135. The first-person plural is used as the dative object of revelation and also as the subject of preaching. "..., qui nobis revelavit?" WA 45:90.19; "... praedicamus sapientiam revelatam a Deo e celo." Ibid., 91, 24.

The first plot in the narrative of Trinitarian revelation is caught up in the biblical passage's doxological embrace. The awe filled question, "Who has been his counselor?" (Rom 11:34), has already been answered. It poses as the point of entry into an extended description of the Holy Spirit, the Trinitarian person who reveals the inner Trinity to and in the church. Clothed in the church's poor stammering and few technical terms is the revelation of a subject matter ineffable for words yet compelling towards an eschatological sight. Luther does not stop with a side-glance at the church's language as the Spirit's vehicle of revelation. For Luther, the church's words are the language in which God speaks from God. The marvelous convergence points to the heart of a divine mystery. The divine desire is to be known as the Triune God in eternity and, as such, to be known in a particular way: through the Spirit speaking to the church in its language. Luther wonders at the divine revelation from the "inside-out." Is there another way of knowing God, perhaps from the "outside-in"?

THE HOMILETICAL DISPUTATION: KNOWLEDGE OF GOD
FROM THE "OUTSIDE-IN" OR THE "INSIDE-OUT"?

The sermon's introductory section on the Spirit is interwoven with a disputation that Luther stages as a contrast demanded by the biblical subject matter and its form. Luther rehearses a controversy, centered on Romans 1:18–20, whose point of contention has to do with the knowledge of God. After having established the sermon's scope to be the divine wisdom, Luther stages the opposing position. Natural reason attempts to know the divine wisdom on the basis of an inference from the works in creation to the knowledge of God. In this section, the opponent's side of the homiletical disputation will be discussed as the knowledge of God from the "outside-in."[136] I represent Luther's interpretation of whom he considers to be

---

136. The disputation woven into this sermon is couched in terms of a dangerous polemic that Luther launches against the religions of Islam and Judaism. Luther intends to contrast the Trinitarian article that is revealed to the church with the Muslim and Jewish religions. In the genre of the sermon, Luther's intense polemic against other religions contrasts with an almost negligible amount in the genre of the disputation. In the disputation, the position of the opponent is constructed primarily at the boundary between the theological and the philosophical regions; Aristotle, Plato, Cicero, Scotus, and Ockham figure significantly in the disputations discussed in ch. 2. The disputation represents a more sophisticated view of the philosophical positions that, in the genre of the sermon, are flattened for the purpose of contrast. In the genre of the sermon, the intermingling of a theological claim with a religio-political position is characteristic not only of Luther's later years, but is also representative

the "people" (*gentes*) of Romans 1:18 and how he flattens the differences between the "people" in order to claim that natural reason is incapable of knowing either the inner-Trinitarian essence or its convergence with the divine desire.

At this juncture in the sermon, Luther's style can be compared to and analyzed according to its disputational form. It is not an anomaly that Luther structures even this sermon in the form of a disputational argument.[137] Often woven into the fabric of his preaching, the antithetical form is declared by Luther to reflect the subject matter that affirms "heaven" while negating its opposite, "hell."[138] Although Rörer imposes his own logical structure on Luther's preached sermon, Luther's disputational style is adapted to the sermon through a dialogue, giving the impression that Luther is refuting his opponents in a line-by-line unfolding of his own claims.[139] In addition to Luther's argumentative idiosyncracy, the sermon's presentation of the biblical subject matter imitates the diatribe form of Paul's Letter to the Romans, in which Paul seems to confront actual

---

of a late-medieval historical ethos. In light of a contemporary study of Luther's Trinitarian understanding, a critical reception of the polemic might challenge the way in which Luther conceives the relation between the inner-Trinitarian essence and its soteriological center. In this section, I choose to focus on the position Luther sustains, the revelation of the Trinity to Christians, and the general position he negates, the incapacity of those outside the boundaries of the Christian faith to know the Trinity.

137. Lohse states that Luther consistently makes use of the disputational form in genres other than in the disputation. Lohse, "Luther als Disputator," 233.

138. Luther discusses the theological reason for using the rhetorical strategy of the antithesis in the genre of the sermon. "Ad maiorem confirmationem non solum affirmativam, sed etiam negativam ponit. Omnis homo currit. Universalem negativam wil ich simpliciter heissen Antithesin in oppositionibus. Quando facio praedicationem, acccipio Antithesin, ut hic Christus facit. Vitam aeternam habet et non hel." WA 36:183.17–21 (Hauspredigt am Pfingstmontag, May 20, 1532). Current researchers on Luther's rhetoric have noticed Luther's homiletical-antithetical style. Stolt sees Luther's "antithetische Zweigliedrigkeit," both at the microlevel of contrasting sentences and at the macrolevel of the argument. Stolt, *Wortkampf*, 36. Mayr calls Luther's style an "'argumentativen Spannungsbogen', d.h. eine rhetorisch-kunstfertig gegliederte Aussageeinheit." Ruppert Mayr, "'Einfeldig zu predigen, ist eine große kunst': Zu Luthers Sprache in seinen Predigten," 92. The rhetorical form of contrast intensifies the affective dimension. The passion of the homiletical disputation is evoked by the dialogical tools Luther uses to stage his argument. Bieritz shows that Luther's dialogical style, evident in the use of pronouns, intensifies the dramatic force of his sermons. Bieritz, "Verbum facit fidem," 483. Winkler discusses the power of dialogue in Luther's assertions of Christ's victory against demonic attack. Winkler, "Luther als Seelsorger und Prediger," 237.

139. "Rörer subsumiert in der Regel mehrere Hauptsätze in eine Satzeinheit." Mayr, "'Einfeldig zu predigen, ist eine große kunst," 91n40.

debating partners.[140] The diatribe shapes the controversy in Romans 1:18–3:20, which articulates competing claims concerning the knowledge of God. Luther summarizes his own position. From the perspective of the Spirit's revelation, the controversial Romans passage is interpreted by cross-referencing Romans 11:33–34 with 1 Corinthians 2:9–11 in order to claim that Christians know both the inner Trinity and the outer-Trinitarian works in creation.[141] They know God from the "inside-out." What is the position contrasted with revelation? For Luther, it is the kind of knowledge of God available to natural reason from the "outside-in."

Luther makes passionate use of a favorite and distinctly medieval disputational form in order to maximize his position in contrast to natural reason. Luther begins to define his opponents by appealing to Paul's term in Romans 1:18, the "people" (*gentes*). For Paul, who appropriates Stoic natural theology when writing this famous verse, the "people" (*gentes*) designate all people who ask one fundamental question.[142] In asking a common question, the natural reason of the "people" (*gentes*) is exposed. The question is concerned with the knowledge, on the basis of what God has revealed, of the "eternal power and divinity" (Rom 1:20). In a sermon at home on the articles of faith, also preached in 1537, Luther makes a similar point. The question that is as old as Aristotle perplexes all people concerns the origin of the world and of every person.[143] The question demands an answer that, as Luther states in the Schmalcald sermon, cannot be found.[144] In the Romans 11:33–36 sermon, Luther at least constructs a thought experiment in order to conjecture what his opponents' answer might look like. What would the form of the answer take, and what would the answer be, if the question were posed by two representatives of natural reason—the

---

140. Brevard S. Childs, *The New Testament as Canon*, 260.

141. In this disputational-argumentative section, Luther aims to show how Christians know Christ from both the inside-out and from the outside-in. "Ideo videmus Christum foris et intus. Soli Christiani recte loquuntur de personis, cogitationibus et operibus, wie ers aussen machen cum creaturis, praesertim piis, quia audiunt ex revelatione spiritus sancti." WA 45:90.20–22.

142. "Apud Summos gentiles. ..." Ibid., 89.28.

143. "Denn darumb haben sich alle weise leute je und je bekummert, wo her die welt und wir kommen." Ibid., 12.17–19 (Schmalcald, 1537).

144. "... haben es aber nicht konnen finden." Ibid., 12.19.

philosophers Aristotle and Plato?[145] Luther's initial appeal to these philosophers soon accelerates him into a head-on encounter with other representative thinkers, especially those from the late Middle Ages.

Luther reconstructs the answer to the question concerning the knowledge of God from the works of creation in the form common to medieval
science. The inference from the works in creation to the divine essence is
already suggested by Romans 1:20. Luther appropriates this form in order
to represent his opponents and specifies it with elements appearing in a
late medieval discussion. According to Luther's version, the inference has,
as its premise, the one created world that implies the dominion of one God.
"They have seen heaven and earth so wisely governed and, from there, they
have made a weak inference from the external regiment and essence of the
creature that there is one God."[146] With this inference, Luther steps into
the wider arena of philosophy and theology concerned with the proofs for
the existence of God.[147] The proofs can be understood to represent, for a
particular thinker, her construal of the relationship between theology and
philosophy as they configure the kind of inferences based on the created
works. In the medieval trajectory, the debate turns on the issue of whether
the premises can imply only a philosophical concept of God, such as a first
cause, or also the Christian God. Luther is wholeheartedly engaged in the
thicket of the medieval debate when he appeals to a particular inference
as a strategy in interpreting Romans 1:18-20. How Luther orients his own
position in view of the inference strikes at the heart of his own understanding, in the homiletical genre, regarding the incapacity of natural reason to
infer the Triune God from creation.

Luther's inference can be interpreted in proximity not to Aristotle but
to William of Ockham. The way Luther characterizes his opponents seems
to come remarkably close to Ockham's own criticism of specific proofs for

---

145. "Aristoteles et Plato. ..." Ibid., 91.2.

146. Ibid., 90.2-4.

147. The proofs for the existence of God preoccupied medieval philosophers and theologians, who were concerned with demonstrating the finitude of creation, in contrast to
Aristotle, who held onto the eternity of the world. In the *Hauspredigt*, Luther represents
Aristotle's position in contrast to the Christian understanding of the creation from nothing.
"Der weisse man Aristoteles schleusset vast dahin, es sey die welt von ewikeit gewesen. Da
mus man je sagen, er habe gar nichts von diser kunst gewust. Darumb wenn man sagt, himel
und erden sey ein geschopf oder werck, das gemacht sey von dem, der da heist ein einiger Gott
und aus nichts gemacht, das ist ein kunst uber alle kunst." Ibid., 13.9-13 (Schmalcald, 1537).

the existence of God—namely the proof from perfection and the proof from final causality. For Ockham, the former can, at best, be used to show a number of possible species satisfying the description, while the latter is rejected entirely.[148] Only one inference, Ockham admits, can prove the unity of a first cause. This is the proof of a first efficient cause by conservation.[149] A *per accidens* series of producing causes cannot demonstrate what the proof of conservation can: that a chain of conserving causes terminates "with something different in kind from the things with which it started," meaning not produced and needing a conserver.[150] When Luther mentions the key word, "to be governed," in his rehearsal of the opponent's position, he is most likely appealing to Ockham's approval of the proof from conservation.[151] Ockham, however, does not place complete confidence in this proof to demonstrate the existence of the Christian God. When regarding the heavenly bodies, the subject matter of Aristotelian physics, Ockham concludes that the same proof can be used to demonstrate a plurality of unconserved conservers.[152] A similar argument is found in Biel who, following Ockham, concludes that the oneness of God cannot be demonstrated by natural reason; it is to be taken on faith.[153] In his sermon, Luther's criticism of the proof from conservation can be seen to dovetail with both Biel's and Ockham's positions. For Luther, the proof can, at best, weakly imply that there is one God on the basis of the external government, but it cannot demonstrate who God is in his essence.[154] If natural reason

---

148. McCord Adams, *Ockham*, vol. 2, 972–79.

149. "Ad argumentum principale dico quod per efficientiam, secundum quod dicit rem immediate accipere esse post nonesse, non potest probari primum efficiens esse, sed per efficientiam secundum quod dicit rem continuari in esse bene potest probari hoc esse per conservationem." Ockham, *Quaestiones in libros Physicorum Aristotelis*, q. 136 [*OPh* VI, 769].

150. McCord Adams, *Ockham*, vol. 2, 971.

151. WA 45:90.2.

152. McCord Adams, *Ockham*, vol. 2, 971–72.

153. "Conclusio tertia: Tantum unum esse Deum est creditum et non demonstratum ratione naturali nobis in via possibili, tametsi multae probabiles rationes ad huius veritatis ostensionem possint adduci." Biel, *Sent.* I d. 2, q. 10, art. 2, c. 3 [vol. 1, 189]; "Sciendum tamen quod potest demonstrari Deum esse, accipiendo 'Deum' secundo modo prius dicto. ... Sed ex hoc non sequitur quod potest demonstrari quod tantum est unum tale, sed hoc tantum fide tenetur." Ockham, *Quodl.* 1, q. 1, c. 4 [OTh IX, 3].

154. "Apud Summos gentiles conclusum est krencklich." WA 45:89.28; "... et inde schwechlich concluserunt." Ibid., 90.2–3; "Sed huc non venerunt nec potuerunt venire, quid sey Gott in seim gottlichen, abgrundlichen wesen sey." Ibid., 89:29–90.2.

cannot demonstrate the oneness of God on the basis of the divine works in creation, then neither can it reach the triune essence. Luther's appeal to Ockham's argument establishes the contrast Luther sets up between the incapacity of natural reason and the Spirit who reveals both the Trinitarian nature and the divine soteriological desire.

Luther captures the incapacity of natural reason in the colloquial form of the idiom. Appearing in other sermons making a similar argument, a stock idiom in Luther's vast repertoire assumes the "one house, one house-holder" rule.[155] Luther appeals to two popular expressions, "Just as there cannot be two roosters, there cannot be two heads of the house" and "Two rulers cannot endure each other in one house," to caricature the common position of the "people" (*gentes*) seated outside the Christian religion.[156] The two idioms are strategically used to introduce the two other religions claiming the unity of God, Judaism and Islam, yet their use characterizes Luther's polemically dangerous style marking his later years. Although Mayr softens Luther's vitriol by suggesting that Luther is typologizing his opponents, the unfortunate tone of this passage is uttered against the backdrop of personal relations, the political exile of Jews from Saxony, and the fear of the Ottoman invasion.[157] After being used to caricature the religions outside

---

155. WA 34,1:499.24 (Trinity Sunday, 1531); WA 36:410.28 (Predigt am Tage Johannes des Evangelisten, Dec. 27, 1532, to John 1:1); WA 37:38.30-31 (Torgau, 1533).

156. WA 45:90.25-26, 91.1. In Rörer's transcription, the first idiom is preceded by a summary of the Jewish and "Turkish" positions regarding the Christian faith in three gods (Ibid., 90.23-25). The second idiom is attributed to the "Iudei et gentes." Ibid., 90.31-91.1. The repertoire of Luther's idioms is astounding. His works are full of popular idioms, expressions and citations from ancient writers. Luther praised Erasmus' collections, the "Copia" and the 4151 idioms and citations contained in the "Adagia." Luther criticized Sebastian Franck's collection for recording idioms that dishonored both women and marriage. When Johannes Agricola published his collection of idioms in 1529 and reprinted it in 1532, Luther responded, "Der Teuffel ist den Sprichwortten feindt." In Ernst Thiele, *Luthers Sprichwörtersammlung*, xvi-xvii. Close to 500 idioms are collected from Luther's handwritten notes and are documented in Thiele's book. The idioms found in the Rom 11:33-36 sermons are not contained in Thiele's collection. Wander records the idioms in his lexicon as follows: "Zween Hanen können nicht auff einem Mist seyn"; "Zwen hanen vff einer misten vertragen (leiden) sich nit"; "Ein Haus leidet nicht zwei Herren." Karl Friedrich Wilhelm Wander, ed., *Deutsches Sprichwörter-Lexikon*, 268 (no. 183); 269 (no. 190); 401 (no. 112).

157. Mayr, "'Einfeldig zu predigen, ist eine große kunst,'" 99. On Aug. 6, 1537, the Elector issued an edict, exiling Jews from Saxony. Another version of this edict appeared on May 6, 1543. Related to the political exile of the Jews from Saxony, Luther's intensified polemic against Jews took the concrete form of a vendetta against Josel. Wolfgang Capito wrote a letter to Luther about a Jew, Josel, and asked Luther to plead to the Elector on Josel's behalf. Luther refused the request. See the two letters in WABr 8:77.1-78.39 (no. 3152, Capito to Luther);

Christianity, the idiom is immediately related to the argument against the philosophers. Luther explicitly refers to Plato[158] and cites a passage from Aristotle's *Metaphysics:* "It is not valid to posit a plurality of principles. Consequently, there must be only one God."[159] The Aristotle quote seems to be associated, at least by Ockham, with the inference from creation to the existence of one God.[160] Luther's polemic serves to subsume all philosophers and religions under an idiom that, when reviewed from the perspective of his criticism against the proof from conservation, is seen to reflect the sickness and weakness of natural reason. Like Ockham, Luther holds a position that challenges the capacity of natural reason to demonstrate the unity of God on the basis of the data of the world. While the surface level of Luther's preaching sounds as if he is rejecting philosophy, he is, in fact, appealing to Ockham in order to strengthen his own position, which privileges the Spirit's revelation. Like Ockham and Biel,[161] Luther insists on the Trinity as the subject matter of revelation.

Ibid., 89.1–91.63 (no. 3157, Luther to Josel). The army of the Ottoman empire encountered the army of the Holy Roman Empire in December 1537, and the loss sustained by King Ferdinand evoked anxiety throughout his empire for years. See: Brecht, *Martin Luther*, vol. 3, 346–51.

158. It is highly unlikely that Luther read Plato, *The Republic*, IV, 17, in which Socrates discusses the virtue of justice as the one principle of harmony and unity. See: Plato, *The Republic: Books I–V*, 414–15.

159. WA 45:91.2–3. One of Luther's favorite quotes from Aristotle's *Metaphysics* often appears in the context of inferring one Lord on the basis of one creation. "The rule of many is not good; let there be one ruler." *Met.* XII (10), 1076a, 4 [vol. 2, 1700]. The quote is originally from Homer's *Iliad* II, 204, that is cited in WA 45:91n2. "οὐκ ἀγαθὸν πολυκοιρανίη, εἷς κοίρανος ἔστω." Luther also adds the feminine form of *domina* to his argument. "Quando 2 dominae in una domo regunt. ..." WA 45:91.3.

160. "Quod sic: Quia unius mundi est tantum unus princeps, XII *Metaphysicae*." Ockham, *Quodl.* I, q. 1 [*OTh* IX, 1].

161. Knowledge of the inner Trinity is, for Luther, as well as for the medieval theologians of the Christian tradition, an article of faith revealed to the church. "Ad argumentum igitur dico quod sicut illa conclusio in qua praedicatur esse trinum et unum de quocumque conceptu Dei non potest probari in diversis scientiis sed solum probatur in theologia praesupposita fide." Ockham, *Quodl.* V, q. 1, ad. inst. 1 [*OTh* IX, 478]. "Secundo sequitur quod veritatum theologicarum aliquae sunt naturaliter notae, aliquae sunt supernaturaliter cognitae et tantum fide creditae, ut 'Deus est trinus et unus', 'Deus est incarnatus' etc." Biel, *Prol.* q. 1, art. 1, nota 3, col. 2 (D) [vol. 1, 13]; "Nam in primo praesens est Deus aliis, quibus se revelavit, quorum auctoritati credimus. 'Quod enim credo Deum esse trinum et unum, hoc credo Dei Filio, qui hoc enarravit et praedicavit, et Spiritui Sancto, qui hoc' patribus 'inspiravit.' " "In secundo modo 'est praesens in effectu proprio'; qui modus 'tanto est eminentior quanto effectum divinae grataie magis sentit in se homo vel etiam quanto melius scit considerare Deum in exterioribus creaturis'." Biel, *Sent.* II, d. 23, q. 1, art. 3, dub. 2 (G) [vol. 2, 468].

In the Cruciger version of Luther's sermon, a similar position is advanced that is clothed in almost Kantian-sounding terminology. Not found in Rörer's transcription, Cruciger couches Luther's argument in a language distinguishing between *a priori* and *a posteriori* knowledge of God.[162] In medieval terminology, the contrast is referred to as the distinction between the demonstration on account of which (*demonstratio propter quid*) and the demonstration that (*demonstratio quia*).[163] A posteriori knowledge of God, or the demonstration that (*demonstratio quia*), characterizes the type of knowledge accessible to natural reason, which sees God from the outside, the works, and government. On the other hand, the knowledge of God that is invisible to human wisdom, God's inner essence, is considered to be *a priori* knowledge, or the demonstration on account of which (*demonstratio propter quid*). The appeal to the distinction between *a priori* and *a posteriori* was known to medieval theologians, who commonly mapped the distinction onto theological proofs. *A priori* knowledge, typically associated with Anselm, argues from the description of the divine essence to the existence of God. When Luther, according to Cruciger, preaches on the distinction, he aims to convince his hearers that the *a priori* knowledge of the inner side of God must be revealed by the Spirit.

At the heart of Luther's sermon is a controversy exegetically concentrated on Romans 1:18–20. The controversy is staged between the knowledge of the inner Trinity revealed by the Spirit and the question of natural reason regarding the origin of the world that is, at best, answered by the concept of a householder or ruler. Luther contends that, for Christians, the Spirit's revelation of the Trinity is the starting point for knowing the inner side of God. This position is contrasted with any *a posteriori* inference from the data of the world to the unity of God. Luther rejects any proofs

---

162. Cruciger, not Rörer, uses the terminology of the *a priori* and *a posteriori* knowledge of God. "Das ist ein Erkentnis (A posteriore), da man Gott von aussen ansihet an seinen wercken und Regiment, wie man in ein Schlos oder Haus auswendig ansihet und dabey spu(e)ret den Herrn oder Haus Wirt. Aber (A priore) von inwendig her hat kein menschliche weisheit noch nie ersehen ko(e)nnen, was und wie doch Gott sey in jm selbs oder in seinem innerlichen wesen, Kan auch niemand etwas davon wissen noch reden, denn welchen es offenbart ist durch den heiligen Geist, Denn gleich wie niemand weis (spricht S. Paulus j. Kor. ij)." WA 21:509.18–25.

163. "Propter quod oportet scire quod quaedam est demonstratio cuius praemissae sunt simpliciter priores conclusione, et illa vocatur demonstratio a priori sive propter quid." Ockham, *SL* III-2, 17 [*OPh* I, 533]; "In metaphysica demonstrantur demonstratione quia, in theologia propter quid." Biel, *Prol.* q. 1, art. 1, nota 3, col. 1 (D) [vol. 1, 13].

of natural reason for the divine existence in order to leave room for the Spirit to reveal the inmost depths of God. How this revelation proceeds by incorporating its hearers into the Spirit's way with the church will be discussed in the next section.

THE HOMILETICAL WORD AND THE NARRATIVITY OF INCORPORATION

The view to the sermon's central theme should not be blurred by Luther's polemical force. Although sometimes hidden amid the smoke, the theme of the Spirit's revelation will now be brought back into focus, particularly in light of the doxology shaping the entire sermon. In this section, I will explore the final aspect to Luther's understanding of the Holy Spirit. The Spirit is the person who reveals the divine wisdom, both as the knowledge of the inner Trinity and as the way of God with the church (Rom 11:33). Luther conceives the sermon according to an incorporation of hearers into the subject matter of preaching. The section will conclude with my proposal regarding the relation between the divine word and the preached word that takes into account a doctrinal component as well as the human as a subject of speech.

Not to be forgotten is the fact that a doxology orients the focus of Luther's sermon. In spite of various disputational interruptions, Luther reminds his hearers of the sermon's doxological impulse by weaving in repetitions of the Romans 11:33–34 text. With Paul, Luther asks, "Who has been his counselor?" "Who has known?" (Rom 11:34; Isa 40:13; Jer 23:18; 1 Cor 2:16), and sighs an awe-filled, "Oh, the depth!"[164] The questions and the sigh are uttered in the first part of the sermon, one that until now has been discussed according to the rubric of the Holy Spirit. Surrounded by the doxological embrace, the first site in the narrative wonders at the content of the Spirit's revelation, the divine wisdom, spoken of in Romans 11:33–34.[165] By infusing the sermon with the doxological wonder at the divine wisdom, Luther builds an exegetical bridge between the content of the revelation, the inner Trinity, and the particular way in which this revelation proceeds.

---

164. WA 45:91.23–24, 93.13–14, 92.34.

165. "Non praedicamus rationem, sed sapientiam, quae non potest comprehendi, sed so tieff, ut dicat: 'Quis eius consiliarius?' praedicamus sapientiam revelatam a Deo e celo, foris revelatur per verbum, intus revelat in corde." Ibid., 91.22–25.

The doxology expresses an awe of the divine wisdom that is manifest as the particular way of the Spirit to the church.

The divine wisdom is determined by another word taken from the sermon's biblical foundation. It is not a coincidence that the word "way" (Rom 11:33) appears explicitly in the sermon. Luther turns to this particular word, found in Romans 11:33 (Isa 45:15; 55:8–9). "'Ways,' his counsel, the ways he desires to be with us."[166] The divine ways are equivocated with the divine "decision," or wisdom that is explained as the ways in which God desires to be "with us." When the word "way" is read to interpret the Spirit's plot, one discovers that, from the onset, the sermon's own movement is constituted by the process in which the Spirit's revelation occurs. The content of the divine wisdom is revealed to be the inner Trinity, and this content converges with the way in which this action proceeds. By speaking of the inner Trinity, the Spirit points to the church as the particular site at which God is "with us." The first site of the divine wisdom is plotted by a convergence between the Spirit and the church.

The convergence is constituted by the act of preaching. The sermon's movement betrays the convergence that takes place during its rehearsal, particularly through the shift detected by the pronouns. In the early part of the sermon, Luther uses the third-person singular or plural and attributes the revelation to the Spirit.[167] A gradual shift takes place by specifying the third-person plural to be Christians as the recipients of revelation.[168] Luther then switches the pronoun to the first-person plural, thereby defining the Christians, or "us," to be his hearers.[169] The sermon's development is marked by an increasing frequency in the use of the first-person plural,

---

166. Ibid., 93.18–19.

167. The Trinity "… fide cognoscatur et maneat." Ibid., 89.18–19. "Ideo quando ista sublimis praedicatio praedicatur." Ibid., 90.22–23. The revelation is "foris revelatur per verbum, intus revelat in corde." Ibid., 91.24–25. The same theme appears in the *Hauspredigt* in which Luther preaches on the external and internal revelation of the Spirit. "Das heist nu des heyligen geistes regiment auff erden, Das die leut so gewiß werden und alles gern und willig drub leyden, und das heist den heyligen Geist haben, die schopffung und erlosung also fulen und In das hertz schreyben, Denn solchs thet allein der heylig geist, welchen man sihet durch die tauff, Sacrament und predigt, das ein Christ den andern trostet, straffet, unterweyset." Ibid., 23.1–6 (Schmalcald, 1537).

168. "Hoc Christianis revelatum e celo." Ibid., 89.26–27.

169. "Sic nemo agnoscit Deum ut nos Christiani. Nobis per spiritum sanctum deus revelavit." Ibid., 90.8–9.

so that the preacher and congregation emerge as the subjects of seeing, speaking, preaching, and revealing.[170] Formerly attributed to the Spirit, the verbs are now, through a displacement of pronouns, attributed to human subjects. At this literary level, the sermon mirrors the convergence that is taking place. What is occurring is the actualization of the convergence as the Spirit opens the inner Trinity to hearers who are gradually incorporated into this particular way of revelation. As the hearers are gathered into the Spirit's view, they learn to speak about what they have been shown.

The incorporation is reflected in speech. Not just a passive hearing but an active seeing prompts the "right speaking" that exposes an increase in the knowledge of God. The theme of right speaking emerges when an account can be provided for a shift in the subjects of speech. For Luther, a "new church" is born when the "first principles" are preached.[171] Christians, who are incorporated into the site of the Spirit's revelation, know the mind of God so intimately that they can "rightly speak" about the inner-Trinitarian persons, their thoughts, and the outer-Trinitarian works.[172] The subjects of speech are Christians who have been incorporated into the divine wisdom of which the Spirit speaks. The Spirit reveals by incorporating those who hear into the revelation that is articulated in the language available in the church. God's way with the church is manifest as a

---

170. "Ideo videmus." Ibid., 90.20; "Ideo quando dicimus." Ibid., 90.31; "Habemus igitur unicum deum, sed revelationem habemus." Ibid., 91.5; "... praedicamus sapientiam revelatam a Deo e celo" Ibid., 91.24; "... et tamen nihil aliud praedicamus quam dei filium." Ibid., 92.18-19.

171. "Man sol auff der cantzel die zitzen herauß ziehen vnd daß volck mit milch trencken, den eß wechst alle tage eine newe kirch auff, quae indiget primis principiis." WATr 3:310.5-7 (no. 3421, Tischreden aus verschiedenen Jahren).

172. "Soli Christiani recte loquuntur de personis, cogitationibus et operibus, wie ers aussen machen cum creaturis, praesertim piis, quia audiunt ex revelatione spiritus sancti." WA 45:90.20-22. Emerging out of a controversy at the Wittenberg faculty in 1537, the theme of the "right speaking" of Christians is mentioned at a more explicit level in Luther's later disputations and sermons. Cordatus, a student of Cruciger, had disputed with his professor on the legitimacy of using the discourse of formal causes when discussing the theological theme of justification. The controversy implicated Melanchthon who had written Cruciger's lecture script. The affair of accusation and defense lasted until mid-April when Luther appealed to Cruciger, asking him to omit the precarious sentence in the latter's commentary on 1 Timothy. A section in the doctoral disputation (Promotionsdisputation) of Palladius and Tilemann (WA 39,1:202-257, esp. 227-233), taking place on June 1, 1537, and Luther's speech five days later on the occasion of Palladius's Promotion (WA 39,1:260.1-263.21), deals with this issue of recte loquuntur. "Sapientia igitur a Christo promissa et donata ... sicut os ab ipso promissum nova loquela et linguae novae sunt, et tamen sunt omnium gentium nativae linguae." WA 39,1:262.15, 18-19. For a detailed account and a bibliography of the Cordatus controversy, see: Streiff, "Novis Linguis Loqui," 35-39.

right speaking in a language attributed simultaneously to the Spirit and to the church.

The rhetorical prowess of Luther's sermons witnesses to his conviction that "right speech" arises when the human hearer experiences the entire range of what is seen. The rhetorical component plays an enormous role in Luther's preaching style.[173] Luther draws on the wealth of his rhetorical repertoire in order to convey the sermon in a way alive to the full extent of human subjectivity, not solely of the transcendental "I."[174] Recalling Christ's homiletical example, Luther tailors his sermons to accomodate to the cognitive and affective aspects of the concrete human hearers he is addressing:[175] the students and theologians, but more importantly, the women, children, and men of Wittenberg.[176] Excluded from his hearers are those who are as coarse as pigs.[177] These people, whom Luther caricatures as those fixed only on filling their bellies, have no interest in seeking God and God's justice and act in ways committing crimes against others.[178] In contrast, other hearers

---

173. There has been a flurry of recent literature on the relation between Luther's rhetoric and dialectics. Bieritz, Haustein, and Winkler write on the uses of rhetoric to move the will. Bieritz, "Verbum facit fidem," 488; Manfred Haustein, "Luther als Prediger," 94; and Winkler, *Impulse Luthers für die heutige Gemeindepraxis*, 71, 82.

174. In one of his most famous Table Talks, Luther refers to the Father as the *grammatica*, the Son as the *dialectica*, and the Spirit as the *rhetorica*. WATr 1:563.26-29 (no. 1143, first half of 1530s).

175. A Table Talk exposes Christ as Luther's example for preaching. "Christus mit seinem predigen ist fluchs in parabel hinein gefallen vnd hatt von schaffen, hirten, wolfen, weinbergen, feigenbaumen gesagt, von samen, ackern, pflugen; das haben die armen laien konnen vernemen." WATr 2:163.21-23 (no. 1650, June 12 to July 12, 1532). In another Table Talk, Luther speaks of accomodating the sermon to his hearers. "Man mus nicht predigen, tapffer herfahren, mit großen worten, prechtig vnd kunstreich, das man sehe, wie gelert man sey, vnd seine ehre suchen [Luther is referring to Bucer and Zwingli!]. Non est locus ibi. Man sol sich aldohin accommodiren ad auditores, vnd das feilet gemeiniglich allen predigern, das sie predigen, das das gemeine volck gar wenig daraus lerne." WATr 4:447.11-15 (no. 4719, July 23, 1539).

176. Werdemann has reconstructed Luther's Wittenberg congregation in light of Luther's remarks and the rhetorical strategies Luther uses to appeal to the vast array of personalities standing before him. See: Hermann Werdemann, *Luthers Wittenberger Gemeinde Wiederhergestellt aus seinen Predigten*. The lower center panel of the altar painting in the Wittenberg city church by Lucas Cranach the Elder (1547) depicts Luther on the chancel. Luther is pointing to a figure of Christ on the cross and is preaching to his congregation, in which his wife, Katherina von Bora, and his son Hans are sitting in the first row.

177. "... gar rohe als sew: illis non opus praedicare." WA 45:95.1.

178. "... tantum nati, ut bauch fullen, aliis schaden thun, gar nach Gott nichts fragen, et tales hodie plures inter cives, nobiles et rusticos. Nihil curant eius iudicia etc. Et illos deus non curat, lesst auch hin gehen. Non quod cogimur ferre eorum maliciam mit stelen, rauben etc. Die ghet der Text nicht an." Ibid., 95.2-6.

of Luther's sermon are those endowed with natural reason, who ask the question concerning the nature of the divine essence and the works which can be predicted to merit God's rewarding justice.[179] These "people" (*gentes*; Rom 1:18) could be one group of hearers in Luther's congregation. Other hearers are those who, like his children, are coaxed, cajoled, and invited to see the things of which he preaches. The variation in styles uncovers Luther's work to incite an affective and cognitive experience of the sermon. Luther's rhetorical fitness and dialectical force as well as his concern for an increase in right speaking are aspects of his preaching activity that appeal to an experientially diverse notion of human subjecthood.

The theme of "right speaking" challenges the instrumental concept of the preached word. When humans are regarded as subjects of speech, their active ability to speak rightly demands an understanding concerning the things spoken about. Luther's sermon offers a representative example of active articulation, not passive reception, of the subject matter at hand. His sermon privileges doctrine as the knowledge of God that must be taught and then subsequently articulated by those who grow in understanding. Luther's position regarding the language used throughout the church's history of Trinitarian reflection witnesses to the "right speaking" that accompanies new insights. This language is correctly predicated of the church. Revelatory language is rightly spoken by Christians, by "us." When humans are determined as subjects according to experiential, cognitive and religious capacities, then the words they speak cannot be narrowed to a passive instrument directed at a transcendental "I."[180] Their incorporation into the Spirit's speech is mirrored by their contribution to that speech. Regarded as subjects of speech, humans speak of the object of faith in a way that can be passionate in its witness to mystery and creative as it encompasses all of human experience.

The "right speech" surfaces at an intersection between the Spirit and the church. At the first site of Luther's sermon, the relation between the Spirit and the church is concentrated in the preaching performance. Preaching

---

179. "… qui cogitant, quomodo liberari debeant a peccatis et libenter vellent scire, quae dei iudicia, viae, quid damnet, quid non." Ibid., 95.6–8. "Is vult dei consilarius esse et ei prius dare." Ibid., 95.19–20.

180. In discussions of Luther's homiletical theory, the term "instrumentality" is commonly ascribed to the human word as the passive vehicle of the divine word. For example, see: Beutel, *In dem Anfang war das Wort*, 469.

is the site at which the revelation is attributed to the Spirit, but the perseverance of the Trinitarian article is solely assigned to the church. The speaking of the Spirit and the discourse of the church are bound together in an intriguing structure of mutual predication. The church confesses the subject of speech to be the Spirit, and the Spirit points to the church as the location of revelation. From the former perspective, the church's contribution can be correctly described to be "instrumental." To the Spirit is attributed the knowledge of God from the "inside-out"; any other attempt to know God would be the illusion of natural reason. From the converse perspective, that of the words spoken and heard, the Spirit's speech is predicated of the church. The Spirit points to the words of the prophets, the psalmist, the church councils, and the church's preaching as the language of revelation. Despite the stammering, the church is represented by this model of mutual predication as the site at which the divine wisdom is revealed. The way of the divine wisdom is the Spirit to the church; in the church, the Spirit reveals the inner Trinity in the church's language. In light of this mutual predication of speech, the doxology arises as a fitting acknowledgment of wonder at the convergence between the inner-Trinitarian revelation and the way this knowledge is revealed in the church.

THE HOLY SPIRIT: CONCLUSION

Luther's understanding of the Holy Spirit was the first site in the narrative of Trinitarian revelation. The exegetical perspective was shaped by the theme of Romans 1:18-20, the knowledge of God, that Luther interpreted from the doxological perspective of Romans 11:33-34. The latter passage wondered at the divine wisdom, revealed by the Spirit. Contrasted with the knowledge of God from the "inside-out" was the incapacity of the "people" (*gentes*; Rom 1:18) to attain the triune essence. For the purpose of rhetorical force, Luther seemed to flatten philosophical knowledge from the "outside-in" to a popular idiom. When the deeper dimension of his polemic was analyzed more closely, it appeared that Luther did not deviate from a familiar position—that of William of Ockham. Furthermore, the homiletical disputation was seen to inform Luther's preaching style. Luther did not shy away from preaching about the inner Trinity. In fact, he explained how the Spirit reveals the "unfathomable way" of God "with us," and theology teaches Christians how to speak rightly about the inner Trinity.

THE INNER AND OUTER TRINITY

Until this juncture, Luther's sermon has plotted the Spirit's revelation as the site of mutual predication between the Spirit's speech and the church's language. The narrative of Trinitarian revelation continues to unfold at other sites. In this section, I intend to follow the sites Luther plots in the narrative from the inner to the outer Trinity and to show that Luther privileges a specific speech structure at sites revealing the Father, the Son, and the triune essence in baptism. By setting up the speech of both Father and Son to consist of a revelatory content together with the particular way "with us," Luther develops a grammar for reading the Trinitarian revelation in both the work of baptism and, ultimately, in the created works; that is the theme of this chapter's final section.

This section begins at the most original point in eternity. Here, another sermon is preached; in the inner Trinity, the Father's voice is heard. Discussed under the rubric of the Father will be the speech structure revealing God's beloved Son and anticipating the Son's incarnation as the way God desires to "be with" humans. The second section focuses on the revelation of the outer Trinity, which occurs at three sites: at Christ's baptism, at Christ's incarnation, and at the rite of baptism. Each of these will be discussed according to a distinctive speech structure that reveals the convergence between knowledge of the Trinity and the way God is "with us." The section concludes with an interpretation of the hidden God (*deus absconditus*) in light of the sermon's theme. By following Luther's sermon from the speech structures in eternity, through the incarnation, and then to the divine work of baptism, a full narrative picture of Luther's Trinitarian understanding is gained.

THE CROSS AS THE ETERNAL SERMON OF THE FATHER

The narrative arrives at a site brought into view by the Spirit. The Spirit preaches a sermon, as Luther states early during his own sermon.[181] What do the hearers of the Spirit's sermon hear? Luther responds: they hear an eternal sermon, preached by the Father.[182] Located in eternity is the genre of the sermon shaping the Father's word. In his own sermon, Luther

---

181. The explicit mention of the word, "sermon," is located earlier under the revelation of the Spirit. "Ideo quando ista sublimis praedicatio praedicatur." WA 45:90.22–23.

182. "... et quod haec aeterna praedicatio a patre." Ibid., 93.28–29.

formulates the "word" of the Father's sermon in the language of the confession of faith. "All scripture and especially the second article (I believe in Jesus Christ) compels us [to confess that God is three persons]."[183] The Father's sermon is the word himself, Jesus Christ. Luther's second reference to the Father's sermon uncovers more content. The Father's word is specified as Christ's incarnation and resurrection, and further, the sermon contains the *promissio* of "salvation for those who believe in him."[184] It remains an intriguing coincidence that the Father's word is articulated in confessional language and that it contains the only reference to the resurrection in Luther's entire sermon. In view of its narrative site, this coincidence is theologically of interest. Luther locates the Father's sermon, fittingly, after the Spirit's sermon in order to show that only the Spirit opens a view to the inner Trinity in a way eliciting the confession of faith in Christ. Luther places the resurrection in the Father's speech in order to underline the theological point that the Father's redemptive will for the sinner is bound together with the life of God's own Son.

The relation of the Father to his word, or sermon, is conceived according to a particular model. Two key biblical passages make up the constellation in which Luther construes the word in the inner Trinity. Both John's prologue and Genesis 1 serve as the crucial texts for disclosing the Father's coexistence with his word. The prologue is the powerful statement on the "greatest article of our holy Christian faith."[185] For Luther, John speaks of the same subject matter as Moses, yet the New Testament author is more explicit than his Old Testament counterpart by locating the word at a site preceding the will to create.[186] Outside any creature, the Father speaks

---

183. Ibid., 91.8–9. Preceding this confession is a remark made concerning the divine nature that is constituted by "ein dreyfeltige person." Luthers shows imaginative flexibility in describing the Triune nature as "ein dreifeltige person," in "seiner Gottlichen natur sey er ein dreifeltige person: Ein vater, son und heiliger geist." Ibid., 91.6–7. Luther does not mean one person divided into three parts of Father, Son, and Spirit!

184. "Ist zu tieff, hoch, et illa revelatur per spiritum sanctum in Euangelio, quod credo, quod 1 deus, sed esse in eo 3 personas, filium a patre et spiritum sanctum a patre, spiritum sanctum, et quod haec aeterna praedicatio a patre, ut filius homo et resurgeret, ut credentes in eum salvi." Ibid., 93.26–30.

185. WA 46:541.5 (Commentary on John 1–2 in sermons of 1537–1538, to John 1:1–3).

186. "... und Sanct Johannes hat es aus Mose genomen, aber Moses feret nicht also heraus, wie S. Johannes, der da spricht, das im anfange, ehe die welt, Himel und erden oder einige Creatur geschaffen, da sey das Wort gewesen." Ibid., 542.34–37. In his translation of the Bible, Luther uses two different pronouns to distinguish between Genesis 1 and John 1. Luther

in eternity, holding a "conversation with himself," as Luther describes.[187] Using the picture of the "word straight from the heart" of the human, which he admits is a "very dark analogy," Luther resorts to the decision of the "holy Fathers" who refer to this inner-Trinitarian conversation as the "word of God."[188] By using the Johannine-Genesis constellation, Luther can place the Holy Spirit as the hearer of the Father's word.[189] According to this model, the Son is not distinct from the word's content. The Father speaks the word, God's Son, that the Spirit hears. The "self-conversation" model of the inner Trinity differs from the "conversation of love" that is under-girded by the prosopographic exegesis of the royal psalms.[190] According to the interpersonal dialogical model, the Father speaks a word that is distinct from the Son, who hears it. This model's difficulty concerning the Holy Spirit's status in the love conversation is resolved by the self-conversation model, in which the Spirit is explicitly assigned the role of hearer. When the content of the Father's word is identified with the Son, what then can the Spirit hear?

---

translates Genesis 1:1 with "Am anfang. ..." [WADB 8:36 (1523)] and John 1:1 with "Im anfang ..." [WADB 6:326 (1522)]. Both Asendorf and Jansen notice the cross-referencing between John 1 and Gen 1 as the exegetical foundation for Luther's understanding of the Trinitarian concept of the word. See: Ulrich Asendorf, *Die Theologie Martin Luthers nach seinen Predigten*, 36–40; Jansen, *Studien zu Luthers Trinitätslehre*, 154–65.

187. "Das aber Gott ein Wort redet oder Gott ein Gesprech mit sich selber hat, wil nie-mand in kopff gehen. ... Darumb sollen wir ... dem heiligen Geist gleuben, der durch Mosen und Joannem geredet hat, das Gott ein Wort bey sich selber habe ausser aller Creatur." WA 46:547.6–7, 12, 13–15.

188. "Weiter sollen wir wissen, das in Gott ein Wort sey, nicht meinem oder deinem wort gleich, denn wir haben auch ein wort, sonderlich des hertzens wort, wie es die heiligen Veter nennen, als wenn ein Mensch bey sich selber etwas bedenckt und vleissig nachforschet, so hat er ein wort oder gesprech mit sich selber, davon niemand weis denn er allein." Ibid., 543.23–27. For Luther, the analogy of the "word of the heart" guards against false speculation, and serves to show how God's Son is the word of the inner-Trinitarian conversation. "Daru(e)mb ist diese Gleichnis von unserm wort genomen seer tunckel und finster, aber gleichwol gibt unser wort, wiewol es nicht mit jenem wort zuvergleichen ist, einen kleinen bericht, ja ursache, der sachen nachzudencken und deste leichter zu fassen, auch die gedancken und speculation des Menschlichen Hertzens gegen diesem Go(e)ttlichem Gespreche und wort zuhalten und zu lernen, wie Gottes Son ein wort sey." Ibid., 544.21–26. Augustine uses the human word as an analogy of the inner word of the Trinity and also discusses the dissimilarity between these two words. The human word lies, whereas God's word never lies; the human word speaks its thoughts that are temporal, whereas God's word is eternal. *De Trin.*, 18, 15 [PL 42:1077–79].

189. WA 46:59.14–25 (Commentary on John 16, 1538, to John 16:13).

190. The prosopographic type of inner-Trinitarian understanding is biblically based on the royal psalms. This model is observed in the hymn, "Now Rejoice, Dear Christians," and is discussed in ch. 3, "The Inner-Trinitarian Speech of the Father."

In his self-conversation, the Father speaks of a subject matter similar to the one written into the conversation of love. Whether the Father addresses a distinct word to the Son or identifies the word with the Son, the content is the same. The Father preaches on the Son's incarnation.[191] In an interesting twist to Genesis 1:26, Luther portrays the inner-Trinitarian conversation in view of the incarnation.[192] The divine counsel decides, "Let us make the human," and already its intention is formulated, "so that the Son might become a human and that all might believe in him."[193] Explicit in eternity, the incarnation is already bound up with the *promissio*. Salvation is assured to those who believe in Christ.[194] The salvation of the sinner bears a cost that is also written into the divine life. Inscribed in the eternal sermon is the word of death. At this site, Luther refers to Christ's death in the future tense: "Because the Son of God must die, neither the Father nor the Holy Spirit became a human."[195] Luther insists on the Son's death in view of future redemption in order to make a Trinitarian claim. Knowledge of the inner-Trinitarian distinctions is necessary in order to understand that it is precisely the Second Person who is destined to assume human nature without sin and to die.[196] The inner Trinity's Christological center is the

---

191. In the conversation of love described in ch. 3, the Father speaks to the Son in a series of imperatives, telling the Son about the incarnation and death that will set the captive free. See: ch. 3, "The Inner-Trinitarian Speech of the Father."

192. The book of Genesis, on which Luther began lecturing after concluding Psalm 90 on May 31, 1535, represents the final ten years of Luther's teaching career. He lectured on Gen 1 to Gen 3:14 until the outbreak of the plague in Wittenberg in July, 1535. On Jan. 25, 1536, Luther resumed the lectures. The verb in Gen 1:26, "faciamus," presents a point of exegetical controversy. In the commentary to this passage, Luther alludes to an interpretation of the divine counsel that refers the plural to God and to the angels. See: WA 42:43.18. Luther possibly has Lyra's reception of Rabbi ben Ezra's interpretation in mind. See: LW 1:57n90. Luther interprets the plural to mean the three persons of the Trinity. "Secundo verbum 'faciamus' pertinet ad mysterium fidei nostrae confirmandum, qua credimus ab aeterno unum Deum et distinctas tres personas in una divinitate, Patrem, Filium et Spiritum Sanctum." WA 42:43.12–14.

193. "Praedicatio rationis, non von innwendig her aus, wie es Gott in sein Gottlichem rad beschlossen, ubi solus bey im allein, antequam oravimus, fecit, 'faciamus hominem', utque filius fiat homo, ut omnes credentes in eum." WA 45:93.7–10.

194. "... ut credentes in eum salvi." Ibid., 93.29–30.

195. Ibid., 91.10–11.

196. "Ideo oportet habere unterschiedliche person. Ideo die innwendige Gottheit mussen wir wissen, quia fatemur Deum assumpsisse humanam naturam, ut nos, sine peccato. Ibi erzwingt sichs, quod pater alia persona a filio et spiritu sancto." Ibid., 9.11–14; "Ibi oportet scire patrem et spiritum sanctum non factum hominem. Verum: deus vere factus homo, sed

pivot around which turn the revelation of the inner-Trinitarian relations and death on behalf of the sinner's life.

In a manner similar to the section on the Spirit, Luther unfolds the second part of the sermon by weaving in a point of controversy. The matter for debate is the sermon's content. Luther contrasts the "sermon of reason" with the Father's "eternal sermon."[197] Luther picks up the theme of the "divine counsel," introduced by the reference to Genesis 1:26 (see also Rom 11:35; Isa 40:13) in order to contrast two positions. For Luther, natural reason answers the question, "Who has been his counselor?" by predicating the attributes, "good, merciful, just, almighty" of the one God who rules the one world.[198] The contrast focuses on the divine attributes. Another development in Luther's dispute with the philosophers unfolds.

Once again, Luther appeals to the *a posteriori* inference found in discussions of the type inferring the divine nature from the created works. He collapses various philosophical determinations of the divine essence into a sweeping generalization that underlines his contrast: "But in this way: the one God, who rules heaven and earth, is good, merciful, just, and all-powerful."[199] Luther rejects this position in a way reminiscent of and radicalizing Ockham's criticism of the proofs from perfection. For Ockham, if natural reason cannot prove one God—where God is defined as what is nobler than all else—then one cannot prove that "God is good or wise."[200] On the other hand, Ockham is prepared to accept certain metaphysical definitions of the divine essence. According to Ockham, natural reason is limited to predicating the metaphysical concepts of goodness and wisdom under certain natural theological assumptions on the meaning of the

---

nec pater nec spiritus sanctus, sed media persona, et tantum manserunt in 1 gottlich wesen." Ibid., 91.16-19.

197. See 259n193.

198. WA 45:91.31. Luther is collapsing various philosophical determinations of the divine attributes into one sweeping conclusion for the polemical purpose of contrast. See: "The Homiletical Disputation."

199. WA 45:91.30-31.

200. "Unde tales conclusiones 'Deus est bonus', 'Deus est sapiens' etc., sic accepto Deo, non possunt probari in diversis scientiis. Et ratio est quia sic accipiendo Deum, non est naturaliter evidens Deum esse, sicut deducit ratio, et patet in primo *Quodlibet* [I, q. 1], et per consequens non est naturaliter evidens Deum sic acceptum esse bonum." Ockham, *Quodl.* V, q. 1, ad. inst. 1 [*OTh* IX, 478].

concept "God."[201] Regarding the attribute "almighty," Ockham admits that one cannot prove that God is the cause of everything immediately. He is persuaded to accept this attribute on the authority of John 1:3 and the Creed and by a particular argument of reason.[202] Ockham's position differs from that of Biel. For Biel, natural reason can know that God exists, that he is a living God and a wise God.[203] Luther possibly has Biel in mind when he rejects any determinations of the divine attributes from the "outside-in." Luther radicalizes Ockham's position against Biel by stressing the incapacity of natural reason to attain any knowledge of the divine attributes. While Luther undermines Ockham's limited metaphysical deference to natural reason, he is maximizing Ockham's own theological appeal to the authority of Scripture and the Creed.

The discussion of attributes plays into the controversy regarding the divine counsel. Luther addresses the question, "What is pleasing to God?" For Luther, the position of natural reason attempts to determine the way God acts with respect to human efforts. Reason determines the kind of works that are pleasing to the God who will reward them.[204] In his Isaiah commentary of 1527–1530, Luther makes a similar point. He accuses reason of playing the "divine counselor" by prescribing to God the divine attributes, and he connects the idolatry of reason with its self-righteous

---

201. "Sed ex hoc non sequitur quin aliqua conclusio in qua 'bonum' vel 'sapiens' praedicatur de conceptu Dei, ut per illum intelligimus quod est aliquid quo nihil est perfectius nec prius—quia sic potest demonstrari Deum esse ... vel etiam potest demonstrari conclusio in qua praedicatur 'bonum' de prima causa vel de quocumque alio conceptu Dei ad quem philosophus potuit naturaliter devenire—possit probari in theologia et in aliqua scientia naturali." Idem, *Quodl.* V, q. 1, ad. inst. 1 [*OTh* IX, 479].

202. "Circa secundum dico primo quod Deus est causa omnium mediata vel immediata, licet hoc non possit demonstrari. Tamen hoc persuadeo auctoritate et ratione." Idem, *Quodl.* III, q. 4, a. 2, c. 1 [*OTh* IX, 215]. "Praeterea per rationem hoc probo primo sic: omnia dependent essentialiter a Deo; quod non esset verum nisi Deus esset causa illorum. Praeterea si non sic, tunc aliquid aliud a Deo esset incausatum, vel esset processus in infinitum in causis. Quia accipio aliquid quod non ponis causari a Deo, et quaero utrum sit causatum aut incausatum; si primo modo, igitur causatur ab aliquo; et de illo quaero, et erit processus in infinitum. Si detur secundum, habetur propositum, quia tale est Deus." Ibid. [OTh IX, 216].

203. "Ex illo sequitur quod aliquae veritates naturaliter notae sunt theologicae, ut 'Deus est bonus, vivens, sapiens, intelligens', quas etiam *Philosophus* demonstrat XII Metaphysicae. Et per hoc veritates illae pertinent tam ad metaphysicam quam ad theologiam. In metaphysica demonstrantur demonstratione quia, in theologia propter quid." Biel, *Prol.* q. 1, art. 1, nota 3, col. 1 (D) [vol. 1,13].

204. "... qui nunc from ist und gut werck hat, dem wird ers belohnen." WA 45:92.1.

attitude.[205] In the sermon, the contrast is achieved by answering the doxological question, "who has ever given [God] anything?" from the perspective
of the divine counsel in eternity. At this location where God is "by himself,"
God is not determined by a structure of payment.[206] There, the divine attribute of mercy is disclosed as the ground for the Father's decision to send
his Son, "that he was born, died for us ... without our merits."[207] By weaving the Genesis 1:26 passage into the doxological question of Romans 11:35,
Luther preaches on the divine counsel from the "inside-out," the divine
mercy shown in Christ's birth and death, for "us."

The Father's sermon shapes the way the divine wisdom is revealed at
this site. A convergence can be observed in Luther's portrayal of the particular way in which the Trinitarian essence is revealed at this site together
with the way in which the essence circumscribes a soteriological intention.
In order to underline the convergence, Luther strategically uses the same
word, "eternity," in two distinct places, each referring to the same content.
Luther explicitly refers to the generation of the Son from the Father "from
eternity" and to the divine cognition "from eternity" of Christ's incarnation.[208] By duplicating the term "from eternity" in the contexts of the Son's
eternal generation and of the inner-Trinitarian view of the incarnation,
Luther establishes a convergence in the Father's sermon between the Triune

---

205. "'Aut quis consiliarius eius docuit eum?' Iterum quaestio contra iusticiarios, qui
dicunt: Nos consiliarii eius, quia scio hanc regulam meam, cucullam meam illi placere, quia
ego elegi. Seyt uns Got wyll kummen. Difficile est illos iusticiarios confundere ideo copiosis
verbis, Quia ipsi volunt esse dii." WA 31,2:275.1-5 (Lectures on Isaiah, 1527–1530, to Isa 40:13).
For Luther, the efforts of natural reason to determine the divine attributes, and then to infer
what human actions are pleasing to God, mark the religions outside Christianity as well as
various groups within the boundaries of Christianity. With respect to the latter group,
Luther mentions in his sermon: the pope, the bishops as well as the robes, cowl, and rule of
the Franciscans. WA 45:92.17, 23, 25, 27–28; 93.3-4.

206. "... ubi solus bey im allein..." Ibid., 93.8. "Er darff niemand bezalen, quia nemo dedit
ei aliquid, quia nemo fuit." Ibid., 93.2-3.

207. Ibid., 92.16; 93.31. For Luther, the divine attribute of mercy is integrally connected
to the show of mercy, "sine meritis." Luther refers to the attribute of mercy later on in the
sermon. "Hanc mentem Dei nemo agnovit etc. sed ex mera misericordia fecit." Ibid., 92.19-20;
"... quod sic suam misericordiam effudit." Ibid., 93.11. The reason for showing mercy is the
divine essence of mercy itself. For an extended discussion of the divine mercy in the genre
of the hymn, see: ch. 3, "The Inner-Trinitarian Essence."

208. "Sed pater ab eterno genuit filium. Et illa divinitas habet istam cogitationem ab
eterno, quod filius sol die menscheit anziehen et venire et crucifigi et id propter peccata, ut
auferret ea et sanctificaret nos per spiritum sanctum." WA 45:92.10-13.

nature and the desire to save.[209] In the Father's sermon, the divine wisdom is disclosed in view of a double focus: Christ's eternal relation to the Father as his origin and the decision in eternity for Christ to redeem humanity from sin, death, and hell.[210] The convergence between the Trinitarian revelation and the inexpressible will to show mercy in Christ is also evident in other sermons Luther preached on the divine "abyss."[211] Yet the awe at this convergence surfaces explicitly in his sermon on Romans 11:33-36.[212] Luther wonders at the divine wisdom that discloses the way God desires to be known together with the divine will anticipating human salvation.

The Father's speech does not solely point to the Christological convergence at the inner Trinity. How the Father desires to be known is also an aspect to the divine wisdom. This knowledge is accessible through the distinct speech structure plotted at this site. When preaching his sermon, the Father reveals the Son both as his only Son and as the anticipated Savior of the world. The Father looks to his Son, not to himself. The Father also places the Spirit in relation to his speech. The speech reveals the word to be the Son, and the word situates the Spirit as its hearer. By directly revealing the persons of the Son and the Spirit in relation to his speech, the Father indirectly shows himself in light of the word. The Father shows himself in the way he desires to be known, as the Father of the Son and as the origin

---

209. "... sed in scriptura, quae dicit: deitas sint 3 personae et filius descenderit factus homo ex virgine et in humanitate gesserit omnia peccata et erwurget et sedeat ad dexteram, et si credam in eum, salver." Ibid., 92.29-31.

210. In referring to the incarnation, Luther emphasizes the divine intention to redeem humanity from sin, death, and hell. "... ut nos, sine peccato." Ibid., 91.13; "... ut redimat a peccato, morte, helle et ut daret suam vitam sine nostro merito," Ibid., 91.29-30; "... et venire et crucifigi et id propter peccata." Ibid., 92.12; "... et in humanitate gesserit omnia peccata et erwurget." Ibid., 92.30-31.

211. In the following two quotes from sermons, Luther preaches on the Christological center of the inner Trinity as the eternal love God has "for us" in eternity. Luther preaches on Phil 2:5-12. "Hie schleusst S. Paulus mit eym wort den hymel auff [the obedience of the Son to the Father] und reumet uns eyn, das wyr ynn den abgrund Go(e)ttlicher Maiestet sehen und schawen den unaussprechlichen gnedigen willen und liebe des veterlichen hertzen gegen uns, das wyr fulen, wie Gott von ewickeyt das gefallen habe, was Christus die herliche person fur uns sollte und nu gethan hat." WA 17,2:244.27-32 (Palm Sunday, Fastenpostille, 1525); "... denn da wurde es sehen ynn den abgrund des veterlichen hertzen, ja ynn die grundlose und ewige guete und liebe Gotts, die er zu uns tregt und von ewickeyt getragen hat." WA 20:229.13-15 (Epiphany afternoon, 1526, to Matt 3:17).

212. "Welcher ein tieffer reicher gedancken dei, quod sic suam misericordiam effudit, ut agnosceremus, quid cogitet, quid concluserit, et videamus eius cor per eius revelationem. Das ist ein reiche, tieffe, grundlose weisheit. 'Quis cognovit?'" WA 45:93.11-14.

of the will to save. At this inner-Trinitarian site, the speech structure privileges the Father as the source of revelation. The grammar provided by this structure of revelation will now be traced through subsequent sites in the narrative: in Christ's incarnation and then in the work of baptism.

THE SITES OF MUTUAL REVELATION

Until now, the Spirit's sermon and the Father's voice have been heard to reveal the inner Trinity. It is at this time that the narrative turns outward to how the outer Trinity also reveals God's essence. There are a number of sites at which this revelation takes place. Yet these sites have a distinctive narrative order—from baptism to cross, and then finally to the revelation of the Triune essence in the work of creation.

I begin with Christ's baptism, which provides the grammar for an implicit speech structure revealing the Trinity.

The first site of outer-Trinitarian revelation is narrated on a particular occasion. Luther praises the story of Christ's baptism in Matthew 3:13-17, the gospel text for the feast of Epiphany, to be the occasion for the "illustration and presentation" of the divine majesty in a most "sweet, comforting and friendly" way.[213] Heard by the Jordan River, the Father's voice structures the revelation of the three Trinitarian persons. The speech of the Father does not directly draw attention to himself, but reveals the beloved Son: "'THIS IS MY BELOVED SON, in whom I am well pleased.'"[214] "Listen to him."[215] By pointing to the Son in whom he is well pleased, the Father distinguishes himself from his Son. The Third Person of the Trinity is also

---

213. "Und erstlich sehen, das bey der Tauff CHRisti die Allmechtige, ewige Go(e)ttliche Maiestet selbs wunderbarlicher weise ist, Ja ist nicht allein darbey, sondern bildet sich hie in dreien unterscheidenen Personen sehr lieblich und tro(e)stlich, freundlich ab. ... Dieweil denn nu unser lieber Herrgott selbst darbey und mit ist und sich so scho(e)n, herrlich und lieblich in dreien Personen abbildet und darstellet." WA 51:110.17-20, 22-23 (Epiphany, 1546).

214. Ibid., 110.31-32. A similar passage is found in an Epiphany sermon (1541). "'Hic est filius meus dilectas'. Ibi vide revelatam lucem, in qua pater se offenbaret per vocem suam." WA 49:202.2-3.

215. "Ibi clarum, quod pater loquitur non de seipso, sed de filio: 'Hunc audite'." WA 46:433.13-14 (Trinity Sunday, 1538). The Father speaks the imperative at the transfiguration of Jesus in Matt 17:5. In the Major *disputatio*, the first thesis alludes to this biblical passage. "Disputationes de articulis fidei exstinctas voluit Deus pater, dum dicit de Deo filio suo: Hunc audite." WA 39,2:287.5-6 (Major, thesis 1).

revealed in the context of this "greatest sermon."[216] Appearing in the form of a dove, the Holy Spirit is revealed as the "greatest student and hearer" of the Father's speech.[217] Symmetry can be observed in many of Luther's sermons on Christ's baptism. At both the inner- and outer-Trinitarian sites, the Father's speech structures the way in which the other two persons are related to him. Using the metaphor of the sermon, Luther describes the Father as the preacher at both Trinitarian sites, preaching the Son as his sermon that is heard by the Spirit.[218] At both locations, the Father's voice is heard, pointing to the other two persons and assigning them their roles in relation to his speech. The only difference is that the imperative, "Listen to him," is addressed at the outer-Trinitarian site. Here, the Spirit hears the Father as well as all those present.

The Father's sermon is representative of a speech structure that Luther uses to develop his own Trinitarian hermeneutic. Luther understands the concept of "person" in relation to an exegetical principle founded on this type of Trinitarian revelation. Read according to this hermeneutic are biblical passages in which one divine person addresses another, such as the royal psalms, texts describing the divine counsel (Gen 1:26; John 1:1-4), or the pericope on Christ's baptism. Luther notices that in these passages, the speech of one person reveals another person, thereby distinguishing the speaker from the person spoken about. This observation is aptly summarized by the following excerpt from a sermon preached in 1538: "The forms are so completely different from one another, that one is the Father who speaks, the other the Son about whom the Father speaks, and the other the Holy Spirit who is in the form of a dove."[219] The revelation of God as a Trinity is grounded in this speech structure.[220] When one person

---

216. In one of his last sermons, Luther cannot find enough adjectives to praise the "highest" and "greatest" sermon: the Father's speech at the baptism of Christ. "So ist auch diese seine predigt die ho(e)chste predigt, und ist kein ho(e)here predigt nicht in die welt komen dan die." WA 51:110.37-38 (Epiphany, 1546).

217. "So ist auch der gro(e)ste Schuler und zuho(e)rer dieser Predigt der heilige Geist selbst, die dritte person Go(e)ttlicher Maiestet." Ibid., 111.1-3.

218. "Das sind je hohe Prediger, Predigt und zuho(e)rer und ko(e)nnen nicht gro(e)sser sein." Ibid., 111.3-4.

219. WA 46:433.11-13 (Trinity Sunday, 1538).

220. In Rörer's transcription of a 1544 sermon, Luther offers the exegetical rule for understanding the speech of one person to reveal the Trinity. "Dominus de alio etiam tertio loquitur, ut putes alium de alio loqui, qui non eins sind." WA 49:466.16-17 (Trinity Sunday, 1544).

speaks, the speech reveals the other two persons. Luther's exegetical insight into the Trinitarian constitution of divine speech is formed materially by the order of the relations; the order of speaking mirrors the order of the inner-Trinitarian relations. For example, when the Father speaks, he reveals the word to be his Son, and conversely the Father discloses himself to be the Son's origin. By situating the Spirit as the sermon's hearer, the Father points to the Spirit as the Third Person, who is related both to the Father and to the word. The Father's speech reveals both the Triune nature and determines the three persons as either subject, subject matter, or hearer of speech. It remains to be shown how Christ modifies the Father's speech structure.

After a long and gradual approach, Luther finally turns to Christ's outer-Trinitarian manifestation. In his sermon on Romans 11:33–36, Luther spends the greater part in preaching on the Spirit and the Father, who each point to the Christological center of the Triune relations. Even they preach on a subject matter that must ground all proclamation. As Luther says, "We preach nothing other than the Son of God."[221] In the middle of his own sermon, Luther takes leave of eternity in order to preach on the moment of Christ's incarnation: "Christ was made manifest in the flesh."[222] Compared to the preceding two sections on the Spirit and the Father, the few remarks that Luther devotes to Christ are uncharacteristically brief. In just a few lines, Luther brings his sermon to its apex by describing Christ's speech. It is of note that, at this site, the genre of the sermon appears, this time in Christ's mouth: "But see how Christ is born, preaches, and says 'Come to me' and dies."[223] This is Luther's brief summary of Christ's sermon that discloses the same content as the Father's speech in eternity. In the inner Trinity, the Father had revealed the Son by anticipating Christ's incarnation. At the outer Trinity, the bounds of the incarnation, birth, and death appear in Christ's sermon. The symmetry in content assures that the incarnate Christ is the same person as the one of whom the Father spoke. Recapitulated at its outer-Trinitarian site is the subject of the Father's sermon, the content of which is Christ himself.

---

221. WA 45:92.18–19.

222. Ibid., 93.16.

223. Ibid., 97.3–4.

The foundational structure of mutual revelation is reflected in Christ's speech. Christ's primary intention is to reveal not himself, but his Father. In his sermon, Luther achieves this aim by resorting to the language of love that appears together with the central theme of knowing God. In a conversation of love, Christ addresses his hearers. "Thus come with joy that you may know what God thinks. God the Father ... loves you because he loves me. There is no other way."[224] In this passage, Luther reworks the Father's address, spoken at Christ's baptism, into Christ's sermon. The Father's words to his beloved Son are now issued by Christ. To his hearers, Christ reveals the Father as the one who loves him. By referring Christ's speech to the Father, Luther marks this site with the stamp of mutual revelation common to the Trinitarian speech structure. There is, however, a unique characteristic. At this site, the Son's revelation of the Father is the occasion for speaking the *promissio* of love to his hearers. The Father's love for the Son is proclaimed to be so great that it includes those who hear. At this outer-Trinitarian site, Luther orients the Father's anticipation of salvation to its actualization. The exclusivity of the Father's inner-Trinitarian speech is inclusive at its outer-Trinitarian site. It is addressed to those gathered to hear. Luther concludes the short statement by asserting, "There is no other way." There is no other way to the Father's love except through the way by which God desires to be known in Christ.

Luther explicitly mentions the word "way" to alert his hearers to the theme in Romans 11:33–36. The way of Christ is disclosed as "the way he wants to be with us."[225] Similar to the rubrics of the Spirit and of the Father, the Christological site also represents the divine wisdom according to a convergence. The divine wisdom is revealed by Christ as the way in which the Trinitarian revelation proceeds at its outer-Trinitarian extreme. Christ's incarnation is the way by which God has chosen to reveal the knowledge of God's Triune essence. In addition, the revelatory site coincides with what has previously been located in the inner Trinity: the soteriological import of Christ's way with us—that is, through his death.

An intriguing speech structure represents the divine wisdom at the Christological site. Through a subtle narrated flow, Luther orients this

---

224. Ibid., 97.5–7.

225. Ibid., 93.19.

section of the sermon to Christ, who is brought to view. Luther begins by pointing to Christ. He intersperses the sermon with appeals, invitations, and pleas to go to the manger, the cross, the wounds of Christ. There, Luther persuades his hearers, where God is revealed "to you,"[226] "then you have him in whom all treasures are contained."[227] All the treasures of the divine wisdom are found in Christ, as Luther witnesses by referring Romans 11:33 explicitly to Christ. Once the focus is directed to this person, Luther locates a distinct speech in Christ's mouth. Citing John 14:6, Luther isolates the only way by which God can be found: "Therefore abide in him who says: 'I am the way', then you will learn who God is."[228] The word that has guided the entire sermon is recapitulated in a direct address. Christ speaks, "I am the way." The divine ways of Romans 11:33 are concentrated in a compact self-disclosure, taken from John 14:6. Christ reveals himself as the *promissio* of God.

Luther unfolds Christ's speech in such a way as to situate the *promissio* in a structure of mutual witness. The *promissio* is not limited to self-definition. Rather, Christ uses his address to direct his hearers to the Father. There, in Christ, "you will find God." With this short statement, Luther brings the sermon to its culmination. The speech structure captures the convergence characterizing the divine wisdom: the coincidence between the knowledge of God and the divine way. At the Christological site, the knowledge of the Father through the Son's witness appears together with the *promissio* as Christ's way "with us." The Father's inmost thoughts in eternity are actualized when Christ speaks.

Christ's *promissio* is, for Luther, intimately bound together with the narrative of his incarnation. For Luther, the theme of the divine wisdom in Christ captures the *promissio* together with the narrative extension of Christ's birth and death. In his sermon on Romans 11:33–36, a minimal mention is awarded to Christ's narrative. Luther mentions the terms "to be born" and "to die."[229] Birth and death summarize the bounds of Christ's

---

226. "Si vis in seinen heimlichen rat kriechen, so lasse deine cogitationes faren et vade in praesepi et in cruce cum vulneribus, quae tibi revelata." Ibid., 96.4–6; "Ideo halt dich der revelationis, quae gethan ist." Ibid., 96.10–11; "Ideo wil bleiben hie niden contentus revelatione, quae facta per Christum." Ibid., 96.11–12.

227. Ibid., 96.16.

228. Ibid., 97.8–9.

229. See 266n223.

incarnation to fill the content of the pivotal word, "way." God's way, located in the *promissio*, is defined in terms of the person of Christ, who comes to creation as a story that is told. Luther's homiletical gesture to the *promissio's* narrative embrace can be supplemented by what he defines in his Large Catechism to be the content of faith in Jesus Christ.[230] In the explanation to the second article of the Creed, Luther rehearses the stages on the way Christ accomplishes the redemption of human nature from captivity to sin, death, and devil. At each narrated site, Christ wins redemption "for you."[231] The description of each stage is reserved for sermons preached on the great feast days of the church year, as Luther notes.[232] Although the narrated content is kept to a minimum in his Romans sermon, Luther points to an insight he has worked out in his understanding of the confession of faith. In order to expose the Christological center of the divine wisdom, the narrative elements are coupled with the *promissio*. This link determines the divine wisdom as the revelation of the Trinitarian person that coincides with the soteriological intention of his life and death.

During his preaching, Luther incorporates his hearers into the speech structure by using the rhetorical strategy of feigned speech.[233] While Luther points to Christ, he can also speak in the person of Christ, who is heard to address the congregation. Luther's own sermon is performed as an inclusion into the site of the speech structure by which the divine wisdom is

---

230. Luther weaves the summary statement of the second article of the Creed into his sermon, "Credo in Iesum Christum." WA 45:91.9.

231. After describing at length the correlation between Christ as Lord and his work of redeeming human nature from sin, death, and devil, Luther concludes his explanation to the second article of the Creed in the Large Catechism by stating that the right knowledge of Christ is preached on particular feast days of the church year. Each feast day celebrates the sub-articles as stages of "my" redemption. "Aber diese eynzele stu(e)ck alle sonderlich auszustreichen geho(e)ret nicht ynn die kurtze kinderpredigt sondern ynn die grossen predigte uber das gantze iar, sonderlich auff die zeit zo dazu geordnet sind ein yglichen artickel ynn die lenge zuhandlen: von der gepurt, leiden, aufferstehen, hymelfart Christi etc." WA 30,1:187.10–14 (1529).

232. "Die stu(e)cke aber, so nacheinander ynn diesem artikel folgen, thuen nichts anders, denn das sie solche erlo(e)sung verkleren und ausdru(e)cken," Ibid., 186.32–33.

233. The rhetorical strategy of "feigned speech" creates the dialectical character of Luther's sermons. Mayr, "'Einfeldig zu predigen, ist eine große kunst,'" 97. The flexible use of pronouns is a mark of Luther's distinctive preaching style, as has been noticed by some Luther scholars. Bieritz states that the use of personal pronouns increases the sermon's intensity. Bieritz, "Verbum facit fidem," 483. Winkler writes that Luther's use of pronouns exposes the preacher's deep identification with his congregation. Winkler, "Impulse Luthers für die heutige Gemeindepraxis," 77.

revealed. When Christ is preached, hearers are taken up to view both aspects to the divine wisdom: the knowledge of the Father through Christ and the way of salvation that is the person of Christ. The *promissio* of the Father's own sermon, spoken in eternity, is actualized in time as the proclamation of salvation to those who believe in Christ. The understanding of Luther's sermon in terms of incorporation attempts to take seriously the narrative dimension of Christ's life to be constitutive of the *promissio* while also providing an account for the mutual speech structure of the sermon. Luther attributes the preached word to Christ while, at the same time, he speaks in the person of Christ in order to communicate salvation to his hearers. Complex in its narrative movement and sophisticated in its stress on knowledge, Luther's sermon preaches Christ in a way orienting the hearers to receive the power of the Triune God to raise the dead.

During the incorporation, minds are renewed. At the beginning of his sermon, Luther announces that only Christians speak rightly of the Trinitarian persons, thoughts, and works.[234] This claim is realized through the preaching. Luther refers to this realization at junctures in his own sermon. To know Christ is to acquire his mind, to think like God,[235] and to speak rightly in the Spirit. The new understanding is reflected in one's actions, as Luther remarks.[236] Through the incorporation into the *promissio*, thoughts, actions, and speech exhibit the effects of renewal. At this site, the revelation of the three Trinitarian persons and their particular ways of advent are complete. What remains is the revelation in the unity of the work that does not explicitly contain a subject of speech.

A final outer-Trinitarian site reveals the Trinity according to an implicit speech structure. If all created works are to be gradually regarded as sites of revelatory potential, as the Romans 11 text intends, then one work is to be represented as the grammar. This occasion, as Luther points out in other sermons on the Trinity, is the outer-Trinitarian work of baptism. In baptism, one person is not designated as a speaker who reveals another.

---

234. "Soli Christiani recte loquuntur de personis, cogitationibus et operibus, wie ers aussen machen cum creaturis, praesertim piis, quia audiunt ex revelatione spiritus sancti." WA 45:90.20–22.

235. "Non invenitur ratione, quid deo placeat, sed cogitandum, ut Christi mentem acquiratis." Ibid., 96.24–25.

236. "Crede in Christum, postea bene operare, mane cum uxore, liberis." Ibid., 97.14–15.

Rather, an implicit speech structure undergirds the mutual revelation taking place in the work accomplished by the unity of the essence. In a sermon on Pentecost, Luther discusses the baptism in the Spirit by locating the relevant biblical passages in the speech of both the Father and the Spirit. The Father reveals the Spirit by speaking, "I will pour [the Spirit] out upon all flesh [Acts 2:17, Joel 3:1]."[237] Conversely, the Spirit witnesses to its unity with the Father by claiming, "The Lord is one God."[238] At this site, the mutual revelation between the Father and the Spirit implicitly figures into the event of the Spirit's advent. In his notes to John 3, Luther speaks of baptism in a similar fashion. Luther shows how Christ and the Spirit witness to each other in a speech structure that is implicit when someone is baptized. Christ speaks, "And by the Spirit" to reveal the Spirit's presence in the water of baptism.[239] Conversely, the Spirit reveals the unity of the Trinity at work in baptism by pointing to Christ's command in Matthew 28:19 to baptize in the name of Father, Son, and Spirit.[240] Luther's understanding of baptism according to an implicit structure of mutual revelation is patterned by an explicit motif. The speech of one person attributes the work to another person, thereby revealing the presence of the other person in the work accomplished by all three. Baptism provides the grammar of reading the mutual Trinitarian revelation through the representative work of creating anew. In this light, the work is seen through the lens of the new creation that coincides with revelatory speech.

The three outer-Trinitarian sites unfold a narrative of Trinitarian revelation. The narrative extends from the event most symmetrical with the inner Trinity, the Father's witness at Christ's baptism, through the *promissio* spoken personally by Christ and then ending with the work of baptism.

---

237. WA 49:465.1 (Trinity Sunday, 1544).

238. Ibid., 466.7. In this text, Luther attributes the verb, "preaching," to the Spirit. "Et tum in eo sermone palam facit se pater distincte, sic filius, sic Spiritus sanctus: 'Effundam de Spiritu', qui praedicabit de Domino: Est unus Deus Dominus." Ibid., 466.5-7.

239. WA 45:447.14 (Conciunculae quaedam D. Mart. Lutheri amico cuidam praescriptae, 1537). Christ reveals the Spirit's work: "... sed spiritu coniuncto et cooperante eduntur filii regni caelorum." Ibid., 447.16. In a Trinity Sunday sermon, the same point is made. "Sed quando secundum Christi institutionem baptiso, Ibi in et cum aqua spiritus sanctus et ex illa aqua et spiritu sancto fit novus homo." WA 37:417.18-20 (1534).

240. "Quia spiritus cum aqua iungi non potest nisi per verbum hominis a Christo traditum ... Hoc medium autem est praeceptum illud verbum a Christo: 'Ite', baptisate in nomine Patris et Filii' etc." WA 45:447.18-19, 23-25 (Conciunculae, 1537).

At each site, a common speech structure is seen to determine the divine wisdom (Rom 11:33). Representing a convergence between the knowledge of the Triune God and the way that God is "with us," the divine wisdom is revealed through a structure in which one person reveals another and, by so doing, points to the way in which that person is "with us." At each site, hearers are progressively incorporated into the speech in order that they might know how God desires to be known, as the Triune God. As they are incorporated into this knowledge, the hearers experience the way each of the three persons contributes to the soteriological effect of the God "with us." The symmetry between the sites is achieved by the Christological center. The differences are explained by the distinctions between persons as subjects of speech. To review, the Father's address at Christ's baptism reveals his Son. In his own speech, Christ reveals the Father. Although implicit in baptism, the speech structure provides the grammar for reading the Trinitarian revelation together with the explicit work of creating anew. By plotting distinct structures at various points in the narrative, Luther aims to show that Christians know not only the inner side of God but also the outer-Trinitarian essence revealed in all of creation. It is to this final theme that the entire narrative is oriented. The eschatological dimension to revelation, however, cannot be studied without first looking at the danger posed to the revelatory word. The narrative's other side surfaces with the issue of the hidden God (*deus absconditus*).

THE HIDDEN GOD (*DEUS ABSCONDITUS*) IN THE
NARRATIVE OF TRINITARIAN REVELATION

In the Christological section of the sermon, Luther addresses an issue that has intrigued and horrified scholars studying Luther's concept of God. Woven into this section is a contrast between Christ and a theme commonly referred to by Luther scholars as the hidden God (*deus absconditus*). Regarded as a crucial element in Luther's understanding of God, the divine hiddenness has emerged in the history of Luther interpretation as the subject matter of theological fascination and philosophical study, particularly in the trajectory of Böhme, Hegel, and Schelling.[241] It is not surprising that

---

241. Rudolf Köhler, "Der Deus Absconditus in Philosophie und Theologie," 47. The theme of the *deus absconditus* in Luther's theology strikes at the heart of Luther's understanding of God. Dillenberger classifies interpretations of Luther according to various degrees of divine

a significant part of Luther's sermon, devoted to the theme of the incomprehensible ways of God, includes the rejection of speculation on what has not been revealed. The same text on which the sermon is based, Romans 11:33–36, crops up in *The Bondage of the Will* when Luther discusses the incomprehensibility of the divine judgment concerning reprobation.[242] In his sermon, Luther uses the terms "divine Majesty" and "essence" to refer to the Trinitarian essence. These same terms surface when Luther discusses the divine hiddenness in his famous theological treatise.[243] In the following section, I will show how Luther draws the distinction between "right speculation" on the inner Trinity and a type of speculation that incites the divine anger.

In order to adequately determine what Luther might mean by the "hidden God," the context must be clarified. The sermon to this point orients the incomprehensibility of the divine wisdom (Rom 11:33) to Christ.

---

hiddenness. In the Ritschlian trajectory, the divine attribute of love is privileged, and a version of the *deus absconditus* is dismissed as a vestige of nominalism. Three other types of interpretation are developed. Expounded by Emanuel Hirsch is the hiddenness of God behind history. Erich Seeberg's "metaphysics of opposites" concerns the divine revelation in its antithesis. Both Althaus and Elert refer the *theologia crucis* to the hiddenness of God in Christ's death. See: John Dillenberger, *God Hidden and Revealed*, 1–69. A monograph thematizing Luther's concept of the *deus absconditus* at the various sites of the cross, the divine counsel, and history is Bandt's dissertation. See: Helmut Bandt, *Luthers Lehre vom verborgenen Gott*. In an article, Geißer argues that the divine hiddenness is structured by two poles. At one pole, God is not hidden in the sense of a transcendent reality, but is hidden as a continuous transcendence in the work of creating. The second pole is the divine hiddenness on the cross. Hans Friedrich Geißer, "Zur Hermeneutik der Verborgenheit Gottes," 164.

242. Luther uses Rom 11:33 to debate Erasmus on the point of the incomprehensibility of the divine judgments. In the sermon, the incomprehensibility of the divine nature is subsumed under the rubric of the ways in which the divine counsel has decided to reveal the essence of mercy in Christ. In the theological treatise, "De servo arbitrio," Luther cites Rom 11:33 in the context of God's omnipotence and its relation to the will of the ungodly. "Reliqua igitur sunt, ut quaerat quispiam, cur Deus non cesset ab ipso motu omnipotentiae, quo voluntas impiorum movetur, ut pergat mala esse et peior fieri? ... Hoc pertinet ad secreta maiestatis, ubi incomprehensibilia sunt iudicia eius. Nec nostrum hoc est quaerere, sed adorare mysteria haec." WA 18:712.19–22, 25–26. At the end of the treatise, Luther cites Rom 11:33 in the context of comparing human justice with the incomprehensible justice of God. Luther begins with the premise that God justifies the ungodly and then asks why some of the ungodly are not justified. "At cum sit Deus verus et unus, deinde totus incomprehensibilis et inaccessibilis humana ratione, par est, imo neccessarium est, ut et iustitia sua sit incomprehensibilis, Sicut Paulus quoque exclamat dicens: O altitudo divitiarum sapientiae et scientiae Dei; quam incomprehensibilia sunt iudicia eius et investigabiles viae eius." Ibid., 784.11–15.

243. In the sermon, the term "Majesty" refers to the "intus 3 personae" (WA 45:93.15), whereas in "De servo arbitrio," the term refers to the extreme hiddenness of God. See: footnote 49.

In the tradition following Lombard, however, the text is also cited in the context of God's predestining will.[244] Early in the sermon, Luther shies away from preaching on predestination: "the text does not lead us to predestination, as it is interpreted."[245] Luther's intention is to preach on the Christological center of both the inner and the outer Trinity. A subject matter that extends beyond the boundary established by revelation is initially erased from view.

In the sermon held a week later, Luther's focus changes slightly. Luther discusses two groups in view of Christ's revelation. The distinction he draws between the groups serves to clearly assign the theme of divine hiddenness to one location. For the first group, Luther contrasts the revelation of the divine will with the efforts of natural reason to determine the divine nature.[246] This first position rehearses, under the Christological section, the same controversy we have encountered under the Holy Spirit. Luther rejects the position of those people who strive to counsel God by determining what is pleasing to God from the "outside-in."

The second group consists of another set of hearers. Luther defines this group by referring to persons commonly mentioned in medieval discussions of predestination and divine foreknowledge. For Luther, the examples of Paul's agony in Romans 9–11 over the reprobation of the Jews and the salvation of the Gentiles, as well as the rejection of Judas and the acceptance of Peter, touch the heart of the issue concerning the incomprehensible judgments of God: why God rejects saints and forgives sinners.[247] Luther's

244. In *Sent.* I, d. 40-41 [284-93], Lombard discusses God's plan for justification with respect to the election of the saints and the reprobation of sinners.

245. WA 45:92.34-35.

246. "Das heist unserm herr Gott furmalen, was er im sol gefallen lassen." Ibid., 95.21-22.

247. "Sicut Paulus hoc einfu(e)ret nach dem hohen verstand, quare Juden gestrafft et gentes angenomen, reiicit Sanctos et accipit peccatores, Iudam deserit et Petrum suscepit." Ibid., 96.2-4. The issue appears in the Palladius *disputatio* of 1537 in the context of discussing justification by works. In an argument, Luther appeals to the examples of Judas and Peter to show that, although both were contrite, only one was justified. Luther concludes that humans are justified, not by the law, but by grace. "Non est hic quaestio, quid requiratur, sed quid iustificet coram Deo. Exemplum de Iuda et Petro. Iudas et Petrus uterque contritus adfuit, sed non uterque iustificatus est. Neutrum Deus iustificavit per opera legis. Si lex iustificaret, tam Iudam quam Petrum iustificasset, quia uterque sensit legem et vim legis, maximissime autem Iudas, qui tamen damnatus est." WA 39,1:210.4-12 (witness A). McCord Adams discusses the example of Peter in Ockham's view regarding future contingent propositions and God's infallible foreknowledge of future contingents. See: William Ockham, *Predestination, God's Foreknowledge, and Future Contingents*, 9-12, 15-16. Oberman states that the examples of Judas

use of classic examples points out a characteristic common to this group. To those who have heard the revelation of the Trinity's Christological center is presented the temptation to refuse to acknowledge this way of God in Christ. These people are tempted to climb above the revelation and search out the divine ways that have not been revealed.[248] Luther mentions the danger and swiftly turns to its source.

The most extreme antithesis to Christ lies at the temptation's root. Luther explicitly names the angel who fell from grace: "It is the greatest temptation of the devil to lead people away from the way revealed to them."[249] Luther gives the original example of Satan, who, using his own wisdom, inquired into the depths of the divine majesty and fell into the abyss.[250] Satan attempted to search those aspects of God that "were not to be known."[251] In his sermon, Luther alludes to Satan in the context of a passage that he interprets in his Isaiah commentary (1527-1530) to refer to the Babylonian king.[252] Isaiah 14:12-13 (see also Luke 10:18; Rev 12:9) speaks of

---

and Peter were common in medieval discussions of divine foreknowledge and predestination. Oberman, *Spätscholastik und Reformation*, 199.

248. "3. [the third group] sunt Christiani, qui wollen hinuber uber diese offenbarung et volunt iudicia ergreiffen und wege erforschen, quas non revelavit." WA 45:95.29-31. The object of the *exhortatio* are the Christians who have already been given the revelation. "Prius dixi ex revelatione aliquo modo nos scire, quae iudiciae et viae." Ibid., 95.31-32.

249. Ibid., 96.20-21.

250. "Sicut Satan suam sapientiam, quid deus sit, ideo in abgrund." Ibid., 96, 9-10.

251. Ibid., 96.28-29. Similar to: "… et volunt iudica ergreiffen und wege erforschen, quas non revelavit." Ibid., 95.30-31.

252. "Illi dicunt cum Lucifero: 'Ascendam'." Ibid., 96.30-31. In the Isaiah commentary of 1527-1530, Luther determines the subject of the verb, "to fall," in Isa 14:12 to be, not Lucifer, but the Babylonian king. "'Quomodo cecidisti de celo, Lucifer.' Haec non sunt dicta de angelo prius deiecto e celo, sed de rege Babylonis, et est figurata loquucio." WA 31,2:99.34-35. The metaphor "to ascend into heaven" is frequently used by Luther to refer to the demonic attack against God or the demonic striving to be like God. The metaphor is taken from Isa 14:14. "'De celo' i. e. altissimo imperii. 'In terram' i.e. in imum. Voluisti deum nostrum conculcare, id quod est Ascendere super nubes et celos, quorum ipse dominus est." Ibid., 100.5-7. Those who attempt to ascend into heaven, striving to be like God, will perish. See: Ibid., 101.1-3. In "De servo arbitrio," Luther refers to 2 Thess 2:4 in order to illustrate the demonic attack against God. The antichrist attempts to rise above the divine word and encounters the God who is not preached: God in his nature and majesty. "Hic enim vere valet illud: Quae supra nos, nihil ad nos. Et ne meam hanc esse distinctionem quis arbitretur, Paulum sequor, qui ad Thessalonicenses de Antichristo scribit, quod sit exaltaturus esse super omnem Deum praedicatum et cultum, manifeste significans, aliquem posse extolli supra Deum, quatenus est praedicatus et cultus, id est, supra verbum et cultum quo Deus nobis cognitus est et nobiscum habet commercium, sed supra Deum non cultum nec praedicatum, ut est in sua natura et maiestate, nihil potest extolli, sed omnia sunt sub potenti manu eius." WA 18:685.6-14.

the king who attempts to storm heaven, only to fall from it. What Luther insists to be the demonic threat is the forcing of the separation of God from God's revealed way. The revolt could entail the question of personal salvation, as Luther remarks, but the revolt seems more to be associated with the larger aspect of the demonic attack against revelation.[253] If the pronouncement "there is no other way"[254] exhausts all the divine treasures, then, for Luther, there is no other way by which God can be known.

The intensity in this section is created by its rhetorical form. Luther regards the temptation to pose a serious threat to his hearers. Even Christ, Luther speaks, was not immune to the devil's attack on the pinnacle of the temple (Matt 4:5).[255] In order to address the imminent danger, Luther directly warns his congregation. An exhortation, not a disputation, appears as the form in which the contrast between Christ and antichrist is achieved.[256] Luther exhorts his hearers to stay away from the devil, who attempted to speculate on the way in which God is "with you" apart from the Trinitarian revelation.[257] He warns his congregation not to climb the "ladder" with the intention to search what has not been revealed.[258] The result, illustrated by Adam and Eve's example, is fatal:[259] the breaking of one's neck or being hit by lightning.[260] When Luther preaches that there is

253. Only once in this section does Luther explicitly refer to the issue of climbing above the revelation and inquiring into the question of one's salvation. "Ibi Satan iubet tales hoher steigen, quam deus wil haben, ut forschen, an sint versehen, obs selig sollen werden, und faren ex revelatione, quam deus revelavit, in alia somnia, quae non revelavit." WA 45:95.32–96.1.

254. Ibid., 97.6–7.

255. "Christus in pinnam, et Paulus in solch gedancken gefuret, Da wissen wenig leute von." Ibid., 96.19–20.

256. Luther defines preaching as a combination of *doctrina* and *exhortatio*. See 226n67. Both types of speech shape the subject matter in distinct ways. The function of *doctrina* is to teach; the rhetorical strategy of the *exhortatio* aims to persuade. Clear boundaries between these two types of speech are, only in the rarest cases, drawn. Mayr, "'Einfeldig zu predigen, ist eine große kunst,'" 95.

257. "Si vero gehest den holtzweg et specularis, quomodo deus tecum und magst eigen bru(e)cke, sequeris satanam et rues cum ipso." WA 45:97.7–8. "Si autem quaeris, quare deus hoc faciat etc. tum wird dich der Teufel fu(e)ren auff die hohe, de quo praecipitatus ipse." Ibid., 96.17–18.

258. "Econtra prohibet, ut non steigen in die hohe extra leyter et revelationem in ea, quae non revelata." Ibid., 96.26–27.

259. "Sic Adam et Eva. ..." Ibid., 96.29.

260. "Si extra Christum per tuas cogitationes vis scire, quomodo deus tecum mit dir, so brichstu den hals. Qui scrutatur, den schlecht der donner." Ibid., 96.7–9.

an aspect to God that God desires to remain hidden, he is not referring to a remainder that is held back in the revelation of the Christological center of salvation.[261] Uttered in the context of the doxology in Romans 11:33-36, Luther's insistence on the danger is not intended to compromise the entire revelation in Christ. Rather, Luther recognizes the temptation for those who have heard the word to disobey it, like Satan, who attempted to build his own bridge to heaven.

The exhortation does not only address illegitimate speculation on the divine way "with you." For Luther, the demonic attack poses a continuous challenge to the knowledge of God. In other sermons on the Trinity, Luther traces the church's history as the defense of the Trinitarian article. The writing of the New Testament, particularly John's Gospel, is a defense of Christ's divinity against Cerinth's challenge.[262] From Genesis 3:1 to Revelation 17:14, Scripture narrates the story of the devil's disputation with God's word.[263] The church fathers—primarily Alexander of Alexandria, Augustine, and Hilary—defend the divinity of Christ and the Spirit against those who dispute the chief article of the church, such as the Arians and the Macedonians,[264] Sabellius,[265] and Paul of Samosata.[266] The defense is accompanied by miraculous signs: Arius's untimely death[267]

---

261. Luther refers to members in group three, who desire to see what they assume God to have kept hidden from them. "... quid faciat in corde, da ers verborgen wil haben." Ibid., 96.30.

262. "Das also dieser Artickel von der Apostel und veter zeit bis auff diesen heutigen tag stets ist angefochten worden, wie denn die historien zeugen und sonderlich das Euangelion S. Johannis, welchs S. Johannes allein zur bekrefftigung dieses artickels hat schreiben mu(e)ssen wider Cherinthum den ketzer." WA 41:270.28-32 (Trinity Sunday, 1535).

263. "In Apocalypsi Agnus. 1. necesse est ante omnia, ut claudatur ratio et nemo trachte nach dem artikel. Nam heretici habens wollen ermessen, wies muglich sey. Sic Satan proponit verbum dei alicui et quaerit: wie reimt sichs? ... Sic gedacht sie [Eva] der sache nach et volebat de eo disputare. Statim successit ei." WA 34,1:500.1-4, 6-7 (Trinity Sunday, 1531).

264. WA 27:187.4 (Trinity Sunday, 1528).

265. WA 46:531.16 (Predigt am Sonntag nach Weihnachten, Dec. 29, 1538).

266. Ibid., 533.11.

267. Luther preaches on the fatal outcome in Arius' controversy with Alexander, Bishop of Alexandria. On the day when Alexander must either embrace Arius or lose his bishop's office, the fateful event occurs. Arius walks to the meeting with all pomp and circumstance. "Als nu die pompa auff der gassen verzeuhet und nach jm harrete, kompt botschafft, wie er auff dem gemache gestorben, und lung und leber von jm weg sey gangen, das es die historia billich heisst mortem dignam blasphema et foetida mente." WA 41:279.18-21 (Trinity Sunday, 1535).

and Cerinth's drowning in the bath.[268] Luther sees Scripture, the Creed, and the theological tradition of their interpretation in terms of God's defense of the Trinitarian article against both the devil and the "world."[269] The polemic in these texts seems to dovetail with the exhortation in the Romans 11 sermon. Directed against those who have already heard God's word, Luther's charge combines the element of wrong speculation with the erosion of the Trinitarian article. Luther connects the attempt to separate God from the way revealed to be "with you" with the denial of the Triune essence. Against the two-headed spear of the demonic attack, God rises up in defense. The aspect of God that arises is, as Jüngel has shown, the place where God has not defined himself in his word.[270] It is the God who encounters the devil as enemy.

In order to avoid generalizing the theme of divine hiddenness as a static element in Luther's doctrine of God, it is imperative to closely observe the context in which Luther brings this topic to the fore. The theme of divine hiddenness is properly assigned a site in relation to revelation. Luther's entire sermon is structured by the context of the knowledge of God and its convergence with the *promissio.* For Luther, the divine hiddenness cannot be understood to compromise any aspect to the divine revelation. Yet he assigns a site to that divine aspect that remains hidden, only to reveal itself to be at enmity with those who challenge God directly. For Luther, even the seeming hiddenness is determined by the context of revelation. The context is also suggested by the form in which these statements take place. Luther uses the exhortation to warn those who hear the revelation not to

---

268. "Wie sie nu itzt aus dem bade gangen waren, fellet die bade stuben ein und erschlegt Cherinthum mit seinem anhang, das nicht einer davon kame." Ibid., 278.25-27.

269. "Darumb hat Gott also druber gehalten, das der Artikel allein durchs wort erhalten ist und so bestetigt, das alle Teuffel und wellt, ob sie jn wol redlich angefochten, dennoch haben mu(e)ssen lassen stehen und bleiben jnn der Christenheit." WA 37:41.25-28 (Torgau, 1533).

270. Jüngel interprets the theme of the *deus absconditus* in terms of the demonic attack. The "tum" in "Neque enim tum verbo suo definivit sese, sed liberum sese reservavit super omnia" (WA 18:685.23-24), often omitted in citations, states specifically the location at which God has not defined himself. "Der Sinn ist vielmehr: der verborgene Gott hat sich *in der Verborgenheit* seiner *Majestät* (tum) nicht definiert. ... In seinem Wort hingegen, das ist die Prämisse der Formulierung Luthers, hat Gott sich definiert." Jüngel, "Quae supra nos, nihil ad nos: Eine Kurzformel der Lehre vom verborgenen Gott—im Anschluß an Luther interpretiert," 230. "Wer danach trachtet, muß Gott zum Feind haben, weil er sich zum Feind Gottes *macht.*" Ibid., 240. [Italics in original text.] Luther's invitation to rightly speculate on the Trinitarian mystery has nothing to do with his understanding of that aspect of God encountering the devil as his enemy.

heed the devil's whisper. The temptation of disobedient denial is presented to those who already know God. To these hearers, Luther directs an entire sermon that focuses on proclaiming all what is needed to know concerning the divine way and its judgments.[271] The incomprehensible divine essence presents enough of God to study in this life and in the eternal sight of the Trinity that the angels now enjoy.[272] In preaching on the Father's eternal love for the Son, Luther reveals God according to the divine desire and the divine pleasure that is announced to those who dwell in that revelation.

THE INNER AND OUTER TRINITY: CONCLUSION

Luther's sermon traces a narrative of Trinitarian revelation that casts the theme of Romans 1:18-20, the revelation of the divine essence in creation, from the perspective of Romans 11:33-36. The deep riches of both the divine knowledge and wisdom set the doxological stage for Luther's preaching on God's desire to be known as the Triune God through the ways the divine counsel has, at a location in eternity, decided to be "with us." This revelation proceeds through various structures of mutual revelation. At each narrative site, a speech structure exhibits both a Trinitarian person as the subject of a speech and the speech's content as the *promissio* of salvation. Through speech, one person is revealed indirectly by pointing to another directly. By mutual revelation, the triune essence is shown to converge with its soteriological motivation.

The various sites unfolded according to a narrative from the inner to the outer Trinity. After the Spirit's revelation of the inner Trinity to the church, the Father reveals the Christological center of the inner Trinity by preaching an eternal sermon. The Father points to his Son as the person who will accomplish the salvation of those who believe in him. Outer-Trinitarian sites determine the actualization of the eternal sermon in time. Christ's baptism reveals the symmetry between the inner and the outer Trinity by a structure that duplicates the inner-Trinitarian speech of the Father. As the incarnate Son, Christ speaks the *promissio* in such a way as

---

271. "Loquitur ergo de doctrinae via, iudiciorum, quae nemo novit, sed tamen revelata." WA 45:96.31-32.

272. "Da hastu gnug zustudieren. Petrus: Angeli haben lust dran, quod nobis revelatum, quod dei filius homo factus etc. et tamen angeli sehen sich selig dran und eitel freude und wonne dran [1 Pet 1:12]." Ibid., 96.12-15.

to extend its soteriological content into the narrative of his life and death. The baptismal rite is understood according to an implicit speech structure that provides the grammar for reading the revelation of the Triune essence in a representative work of creating anew. Finally, I have described these sites in terms of an incorporation: hearers are incorporated into the sermon's speech structures as they grow in the knowledge of the Trinity and of the Trinitarian ways of God "with us" as well as in the right speech about what they have come to know. Luther's exhortation is contrasted with the sermon's focus on Christ. He prohibits his hearers from wrongly speculating on the subject matter of his sermon, the right knowledge of the Triune God and the divine works. The discussion in this section ends where the sermon began. Implied by Romans 1:19–20, the question of the "people" (*gentes*) concerns the inference from the works in creation to the divine essence. From the site of baptism, a preliminary answer has been given. The implicit speech structure reveals all three persons in the unity of a work in creation. Not yet fully answered is the question of how the Trinitarian essence is revealed in all the created works if it encounters creation in the unity of its essence. It is the theme of creation's glorification of the Triune God with which Luther concludes his sermon.

THE GLORIFICATION OF THE
TRIUNE GOD IN CREATION

The final site of the narrative of Trinitarian revelation, and the final section of this chapter, is oriented to the exegetical configuration marked at the very beginning of Luther's sermon. Throughout the sermon, the exegetical direction of interpreting Romans 1:18–20 from the perspective of Romans 11:33–36 has moved the sermon along sites, plotting the particular viewpoints of the Trinity. The final outer-Trinitarian site focuses on Romans 1:20: the revelation of the "eternal power and divinity" in the works of creation. At the end of the second part to his sermon, Luther finally addresses the controversial passage. From the "inside-out," he gives an answer to how the "people" (*gentes*) can legitimately infer the traces in creation to reflect Trinitarian glory. The question to be answered in this section concerns the outermost site of Trinitarian revelation. How is the inner-Trinitarian essence revealed in the created works that it accomplishes through the unity of its essence? The answer will be offered in two parts. I will look first at how Luther locates the attribute "to create" in the inner Trinity and how he then draws the distinction between Creator and creature. In the second part, I will show that the Creator-creature distinction grounds Luther's understanding of the Trinitarian traces in creation that are articulated by the prepositions "from, through, in" in Romans 11:36. Luther's sermon ends with a vision of the convergence between the Trinitarian revelation in creation and the blessed sight of the three persons in the one essence.

THE TRINITARIAN STRUCTURE OF REVELATION IN CREATION

In order to determine how the Trinity is revealed in creation, Luther begins where he has begun before. As was the case with the inner-Trinitarian decision to redeem, so too does he now privilege the inner-Trinitarian revelation in the decision to create. If the traces in creation are to be understood as the bearers of Trinitarian revelation, then Luther must first secure the knowledge that creation is, in fact, an extension of the divine will in eternity. This knowledge is not self-evident, as the controversy with the "people" (*gentes*) has pointed out. The revelation of the Triune God from the "inside-out" must also include the knowledge that this God is the creator of all that exists. In his commentary on John (1532), Luther locates this knowledge in the inner Trinity. He isolates a site in eternity as far back as Genesis 1, Psalm 33, and John 1:1 permit, which the Holy Spirit reveals to Moses, David, and John, who could not have witnessed the scene.[273] At this location in eternity, the Father speaks, and his speech adds another determination to the word; the Father decides to create heaven and earth.[274] Luther receives the Johannine model of the inner-Trinitarian self-conversation in order to show the convergence between the word's generation and the decision to create.

---

273. "... sondern dem heiligen Geist gleuben, der durch Mosen und Joannem geredet hat, das Gott ein Wort bey sich selber habe ausser aller Creatur." WA 46:547.13–15 (Commentary on John 1–2 in sermons of 1537 and 1538, to John 1:1–3). "... zwar die Propheten, und sonderlich David Psalm 33. [Ps 33:6] habens auch geru(e)ret, aber nicht so klar und deutlich wie Moses." Ibid., 547.9–11.

274. "Also hat Gott auch in ewigkeit in seiner Maiestet und Go(e)ttlichem wesen ein wort, rede, gespreche oder gedancken in seinem Go(e)ttlichen Hertzen mit sich selber. ... dadurch GOTT geschlossen hat Himel und Erden zu schaffen [Gen 1:1–3]." Ibid., 544.3–5, 6–7.

A difficulty is presented by Luther's turn to the inner Trinity. Already located there by the narrative of revelation is the Christological center that converges with the divine will to redeem. If the eternal word is already occupied with the decision to redeem, how does Luther relate it to the decision to create? The answer to this question points to a central moment in Luther's Trinitarian understanding. Luther resists speculation on this point. He does not allocate the two decisions to two temporally disjunct points in the Son's eternal generation.[275] Rather, a distinction is established by an overlay motif. In the sermon on John 1, Luther preaches that "no one knew of the will to create until the word became flesh."[276] Without the incarnation, the will to create remained hidden; the decision to redeem is overlaid with the decision to create. The primary intention of the overlay rubric is to privilege the inner-Trinitarian revelation from the perspective of the Son's incarnation and death. Creation, in and of itself, does not convey the revelatory potential of the inner-Trinitarian distinctions without the prior revelation of the Son. Luther privileges the soteriological significance of the Trinitarian revelation while also insisting that the divine will to create is part and parcel of the eternal good pleasure. Both decisions are regarded as the content of the Father's speech that reveals the Son, in whom the salvation of humankind is accomplished and through whom all things were made.

If the decision to create is located in the eternal will and bound together with the Son's generation, then an account must be given for the way each person is related to the attribute "to create." Luther describes this relation by reviewing the Trinitarian manifestations in creation. In a brief statement, Luther distinguishes between the three persons and their particular appearances in creation: "God created heaven and earth, the Son was made human, the Holy Spirit appeared in the form of a dove."[277] From this sentence, the premature conclusion can be drawn that Luther locates the

---

275. A matter for further study could be to compare Luther's resistance to speculation on this point with the position of Duns Scotus.

276. "Aber von solchem willen GOTTES hat nie kein Mensch gewust, bis so lange dasselbige Wort fleisch wird, und verku(e)ndiget uns, wie hernach folget: 'der Son, der im Schos des Vaters ist, hats uns offenbaret [John 1:18]'." WA 46:544.7-10. The movement in this sermon on John follows the same movement as Luther's sermon on Rom 11:33-36. Luther preaches on the Trinity's Christological center first in terms of redemption and then in terms of creation.

277. WA 45:91.15-16.

Trinitarian distinctions at the outer Trinity. On closer look, the statement explicitly joins the Second Person to the incarnation. Even a statement thematizing the outer Trinity shows a consistent privileging of the Trinitarian revelation from the perspective of the incarnation. In this remark, the attribute "to create" is predicated of God in a way differing from the Son's personal characteristic, "was made human." The difference becomes explicit later in the sermon, when Luther distributes "to create" to both Christ and the Spirit. Luther preaches, "Christ created heaven and earth ... the dove created heaven and earth."[278] Luther can predicate the same attribute to Christ and the Spirit while also predicating it of God. In his explanation to the first article of the Creed, Luther specifies that the article on the Father sheds light on creation.[279] While the noun might appear to point to the Father's special work, other statements, such as the one found in his sermon, show how Luther can distribute the same attribute to all three persons. The logic of the *totus* and *solus*, discussed in chapter two, explains that an attribute, predicated of each person but not to the exclusion of the others, is an essence attribute.[280] Luther is not content with preaching on the logic of Trinitarian predication. He returns to the Romans text and translates the logic into a doxology.

The doxological part of the sermon begins with a distinction that makes no mention of the Trinity. Luther concentrates on the first preposition appearing in Romans 11:36, "from him."[281] For Luther, the one preposition is sufficient to explain that "God has created all things and from him come all things."[282] It refers to the entire divine nature and not to one particular

---

278. "Christus fecit celum et terram, infans etc. Columba descendit et cum brausen descendit in die pentecostes, qui creavit celum et terram." Ibid., 91.19-21. Schwarz has shown that Luther follows both Ockham and Biel, who predicate divine attributes of the divine person carrying human nature in a supposital union. See: Reinhard Schwarz, "Gott ist Mensch," 319.

279. WA 30,1:183.5.

280. See: ch. 2, "The Logic of the *Totus* and *Solus*."

281. WA 45:94.2.

282. Ibid., 94.5. The entire sentence reads, "'Von im' etc. dicit Paulus. Es were gar sat und gnug geredt, si dixisset: Ex ipso omnia, quia tantum dixisset, quod nulla creatura a seipso, sed quod suam originem per deum, et per hoc satis dictum de creatione, quod deus omnia crearit et ab ipso veniant omnia." Ibid., 94.2-5. In another Trinitarian sermon, Luther preaches that it is the nature of the Triune God to create and to make alive. "Ista opera urgent, quod tres unterschieden personen, ein einiger Gott sey, quia scriptura sancta dicit, quod unicus sit creator, vivificator." WA 46:437.16-18 (Trinity Sunday, 1538).

person. By appealing to this preposition, Luther points to a crucial distinction between God and all creatures. All creatures are defined as owing their existence to God; no created entity has its nature from itself. Conversely, God is the one who creates all things. The preposition "from" points out the difference between that which proceeds from God, and God. This distinction is most difficult to draw, as Luther preaches in another Trinitarian sermon. It is an "art above all art."[283] In the Romans sermon, Luther curiously says that this knowledge is sufficient.[284] A few moments later, Luther qualifies this statement, asserting that not only has God created all things, but that God has revealed the Triune essence.[285] The distinction between Creator and creature serves to establish the work of creation in an outer-Trinitarian symmetry with the inner Trinity's decision to create. The preposition "from" suffices to show the unity of the essence in the created works, because it connotes the difference between Creator and creature. What remains to be thematized is how the Trinitarian essence is revealed in creation. Luther will respond to the controversy with the "people" (*gentes*; Rom 1:18-20) by turning to the full doxology in Romans 11:36.

DOXOLOGY AS ESCHATOLOGICAL IMPULSE

The final section of Luther's sermon contains some of Luther's most poignant passages on God's desire to be known as triune Creator by all creatures. Luther pauses initially at the word "from" (*von*; Rom 11:36a). The preposition suffices to define the Creator as the one who creates through the unity of the divine essence. Luther's focus on the Trinity drives the sermon to its conclusion. He is intent on answering the question of how all created works can reflect the Trinitarian glory. The answer is given by the complete doxology in Romans 11:36.

Luther reads the remaining prepositions in Romans 11:36 to denote the Trinitarian distinctions. The divine essence that creates all things is differentiated by the three prepositions. Luther preaches, "But [Paul] does not merely say 'from him,' but he adds: 'through and in him.' In this way

---

283. "Darumb wenn man sagt, himel und erden sey ein geschopf oder werck, das gemacht sey von dem, der da heist ein einiger Gott und aus nichts gemacht, das ist ein kunst uber alle kunst." WA 45:13.11-13 (Schmalcald, 1537).

284. Ibid., 94.3-4. See 283n282.

285. "Non solum creavit omnia, sed seipsum nobis revelat." WA 45:94.12.

he composes a threefold God and still ascribes all things to the three persons."[286] From the three prepositions "from, through, in," Luther locates a "threefold God" within the divine essence that creates. Corresponding to the definition that all creatures owe their existence to God is the definition of the Creator who creates in three ways.

Later in the sermon, Luther correlates the three prepositions with the three persons. In Rörer's transcript, the prepositions introduce the three persons as they each contribute to the one work of creating. "These words testify to the Trinity in the Godhead. From the Father is everything, through the Son is everything, and in the Holy Spirit are all things."[287] "From, through, and in" are referred respectively to, "Father, Son, and Spirit." Cruciger's text also correlates the prepositions in this way.[288] In other Trinitarian sermons, Luther similarly notes the relevance of the Romans 11:36 text for reading the Trinitarian revelation in the work of creating.[289] Luther privileges the inner-Trinitarian relations of origin in order to articulate the correlation. By correlating the prepositions with their order in the inner-Trinitarian relations of origin, Luther can assure

---

286. Ibid., 94.5-7.

287. Ibid., 97.19-20. Luther quotes the doxological stanza in Peter Abelard's hymn "O Quanta Qualia": "Perenni domino perpes sit gloria / ex quo sunt, per quem sunt, in quo sunt omnia / ex quo sunt, Pater est, per quem sunt, Filius / in quo sunt, Patri et Filii Spiritus"; in English, "To the eternal Lord be perpetual glory / from whom are, through whom are, in whom are all things / from whom [all things] are, is the Father, through whom [all things] are, is the Son, in whom [all things] are is the Spirit of the Father and the Son." I thank Aaron Moldenhauer for pointing out this reference.

288. "Nemlich also, das alle ding von Gott dem Vater und durch den Son geschaffen (wie er denn durch den Son alle ding thut) und in dem heiligen Geist durch Gottes wolgefallen erhalten werden." WA 21:521.32-35. Cruciger adds two biblical passages on which his text is based. He cites 1 Cor 8:6, a passage including the first two prepositions. "'Wir haben nur einen Gott, den Vater, von welchem alle ding sind, Und einen HErrn, Jhesum Christum, durch welchen alle ding sind' etc." Ibid., 521.36-38. Cruciger uses Gen 1:31 in order to show that the preposition "in" refers to the Holy Spirit. Ibid., 521.38-39.

289. "Discrimen: vom vater, durch den sun et a nulla procreatur. Im heyligen geist. Ita Paulus: distinctae personae, una essentia, omnia creata a patre per filium in spiritu sancto. Hactenus nobis licet loqui, sofern uns got furschlegt, si progredimur, fiet, quod olim hereticis, qui totum ferme orbem seduxerunt. Arriani etc." WA 17,1:280.8-12 (Trinity Sunday, 1525). Ps 33:6 is cited to show that all things are created by the word. Ibid., 279.14. The attribute, "to create," is only predicated of God. "Hoc non potest imputari creaturae, nulla est quae possit creare omnia." Ibid., 279.16-17. Luther alludes to Gen 1:6 in order to attribute "ornare" to the Spirit. "Gen. Vides neminem celum ornare quam deum, qui dixit. Et hic per os spiritus etc. ergo spiritus sanctus est verus deus, qui creat omnia." Ibid., 279.17-19. Luther cites Rom 11:36 in another Trinity Sunday sermon (1538). "Item Paulus: omnia per ipsum facta." WA 46:437.10.

symmetry between the inner and the outer Trinity. As the Christological symmetry between inner and outer Trinity is established by the Father's speech, so too does the inner-Trinitarian differentiation serve to determine the outer-Trinitarian order in the one work of creating. The Father, the origin of the Son's eternal generation, creates in the unity of the essence as the origin of all things. The Christological center of the inner Trinity is the Son, through whom all things are created, and the Spirit, who hears the Father's inner-Trinitarian word.

Luther does not stop at the symmetry between the inner and the outer Trinity. He continues in his sermon to locate the prepositions as Trinitarian traces in creation itself. Not only does God create from nothing, but God preserves and sustains the creatures.[290] Luther uses an example from 1 Corinthians 15:37 in order to show how God continues to create, even raising new life from a dead seed.[291] Without the continuous activity of God, all creatures would be lost.[292] With this extended definition of God's creating work, Luther correlates the Trinitarian essence with creation as the latter's beginning, middle, and end.[293] The age-old question concerning the origin and goal of creation is answered by the revelation of the Triune God as the beginning, middle, and end of creation.[294] At this juncture, Luther answers the question posed by all the "people" (*gentes*) in Romans 1:19-20.

290. "Nulla creatura a seipsa, sed a deo, cum coepta per eum, erhalten, ut so gros, weit etc. und wens auffhoren sol etc." WA 45:97.21-23.

291. "Sicut inspice granum, sein anheben ist ex mortuo grano, so hebts an, postea wechsts her aus et fit halm." Ibid., 97.23-24. Luther uses Paul's example of the dead seed from which new life grows in order to preach on the nature of God. The attribute of the divine nature "to create" is immediately referred to the attribute, "to raise from the dead." In a study of a sermon on 1 Cor 15, Beutel relates Luther's use of the example of the seed to his understanding of the "new language" that Christians speak. See: Beutel, "Offene Predigt," 526-28. The choice of analogies that Luther uses to illustrate his preaching demonstrates his commitment to staying as close to Scripture as possible. Most of his analogies are taken from Scripture. In a Table Talk, Luther speaks of following Christ's example of preaching. "Einfeldig zu predigen, ist eine große kunst. Christus thuts selber; er redet allein vom ackerwerck, vom senffkorn, vnd braucht eitel grobe, pewrische similitudines." WATr 4:447.19-21 (no. 4719, July 23, 1539).

292. Quando ipse cessat, nihil fit, et si non incrementum dat, auch verlorn, es mus alles per et in." WA 45:97.26-27. "Sic creavit mundum, non ut faber aut sutor calceum, nihil curat, an domus ab aquis rapiatur, igni comburatur." Ibid., 97.33-34. Luther even eliminates the secondary cause of the human "medium" in attributing the traces to the work of the Creator. "Homo non potest medium facere, nisi velim velim abscindere calamum, tum etc." Ibid., 97.28-29.

293. "Er ist anfang, mittel, ende." Ibid., 97.32.

294. "Hie wurdt uns am ersten furgehalten, Das wir wissen und lernen sollen, wo wir her kommen, was wir sind und wo hin wir gehoren ... Darumb lerne hie zum ersten, wo her

He even sharpens his designation of the "people (*gentes*)" as those who are incapable of attaining even the slightest bit of knowledge concerning not only the Creator but also the creature.[295] From the doxology in Romans 11:36, Romans 1:18-20 becomes fully explicit as the Trinitarian traces in creation's own narrative.[296] This foundational knowledge further opens up the possibility of seeing traces of the Trinity in all the created works—more than Augustine could ever have imagined![297] Suspended in the narrative of Trinitarian revelation is the narrative of creation and of every living creature; beginning, middle, and end are attributed to the Creator.

Luther uses the claim of the Trinitarian traces in order to launch the concluding doxology. He locates his interpretation of Romans 11:36 in the tradition of the early church fathers. "[According to] the Fathers: the beginning, middle, and end are from God."[298] The Trinitarian interpretation of this passage is not self-evident, as the history of its thematization shows. Both Basil of Caesarea and Gregory Nazianzen give evidence for an Arian

---

du kombst, Nemlich von dem, der da heist ein schopffer himels und der erden." Ibid., 12.16-17, 13.22-23 (Schmalcald, 1537).

295. "Si ista 2 non intelligis, quae extra deum, 1. das geringst in creaturis, 2. das geistlich wesen, quomodo solt selig, quomodo intelligeres hoc, quod non in creaturis nec 2. nec revelatum est?" Ibid., 94.29-31. No one can explain how the eyes see and how the tongue utters intelligible speech. "Nemo potest dicere, wie es zugehet, quomodo oculi videant, aures audiant et lingua so verstendlich laute, ut von 3, 4 milibus intelligatur." Ibid., 94.16-17.

296. The three prepositions in Rom 11:36 can be read together with the three verbs in Acts 17:28: "in ipso enim vivimus et movemur et sumus" (*Vulgata*).

297. "Sic postea in omnibus creaturis viel mher gleichnis ut Augustinus." WA 45:97.31-32. In another sermon on the Trinity, Luther preaches that not even Augustine could add to the illustration of the Trinity in Rom 11:36. "Setzt zu, quod spiritus sanctus vernewert, per filium ausgerichtet pater fast, pater facit per filium in spiritu sancto. Nemo kans aufgrunden. Augustinus et alii, sed nicht weiter bracht, den da die schrifft gelassen. Von, durch, in im ist alles. Da lests scriptura sacra stehen, praecipue Paulus, wie wol mher hoher ansticht, quod ewig bild filius patris. Ibi pater, von dem alle, filius, per quem, spiritus sanctus, in quo omnia creata et tamen creatio unum opus." WA 45:181.18-24 (Gallustag, 1537). An extended discussion of the traces of the Trinity in creation is included in Luther's lectures on Genesis. "Quia divinitatis vestigia sunt in creatura." WA 43:276.28 (Lectures on Genesis, 1535-1545, to Gen 23:1-2). The first trace is the trace of the Father in the substance of things. The trace of the Son is in their form, and the trace of the Spirit is in their beauty. The traces are seen by the godly in the works of creation and in their *usum*. On the contrary, the ungodly neither see God in creation nor give him the glory and cannot enjoy creation. Ibid., 276.28-42.

298. WA 45:97.21. A little later on, Luther repeats this allusion. "Sic secundum veteres interpretes exposita verba Pauli." Ibid., 97.25-26. The precedent for the medieval tradition of a Trinitarian interpretation of this text is set by Lombard, who mentions the text in the context of creation. Lombard remarks on Rom 11:36. "Quod idem est omnia esse ex Deo et per ipsum et in ipso." *Sent.* I, d. 36, c. 3 (161) [261].

interpretation of this passage. According to the Arians, the prepositions διά ("through") and ἔν ("in") connote degrees of subordination to the Father.[299] In his treatise *De Spiritu Sancto*, Basil argues against the Arians that glory must be given to all three persons of the Trinity. When the prepositions of the passage are substituted with καί ("and") or μετά ("with"), then the distinctions between the *hypostases*, as well as the inseparability of their fellowship are assured.[300] Glory is offered to the Father, through (διά) the Son, and in (ἔν) the Holy Spirit.[301] John of Damascus alludes to Gregory Nazianzen's *Fifth Theological Oration* in order to show that the prepositions do not multiply the natures but that they refer to the three "properties" of the indivisible divine nature.[302] In his *De Trinitate*, Hilary understands the prepositions to mean the coequality of all three persons in the unity of the work.[303] Augustine warns against confusing the three prepositions with three gods.[304] The prepositions in Romans 11:36 must be correctly understood to refer to three coequal persons. If this meaning is assured, then the doxology can fittingly glorify the three persons of the Trinity.

Luther also thematizes the tradition's concern with rightly interpreting Romans 11:36. The way he understands this text shows how seriously he takes the Trinitarian traces in creation to reflect the glory of the divine essence. He advances an argument from the text's grammatical level. The passage's final clause attracts his attention: "To him be the glory."[305] Luther argues that Paul does not use the third-person plural dative, "to them" (*quibus*), but the third-person singular dative, "to him" (*cui*). "He does not

---

299. Basil of Caesarea, section 6 (13) in *De Spiritu Sancto* [NPNF, vol. 8, 8]; Gregory Nazianzen, section 20 in *The Fifth Theological Oration: On The Holy Spirit* [NPNF, vol. 7, 324].

300. Basil, section 25 (59) in *De Spiritu Sancto* [NPNF, vol. 8, 37].

301. Ibid., section 7 (16) [NPNF, vol. 8, 10]; section 26 (63) [NPNF, vol. 8, 39–40].

302. John of Damascus, *Exposition of the Orthodox Faith*, 10 [NPNF, vol. 9, 54].

303. Hilary of Poitiers, *De Trinitate*, 8 (37) [NPNF, vol. 9, 148].

304. Augustine cites Rom 11:36 at the end of book six in the *De Trinitate*. "Quoniam unus est Deus, sed tamen Trinitas. Nec confuse accipiendum est, Ex quo omnia, per quem omnia, in quo omnia: nec diis multis, sed ipsi gloria in saecula saeculorum. Amen." *De Trin.*, 6, 10 (12) [PL 42:932]. He also quotes Rom 11:36 when discussing both the *creatio ex nihilo*, and the attribution of sin, not to God, but to the human will. *De Natura Boni Contra Manichaeos*, 26 and 28 [PL 42:560].

305. WA 45:94.11. "Et schleust in fine, quod tantum unus deus." Ibid., 94.7. "Teilet in inn drey et tamen bringts wider zusamen inn ein." Ibid., 94.8–9.

say: 'to them be the glory', but to 'him'."[306] The Trinitarian unity is revealed by the term "to him" (*cui*) after the three persons have been distinguished. Cruciger's variant differs slightly from Rörer's record on this point. Rather than appealing to the text's grammar, Cruciger grounds the Trinitarian unity in the classic doctrine that the three persons are one and the same as the divine essence.[307] According to Rörer, Luther begins with the Trinitarian traces and then reverts back to the unity. By this move, Luther establishes the Trinitarian traces as the locations at which God is glorifed. The "to him" (*cui*) suspends the traces in the doxology that is reserved for God alone.

The final moment of Luther's sermon brings the narrative to a doxological high point. Luther picks up a theme he left off after preaching on the Trinitarian revelation in explicit speech structures. Each speech structure reveals the divine wisdom as the convergence between knowledge of the Trinity and the way a particular person is "with us." At the site of creation, Luther plots a distinctive convergence as the sermon's climax. An eschatological vision secures the convergence between knowledge of the Trinity and the Trinitarian traces as God's way with creation. On that final day, both will be seen: the sight of the Trinity and God as creation's beginning, middle, and end. "That on the last day we will see how God is the beginning,

---

306. Ibid., 94.8. A similar argument is advanced in the Gallus Day sermon. Alluding to Isa 48:11, Luther preaches that God does not give his glory to anyone. The work of creation is attributed to God; attribution is converted to glorifying God as Creator. "Meum opus, ehr sol nemo haben nisi is, qui deus." Ibid., 182.24-25 (Gallustag, 1537). In this sermon, Luther refers to other passages in Scripture that distinguish between the three persons as well as uniting them in the essence. Matt 28:19 distinguishes between the names of Father, Son, and Spirit, and baptism is performed "'In nomine', non in viel namen, sed in einigen namen, laut 3 namen et tamen l." Ibid., 182.34-35. There are three persons who work salvation, but only one Savior, Jesus Christ (Titus 3:4). Ibid., 182.17-19. Referring to John 5:19 ("pater vivificat"), Luther says, "Ergo alls ein werck, leben et unus deus vivificans, et tamen 3 personae." Ibid., 182.27-28. Also in John 1:16, the term, "'Cuius' nimbt die 3 person zu samen." Ibid., 183.10. In this sermon, Rom 11:33 is cited in the context of glorifying the three persons as one God. "Item ad Ro. von vel aus, in, durch, in im, in dem selben etc. Ziehet 3 person in unum wesen und ehr, qui heisst drey person in 3 wesen. Non possum laudare patrem, nisi etiam filium et spiritum sanctum." Ibid., 182.35-38.

307. Cruciger's text interprets the first article of the Creed in terms of the unity of the essence in the one work of creation, a unity that is, on the inner side of God, one and the same as the three persons. "Also leret uns die Schrifft, das wol das werck der Schaffung aller Creaturn ist des einigen Gottes oder der gantzen Gottheit, und doch in dem einigen wesen die drey Personen also unterschieden, das man recht sagt, Das alles herkompt, bestehet und bleibt vom Vater, als von der ersten Person durch den Son, der vom Vater ist, und in dem heiligen Geist, beide, vom Vater und Son ausgehend, welche doch alle drey in einer unzertrenneten Gottheit bleiben." WA 21:522.1-7.

middle, and end of all creatures and we will see how [there are] three persons of the Godhead, etc."[308] Based on Romans 11:36, the prepositional symmetry between the inner-Trinitarian relations of origin and the outer-Trinitarian determination of the origin and consummation of creation moves towards the sight of the Trinity that coincides with the sight of the Trinitarian traces as God's way in all of creation. The eschatological sight draws the revelation of God in creation together with the divine desire to be known as God is, in eternity. All creation will be revealed in light of the Creator, who desires that all creation reflect the divine glory. Luther ends his sermon on a doxological note.[309] The incomprehensible wisdom of God—the inner-Trinitarian essence and the outer-Trinitarian way of God in creation—is revealed in creation as the object of eternal glory.

The question addressed in this section is one that had been posed early in the chapter but that could only be answered in full once the entire narrative of Trinitarian revelation was told: how does creation reveal the Trinity when the Trinity creates through the unity of the essence? Luther began by situating the divine will to create in the inner Trinity. The distinction between the soteriological will and the decision to create secured the claim that only the former reveals the Trinitarian essence through speech. When the will to create was laid over the decision to save, the revelatory potential was transferred into the works of creation. The Creator-creature distinction functioned to show that the created works reveal the Trinitarian traces. By calling on the correlation in Romans 11:36 between the prepositions and the Trinitarian persons, Luther then moved the doxology into the eschatological sight of the Trinity and its glory, reflected in all of creation.

---

308. WA 45:98.2–4. A similar eschatological impulse is articulated in the Gallus Day sermon. "Morere in hac fide: in extremo die videbis." Ibid., 182.15 (1537).

309. Luther gives Anton Lauterbach some advice on preaching. A sermon is preached to the glory of God. "Wen ir wolt predigen, so redet mit Gott vnd sprecht: Lieber Herr Gott, ich will dir zu ehren predigen; ich will von dir reden, dich loben, dein nhamen preisen. Ob ichs nicht wol vnd gutt kan machen, mach du es gutt. Vnd seht weder Philippum, Pomeranum, mich vnd kein gelerten an vnd last euch duncken, ir seit der gelertest, wen ir redet auf der canntzel." WATr 2:144.11–16 (no. 1590, May 20 to 27, 1532).

CONCLUSION

Luther's understanding of the Trinity as it is articulated in the genre of the sermon is studied in this chapter according to a sermon he preached on Trinity Sunday and on the first Sunday after Trinity in 1537. Chosen as a representative text of this genre, the sermon on Romans 11:33-36 is a narrative of Trinitarian revelation that locates the *promissio* at various sites. The sermon's exegetical shape is established by Romans 1:18-20—the knowledge of God revealed in creation—and this theme is read from the doxological perspective of Romans 11:33-36. The Spirit plots the first site in the narrative by revealing the inner Trinity. God's desire to be known as God is—the Trinity in eternity—is revealed by the Spirit to the church. At its first narrative point, the "incomprehensible way" of the divine desire consists of the Spirit's incorporation of Christians into the knowledge and right speaking of the eternal Trinitarian relations. The second site in the narrative discloses the Father's eternal sermon to be the convergence between the Son's eternal generation and the divine counsel's decision for the salvation of humankind in Christ. At the third site oriented to Christ's incarnation, the outer Trinity is revealed in speech structures at Christ's baptism, Christ's sermon, and the baptismal rite. The outer-Trinitarian sites focus on Christ's *promissio*, communicating salvation to those who believe in him. The sermon's final site recapitulates the theme of the Trinitarian revelation in creation. From the doxology of Romans 11:36, creation is seen to be sustained by the Triune God as its beginning, middle, and end. Permeated with divine traces, the created works look towards the eschatological vision of convergence between the sight of the Trinity and the glorification of the Triune God in all creation.

In this chapter, two aspects of Luther's Trinitarian understanding are used to challenge the "word-event" approach to Luther's sermons. In order to expose the dogmatic reduction of this approach, I stressed the doctrinal dimension that is far from absent in Luther's sermons on the Trinity. The sermon on Romans 11:33-36 represents what is found in other sermons: Luther's privileging of knowledge concerning the inner Trinity. Only through the revelation of the inner Trinity is knowledge concerning the Triune God obtained. Luther's doctrinal emphasis corrects the one-sided view of the metaphysics of effects that tends to stress the outer-Trinitarian revelation in the works of creation, redemption, and sanctification. It also shows that the outer-Trinitarian works can be appropriated to the three persons only on the basis of the inner-Trinitarian revelation.

If the inner Trinity is allocated the site Luther assigns to it, then it can be seen as the starting point for revelation as both knowledge and as God's way with creation. As a narrative starting point, the inner Trinity cannot be collapsed from the onset into the relation that limits the content of revelation to a soteriological effect. There is knowledge of the Trinity that, although not separated from soteriology, adds another dimension to it. I have used the terminology of incorporation to show that the sermon is not crystallized into a kerygma, to be appropriated existentially by faith, but that it invites a full immersion into learning, speaking, and glorifying the Trinity. The soteriological dimension funds every sermon. Building on this foundation, I propose that incorporation opens up the homiletical arena to the many ways God reveals the knowledge of the divine essence through God's way with the church. Preachers are incorporated into this knowledge as they grow in learning, and hearers are incorporated into richer experiences of the word. The word is attributed to God, and it is incarnate in concrete sermons, preached to and by human subjects. The incorporation motif also points out that creation and redemption are not two distinct plots to be appropriated to outer-Trinitarian works but are intimately bound up with the inner-Trinitarian essence as the content of its will. In this way, all of creation will be incorporated into the glorification of the Triune God, who is the beginning, middle, and end of all that is.

5

Conclusion

More rooted in the medieval tradition than some Luther scholars have until now admitted and radical in their ability to provoke contemporary thought, Luther's texts continue to offer visionary glimpses of a divine reality that is ultimately beyond human understanding. The theme of my investigation was Luther's understanding of the Trinity in his works from 1523 to 1546, as articulated in representative texts of three genres: the disputation, the hymn, and the sermon. A topic more typically coupled with the early church's struggles against heresies and sometimes caricatured as a petrified vestige of medieval scholastic metaphysics, Luther's Trinitarian understanding was a contribution to the history of this doctrine. The exegetical richness of Luther's Trinitarian canon, his invitation to "right speculation" on the eternity of God, the narrative recital, and the *promissio* at the center are elements shaping a commitment to the doctrine of the Trinity that uniquely balances a passion for the old with the excitement of the new.

I focus on the ways in which genre is related to Luther's articulation of his Trinitarian understanding. As a theological category, genre is determined by its proximity to genres found in Scripture and in the liturgical tradition of the church. Examples of this type are the hymn and the sermon. In the case of the disputation, the theological legitimacy of an academic site is undergirded by Luther's own rootedness in a medieval milieu that sees the necessity of seeking an understanding of the truth and defending it against attack. The subject matter is given a distinctive shaping by the respective genre. In the disputation, the view to the inner Trinity is fixed by the proposition that three *res* are one and the same as one *res*. Although the exclusive focus on the inner Trinity is established in this genre, the central element of the infinity associated with the Triune essence surfaces as the starting point for narratives found in other genres. The hymn of praise sings first of the Father's inner-Trinitarian turn to the

Son and then of the turn to the outer-Trinitarian show of mercy. In the sermon, hearers are invited to listen to the Father's sermon in eternity and then to Christ speak in time. Genre distinctions acknowledge the differing facets of distinct life spaces that bring the Trinity to view. Sometimes the genre is fragmented, as in Luther's hymn, "Now Rejoice, Dear Christians." The lament interrupts the joy-filled hymn of praise. Yet these broken spaces witness to their potential for transformation by the one who embraces all creation and whose advent ultimately makes all things new.

The issue of language accompanies the discussion of genre. For Luther, any talk of the Trinity is to be attributed to God. Luther insists, as does Hilary of Poitiers before him, that it is God's nature to speak from himself. In all three genres, this insight is initially worked out under the rubric of the Holy Spirit. To the Spirit is attributed the language of the prophets, the psalmist, the church's conciliar decisions, and its ongoing proclamation, which reveals a mystery transcending creaturely comprehension. Although Luther seems to maximize a novel insight regarding the pneumatological source of theological language, his focus reflects what his theological predecessors had already acknowledged. For Aquinas, Scotus, Ockham, and Biel, the Trinity is not accessible by natural reason; it is the subject matter of revelation.

Luther's conviction regarding the divine status of the word emerges as a determinative factor in his Trinitarian understanding. The word is conjugated across the three persons in order to identify each person as a subject of speech. The identification of a person with the word is part and parcel of a Trinitarian hermeneutic that Luther sees rooted in Scripture and in the history of its interpretation. In the hymn, the inner-Trinitarian conversation of love is conceived according to a prosopographic exegesis of the royal psalms. This structure distinguishes between the speech's content and the Son as addressee of the Father's word. In the sermon, a self-conversation is observed to be exegetically linked to Genesis 1 and John's prologue. According to this model, the Father speaks the word, the content of which merges with the Son's eternal generation. Both models for conversation reflect a similarity regarding the way in which speech structures the Trinitarian relations. When one Person speaks, another is revealed, and a third Person listens. By exposing the divine nature in light of a mutual pointing, Luther clarifies the locations of speech as relations of origin. The

Son is distinguished from the Father when the latter's voice is heard: "This is my beloved Son" (Matt 3:17; 17:5). In his theological development after 1528, Luther locates the Spirit as the word's hearer in order to show how the Spirit receives the divine essence from both the Father and the Son.

The subject matter of speech is identified with the *promissio*. At three sites of the word, the *promissio* is spoken in ways directly pointing to Christ and indirectly disclosing the speaker in relation to him. Eternity is filled with the Father's speech, which points to his beloved heart, his Son. The Father is also heard to locate the promise of life for the sinner in the Son's death. The fulfilled time of Christ's advent is anticipated by the prophets' words, through which the Spirit speaks, and it is actualized when the Spirit leads the community to hear Christ's address of salvation. For Luther, the *promissio* is inseparably conjoined with Christ's incarnation. Defined as the identity between *res* and word, the *promissio* is localized in the present tense when Christ speaks. In speaking the *promissio* to those who cannot hear, Christ creates hearers of his word and communicates all the "divine treasures" (Col 2:3) to them. The address of salvation, however, is sustained through a divine silence to which there is no discursive access. At the center of the Trinity is the silent mystery of the beloved Son's death, a silence that has become the *promissio* of life "for us."

Focused through the lens of the divine word, Luther's Trinitarian understanding is articulated in human words. Rehearsed in a variety of discourses, the *promissio*'s identity between *res* and word is opened by the differential to the possibilities of exploring how reason, illuminated by faith, is used to articulate the Trinity. By the term "differential," I intended to mark the identity between the divine word and the human word that, for Luther, is explicit in the homiletical genre. Luther can state "This the Lord has said" after every sermon he preaches. The concept of identity, however, cannot be seen to limit the many ways in which Luther speaks, disputes, determines, and illustrates his understanding of the Trinitarian *res*. In the chapter on the sermon, I developed the idea of incorporation in order to show how Luther construes the historical and personal growth in learning and speaking about the Trinity. Under the rubric of the Spirit, the church is incorporated into the divine defense of the Trinitarian article against heresy. Throughout its history, the church is guided by the Spirit in clarifying its understanding of the Trinitarian nature of God and in articulating that understanding. On the personal level, each Christian grows in the knowledge of faith's object and begins to speakly rightly about divine matters. The idea of incorporation was intended to provide an account for the convergence between the historical development in formulating the Trinitarian doctrine and the soteriological center of the divine nature. Read through the structure of mutual revelation, incorporation suggested how Luther could attribute the word wholeheartedly to God while being simultaneously committed to speaking many words in concrete genres and in historical situations. The mystery of the word made flesh, incarnate in Christ, is embodied in human words.

In all genres of this study, the fundamental category structuring Luther's conception of the Trinity is shown to be the distinction between the inner and the outer Trinity. Using Luther's own terminology, the "inner" and "outer" sides of God are mapped as two locations of the Trinity that are distinguished from each other by the persons who are heard to speak and listen. To first gain access into the Trinity, the Spirit's outer-Trinitarian speech surfaces as the starting point. Luther's appeal at the beginning of every genre points to the Spirit as the source of right speaking and understanding. In both the hymn and the sermon, the inner Trinity is the site at which the Father is heard to speak. Either construed according to the model of the royal psalms or the Johannine model, the Father's speech is bound up with the Son's eternal generation and with the Spirit as the intent hearer. The inner Trinity is also the site of another subject of speech. After his ascension, Christ is heard at the eternal mercy seat to plead before the Father on behalf of the church and individual penitents. Couched in the language of the penitential psalms, Christ's inner-Trinitarian speech is heard by the Father alone. There are outer-Trinitarian sites at which the three persons can be heard by hearers other than the Spirit. The Father's voice is heard once by those gathered as witnesses to Christ's baptism. Christ is the central figure who speaks at the outer Trinity. In the hymn and the sermon, Christ concentrates his address in the *promissio*, extending it through the narrated stages of his incarnation, death, resurrection, and ascension. Also located at the outer Trinity is the Holy Spirit, whose words are identified with the church's history of speaking and singing about the Trinity. The still, small voice is hidden amid the church's proclamation and the praises sung to God.

The distinction between the inner and the outer Trinity overarches the distinction between Creator and creature. For Luther, the Trinity's posture with respect to creation is established by the two sides of the Creator. In the disputation, the infinity of the inner Trinity is determined in order to prohibit any importation of temporally understood creaturely terms into the eternal relations. By locating the Trinitarian relations on the inner side, Luther can resist the modalism attached to viewing the Trinity as three ways in which the Creator encounters creation. Luther continues to privilege the inner Trinity as the starting point for any movement towards its outer side. When the Creator encounters creation through the unity of the essence, the revelation of the inner side becomes significant as the only way by which the Creator is known to be constituted by three persons. The symmetry between the inner and outer sides is established by the Christological center. At both locations, the Christological center assures that the God in eternity is the same God who works life through the death of Christ.

I have applied the category of narrative throughout Luther's understanding of the movement in the inner Trinity. The time of the inner-Trinitarian turn is told as a story. The study of the disputation shows Luther's engagement to precisely determine the type of infinity characterizing the relations of origin. Yet, in the genre of the hymn, the same infinity is told as a narrative of the Father's inner-Trinitarian turn to the Son preceding the outer-Trinitarian advent in creation. Narrative cannot be interpreted to undermine the disputation's discourse of infinity. Rather, narrative construes the incomprehensibility of a show of mercy without accounting for a conceptual justification. The origins of the divine mercy shown to creation turn on the attribute of mercy that cannot be grounded in any element other than the divine attribute itself. A perspective complementary to the disputation is offered by the hymn. Established by the disputation's focus is the infinity of the attribute that grounds the hymn's recital of the mercy shown "to us" in Christ as a truth claim according to the modality of necessity. In the hymn, the divine mercy becomes the object of eternal praise.

A specific order among the three persons is presented by the narrative structured by two extremes. In the movement from the inner to the outer Trinity, the Father is located at the origin. The Father sends the Son to redeem humanity from captivity and, together with the ascended Christ, pours out the Spirit. In this narrative, the Trinitarian order reflects the relations of origin. It is also marked by immediacy. The Son's immediate obedience to the Father and the Spirit's complete fulfillment of Christ's *promissio* are elements that secure the uninterrupted continuity of advent from the inner to the outer Trinity. The narrative of incorporation is a story in the reverse direction. Beginning with the Spirit, those who hear the story are led to Christ, who addresses his *promissio* of salvation to them and includes them in the Father's love for the Son. The narrative from the outer to the inner Trinity is marred by the ruptures of human sin and captivity, demonic attack, and the incapacity of natural reason to know either the Triune God or the *promissio* of redemption. The ruptures are the open wound of a Trinitarian understanding that admits the divine silence at its Christological center, confesses the power of the divine speech to heal broken reality, and bows before the divine majesty who alone works all in all.

The genre-language approach opens up possibilities of conceiving Luther's understanding of a theological subject matter in light of his rootedness in a trajectory of medieval thought. Particularly the disputation reflects Luther's location in a history of "holy speculation" on the inner Trinity. Lying below the rhetorical surface of Luther's writings is a sophisticated reception of medieval logic, semantics, and metaphysics. When disputing on the formal and real distinctions, for example, Luther's criticism against Scotus veers remarkably close to a position Ockham held a few centuries earlier. By orienting Luther in sight of a critical appreciation for, rather than an outright rejection of, academic tools of reason, the elements considered to be novel to Luther may be worked out with greater precision in their relation to the "old."

Rather than defining the "new" in terms of static principles, such as the law-gospel distinction or even that emblem of the Reformation, the doctrine of justification, the foundational asymmetry is developed from Luther's understanding of the divine nature. In all three genres, the Triune essence is articulated in relation to the divine attributes of infinity and mercy. Once the central attribute of mercy is fixed together with the eternal Trinitarian essence, the contours of other elements, such as law or hiddenness, are assigned locations in relation to the primary determination. For example, when the hymn "Now Rejoice, Dear Christians" is perceived as a hymn of praise, its literal starting point, the advent of the Spirit, assigns a location to the lament. The narrative of Trinitarian advent retains the lament as rupture while suspending it both pneumatologically and Christologically as speech. The anthropological view resulting from the rigid application of the law-gospel relation is displaced by the Trinitarian-theological privileging of the divine mercy. Even the theme of the hidden God (*deus absconditus*) that is often misunderstood by Luther scholars to either dissuade speculation on the Trinitarian essence or to drive a rift between the "special" revelation of the Trinity and the "hidden" judgments is allocated a place in the genre of the sermon. Luther situates the theme in an exhortation against the demonic antithesis to the divine revelation without petrifying it as a static principle in the doctrine of God. The idea of incorporation is introduced to challenge an understanding of the identity between the divine word and the human word that limits the latter to "instrumentality." The sheer performance of Luther's sermon witnesses to his appeal to the cognitive, experiential, and ethical dimensions of the word that is communicated in a distinct speech situation. Further work investigating the radical seriousness with which Luther takes the concrete word might use another category. Incorporation is chosen to gesture in this interpretational direction.

The postcritical anxiety marking the relationship of systematic theology to Scripture might be soothed by reorienting the method of "system" to a study of genres and their proximity to exegetical constellations. By viewing genre in terms of its location in Scripture, in the liturgy of the church, and in the history of its theological reception, possibilities of studying the mutual relationship between dogma and Scripture are presented. I have discussed Luther's privileging of the inner Trinity to be formed by an exegetical constellation of passages: John's prologue, Genesis 1, Psalms, Romans 1:18-3:20, and Romans 11:33-36. Each genre presents a distinct nuancing of these biblical passages within an overarching rubric. The shaping of the biblical interpretation occurs in relation to confessional formulations and to the history of theology that follows in the footsteps of Lombard. The genre approach prohibits reducing all constellations to one dogmatic shape and prevents relegating Scriptural passages to the status of proof-texts to warrant a particular position. A rehabilitation of the relationship between Scripture and dogma would recover the full range of the canon. In contemporary systematic theology, biblical passages in the Old Testament that have been traditionally associated with the Trinity have fallen victim to historical-critical scholarship that limits its Trinitarian hermeneutic to the New Testament. When the move from Scripture to dogma is viewed from the perspective of the "material dogmatics" at work in Scripture itself, the canon is opened to engage serious reflection on diverse exegetical configurations that each offer differing perspectives on the doctrine of God.

A doctrine as allegedly esoteric as the Trinity is offered new potential for pastoral situations in light of the genres in which Luther articulates his Trinitarian understanding. The question of invocation in prayer is understood by Luther according to the logic of the inner-Trinitarian proposition and the model of the penitential psalms. When one person is addressed in prayer, all three persons are invoked through the whole essence that constitutes each person. From the Trinitarian perspective of the psalms, the Spirit reveals Christ, who prays before the Father on behalf of those for whom he died. Luther does not shy away from preaching on the inner Trinity. In order to open up the cognitive dimension to faith, Luther stresses doctrine. He is committed to educating his hearers in the meaning of the Trinitarian article and the truth of the confession of faith. In sermons preached on Trinity Sunday and on the feast of Epiphany, dogma is narratively unfolded in a way revealing the passion and wisdom of God, from its origins in eternity to its outer-Trinitarian extreme in the incarnation of Christ. Catechetical sermons privilege the revelation of the "inner side" of God, the three persons to whom the outer-Trinitarian works of creation, redemption, and sanctification are appropriated. Ultimately, the Triune God is the object of praise. The gratitude for the Trinity's turn to accomplish the "sweet act of wonder" is fittingly expressed in the hymn of praise. Gathered by the Spirit, the community of Christians sings and looks forward to the new song when all creation will glorify the Triune God.

Bibliography

Abbot, Ezra. "I. John V. 7 and Luther's German Bible." In *The Authorship of the Fourth Gospel and other Critical Essays*, 458-63. Boston: G. H. Ellis, 1888.

Adams, Marilyn McCord. *William Ockham*. 2 Vols. Publications in Medieval Studies at the Medieval Institute of the University of Notre Dame 26. Notre Dame, IN: University of Notre Dame Press, 1987.

Ailliaco, Petrus de. *Quaestiones super libros sententiarum cum quibusdam in fine adjunctis*. Strasbourg, 1490. Reprint, Frankfurt: Minerva, 1968.

Aland, Kurt, ed. *Luther Deutsch*. Lutherlexikon Supplement 3. Stuttgart: Klotz, 1957.

Alpers, Paul. "'Nun freut euch, lieben Christen gmein' im Liederbuch der Anna von Köln." *Jahrbuch für Liturgik und Hymnologie* 5 (1960): 132-33.

Althaus, Paul. *Die Theologie Martin Luthers*. 6th ed. Gütersloh: Gerd Mohn, 1983.

— — —. "Luther auf der Kanzel." *Luther: Mitteilungen der Luther-Gesellschaft* 3 (1921): 17-24.

Ameln, Konrad. "Das Achtliederbuch vom Jahre 1523/24." *Jahrbuch für Liturgik und Hymnologie* 2 (1956): 89-91.

— — —. "Luthers Liedauswahl." *Jahrbuch für Liturgik und Hymnologie* 5 (1960): 122-125.

Andresen, Carl. "Zur Entstehung und Geschichte des trinitarischen Personbegriffes." *Zeitschrift für die Neutestamentliche Wissenschaft und die Kunde der Älteren Kirche* 52 (1961): 1-39.

Angelelli, Ignacio. "The techniques of disputation in the history of logic." *The Journal of Philosophy* 67 (1970): 800-815.

Aristotle. *The Complete Works of Aristotle*. The Revised Oxford Translation. 2 Vols. Edited by Jonathan Barnes. Princeton: Princeton University Press, 1991.

Arndt, William F. and F. Wilbur Gingrich. *A Greek-English Lexicon of the New Testament and Other Early Christian Literature: A translation and adaptation of the fourth revised and augmented edition of Walter Bauer's Griechisch-Deutsches Wörterbuch zu den Schriften des Neuen Testaments und der übrigen urchristlichen Literatur*. 2nd ed. Chicago: University of Chicago Press, 1979.

Asendorf, Ulrich. "Die Bedeutung der Predigt für Luthers Theologie." In *Luther als Prediger*, 89–101. Veröffentlichungen der Luther-Akademie e.V. Ratzeburg 9. Erlangen: Luther Verlag, 1986.

———. *Die Theologie Martin Luthers nach seinen Predigten*. Göttingen: Vandenhoeck & Ruprecht, 1988.

———. "Die Trinitätslehre als integrales Problem der Theologie Martin Luthers." In *Luther und die trinitarische Tradition: Ökumenische und philosophische Perspektiven*, 113–30. Veröffentlichungen der Luther-Akademie e.V. Ratzeburg 23. Erlangen: Luther Verlag, 1994.

Ashworth, E. J. "Traditional logic." CHRP 143–72.

Auer, Johann. "Die aristotelische Logik in der Trinitätslehre der Spätscholastik: Bemerkungen zu einer Quaestio des Johannes Wuel de Pruck, Wien 1422." In *Theologie in Geschichte und Gegenwart: Michael Schmaus zum 60. Geburtstag*, edited by Johann Auer and Hermann Volk, 457–96. Munich: K. Zink, 1957.

Bainton, Roland. *Hunted Heretic: The Life and Death of Michael Servetus 1511–1553*. Boston: Beacon, 1960.

Bakhtin, M. M. "The Problem of Speech Genres." In *Speech Genres and Other Late Essays*, 60–102. Translated by Vern W. McGee. Edited by Caryl Emerson and Michael Holquist. Austin: University of Texas Press, 1986.

Bandt, Helmut. *Luthers Lehre vom verborgenen Gott: Eine Untersuchung zu dem offenbarungsgeschichtlichen Ansatz seiner Theologie*. Berlin: Evangelische Verlagsanstalt, 1958.

Barth, Christoph. *Die Errettung vom Tode: Leben und Tod in den Klage- und Dankliedern des Alten Testaments*. Edited by Bernd Janowski. 3rd ed. Stuttgart: Deutsche Bibelgesellschaft, 1997.

Barth, Hans-Martin. "Luthers Predigt von der Predigt." *Pastoraltheologie. Wissenschaft und Praxis* 56 (1967): 481–89.

Barth, Karl. *Die kirchliche Dogmatik*, vol. I/1, *Die Lehre vom Wort Gottes: Prolegomena zur kirchlichen Dogmatik*. Zurich: Evangelischer Verlag, 1964.

———. *Die kirchliche Dogmatik*, vol. I/2, *Die Lehre vom Wort Gottes: Prolegomena zur kirchlichen Dogmatik*. Zurich: Evangelischer Verlag, 1975.

———. *Die kirchliche Dogmatik*, vol. II/1, *Die Lehre von Gott*. Zurich: Evangelischer Verlag, 1948.

Baur, Jörg. "Luther und die Philosophie." *Neue Zeitschrift für systematische Theologie und Religionsphilosophie* 26, no. 1 (1984): 13–28.

Bayer, Oswald. *Aus Glauben Leben: Über Rechtfertigung und Heiligung*. 2nd ed. Stuttgart: Deutsche Bibelgesellschaft, 1990.

———. *Autorität und Kritik: Zu Hermeneutik und Wissenschaftstheorie*. Tübingen: Mohr, 1991.

———. "Das Sein Jesu Christi im Glauben." *Theologische Literaturzeitung* 118, no. 4 (April 1993): 275–84.

———. *Freiheit als Antwort: Zur theologischen Ethik*. Tübingen: Mohr, 1995.

———. *Leibliches Wort: Reformation und Neuzeit im Konflikt*. Tübingen: Mohr, 1992.

———. "Poetologische Trinitätslehre." In *Zur Trinitätslehre in der lutherischen Kirche*, 67–79. Veröffentlichungen der Luther-Akademie e.V. Ratzeburg 26. Erlangen: Luther Verlag, 1996.

———. *Promissio: Geschichte der reformatorischen Wende in Luthers Theologie*. 2nd ed. Darmstadt: Wissenschaftliche Buchgesellschaft, 1989.

———. *Schöpfung als Anrede: Zu einer Hermeneutik der Schöpfung*. 2nd ed. Tübingen: Mohr, 1990.

———. *Theologie*: Handbuch Systematischer Theologie 1. Gütersloh: Gütersloher Verlagshaus, 1994.

———. "Worship and Theology." Translated by Alan Suggate. In *Worship and Ethics: Lutherans and Anglicans in Dialogue*, edited by Oswald Bayer and Alan Suggate, 148–61. Berlin: de Gruyter, 1996.

Beckmann, J. "Trinitatisfest." RGG 6:1041–42.

Beintker, Horst. "Luthers theologische Begründung der
　　Wortverkündigung: Eine Anregung für die Verkündigung
　　heute." In *Wort und Welt: Festgabe für Erich Hertzsch zum 65.*
　　Geburtstag, edited by Manfred Weise, 19-27. Berlin: Evangelische
　　Verlagsanstalt, 1968.

Bell, Theo. *Divus Bernhardus: Bernhard von Clairvaux in Martin Luthers*
　　Schriften. Mainz: von Zabern, 1993.

Benrath, Gustav Adolf. "Antitrinitarier." TRE 3:168-74.

Bernard of Clairvaux. *S. Bernardi Opera*. 8 Vols. Edited by J. Leclerq,
　　C. H. Talbot, and H. M. Rochais. Rome: Editiones Cistercienses,
　　1957-1977.

Beutel, Albrecht. *In dem Anfang war das Wort: Studien zu Luthers*
　　Sprachverständnis. Tübingen: Mohr, 1991.

———. "Offene Predigt: Homiletische Bemerkungen zu Sprache und
　　Sache." *Pastoraltheologie* 77, no. 12 (December 1988): 518-37.

Biel, Gabrielis. *Canonis Misse Expositio*. 3 Vols. Edited by Heiko A.
　　Oberman and William J. Courtenay. Wiesbaden: Franz Steiner,
　　1963-1966.

———. *Collectorium circa quattuor libros Sententiarum*. 3 Vols. Edited by
　　Wilfridus Werbeck and Udo Hofmann. Tübingen: Mohr, 1973-
　　1979.

Bielfeldt, Dennis, "Luther, Metaphor, and Theological Language." *Modern*
　　Theology 6, no. 2 (January 1990): 121-35.

Bieritz, Karl-Heinrich. "Verbum facit fidem: Homiletische
　　Anmerkungen zu einer Lutherpredigt." *Theologische*
　　Literaturzeitung 109, no. 7 (July 1984): 481-94.

Bizer, Ernst. *Fides ex auditu: Eine Untersuchung über die Entdeckung der*
　　Gerechtigkeit Gottes durch Martin Luther. 3rd ed. Neukirchen-
　　Vluyn: Neukirchener Verlag, 1966.

———. "Neue Darstellungen der Theologie Luthers." *Theologische*
　　Rundschau 31 (1965/66): 316-49.

Blankenburg, Walter. "Der gottesdienstliche Liedgesang der Gemeinde."
　　In *Leiturgia: Handbuch des evangelischen Gottesdienstes*, edited
　　by Karl Ferdinand Müller and Walter Blankenburg, 4:559-660.
　　Kassel: Stauda Verlag, 1961.

———. "Johann Walters Chorgesangbuch von 1524 in hymnologischer Sicht: Zum Beginn der Geschichte des evangelischen Kirchenliedes vor 450 Jahren." *Jahrbuch für Liturgik und Hymnologie* 18 (1973/1974): 65-96.

Boehner, Philotheus. *Collected Articles on Ockham.* Edited by Eligius M. Buytaert. St. Bonaventure, NY: St. Bonaventure University, 1958.

———. *Medieval Logic: An Outline of Its Development from 1250 to c. 1400.* Manchester: Manchester University Press, 1952.

Boff, Leonardo. *Trinity and Society.* Translated by Paul Burns. Theology and Liberation. Maryknoll, NY: Orbis, 1988.

Bonhoeffer, Dietrich. "Das Gebetbuch der Bibel: Eine Einführung in die Psalmen (1940)." In *Predigten-Auslegungen-Meditationen 1925-1945.* Vol. 2. Edited by Otto Dudzus. Munich: Kaiser, 1985.

Bornkamm, Heinrich. *Luther und das Alte Testament.* Tübingen: Mohr, 1948.

———. "Probleme der Lutherbiographie." In *Lutherforschung Heute: Referate und Berichte des 1. Internationalen Lutherforschungskongresses Aarhus 18-23 August 1956,* edited by Vilmos Vajta, 15-23. Berlin: Lutherisches Verlagshaus, 1958.

Bräuer, Siegfried. "Thomas Müntzers Liedschaffen: Die theologischen Intentionen der Hymnenübertragungen im Allstedter Gottesdienst von 1523/24 und im Abendmahlslied Müntzers." *Luther Jahrbuch* 41 (1974): 45-102.

Braun, Werner. "Die evangelische Kontrafaktur. Bemerkungen zum Stand ihrer Erforschung." *Jahrbuch für Liturgik und Hymnologie* 11 (1966): 89-113.

Braunfels, Wolfgang. *Die Heilige Dreifaltigkeit.* Lukas-Bücherei zur christlichen Ikonographie 6. Düsseldorf: Schwann, 1954.

Brecht, Martin. "Erfahrung—Exegese—Dogmatik. Luthers Lied 'Nun freut euch, lieben Christen gmein'." *Neue Zeitschrift für systematische Theologie und Religionsphilosophie* 32, no. 2 (1990): 94-104.

———. *Martin Luther,* vol. 2, *Ordnung und Abgrenzung der Reformation 1521-1532.* Stuttgart: Calwer, 1986.

———. *Martin Luther,* vol. 3, *Die Erhaltung der Kirche 1532-1546.* Stuttgart: Calwer, 1987.

Brednich, Rolf Wilhelm. *Die Liedpublizistik im Flugblatt des 15. bis 17. Jahrhundert*, vol. 1, *Abhandlungen*. Baden-Baden: Koerner, 1974.

Burba, Klaus. *Die Christologie in Luthers Liedern*. Gütersloh: Mohn, 1956.

Chenu, M.-D. "Contribution à l'Histoire du Traité de la Foi: Commentaire historique de IIa IIae q. 1, a. 2." In *Mélanges Thomistes*, 123–40. Bibliothèque Thomiste 3. Paris: Vrin, 1934.

———. "Grammaire et Théologie aux XIIe et XIIIe Siècles." In *Archives d'Histoire Doctrinale et Littéraire du Moyen Age*, 5–28. Paris: Vrin, 1936

Childs, Brevard S. *Biblical Theology of the Old and New Testaments: Theological Reflection on the Christian Bible*. Minneapolis: Fortress, 1993.

———. *Introduction to the Old Testament as Scripture*. Philadelphia: Fortress, 1979.

———. *The New Testament as Canon: An Introduction*. Philadelphia: Fortress, 1985.

Congar, Yves M.-J. "Regards et réflexions sur la christologie de Luther." In *Chrétiens en Dialogue. Contributions catholiques à l'Oecuménisme*, 453–89. Paris: Cerf, 1964.

Das Erfurter Enchiridion (Ferbefaß 1524) und der Ergänzungsdruck (Erfurt 1525). Facsimile. Edited by Konrad Ameln. Internationale Gesellschaft für Musikwissenschaft, Documenta Musicologica 1/36. Kassell: Bärenreiter, 1983.

Das Klug'sche Gesangbuch (1533). Facsimile. Edited by Konrad Ameln. Internationale Gesellschaft für Musikwissenschaft, Documenta Musicologica, 1/35. Kassel: Bärenreiter, 1983.

Dietz, Philipp. *Wörterbuch zu Dr. Martin Luthers Deutschen Schriften*. 2nd ed. 2 Vols. New York: Olms, 1973.

Dillenberger, John. *God Hidden and Revealed: The Interpretation of Luther's Deus Absconditus and Its Significance for Religious Thought*. Philadelphia: Fortress, 1953.

Doerne, Martin. "Predigtamt und Prediger bei Luther." In *Wort und Gemeinde: Festschrift für Erdmann Schott zum 65. Geburtstag*, 43–55. Aufsätze und Vorträge zur Theologie und Religionswissenschaft. Berlin: Evangelische Verlagsanstalt, 1967.

Ebbesen, Sten. "Ancient scholastic logic as the source of medieval scholastic logic." CHLMP 101–27.

Ebeling, Gerhard. "Das rechte Unterscheiden: Luthers Anleitung zu theologischer Urteilskraft." *Zeitschrift für Theologie und Kirche* 85, no. 2 (May 1988): 219–58.

———. *Evangelische Evangelienauslegung: Eine Untersuchung zu Luthers Hermeneutik*. 3rd ed. Tübingen: Mohr, 1991.

———. "Luther II: Theologie." RGG 4:495–520.

———. *Luther: Einführung in sein Denken*. 4th ed. Tübingen: Mohr, 1981.

———. *Lutherstudien*. Vol. 1. Tübingen: Mohr, 1971.

———. *Wort und Glaube*. Vol. 1. 3rd ed. Tübingen: Mohr, 1967.

Eck, John. *Enchiridion of Commonplaces: Against Luther and Other Enemies of the Church (1541)*. Translated by Ford Lewis Battles. Grand Rapids: Baker, 1979.

Edwards, Mark U., Jr. "The Luther Quincentennial." *Journal of Ecclesiastical History* 35, no. 4 (October 1984): 597–613.

———. "Toward an Understanding of Luther's Attacks on the Jews." In *Luther, Lutheranism and the Jews: A Record of the Second Consultation between Representatives of The International Jewish Committee for Interreligious Consultation and the Lutheran World Federation Held in Stockholm, Sweden 11–13 July 1983*, edited by Jean Halpérin and Arne Sovik, 15–32. Geneva: Lutheran World Federation, 1984.

Ehrlich, Ernst Ludwig. "Luther and the Jews." In *Luther, Lutheranism and the Jews: A Record of the Second Consultation between Representatives of The International Jewish Committee for Interreligious Consultation and the Lutheran World Federation Held in Stockholm, Sweden 11–13 July 1983*, edited by Jean Halpérin and Arne Sovik, 33–48. Geneva: Lutheran World Federation, 1984.

Elert, Werner. *Morphologie des Luthertums*, vol. 1, *Theologie und Weltanschauung des Luthertums hauptsächlich im 16. und 17. Jahrhundert*. 2nd ed. Munich: Beck, 1952.

Elliger, Walter. *Thomas Müntzer: Leben und Werk*. Göttingen: Vandenhoeck & Ruprecht, 1975.

Faber, Zach. *Luth. Defensionswerck*. In the Archives of the Evangelische Stift, Tübingen, n.d.

Forde, Gerhard O. *Theology Is for Proclamation*. Minneapolis: Fortress, 1990.

Fuchs, Ernst. "Das Sprachereignis in der Verkündigung Jesu, in der Theologie des Paulus und im Ostergeschehen." In *Gesammelte Aufsätze*, vol. 1, *Zum hermeneutischen Problem in der Theologie: Die existentiale Interpretation*, 281–305. Tübingen: Mohr, 1959.

Gabriel, Paul. *Das deutsche evangelische Kirchenlied von Martin Luther bis zur Gegenwart*. 3rd ed. Berlin: Evangelische Verlagsanstalt, 1956.

Gandillar, Maurice Patronnier, de. "De l'usage et de la valeur des arguments probables dans les questions du Cardinal Pierre d'Ailly sur le 'Livre des Sentences'." In *Archives d'Histoire Doctrinale et Littéraire du Moyen Age*, 43–91. Paris: Vrin, 1933.

Geißer, Hans Friedrich. "Zur Hermeneutik der Verborgenheit Gottes." *Wirkungen hermeneutischer Theologie: Eine Zürcher Festgabe zum 70. Geburtstag Gerhard Ebelings*, edited by Hans Friedrich Geißer and Walter Mostert, 155–67. Zurich: Evangelischer Verlag, 1983.

Gerber, Uwe. *Disputatio als Sprache des Glaubens: Eine Einführung in das theologische Verständnis der Sprache an Hand einer entwicklungsgeschichtlichen Untersuchung der disputatio und ihres Sprachvollzuges*. Zurich: Evangelischer Verlag, 1970.

Gilson, Étienne. *Jean Duns Scot: Introduction à ses Positions Fondamentales*. Études de Philosophie Médiévale 42. Paris: Vrin, 1952.

Grane, Leif. "Lutherforschung und Geistesgeschichte: Auseinandersetzung mit Heiko A. Oberman." *Archiv für Reformationsgeschichte* 68 (1977): 302–15.

Grassl, Peter. "Der Ratschluss der Erlösung (Phil. 2, 5–8) im Bilde Dargestellt in Dorschhausen, Landsberg, Einsiedeln und von Führich." *Die Christliche Kunst* 30 (1933/34): 121–28.

Grimm, Jacob and Wilhelm. *Deutsches Wörterbuch*. Leipzig: S. Hirzel, 1854–1954.

Grönvik, Lorenz. *Die Taufe in der Theologie Martin Luthers*. Göttingen and Zurich: Åbo Akademi, 1968.

Große Konkordanz zur Lutherbibel. 2nd ed. Stuttgart: Deutsche Bibelgesellschaft, 1989.

Gunkel, Hermann. *Einleitung in die Psalmen. Die Gattungen der religiösen Lyrik Israels (zu Ende geführt von Joachim Begrich)*. 4th ed. Göttingen: Vandenhoeck & Ruprecht, 1985.

Hägglund, Bengt. "Martin Luther über die Sprache." *Neue Zeitschrift für systematische Theologie und Religionsphilosophie* 26, no. 1 (1984): 1–12.

— — —. *Theologie und Philosophie bei Luther und in der occamistischen Tradition: Luthers Stellung zur Theorie von der doppelten Wahrheit.* Lund: Gleerup, 1955.

Hahn, Gerhard. *Evangelium als literarische Anweisung: Zu Luthers Stellung in der Geschichte des deutschen kirchlichen Liedes.* Munich and Zurich: Artemis Verlag, 1981.

Haile, H. G. *Luther: An Experiment in Biography.* Princeton: Princeton University Press, 1983.

Harnack, Adolf von. *Lehrbuch der Dogmengeschichte*, vols. 2–3, *Die Entwicklung des kirchlichen Dogmas.* 5th ed. Tübingen: Mohr, 1932.

Harnack, Theodosius. *Luthers Theologie mit besonderer Beziehung auf seine Versöhnungs- und Erlösungslehre*, vols. 1–2. Munich: Kaiser, 1927.

Haustein, Manfred. "Luther als Prediger." *Standpunkt* 11, no. 4 (April 1983): 93–95.

Heim, Karl. "Zur Geschichte des Satzes von der doppelten Wahrheit." *Studien zur systematischen Theologie: Theodor von Haering zum 70. Geburtstag*, edited by Friedrich Traub, 1–16. Tübingen: Haering, 1918.

Hell, Sylvia. *Die Dialektik des Wortes bei Martin Luther: Die Beziehung zwischen Gott und dem Menschen.* Innsbruck and Vienna: Tyrolia Verlag, 1992.

Henry, D. P. "Predicables and categories." CHLMP 128–142.

Herms, Eilert. "Das Evangelium für das Volk: Praxis und Theorie der Predigt bei Luther." In *Offenbarung und Glaube: Zur Bildung des christlichen Lebens*, 20–55. Tübingen: Mohr, 1992.

Hintikka, Jaakko. *Time & Necessity: Studies in Aristotle's Theory of Modality.* Oxford: Clarendon, 1973.

Hirsch, Emanuel. "Gesetz und Evangelium in Luthers Predigten." *Luther: Mitteilungen der Luthergesellschaft* 25 (1954): 49–60.

―――. *Hilfsbuch zum Studium der Dogmatik: Die Dogmatik der Reformatoren und der altevangelischen Lehrer quellenmäßig belegt und verdeutscht*. 4th ed. Berlin: de Gruyter, 1964.

―――. "Luthers Predigtweise." *Luther: Mitteilungen der Luthergesellschaft* 25 (1954): 1-23.

―――, ed. "Selbstzeugnis." *Luthers Werke in Auswahl*, vol. 7, *Predigten*. 3rd ed. Berlin: de Gruyter, 1962.

Hödl, Ludwig. "'… sie reden, als ob es zwei gegensätzliche Wahrheiten gäbe': Legende und Wirklichkeit der mittelalterlichen Theorie von der doppelten Wahrheit." In *Philosophie im Mittelalter: Entwicklungslinien und Paradigmen*, edited by Jan P. Beckmann, Ludger Honnefelder, Gangolf Schrimpf, and Georg Wieland, 225-43. Hamburg: Meiner Verlag, 1987.

Holcot, Robert. *Exploring the Boundaries of Reason: Three Questions on the Nature of God*. Edited by Hester Goodenough Gelber. Toronto: Pontifical Institute of Medieval Studies in Toronto, 1983.

Holl, Karl. *Gesammelte Aufsätze zur Kirchengeschichte*, vol. 1, *Luther*. 6th ed. Tübingen: Mohr, 1932.

Honemeyer, Karl. *Thomas Müntzer und Martin Luther: Ihr Ringen um die Musik des Gottesdienstes. Untersuchungen zum 'Deutzsch Kirchenampt' 1523*. Berlin: Luther Verlag 1974.

Iwand, Hans Joachim. "Wider den Mißbrauch des 'pro me' als methodisches Prinzip in der Theologie." *Evangelische Theologie* 14 (1954): 120-25.

Janota, Johannes. *Studien zu Funktion und Typus des deutschen geistlichen Liedes im Mittelalter*. Münchener Texte und Untersuchungen zur deutschen Literatur des Mittelalters 23. Munich: C. H. Beck, 1968.

Jansen, Reiner. *Studien zu Luthers Trinitätslehre*. Bern: Lang, 1976.

Janz, Denis R. *Luther on Thomas Aquinas: The Angelic Doctor in the Thought of the Reformer*. Stuttgart: Franz Steiner, 1989.

Jardine, Lisa. "Humanistic logic." CHRP 173-98.

Jenny, Markus. *Luther, Zwingli, Calvin in ihren Liedern*. Zurich: Zwingli Verlag, 1983.

―――. *Luthers Geistliche Lieder und Kirchengesänge: Vollständige Neuedition in Ergänzung zu Band 35 der Weimarer Ausgabe*. AWA 4. Cologne: Böhlau, 1985

Jenson, Robert W. "Die trinitarische Grundlegung der Theologie—
Östliche und westliche Trinitätslehre als ökumenisches Problem."
Translated by Ulrich Asendorf. In *Luther und die trinitarische
Tradition: Ökumenische und philosophische Perspektiven*, 9-23.
Veröffentlichungen der Luther-Akademie e.V. Ratzeburg 23.
Erlangen: Luther Verlag, 1994.

Jüngel, Eberhard. "Das Verhältnis von 'ökonomischer' und 'immanenter'
Trinität. Erwägungen über eine biblische Begründung der
Trinitätslehre—im Anschluß an und in Auseinandersetzung mit
Karl Rahners Lehre vom dreifaltigen Gott als transzendentem
Urgrund der Heilsgeschichte." In *Entsprechungen: Gott—
Wahrheit—Mensch; Theologische Erorterungen*, 265-75. Munich:
Kaiser, 1980.

———. "Der evangelisch verstandene Gottesdienst." In *Wertlose
Wahrheit: Zur Identität und Relevanz des christlichen Glaubens;
Theologische Erörterungen* 3:283-310. Munich: Kaiser, 1990.

———. *Gott als Geheimnis der Welt: Zur Begründung der Theologie des
Gekreuzigten im Streit zwischen Theismus und Atheismus*. Tübingen:
Mohr, 1992.

———. "Metaphorische Wahrheit. Erwägungen zur theologischen
Relevanz der Metapher als Beitrag zur Hermeneutik einer
narrativen Theologie." In *Entsprechungen: Gott—Wahrheit—
Mensch; Theologische Erörterungen*, 103-57. Munich: Kaiser, 1980.

———. "Quae supra nos, nihil ad nos. Eine Kurzformel der Lehre
vom verborgenen Gott-im Anschluß an Luther interpretiert."
In *Entsprechungen: Gott—Wahrheit—Mensch; Theologische
Erörterungen*, 202-51. Munich: Kaiser, 1980.

Jung, Alfred. "'Nun freut euch, lieben Christen gmein.' Eine theologische
Untersuchung des Lutherliedes." *Jahrbuch für Liturgik und
Hymnologie* 19 (1975): 200-209.

Junghans, Helmar. "Interpreting the Old Luther (1526-1546)." *Currents in
Theology and Mission* 9, no. 5 (October 1982): 271-81.

———, ed. *Leben und Werk Martin Luthers von 1526 bis 1546: Festgabe
zu seinem 500. Geburtstag*. 2 vols. Göttingen: Vandenhoeck &
Ruprecht, 1983.

————. "Luther und die Welt der Reformation." *Luther Jahrbuch* 41 (1974): 138–51.

Käsemann, Ernst. *An die Römer*. 3rd. ed. Handbuch zum Neuen Testament 8a. Tübingen: Mohr, 1974.

Kattenbusch, Ferdinand. *Luthers Stellung zu den oecumenischen Symbolen*. Giessen: Wenzel, 1883.

Kenny, Anthony, and Jan Pinborg. "Medieval philosophical literature." CHLMP 11–42.

Knuuttila, Simo. "Modal logic." CHLMP 342–57.

Köhler, Hans-Joachim, ed. *Flugschriften als Massenmedium der Reformationszeit*. Beiträge zum Tübinger Symposion 1980. Stuttgart: Klett, 1981.

Köhler, Rudolf. "Der Deus Absconditus in Philosophie und Theologie." *Zeitschrift für Religions- und Geistesgeschichte*, Sonderdruck 1 (1955): 46–58.

————. *Die biblischen Quellen der Lieder: Handbuch zum Evangelischen Kirchengesangbuch 1/2*. Göttingen: Vandenhoeck & Ruprecht, 1965.

Koopmans, Jan. *Das altkirchliche Dogma in der Reformation*. Translated by H. Quistorp. Munich: Kaiser, 1955.

Kretzmann, Norman. "Syncategoremata, exponibilia, sophismata." CHLMP 211–45.

Kunze, Gerhard. "Die gottesdienstliche Zeit." In *Leiturgia: Handbuch des evangelischen Gottesdienstes*, vol. 1, *Geschichte und Lehre des evangelischen Gottesdienstes*, edited by Karl Ferdinand Müller and Walter Blankenburg, 437–534. Kassel: Johannes Stauda-Verlag, 1954.

Lehmann, Detlef. "Luther als Prediger." *Oberurseler Hefte: Studien und Beiträge für Theologie und Gemeinde* 17 (1983): 5–23.

Lienhard, Marc. *Martin Luthers christologisches Zeugnis: Entwicklung und Grundzüge seiner Christologie*. Translated by Robert Wolff. Göttingen: Vandenhoeck & Ruprecht, 1980.

Lipphardt, Walther. "Ein Mainzer Prozessionale (um 1400) als Quelle deutscher geistlicher Lieder." *Jahrbuch für Liturgik und Hymnologie* 9 (1964): 95–121.

————. "Über die Begriffe: Kontrafakt, Parodie, Travestie." *Jahrbuch für Liturgik und Hymnologie* 12 (1967): 104–11.

Lischer, Richard. "Die Funktion des Narrativen in Luthers Predigt: Der Zusammenhang von Rhetorik und Anthropologie." Translated by Albrecht Haizmann. In *Homiletisches Lesebuch: Texte zur heutigen Predigtlehre*, 2nd ed., edited by Albrecht Beutel, Volker Drehsen, and Hans Martin Müller, 308-29. Tübingen: Mohr, 1989.

Löfgren, David. *Die Theologie der Schöpfung bei Luther*. Göttingen: Vandenhoeck & Ruprecht, 1960.

Loewenich, Walther von. *Luther und der Neuprotestantismus*. Wittenberg: Luther Verlag, 1963.

———. *Luthers Theologia crucis*. 5th ed. Witten: Luther Verlag, 1967.

Lohr, C. H. "The medieval interpretation of Aristotle." CHLMP 80-98.

Lohse, Bernhard. "Luther als Disputator." In *Evangelium in der Geschichte: Studien zu Luther und der Reformation; Zum 60. Geburtstag des Autors*, edited by Leif Grane, Bernd Moeller, and Otto Hermann Pesch, 250-64. Göttingen: Vandenhoeck & Ruprecht, 1988.

———. *Luthers Theologie in ihrer historischen Entwicklung und in ihrem systematischen Zusammenhang*. Göttingen: Vandenhoeck & Ruprecht, 1995.

———. *Martin Luther: Eine Einführung in sein Leben und sein Werk*. Munich: Kaiser, 1981.

———. *Thomas Müntzer in neuer Sicht: Müntzer im Licht der neueren Forschung und die Frage nach dem Ansatz seiner Theologie*. Göttingen: Vandenhoeck & Ruprecht, 1991.

———. "Zur Struktur von Luthers Theologie: Kriterien einer Darstellung der Theologie Luthers." *Jahrbuch der Gesellschaft für Niedersächsische Kirchengeschichte* 83 (1985): 41-53. Reprinted in *Evangelium in der Geschichte: Studien zu Luther und der Reformation; Zum 60. Geburtstag des Autors*, edited by Leif Grane, Bernd Moeller, and Otto Hermann Pesch, 237-49. Göttingen: Vandenhoeck & Ruprecht, 1988.

Lombardus, Petrus. *Sententiae in IV libris distinctae, Tom. I, Pars I, Liber I et II and Tom. II, Liber III et IV*. Spicilegium Bonaventurianum 4. Grottaferrata: Editiones Collegii S. Bonaventurae, 1971-1981.

Luther, Martin. *Die deutschen geistlichen Lieder*. Edited by Gerhard Hahn. Tübingen: Niemeyer, 1967.

Mahrenholz, Christhard. "Auswahl und Einordnung der Katechismus-Lieder in den Wittenberger Gesangsbüchern seit 1529." In *Gestalt und Glaube: Festschrift zum 60. Geburtstag Oskar Söhngen*, eds. ein Freundeskreis, 123-32. Witten: Luther Verlag, 1960.

Maier, Anneliese. "Diskussionen über das aktuell Unendliche in der ersten Hälfte des 14. Jahrhunderts." In *Ausgehendes Mittelalter: Gesammelte Aufsätze zur Geistesgeschichte des 14. Jahrhunderts*, 1:41-85. Rome: Edizioni di storia e letteratura, 1964.

Maierù, Alfonso. "A propos de la doctrine de la supposition en théologie trinitaire au XIVe siècle." In *Mediaeval Semantics and Metaphysics: Studies dedicated to L. M. de Rijk*, edited by E. P. Bos, 221-38. Nijmegen: Igenium, 1985.

―――. "Logique et théologie trinitaire dans le moyen-âge tardif: deux solutions en présence." In *The Editing of Theological and Philosophical Texts from the Middle Ages: Acts of the conference arranged by the department of classical languages Held at the University of Stockholm 29-31 Aug. 1984*, edited by Monika Asztalos, 185-201. Stockholm: Almqvist & Wiksell, 1986.

―――. "Logique et théologie trinitaire: Pierre D'Ailly." In *Preuve et Raisons à l'Université de Paris: Logique, Ontologie et Théologie au XIVe Siècle*, edited by Zénon Kaluza and Paul Vignaux, 253-68. Paris: Vrin, 1984.

Mannermaa, Tuomo. "Grundlagenforschung der Theologie Martin Luthers und die Ökumene." In *Thesaurus Lutheri: Auf der Suche nach neuen Paradigmen der Luther-Forschung: Referate des Luther-Symposiums in Finnland 11-12 Nov. 1986*, edited by Tuomo Mannermaa, Anja Ghiselli, and Simo Peura, 17-35. Helsinki: Finnische Theologische Literaturgesellschaft, 1987.

―――. "Hat Luther eine trinitarische Ontologie?" In *Luther und die trinitarische Tradition: Ökumenische und philosophische Perspektiven*, 43-60. Veröffentlichungen der Luther-Akademie e.V. Ratzeburg 23. Erlangen: Luther Verlag, 1994.

Manns, Peter. "Zum Gespräch zwischen Martin Luther und der katholischen Theologie: Begegnung zwischen patristisch-monastischer und reformatorischer Theologie an der Scholastik vorbei." In *Vater im Glauben: Studien zur Theologie Martin Luthers.*

Festgabe zum 65. Geburtstag am 10. März 1988, edited by Rolf Decot, 441–532. Stuttgart: Franz Steiner, 1988.

Marenbon, John. *Later Medieval Philosophy (1150–1350): An Introduction.* London: Routledge, 1991.

Martikainen, Eeva. *Doctrina: Studien zu Luthers Begriff der Lehre.* Translated by Hans-Christian Daniel. Helsinki: Finnische Theologische Literaturgesellschaft, 1992.

Maurer, Friedrich. *Die Erlösung: Eine geistliche Dichtung des 14. Jahrhunderts.* Leipzig: Wissenschaftliche Buchgesellschaft, 1934.

Maurer, Wilhelm. *Von der Freiheit eines Christenmenschen: Zwei Untersuchungen zu Luthers Reformationsschriften 1520/21.* Göttingen: Vandenhoeck & Ruprecht, 1949.

Mayr, Ruppert. "'Einfeldig zu predigen, ist eine große kunst': Zu Luthers Sprache in seinen Predigten." In *Reformationsgedenken: Beiträge zum Lutherjahr 1983 aus der Evangelischen Kirche im Rheinland*, edited by Joachim Mehlhausen, 83–100. Cologne: Rheinland-Verlag, 1985.

Meinhold, Peter. "Luther und die Predigt." In *Das Wort und die Wörter: Festschrift Gerhard Friedrich zum 65. Geburtstag*, edited by Horst Balz and Siegfried Schulz, 113–26. Stuttgart: Kohlhammer, 1973.

———. *Luthers Sprachphilosophie.* Berlin: Luther Verlag, 1958.

Meller, Bernhard. *Studien zur Erkenntnislehre des Peter von Ailly.* Freiburg: Herder, 1954.

Metzger, Bruce M. *A Textual Commentary on the Greek New Testament.* New York: United Bible Societies, 1975.

Meuser, Fred W. *Luther the Preacher.* Minneapolis: Augsburg, 1983.

Moltmann, Jürgen. *Trinität und Reich Gottes: Zur Gotteslehre.* 2nd ed. Munich: Kaiser, 1986.

Morel, P. Gall, ed. *Offenbarungen der Schwester Mechthild von Magdeburg oder Das Fliessende Licht der Gottheit.* Darmstadt: Wissenschaftliche Buchgesellschaft, 1963.

Moser, Hans Joachim. *Die Melodien der Lutherlieder.* Welt des Gesangbuchs, Die singende Kirche in Gabe und Aufgabe 4. Leipzig and Hamburg: Gustav Schloessmanns, 1972.

———. "'Nun freut euch, lieben Christen gmein': Die wahrscheinliche Vorgeschichte des Lutherliedes." In *Gestalt und Glaube. Festschrift zum 60. Geburtstag Oskar Söhngen*, eds. ein Freundeskreis, 137–144. Witten and Berlin: Luther Verlag, 1960.

Mostert, Walter. "Luthers Verhältnis zur theologischen und philosophischen Überlieferung." In *Leben und Werk Martin Luthers von 1526 bis 1546: Festgabe zu seinem 500. Geburtstag*, edited by Helmar Junghans, 1:347–368; footnotes in 2:839–849. Göttingen: Vandenhoeck & Ruprecht, 1983.

Müller, Christa. *Das Lob Gottes bei Luther, vornehmlich nach seinen Auslegungen des Psalters*. Forschungen zur Geschichte und Lehre des Protestantismus 7/1. Munich: Kaiser, 1934.

———. *Luthers Lieder: Theologische Auslegungen*. Göttingen: Vandenhoeck & Ruprecht, 1936.

Müntzer, Thomas. *Deutsche Messen und Kirchenämter*. Edited by O. J. Mehl with Friedrich Wiechert. Grimmen: Waberg, 1937.

Murdoch, John E. "From Social into intellectual factors: an aspect of the unitary character of late medieval learning." In *The Cultural Context of Medieval Learning: Proceedings of the First International Colloquium on Philosophy, Science, and Theology in the Middle Ages Held in Sept. 1973*, edited by John Emery Murdoch and Edith Dudley Sylla, 271–339. Dordrecht: Reidel, 1975.

———. "Infinity and continuity." CHLMP, 564–91.

Neale, J. M. and R. F. Littledale. *A Commentary On the Psalms from Primitive and Mediaeval Writers; and From the Various Office-books and Hymns of the Roman, Mozarabic, Ambrosian, Gallican, Greek, Coptic, Armenian, and Syriac Rites*. 4 Vols. London: J. Masters, 1874–1884.

Nembach, Ulrich. *Predigt des Evangeliums: Luther als Prediger, Pädagoge und Rhetor*. Neukirchen-Vluyn: Neukirchener Verlag, 1972.

Niebergall, Alfred. "Die Geschichte der christlichen Predigt." In *Leiturgia: Handbuch des evangelischen Gottesdienstes*, edited by Karl Ferdinand Müller and Walter Blankenburg, 2:181–353. Kassel: Johannes Stauda, 1955.

———. "Luthers Auffassung von der Predigt nach 'De Servo Arbitrio'." In *Reformation und Gegenwart: Vorträge und Vorlesungen von Mitgliedern der Theologischen Fakultät Marburg zum 450. Jubiläum der Reformation*, 83–109. Marburg: Elwert, 1968.

Nilsson, Kjell Ove. *Simul: Das Miteinander von Göttlichem und Menschlichem in Luthers Theologie.* Translated by Christiane Sjöberg-Boehncke with Hans C. Deppe. Göttingen: Vandenhoeck & Ruprecht, 1966.

·Normore, Calvin. "Future contingents." CHLMP 358–81.

Nuchelmans, Gabriel. "The semantics of propositions." CHLMP 197–210.

Oberman, Heiko Augustinus. "Reformation: Epoche oder Episode." *Archiv für Reformationsgeschichte* 68 (1977): 56–109.

———. *Spätscholastik und Reformation,* vol. 1, *Der Herbst der mittelalterlichen Theologie.* Translated by Martin Rumscheid and Henning Kampen. Zurich: Evangelischer Verlag, 1965.

———. "Zwischen Agitation und Reformation: Die Flugschriften als 'Judenspiegel.'" In *Flugschriften als Massenmedium der Reformationszeit: Beiträge zum Tübinger Symposion 1980,* edited by Hans-Joachim Köhler, 269–89. Stuttgart: Klett-Cotta, 1981.

Ockham, William. *Predestination, God's Foreknowledge, and Future Contingents.* Translated by Marilyn McCord Adams and Norman Kretzmann. Indianapolis: Hackett, 1983.

O'Malley, John W. "Luther the Preacher." *Michigan Germanic Studies* 10 (1984): 3–16.

———. *Religious Culture in the Sixteenth Century: Preaching, Rhetoric, Spirituality and Reform.* Brookfield, VT: Valorium, 1993.

O'Regan, Cyril. *The Heterodox Hegel.* SUNY Series in Hegelian Studies. Albany, NY: SUNY Press, 1994.

Overbeck, Franz. "Ueber die Christlichkeit unserer heutigen Theologie (1873)." *Franz Overbeck: Werke und Nachlaß,* vol. 1, *Schriften bis 1873,* edited by Ekkehard W. Stegemann and Niklaus Peter with Marianne Stauffacher-Schaub. Stuttgart and Weimar: Metzler, 1994.

Pannenberg, Wolfhart. *Systematische Theologie,* vol. 1. Göttingen: Vandenhoeck & Ruprecht, 1988.

Paul, Hermann, ed. *Grundriss der Germanischen Philologie,* vol. 2/1, Literaturgeschichte: Mittelhochdeutsche Literatur. 2nd ed. Strasbourg: Trübner, 1909.

Perler, Dominik. *Prädestination, Zeit und Kontingenz. Philosophisch-historische Untersuchungen zu Wilhelm von Ockhams 'Tractatus de praedestinatione et de praescientia Dei respectu futurorum contingentium.'* Amsterdam: Benjamins, 1988.

Pesch, Otto Hermann. *Theologie der Rechtfertigung bei Martin Luther und Thomas von Aquin: Versuch eines systematisch-theologischen Dialogs.* Mainz: Grünewald Verlag, 1985.

Peters, Albrecht. "Die Trinitätslehre in der reformatorischen Christenheit." *Theologische Literaturzeitung* 94, no. 8 (August 1969): 561–70.

———. *Kommentar zu Luthers Katechismen,* vol 2, *Der Glaube,* edited by Gottfried Seebaß. Göttingen: Vandenhoeck & Ruprecht, 1991.

———. "Verborgener Gott—Dreieiniger Gott. Beobachtungen und Überlegungen zum Gottesverständnis Martin Luthers." In *Martin Luther: 'Reformator und Vater im Glauben',* edited by Peter Manns, 74–105. Stuttgart: Luther Verlag, 1985.

Pinomaa, Lennart. *Sieg des Glaubens: Grundlinien der Theologie Luthers.* Corrected and edited by Horst Beintker. Göttingen: Vandenhoeck & Ruprecht, 1964.

Plato. *The Republic: Books I–V.* Translated by Paul Shorey. Cambridge, MA: Harvard University Press, 1969.

Posset, Franz. "Bernardus Redivivus: The Wirkungsgeschichte of a Medieval Sermon in the Reformation of the Sixteenth Century." *Cistercian Studies* 22, no. 3 (1987): 239–49.

Prenter, Regin. "Die göttliche Einsetzung des Predigtamtes und das allgemeine Priestertum bei Luther." *Theologische Literaturzeitung* 86, no. 5 (May 1961): 321–31.

———. *Spiritus Creator: Studien zu Luthers Theologie.* Translated by W. Thiemann. Munich: Kaiser, 1954.

Ricoeur, Paul. "Philosophy and Religious Language." *The Journal of Religion* 54, no. 1 (January 1974): 71–85.

———. "Toward a Hermeneutic of the Idea of Revelation." In *Essays on Biblical Interpretation.* Translated by David Pellauer. Edited by Lewis S. Mudge, 73–118. Philadelphia: Fortress, 1980.

Ritschl, Albrecht. *Die christliche Lehre von der Rechtfertigung und Versöhnung,* vol. 1, *Die Geschichte der Lehre.* 3rd ed. Bonn: Marcus, 1889.

——. *Theologie und Metaphysik: Zur Verständigung und Abwehr.* 2nd ed. Bonn: Marcus, 1887.

Rössler, Dietrich. "Beispiel und Erfahrung: Zu Luthers Homiletik." In *Reformation und Praktische Theologie: Festschrift für Werner Jetter zum 70. Geburtstag*, edited by Hans Martin Müller and Dietrich Rössler, 202–15. Göttingen: Vandenhoeck & Ruprecht, 1983.

Rößler, Martin. "Ballade vom Ratschluß Gottes zur Erlösung." *Für Arbeit und Besinnung* 37 (1983): 444–49.

Saarinen, Risto. *Gottes Wirken auf uns: Die transzendentale Deutung des Gegenwart-Christi-Motivs in der Lutherforschung.* Stuttgart: Franz Steiner, 1989.

——. "Metapher und biblische Redefiguren als Elemente der Sprachphilosophie Luthers." *Neue Zeitschrift für systematische Theologie und Religionsphilosophie* 30, no. 1 (1988): 18–39.

Scheel, Otto. Martin Luther. *Vom Katholizismus zur Reformation*, vol. 1, *Auf der Schule und Universität.* Tübingen: Mohr, 1921.

——. *Martin Luther: Vom Katholizismus zur Reformation*, vol. 2, *Im Kloster.* Tübingen: Mohr, 1930.

Schmid, Heinrich. *Die Dogmatik der evangelisch-lutherischen Kirche, dargestellt und aus den Quellen belegt.* Edited by Horst Georg Pöhlmann. 10th ed. Gütersloh: Mohn, 1983.

Schmid, Wolfgang. "Epikur." RAC 5:681–819.

Schmithals, Walter. *Der Römerbrief: Ein Kommentar.* Gütersloh: Mohn, 1988.

Schneider-Böklen, Elisabeth. *Der Herr hat großes mir getan: Frauen im Gesangbuch.* Stuttgart: Quell Verlag, 1995.

——. "Elisabeth Cruciger—die erste Dichterin des Protestantismus." *Gottesdienst und Kirchenmusik*, no. 2 (March/April 1994): 32–40.

Schoch, Max. *Verbi Divini Ministerium*, vol. 1, *Verbum, Sprache und Wirklichkeit.* Tübingen: Mohr, 1968.

Scholder, Klaus. *Ursprünge und Probleme der Bibelkritik im 17. Jahrhundert: Ein Beitrag zur Entstehung der historisch-kritischen Theologie.* Munich: Kaiser, 1966.

Schwarz, Reinhard. "Gott ist Mensch: Zur Lehre von der Person Christi bei den Ockhamisten und bei Luther." *Zeitschrift für Theologie und Kirche* 63 (1966): 289–351.

―――. *Luther*. Göttingen: Vandenhoeck & Ruprecht, 1986.

Schweizer, Eduard. *Der Brief an die Kolosser*. Evangelisch-Katholischer Kommentar zum Neuen Testament 12. Zurich: Benziger, 1980.

Seeberg, Erich. *Luthers Theologie*, vol. 2, *Christus: Wirklichkeit und Urbild*. Darmstadt: Wissenschaftliche Buchgesellschaft, 1969.

―――. *Luthers Theologie in ihren Grundzügen*. 2nd ed. Stuttgart: Kohlhammer, 1950.

―――. *Luthers Theologie: Motive und Ideen*, vol. 1, *Die Gottesanschauung*. Göttingen: Vandenhoeck & Ruprecht, 1929.

Seeberg, Reinhold. *Lehrbuch der Dogmengeschichte*, vol. 4/1, *Die Entstehung des Protestantischen Lehrbegriffs*. Darmstadt: Wissenschaftliche Buchgesellschaft, 1974.

Sommer, Ernst. "Die Metrik in Luthers Liedern." *Jahrbuch für Liturgik und Hymnologie* 9 (1964): 29-81.

Spitta, Friedrich. *'Ein feste Burg ist unser Gott': Die Lieder Luthers in ihrer Bedeutung für das evangelische Kirchenlied*. Göttingen: Vandenhoeck & Ruprecht, 1905.

Steinlein, Hermann. "Luthers Anlage zur Bildhaftigkeit." *Luther Jahrbuch* 22 (1940): 9-45.

Stolt, Birgit. "Germanistische Hilfsmittel zum Lutherstudium." *Luther Jahrbuch* 46 (1979): 120-35.

―――. "Neue Aspekte der sprachwissenschaftlichen Luther-Forschung. Ein kritischer Rückblick." In *Text und Kritik, Zeitschrift für Literatur: Sonderband, Martin Luther*, edited by Heinz Ludwig Arnold, 6-16. Munich: Kaiser, 1983.

―――. *Studien zu Luthers Freiheitstraktat, mit besonderer Rücksicht auf das Verhältnis der lateinischen und der deutschen Fassung zu einander und die Stilmittel der Rhetorik*. Stockholm: Almkvist & Wiksell, 1969.

―――. *Wortkampf: Frühneuhochdeutsche Beispiele zur rhetorischen Praxis*. Frankfurt am Main: Athenäum, 1974.

Strauss, Gerald. *Luther's House of Learning: Indoctrination of the Young in the German Reformation*. Baltimore: Johns Hopkins University Press 1978.

Streiff, Stefan. *"Novis Linguis Loqui": Martin Luthers Disputation über Job 1,14 "verbum caro factum est" aus dem Jahr 1539*. Göttingen: Vandenhoeck & Ruprecht, 1993.

Stump, Eleonore. "Obligations: From the beginning to the early fourteenth century." CHLMP 315-34.

———. "Topics: their development and absorption into consequences." CHLMP, 273-99.

Stupperich, Robert. "Devotio moderna und reformatorische Frömmigkeit." *Jahrbuch des Vereins für Westfälische Kirchengeschichte* 59/60 (1966/1967): 11-26.

Thiele, Ernst. *Luthers Sprichwörtersammlung*. Weimar: Hermann Böhlaus Nachfolger, 1900.

Thimme, Hans. "Martin Luther als Prediger." In *Luther und der Pietismus: An alle, die mit Ernst Christen sein wollen*, edited by Kurt Heimbucher, 23-56. Giessen and Basel: Brunnen Verlag, 1983.

Työrinoja, Reijo. "Nova vocabula et nova lingua: Luther's Conception of Doctrinal Formulas." In *Thesaurus Lutheri: Auf der Suche nach neuen Paradigmen der Luther-Forschung: Referate des Luther-Symposiums in Finnland 11-12 Nov. 1986*, edited by Tuomo Mannermaa, Anja Ghiselli and Simo Peura, 221-36. Helsinki: Finnische Theologische Literaturgesellschaft, 1987.

———. "Proprietas Verbi: Luther's Conception of Philosophical and Theological Language in the Disputation: Verbum caro factum est (Joh. 1:14), 1539." In *Faith, Will, and Grammar: Some Themes of Intensional Logic and Semantics in Medieval and Reformation Thought*, edited by Heikki Kirjavainen, 143-78. Helsinki: Vammalan Kirjapaino Oy, 1986.

Veit, Patrice. *Das Kirchenlied in der Reformation Martin Luthers: Eine thematische und semantische Untersuchung*. Stuttgart: Steiner, 1986.

Vogelsang, Erich. *Die Anfänge von Luthers Christologie nach der Ersten Psalmenvorlesung insbesondere in ihren exegetischen und systematischen Zusammenhängen mit Augustin und der Scholastik dargestellt*. Berlin and Leipzig: de Gruyter, 1929.

Wackernagel, Philipp. *Bibliographic zur Geschichte des deutschen Kirchenliedes im XVI. Jahrhundert*. Hildesheim: Olms, 1961.

———. *Das Deutsche Kirchenlied*. Stuttgart: S. G. Liesching, 1841.

———. *Martin Luthers geistliche Lieder (mit den zu seinen Lebzeiten gebräuchlichen Singweisen)*. Hildesheim: Olms, 1970.

Walter, Johann. *Das geistliche Gesangbüchlein. 'Chorgesangbuch.' Facsimile of 2d ed. Worms 1525*, edited by Walter Blankenburg. Internationale Gesellschaft für Musikwissenschaft, Documenta Musicologica 1/33. Kassel, Basel, Tours and London: Bärenreiter, 1979.

Wander, Karl Friedrich Wilhelm, ed. *Deutsches Sprichwörter-Lexikon: Ein Hausschatz für das deutsche Volk*, vol. 2. Leipzig: F. A. Brockhaus, 1870. Reprint, Darmstadt: Wissenschaftliche Buchgesellschaft, 1964.

Weismann, Eberhard. "Der Predigtgottesdienst und die verwandten Formen." In *Leiturgia: Handbuch des evangelischen Gottesdienstes*, edited by Karl Ferdinand Müller and Walter Blankenburg, 3:1–97. Kassel: Johannes Stauda, 1956.

Werbick, Jürgen. "Trinitätslehre." In *Handbuch der Dogmatik*, edited by Theodor Schneider, 2:481–576. Düsseldorf: Patmos, 1992.

Werdemann, Hermann. *Luthers Wittenberger Gemeinde wiederhergestellt aus seinen Predigten: Zugleich ein Beitrag zu Luthers Homiletik und zur Gemeindepredigt der Gegenwart*. Gütersloh: Bertelsmann, 1941.

Wernle, Paul. *Der evangelische Glaube nach den Hauptschriften der Reformatoren*, vol. 1, *Luther*. Tübingen: Mohr, 1918.

Werthemann, Helene. *Studien zu den Adventsliedern des 16. und 17. Jahrhunderts*. Zurich: Evangelischer Verlag, 1963.

Wetzel, Christoph. "Die Träger des liturgischen Amtes im evangelischen Gottesdienst bei dem Apostel Paulus und bei Martin Luther." In *Leiturgia: Handbuch des evangelischen Gottesdienstes*, edited by Karl Ferdinand Müller and Walter Blankenburg, 4:269–341. Kassel: Johannes Stauda, 1961.

White, Graham. *Luther as Nominalist: A Study of the Logical Methods used in Martin Luther's disputations in the Light of their Medieval Background*. Helsinki: Luther Agricola, 1994.

Winkler, Eberhard. *Impulse Luthers für die heutige Gemeindepraxis*. Stuttgart: Calwer Verlag, 1983.

———. "Luther als Seelsorger und Prediger." In *Leben und Werk Martin Luthers von 1526 bis 1546: Festgabe zu seinem 500. Geburtstag*, edited by Helmar Junghans, 1:225-39; footnotes in 2:792-97. Göttingen: Vandenhoeck & Ruprecht, 1983.

Wolf, Ernst. "Zur wissenschaftsgeschichtlichen Bedeutung der Disputationen an der Wittenberger Universität im 16. Jahrhundert." In *Peregrinatio* 2:38-51. Munich: Kaiser, 1965.

Wolff, Ludwig. "Zu Luthers Lied 'Nun freut euch, lieben Christen gmein'." *Jahrbuch für Liturgik und Hymnologie* 7 (1962): 99-102.

Wolter, Allan B. *The Philosophical Theology of John Duns Scotus*. Edited by Marilyn McCord Adams. Ithaca, NY: Franciscan Institute, 1990.

Yeago, David S. "Gnosticism, Antinomianism, and Reformation Theology. Reflections on the Costs of a Construal." *Pro Ecclesia* 2, no. 1 (Winter 1993): 37-49.

Zahn, Johannes. *Die Melodien der deutschen evangelischen Kirchenlieder, aus den Quellen geschöpft und mitgeteilt*, vols. 3 and 6. Gütersloh, 1890-1893.

Names Index

Scripture Index

NEW TESTAMENT